Modeling Companion for Software Practitioners

Egon Börger • Alexander Raschke

Modeling Companion for Software Practitioners

 Springer

Egon Börger
Dipartimento di Informatica
Università di Pisa
Pisa, Italy

Alexander Raschke
Institute of Software Engineering
and Programming Languages
Universität Ulm
Ulm, Germany

ISBN 978-3-662-56639-8   ISBN 978-3-662-56641-1   (eBook)
https://doi.org/10.1007/978-3-662-56641-1

Library of Congress Control Number: 2018935112

Printed on acid-free paper

This Springer imprint is published by the registered company Springer-Verlag GmbH, DE part of Springer Nature.
The registered company address is: Heidelberger Platz 3, 14197 Berlin, Germany

Preface: What the Book is About

L'armonia sia non signora ma serva del oratione [1]
—The principle of *Perfettione della moderna musica*
Claudio Monteverdi

The target audiences of the book are practitioners who build software-intensive systems, but also students of the field. The book illustrates, by a variety of applications, *a modeling method which helps the practitioner to* **intellectually manage complex software-intensive systems**. This implies a four-fold support for system development, namely support to **BEDER**

Build, **E**xplain, **D**ebug (validate/verify), maintain (**E**xtend/**R**euse)

well-documented models of computational systems deemed to be reliable.

The proposed method provides this support by a combination of its abstraction concept and its operational character: models come as behavioral models in the precise and simple form of *Abstract State Machines* (ASMs), a semantically rigorously defined form of pseudo-code. In the Introduction (Chap. 1) we explain how the most general concept of abstraction inherent in ASMs permits

- to directly **adapt construction and explanation of models to** data and operations at **any desired level of abstraction**, leading from requirements to executable code,
- to rigorously **mediate between levels of abstraction**,
- to construct and debug system models **piecemeal**, in steps and componentwise,
- to establish (formulate, explain and justify) the intended **system behavior properties** at any given level of abstraction, exploiting any useful means of justification, whether by experimental **validation** or by informal, mathematical, formal or machine-supported **verification**.

---

[1] The music should not dictate but follow the prose.
read: The model should not dictate but reflect the problem. See [188, 189].

This book introduces into the modeling method (Part I) and into the available tool support, which makes design models machine executable and debuggable (Part II).

In Part I we show by examples how to construct, explain, debug, explore, extend and reuse accurate system design models, starting from scratch. Here we assume only elementary knowledge of common mathematical (including set-theoretic) notation, as taught in high-schools, and some basic experience with computational processes (systems, programs, algorithms). Therefore we begin with simple, rather elementary examples to introduce the **seven fundamental constructs of Abstract State Machines** which—exploiting the abstraction capabilities offered by the most comprehensive notion of ASM *state*—suffice for modeling and explaining complex sequential as well as concurrent systems:

> assignment, if-then-else, parallelism, forall, choose, let, call

(Chap. 2, 3). In the remaining chapters we illustrate by some more advanced examples the wide range of applicability of the method. We include examples from automatic control systems, equipments operated by software interacting with humans, algorithms, protocols, monitoring networks of communicating agents, semantics of concurrent algorithmic languages, operating system components, software system architectures, meta-modeling for diagrammatic notations, shared memory models, distributed web services, business processes and last but not least control flow, programming and interaction patterns.[2]

Part II is written for system designers and programmers who are interested to see how the ASM modeling method can be supported by implementing **tools which make design models executable and debuggable**. This needs first of all a mathematical definition of the syntax and semantics of ASMs (Chap. 7). We then apply bootstrapping to specify in terms of basic ASMs various extensions of the seven constructs listed above, namely:

- An implementation of ASMs in CoreASM(Chap. 8)—an ASM interpreter tool which makes them machine-executable—together with an extension of CoreASM by a model debugger (Sect. 8.3).

---

[2] We exclude virtual machines, the semantics of common programming languages and their compilation (proven, even mechanically, to be correct!), given that there is a rich and easily available literature on challenging practical applications of the ASM method in this area. These applications include characteristic examples for the main programming paradigms: imperative, object-oriented, functional, logical etc., see the recent survey [43] for details and references. For other applications a comprehensive survey is available for the first ten years of the ASM method (up to 2003), see [76, Chap. 9]. Unfortunately the survey has not been updated so that the interested reader must search to find publications on the numerous theoretical and practical advances of the method since 2003. A good starting point are the Proceedings of the regular international ASM Workshops and since 2008 the ABZ Conferences in Springer's Lecture Notes in Computer Science [55, 239, 24, 74, 5, 66, 46, 114, 91, 205, 11, 82].

- A meta model of ASM *Control State Diagrams* (CSDs) (Chap. 9), a graphical notation which extends the well-known Finite State Machine flowchart notation to ASMs and is used throughout the book.
- Further specific modeling concepts, namely parameterized ASMs, context-aware ambient ASMs and step controlled ASMs (Chap. 4).

To illustrate how to build, debug and maintain (explore and reuse) systems and to explain their construction in a checkable manner, we construct system models from components adopting a **general, problem-oriented refinement method**. The method starts with abstract models and refines them stepwise, incrementally adding further details. This may be through adding components for additional functionality (horizontal refinements) or through specifying a component further by details leading to an implementation (vertical refinement or parameter instantiation) or any combination of the two. The chain of refinements provides a practical system decomposition and documentation which not only supports understanding, debugging (via testing or (dis-) proving behavioral properties) and maintenance (exploration or reuse of components), but it does it at any level of abstraction involved in the refinement steps. It helps to manage (understand and explain) complexity by breaking complex systems into simpler, well understood, well explained, well documented and objectively checkable parts. To achieve this, the ASM method builds upon the intimate connection between refinement and abstraction, two thought processes which complement each other.

Understanding a system is a prerequisite for justifying its well-functioning. We show in this book how the abstraction and refinement capabilities of the ASM method allow the system engineer to accompany (and document for others to check) the component building steps by **accurate intuitive explanations** of the underlying design and implementation ideas. By its abstraction/refinement pair, the ASM method provides the practitioner with a precise instrument to explain complex system behavior in a simple way, including showing in an objectively checkable and documented way the correctness of what has been built. Here *correctness* refers to a concept of high *practical* relevance, meaning that the components do what they are supposed to do and that they interact in the desired way to realize the system.

It is important for the practicability and the wide range of applicability of the ASM modeling method that the models, their refinements and their properties come in rigorous form but are not formalized in a (necessarily restricted) programming or logic language. In fact, 'modeling is not tied to computers' [134]. Nevertheless, where needed, ASMs can be further supported by formally defined executable versions and mechanically supported forms of logical verification. We adhere to the **principle to be as precise as appropriate for the given problem** domain, as detailed as needed to avoid ambiguity and incompleteness but not more, and to use formalization only where unavoidable (e. g. to refine a model to an executable or mechanically verifiable one). There is no absolute notion of accuracy. We avoid in this book any particular formal (programming or logic) description language or logical proof system. Instead we use only basic set-theoretic and algorithmic notation and rigorous reasoning the practitioner works with on an every-day basis when explaining design ideas. The wide-ranging flexibility this yields for mapping ASM models and reasonings about their properties to a variety of logic languages and mechanically supported verification techniques is not the subject of this (but could be the subject for another valuable) book. Meantime the reader who is interested in the theoretical developments around the concept of ASMs, in particular on verification issues (including a logic for ASMs), is referred to [76, Chaps. 7,8]. Also various non-trivial mathematical proofs of behavioral properties for theoretically challenging ASMs can be found there (or in [232]).

How to Use the Book

This book is written for self-study and to serve as reference book, but it can also be used for teaching. Exercises are inserted to help readers to check their understanding of the explained concepts. For many models defined in this book refinements to executable versions can be downloaded for experimental validation from the website of the book

http://modelingbook.informatik.uni-ulm.de

We deposit there also hints and solutions for some of the exercises and more examples. As support for teaching we also make slides on various themes treated in the book freely available; an acknowledgment would be appreciated where the material is used. In the two introductory chapters 2, 3 we have made a particular effort to start from scratch and to explain each concept separately. As a consequence, the reader who wants to learn what ASMs are and how to use them is advised to read these two chapters sequentially, from beginning to end. The remaining chapters can be read selectively. To facilitate this, we add a summary of some notational conventions and a list of frequently appearing symbols and abbreviations.

We make extensive use of footnotes so that the main explanation flow is not disrupted by side remarks and references.

Dependency of Chapters

Chapter 1 explains **why modeling** cannot be achieved by programming alone and in which respects the two activities are methodologically complementary to each other. The chapter is of epistemological character and can be skipped by the reader who is only interested in technical details.

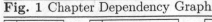

Fig. 1 Chapter Dependency Graph

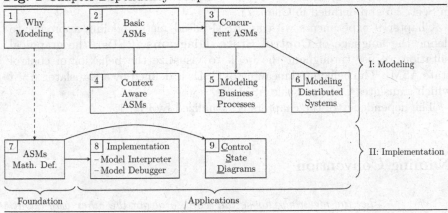

Chapter 2 explains single-agent **basic ASMs**. Technically speaking, it depends on nothing; for its pragmatical motivation it depends on Chapter 1. Chapter 3 explains multi-agent **concurrent ASMs**. It depends on an understanding of the seven basic ASM constructs (which are recapped in Sect. 2.5).

The remaining chapters of Part I can be read independently of each other.

Chapter 4 introduces context-aware ASMs, called **ambient ASMs**, and applies them to model information hiding, programming and communication patterns. It depends on an understanding of basic ASMs (as recapped in Sect. 2.5).

Chapter 5 defines an ASM pattern for modeling web services and a domain specific class of ASM nets, which is tailored for and applied to **model business processes** and their workflows.

Chapter 6 is focussed on **modeling distributed systems**, explained by two characteristic examples: dynamic routing in ad hoc networks and distributed relaxed shared memory management.

Chapters 5, 6 assume an understanding of Definitions 2, 4 (concurrent communicating ASMs) and of concurrent ASM runs (Definition 6).

The chapters of Part II have a technical character and have been written for readers with interest in implementation issues.

Chapter 7 provides a precise, **mathematical definition** (not a formalized one) of the syntax and semantics of ASMs. Technically, this chapter does not depend on any other chapter, but it builds upon the motivations explained in Chap. 1 and Chap. 2. It permits the reader to quickly consult a rigorous, unambiguous, mathematical definition of the few fundamental ASM concepts, should the need be felt when reading the rigorous natural language explanations in the main text.

Chapter 8 defines an ASM model for **CoreASM**, a tool to execute ASMs, together with a specification of a **model debugger** component. It depends on an understanding of the seven basic ASM constructs (which are recapped in Sect. 2.5 and detailed in Chap. 7).

Chapter 9 experiments with an ASM-based metamodeling approach to define the language of **Control State Diagrams** (CSDs), the graphical notation we use throughout the book to visualize the behavior of control state ASMs. The behavioral meaning of CSDs is defined by a translator ASM which translates CSDs to basic ASMs.

The dependency of the chapters is visualized by Fig. 1.

Naming Convention

> *Let the meaning choose the word, and not the other way about.*
> George Orwell[3]

To ease the understanding of models and to facilitate their inspection (see Sect. 1.1.1), we use the following naming convention. To denote objects of some domain and their properties, we use their natural language names (or evocative abbreviations thereof) as formal names, for example

the *color* of a given *table* is *green*

is written as:

$$color(table) = green$$

where the used formal terms *color*, *table*, and *green*, stand for the following:

table $\in$ *Table*	-- *Table* denotes the set of tables
green $\in$ *Color*	-- *Color* denotes the set of colors
color: *Table* $\to$ *Color*	-- *color* denotes the associating function

We treat the same way the predicative version of the statement, 'the table is green' or 'the attribute Green is true for table'. Here 'Green' is considered as attribute which may or may not hold, also called a *Predicate* of *table*. It is written as usual *Green(table)* (read: 'Green' holds for 'table') or *Green(table)* = *true*, interpreting predicates as Boolean-valued functions:

Green: *Table* $\to$ {*true*, *false*} -- Predicates/Sets start with capital letter

In other words, we choose names whose intuitive meaning suggests their intended interpretation and use them to accurately paraphrase the informal descriptions to-be-modeled.

---

[3] See [198].

Acknowledgements

This is the place to express our thanks.

We thank the Abstract State Machines (ASM) community which developed the modeling method explained in this book and since the publication of the AsmBook [76] improved it considerably. In particular we thank those who have helped with detailed critical comments on draft chapters of this book: Paolo Arcaini, Donatella Barnocchi, Don Batory, Alessandro Bianchi, Paolo Dini, Roozbeh Farahbod, Albert Fleischmann, Vincenzo Gervasi, Uwe Glässer, Henri Habrias, Andreas Hense, Felix Kossak, Markus Leitz, Alexei Lisitsa, Klaus-Dieter Schewe, Jacopo Soldani, Kirsten Winter, Simone Zenzaro.

Last but not least we thank the Alexander von Humboldt Foundation, for a grant which supported two stays of the first author at the University of Ulm for our work on the book, and Alfred Hofmann and Ralf Gerstner from Springer for their trust and patience.

Egon Börger
Alexander Raschke
Pisa and Ulm, January 2018

Contents

Symbols and Notations

Notations from Logic

not $(\neg)$, **and** $(\wedge)$, **or** $(\vee)$ -- negation, conjunction, disjunction

iff $(\Leftrightarrow)$ -- logical equivalence: if and only if

forall $(\forall)$ -- universal quantifier

forsome $(\exists)$, **thereissome** $(\exists)$ -- existential quantifier

thereisno $(\neg\exists)$ -- negated existential quantifier

$eval(exp, \mathcal{A}, \zeta)$ -- value of exp in state $\mathcal{A}$ with variable assignment ζ

$eval_\zeta^{\mathfrak{A}}(exp)$, $[\![exp]\!]_\zeta^{\mathfrak{A}}$ -- other notations for $eval(exp, \mathcal{A}, \zeta)$

$eval_{\zeta,env}^{\mathfrak{A}}$, $[\![exp]\!]_{\zeta,env}^{\mathfrak{A}}$ -- extension of $eval$ by an $environment$, Def. 8

$exp(x/t)$ -- result of replacing each free occurrence of x in exp by t

Set/Multiset/List Notation

NAT   -- set of natural numbers $0, 1, 2, \ldots$

$|A|$ -- cardinality of A

$x \in A$ -- x is an element of A

$A \setminus B = \{a \in A \mid a \notin B\}$ -- difference set

$A \cap B, A \cup B, A \times B$ -- intersection, union, cross product

$A \subseteq B$ -- A is a subset of B

$\wp(X) = \{Y \mid Y \subseteq X\}$ -- Power set of X

$\{x \in X \mid P(x)\}$ -- set of all elements of X which satisfy P

$f : A \to B$ -- function f from domain A to range B

$f[a \mapsto b]$ denotes f' **where** $f = f'$ except for $f'(a) = b$

$f_a^b = f[a \mapsto b]$ -- equivalent notation, common in logic

$f(\_) = constant$ -- abbreviates **forall** x $f(x) = constant$

$\epsilon x(P(x))$ -- some x which satisfies P (Hilbert's choice operator)

$\iota x(P(x))$ -- the unique x that satisfies P (Hilbert's ι operator)

$\{\!\}$ -- empty multiset/bag

$\{p_1, p_1, p_2, \ldots, p_n\}$ -- a multiset of $n + 1$ elements

$[]$ -- empty list (or sequence, stream, queue)

$[p_1, \ldots, p_n]$ -- list etc. of n elements, in the given order

$List(Domain)$ -- a list etc. of elements of $Domain$

$head(a)$ -- the first element of a list etc. a

$tail(a)$ -- the list etc. a, except its first element

$concatenate([p_1, \ldots, p_n], [q_1, \ldots, q_m]) = [p_1, \ldots, p_n, q_1, \ldots, q_m]$

$a < b$ -- order relation: a comes before b

$a > b$ -- order relation: a comes after b

ASM Notation. See the definitions in Sect. 7

$Upd(P, \mathcal{A}, env)$ -- update set P computes, given $\mathcal{A}, env$, see Def. 21

$\Delta(P, \mathcal{A}, env)$ -- another notation for $Upd(P, \mathcal{A}, env)$

$Locs(U)$ -- set of locations of updates in an update set U

$\mathfrak{A} + U$ -- sequel state, result of applying to state $\mathfrak{A}$ the updates in U

$S \Rightarrow_P S'$ -- P can make a move from state S to S', See Def. 22

one of ($Rules$)   -- abbreviates **choose** $R \in Rules$ **do** R

SPONTANEOUSLYDO($\mathcal{M}$)   -- see Sect. 3.2.2

import   -- see Sect. 8.1.1

stepwise($P_1, \ldots, P_n$) -- non-atomic sequence operator, see Sect. 4.5.1

P **seq** Q -- atomic sequence operator, see Sect. 4.5.2

$U \oplus V$ -- sequential update set merge, defined p. 171

undef   -- see p. 49

$Instances(P)$ -- set of instances of an ASM P, see Def. 3

COPY($f_1, \ldots, f_n,$ **from** x **to** x') =
     forall $1 \leq i \leq n$ **do** $f_i(x') := f_i(x)$

OtherNotations

DISPLAY   -- output

$RT, RT(a)$ -- Route Table (of agent a)

List of Figures

Part I
Modeling

Chapter 1
Introduction: The Role of Modeling

In this introduction we describe the role of modeling in the process of building reliable software-intensive systems. We explain the conceptual features by which the *Abstract State Machines* (ASM) method, where models take the rigorous meaning of ASMs, permits to realize this role for the development of well documented software for such systems. The rest of the book illustrates this role and introduces the ASM method with modeling examples from various application fields.

The software and the code executing computer are only one part of the ystems we are mainly interested in; the other parts constitute the environment on which the software and computer depend upon and which they affect. As a consequence modeling software components targets two different concerns. One is to accurately formulate the desired software behavior—its intended computational effect when executed in the given field of application—from the *system perspective*. That perspective typically comprises also components of the real world where the software is executed: external actors, sensors, technical equipment, information systems, human users, etc. This requires accurately and adequately relating the relevant real-world system elements and their behavior to abstract model concepts. In this way the abstract model can be 'grounded' in the reality it represents. We call this the **Ground Model Concern**, a crucial, application-domain focussed, epistemological correctness concern characterized in Sect. 1.1. The second concern for an effective modeling method is to provide means to guarantee that the ground model correctness is preserved through the *design steps* taken to vary the high-level requirements model (e. g. for exploration purposes) or to transform it to executable code, possibly passing through some intermediate still partly abstract software models. We call this the **Model Refinement Concern**, a (not only technical) concern for the development of reliable software characterized in Sect. 1.2.

This book illustrates how using ASMs as comprehensive and intuitive notion of 'model', supported by a simple and precise underlying behavioral definition (aka 'semantics' of ASMs), enables coping satisfactorily with these two major software development concerns.[1]

In passing, we mention that the two concerns are essential also when it comes to define standards for software-related concepts and methods and to establish the standard conformance of concrete implementations. Here the standard—an authoritative definition of the desired features—plays the role of the ground model, and every implementation that supports the standard plays the role of a ground model refinement. Standard conformance appears in this context as correctness of the refinement. ASM ground models have been used successfully in various standardization endeavors to accurately define the prescribed behavior. Early examples are the ISO standard for Prolog [151, 68] with its proven-to-be-standard-compliant refinement by the Warren Abstract Machine [69], the IEEE standard for the hardware design language VHDL'93 [150, 57, 58] with its extension to the analog version and to Verilog [211, 210], and the de facto standard for the Kermit protocol [86, 146] which was widely used in those times. Later examples are the International Telecommunication Union standard for the specification language SDL-2000 [154, 103], the de facto standard for Java together with the Java Virtual Machine [232] and the ECMA standard for C# [54] together with the .NET CLR [118]. As recent example we can mention the OMG BPMN 2.0 standard for modeling business processes [196, 166]. Given the complex and special character of these industrial applications of the ASM method, we do not illustrate them in this book and instead refer the interested reader to the cited literature.

1.1 Ground Model Concern

At the beginning of any software project is the task to correctly understand and formulate the real-word problem and the context where the executed software is one among multiple components which together are expected to realize the desired overall system behavior. The task involves three descriptions which together constitute what we call a *ground model*:

- a precise and complete description of the *requirements*, indicating the desired system behavior at the level of abstraction and rigor of the given field of application (also called application domain),
- a *software specification*, i. e. a precise abstract description of the expected behavior of the software when executed by a computer in the system environment,

---

[1] The reader who is eager to see this and is less interested in the foundational aspects of ground model and refinement concern may skip the rest of this introduction and proceed directly to Chap. 2.

- a description of those *domain assumptions* the system designers can rely upon when it comes to justify that the specification satisfies the requirements. The assumptions are assumptions on the structure and behavior of the system components in their environment. The justification is about a behavioral correctness property, namely that the specification will behave as system component the way the requirements demand to solve the given problem. Sometimes, e. g., for simulation purposes, (some) domain assumptions may be formulated in terms of a separate model which describes the assumed behavior of the environment.

The requirements and the domain assumptions are under the responsibility of and have to be formulated by (or in cooperation with) domain experts in application-domain terms. The relevant domain assumptions must be made explicit for the software specification, which is the document the software and the domain experts share and have to agree upon during what is commonly called requirements specification. Through requirements analysis and definition, that portion of application-domain knowledge must become explicit which suffices to establish that the software specification satisfies the requirements under the domain assumptions. This is called the *correctness property*, which is of practical importance and by no means a merely theoretical concern. Thus the software specification stands in between the application-domain-focussed requirements with the related domain assumptions and the software to-be-developed. For the implications on the kind of justification one can expect here, namely to 'explain how the solution (read: the specification) relates to the affairs of the world it helps to handle' [192, p. 254], see the discussion of the *verification method problem* below (Sect. 1.1.1).

The ground model constituents are targeted to reach a common understanding by humans—experts of different fields—of some desired behavior in a portion of the field of application in the real world. Therefore the descriptions must be formulated in a common language both domain and software experts understand (see below the discussion of the *communication problem*, Sect. 1.1.1). These ground model descriptions are not about programming[2] and come prior to it, but they are relevant for the software development. The reason is that poor requirements are still the number one cause of software project and system failures, mainly due to the lack of an appropriate intellectual understanding of the system.[3] Poor requirements typically result in a poor (often completely missing) software specification and/or in an unreliable argument (if any) that under given domain assumptions the software or its specification does what the requirements request and the customer believes it to do.

---

[2] In particular, they are not about classes and their structure where object-oriented approaches to system development tend to put the initial attention.

[3] 'Nearly all the serious accidents in which software has been involved in the past twenty years can be traced to requirements flaws, not coding errors.' [182, Sect. 2.5]

Ground model software specifications represent blueprints of the software component to-be-developed for the system in question. For good reasons they are called 'golden models' in the semiconductor industry. On the one side stakeholders and domain experts can analyze the blueprint—reason about its properties, observe through experiments (testing) its behavior and debug it—prior to its expensive implementation. In this way they can make sure the to-be-developed system is well understood and recognized as correct and complete. On the other side the blueprint provides the authoritative basis—a 'contract'—the software experts (designers and programmers) can rely upon for the further software development via stepwise refinement of model abstractions by executable software components.[4] For this reason a ground model must be:

- *precise* at the level of abstraction and rigor of the problem and of the application domain it belongs to, meaning that it is unambiguous to be correctly understandable by the software designer, in particular in its domain knowledge related features, leaving no gap in understanding,
- *correct*, meaning that the model elements reliably and adequately convey the meaning of what they stand for in the real world,
- *complete*, meaning to contain every behaviorally relevant feature,
- *consistent*, meaning that conflicting objectives which may be present in the original requirements have been resolved.

When a description is precise, its consistency can be checked by rigorous mathematical means, since consistency is about a logical system-internal property. In contrast, for epistemological reasons, the correctness and completeness properties cannot be established by purely linguistic, system-internal means, since they relate precise conceptual features to non-verbal phenomena in the real world. This fact imposes some characteristics on the language used in ground model descriptions, as explained in the next section.

1.1.1 Ground Model Correctness and Completeness

Ground models are conceptual models which relate real-world features to linguistic elements so that their correctness and completeness are properties of epistemological nature. To establish them, the language used to formulate ground models must solve three problems.

First of all, ground models must be understandable for experts of different fields, here application domain and software experts. To solve this *communication problem*, the language used to formulate ground models must have the capability to calibrate the degree of precision of descriptions (read: their level

---

[4] As a consequence, as long as no confusion is to be expected, we often use the term 'ground model' also for the software specification.

of abstraction) to any given application-domain problem. In other words, the language must be able to accurately represent (express)

- any kind of real-world objects with their properties and relations, which constitute arbitrary system 'states',
- arbitrary actions to change the set of objects or to modify some property or relation among them, which constitute arbitrary 'state changes'.

The fact that the **ground model language must embrace a most general notion of state and state change** is contrary to a widely held view. The language must allow domain experts and software experts to reach a common understanding of what states and state changes are.[5] Therefore the language must be a clearly defined, readily understandable portion of natural language, made up from precise and simple but general enough basic constructs to unambiguously represent real-world facts (states of affairs) and state changing events. This is as usual in rigorous scientific disciplines.

The *verification method problem* for ground models stems from the fact that the appropriateness of the association of real-world objects and relations with model elements[6] cannot be proved by mathematical means, for reasons of principle. However **model inspection**, reviewing of the blueprint (not of code!) performed in cooperation by the application-domain experts and the software experts, can provide evidence of the desired direct and adequate correspondence between ground model elements and the features in the world those elements express. In this way, the parties involved can establish the appropriateness of the ground model, in particular the correctness and completeness properties for the software specification. To make such inspections possible, the language to formulate ground models must provide means to express objects, states of affairs and events in the real world *directly*, supporting the correctness link the model inspection has to check. Such direct expressability calls for linguistic support of descriptions at whatever given abstraction level. Even high-level programming languages do not suffice for that because each programming language necessarily is bound to a specific abstraction level determined by the basic data structures and operations it offers.[7] It is important to also recognize, contrary to a widely held view, that the **issue is not whether descriptions are declarative or operational, but at which level of abstraction they are formulated**. Different degrees of detailing serve the multiple roles of abstraction, such as providing an

---

[5] 'The extra communication step between the engineer [read: the domain expert] and the software developer is the source of the most serious problems with software today.' [182, Sect. 2.5]

[6] This is what Leibniz called 'proportio quaedam inter *characteres* ('symbols') et *res* ('things')', the basis of truth: 'Et haec proportio sive relatio est *fundamentum veritatis*' [178].

[7] See the explanations in [134], that 'programming as it exists now forces us to model, but it does so in an unnatural way', and in [227] that we need to become 'able to grasp ... problems directly, without the intermediate muck of code'.

accurate and checkable overall system understanding, or isolating the hard parts of a system, or communicating and documenting design ideas, etc.

Model inspection or review resembles code inspection, which programmers are used to, but it happens at a higher level of abstraction, being based upon the precise ground model descriptions, using domain-specific reasoning and involving domain and software experts. The experimental (as opposed to deductive) character of ground model inspection leads to the *validation problem* for ground models. It must be possible to support their analysis by repeatable experiments aiming to falsify (and in case to debug) expected model behaviour in the Popperian sense [204]. This calls for **executability of ground model software specifications** so that runtime verification and testing become available at the application-domain (often scenario) level of abstraction. By the way, also the request for executability is contrary to the above mentioned widely held view in computer science which wants specifications to be purely declarative. Executability is necessary for reasons of principle, but is important also pragmatically. The high-level debugging potential the executability of models opens, to detect conceptual problems low-level code inspection easily misses, helps to save on the enormous cost of late code-level testing and runtime verification. Furthermore, it offers to use the ground model as application-domain-knowledge-driven 'oracle' to select characteristic test samples and to define their expected behavior. Last but not least model executability supports exploratory software development processes by providing rigorous models coming with well-documented design decisions. Here we use executability in its algorithmic understanding of 'mechanical' execution, performed at the level of abstraction of the model, possibly mentally (by humans who inspect the conceptual model) and not necessarily by machines.

We briefly explain below (Sect. 1.1.2) how Abstract State Machines solve the communication, verification and validation problems for ground models.

1.1.2 Appropriateness of ASMs as Ground Models

As explained in the preceding section, the epistemological character of ground models requires the language used to describe them to satisfy three properties:

easy comprehension: to be readily understandable by experts of different fields,

clear definition: to be clearly defined without unnecessary formalization overhead,

general direct expressivity: to support abstraction using precise and simple but sufficiently general language constructs which allow one to establish a direct correspondence between ground model elements and whatever 'reality' they express.

The ASM method comes with a precise definition of what is a *model*, namely an ASM. As side effect, we can also use the term 'system model' in a rigorous sense as meaning 'set of interacting ASMs'. We call them also 'machines' because in software development applications, on which this book is focussed, ASMs mainly stand for 'software executed by a computer'.

That ASMs are 'easy to understand' is due to the simple generic language in which they are formulated. ASMs come as sets of basic natural language constructs (called rules), essentially of the following form:

if *condition* **then** *action*.

Here *condition* and *action* denote the following:

- *condition* is any unambiguous expression—what is called a 'proposition' or *state*ment—which describes a *state* of affairs. It may involve whatever kind of objects with whatever properties and relations between them.
- *action* is any unambiguous description of whatever kind of *operations* to change the state of the involved objects—their attributes and relations. The *action* has to be performed whenever the *condition* is true in the given state. For this reason such a condition is called the *guard* of the rule.

No translation to a logic language is needed to express such conditions, actions and their effect precisely. Rules of this form do satisfy the above mentioned *easy comprehension* criterion. In fact they represent a common and well understood scheme used in natural, expert and scientific languages to describe actions to be taken, or state-modifying events to occur, when some condition is satisfied.[8]

Not surprisingly, the scheme corresponds to a basic verification scheme, namely

if P **then** Q

also expressed as 'from P follows Q' or 'P implies Q' and studied in logic. It relates the truth value of propositions representing premise and conclusion.[9] The *easy comprehension* property of ASMs is confirmed also by our cooperation with domain and software design experts. We experienced there that the correct intuitive understanding of ASMs *never* was a problem and that this intuitive understanding always was sufficient to correctly apply ASMs in

---

[8] We mention two outstanding examples where instances of the scheme occur in computing. One is Dijkstra's Guarded Command Language [93] whose basic element has the form $P \rightarrow C$ expressing that if the proposition P is true then the command C is executed. The other is Action Systems [17, 203] where basic actions have the form *Guard* $\rightarrow$ *updates* to execute in a given state a finite set *updates* of variable assignments $y := f(y)$ if the *Guard* is true in that state. None of these two languages has the general state concept on which ASM ground models and ASM refinements are based.

[9] For characteristic applications of ASMs in the area of reasoning systems, see the ASM specifications of reasoning patterns in [160, 27, 28], their refinement to an executable version [29], their use to prove the correctness of the implementation [30] and their use in a medical application [31, 26].

practice, without need of any special training. Obviously, if a system at the level of abstraction where we want to describe it is complex, its model, to be faithful, must reflect that complexity. The distinguishing feature of ASM models is that they do not add any complexity of their own.

The second important characteristics of ASM rules is that their meaning—the effect of their execution—is clearly defined in rigorous though not formalized terms. We hope the reader will recognize this when going through the introductory examples in Sects. 2-3 or by looking at the definitions in Chap. 7. The state change resulting from the execution of rules yields an accurate, simple and abstract, state-based concept of runs of ASMs. This provides conceptual executability one can use for accurate high-level validation and debugging. Thus the language of ASMs satisfies the above stated *clear definition* criterion.

The run concept supports the practical understanding of ASMs as a rigorously defined form of abstract process or virtual machine descriptions, or pseudo-code working over abstract data structures. On the other side it is not difficult to give a purely mathematical definition of ASMs and their behavior which supports the intuitive understanding (see Sect. 7). The mathematical definition is necessary as a basis for building tools supporting mechanical execution and validation (high-level model-based testing and runtime verification) of ASMs (see [84, 16]). It also makes mathematical verifications of model properties possible—at all levels of detail, whether by proof sketches or by genuinely mathematical or formalized or machine-checked or interactive machine supported proofs. How detailed a verification should be is a pragmatic issue, what is important is that the modeling method supports the appropriate form of verification in the given context.[10]

Last but not least also the *general direct expressivity* criterion is satisfied by the expression and action language of ASMs. The most widely used instance of the ASM *expression language* is the language of first-order logic, enriched by rigorous application-domain-specific expressions and a few common algorithmic and set theoretic notations. It allows one to directly represent:

- objects of any kind by elements of a correspondingly named domain,
- any object properties or relations by correspondingly named predicates,
- any operations to change objects, their attributes or relations by correspondingly named functions.

---

[10] We point only to a few characteristic ones out of the numerous examples in the literature which document how the ASM method supports mathematical verification at any level of detail in various domains: intuition-supporting traditional mathematical proofs (like in [69, 51, 232, 231, 23]), proof-rule based proofs in a dedicated logic calculus (like in [225, 230]) or machine-assisted interactive proofs (using well-known theorem provers like KIV [218, 128, 219, 142, 141] or PVS [249, 98, 234, 124] or the dedicated ASM-based Theorem Prover AsmTP [228]). Notably [23] explains how the ASM method allows one to couple design and verification in a compositional way, using stepwise refinements. It would be useful to implement the Asm2EventB translation in [62] so that ASM model properties could be verified using the strong mechanical proof support the B [1] and Event-B [2] methods offer.

A *state* of an ASM is therefore an interpretation of its set, predicate and function symbols (which constitute its *signature*) by corresponding sets of objects with their properties, relations and functions in the modeled (the 'real') world. In this simple way, any desired level of abstraction can be captured without any encoding. Which details appear in (or are abstracted away from) a ground model depends on the details an accurate description of the given application-domain problem requires to mention.[11] The ASM method knows no divorce between theory and practice of computing because it is firmly based upon a most general notion of 'state' and 'state change'.

The most widely used concrete instance of the ASM *action language* uses abstract updates of the form $exp := e$, meaning that the value (object) represented in the given state by the *exp*ression is changed to the value (object) represented in the given state by the expression e. To provide a most general notion of state change, *exp*ressions at the left-hand side of an update support a functional form $exp = f(e_1, \ldots, e_n)$, where f is an n-ary function symbol and e_i are expressions, so that results of abstract operations can be denoted in dependency of parameters of whatever desired sort. More abstract actions can be used in ASMs as the reader will see in this book.

The language of ASMs resembles scientific languages in that it is a rigorous but open language, representing a precise conceptual and notational framework that is extendable by whatever accurate concepts are needed in the respective application domain.

1.2 Model Refinement Concern

Refinement is a general methodological principle to manage complexity by piecemeal de-/composing a system into/from its constituent parts which can be treated separately and then (re-) combined. We explain in this section some outstanding methodological properties of the ASM refinement concept. Its definition and applications will be given in the following chapters.

Refinement goes together with the inverse process of abstraction. ASM refinements as introduced in [39] exploit the availability of arbitrary structures to **accurately link data and operations at whatever level of abstraction** is desired. These structures are generalizations of what in computing is called data structures, namely sets of objects with their properties, relations and operations. The freedom of abstraction allows the designer to tailor ASM refinement/abstraction pairs to faithfully reflect any single design decision or reengineering idea.

Successive refinement steps result in an explicit documentation of the set of design decisions that are piecemeal introduced through the respective levels of abstraction. Proceeding by refinement steps allows one to avoid premature

---

[11] This notion of state is what in logic is known under the name of *Tarski structures*, objects of study of the branch of logic known as model theory.

design decisions. Starting the refinement steps with ground model ASMs provides an explicit link of the system architect's view (blueprint) through the designers' module architecture view to the programmer's compilable code view (implementation). Such refinements link the system lifecycle activities from requirements capture to system maintenance in an organic, effectively maintainable way. The executability of ASM models allows one also to link the traditional levels of testing, namely of the entire system, of its constituent modules and of their code components (unit test).

Given the mathematical character of ASMs, each model refinement, besides its validatability, can be mathematically verified to be 'correct', meaning that it models the underlying design idea in the intended way. The ASM framework allows one to adapt the level of proofs of model properties—of which refinement correctness is only one example—to the degree of reliablity requested for the verification. Proofs can be sketched, or be detailed proofs for humans to read, or machine-checkable or machine-generated or interactive machine-supported proofs, each level of verification serving a different purpose and coming with its characteristic costs. A specific strength of the operational ASM framework is that it directly supports, at any level of abstraction, the provision of proofs for behavioral system properties which closely follow and express the underlying computational intuitions without formal overhead. Such proofs are made by the designer for the stakeholders to read, supporting them to understand the designed system and to check the justification of its correctness. We will illustrate this feature with numerous examples in this book.

Often we apply stepwise ASM refinement also at the ground model level, capturing the given requirements piecemeal by components and their refinements. This supports formulating conceptually, in problem-centered rather than programming language terms, the ideas which contribute to a solution of the problem the requirements demand to solve.[12] Furthermore stepwise development of ground models also reduces the complexity of the inspection process, in accordance with Parnas' code inspection guidelines.[13] Combining ASM ground model inspection with provably correct ASM refinements provides the possibility to develop software that can be certified to exhibit the desired behavior.

A pragmatically important side effect of the ASM refinement method is that it allows the designer to separate orthogonal concerns, namely by horizontal or by vertical refinements. *Horizontal refinements* permit to accu-

---

[12] In this way ground models support a major concern of Language Oriented Programming [97].

[13] 'the key to inspection of any complex product is a policy of *divide and conquer*, i. e., having the inspector examine small parts of the product in isolation, while making sure that 1) nothing is overlooked and 2) that the correctness of all inspected components implies the correctness of the whole product. The decomposition of the inspection into discrete steps must assure that each step is simple enough that it can be carried out reliably and that one inspection step can be carried out without detailed knowledge of the others.' [200]

Fig. 1.1 Models and methods in ASM-based software developments [76]
© 2003 Springer-Verlag Berlin Heidelberg, reprinted with permission

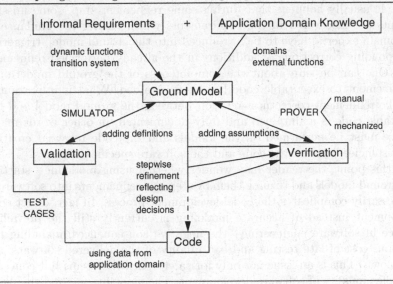

rately introduce piecemeal extensions (e. g., upgradings of functionality[14]) and adaptations (e. g., to changing requirements or environment conditions). This supports *design for change* and system *maintenance* in the sense that later changes can be introduced without complete redesign and without losing the correctness relation between the models that are involved, including the ground model and the code. *Vertical refinements* permit to stepwise introduce more and more details for model elements (domains, functions, rules). This supports *design for reuse* and development of design patterns which offer to introduce model variations. The refinement relation between ground model and code supports the *traceability of requirements* and thus facilitates also the writing of user manuals, relating software behavior to real-world phenomena. Last but not least *design communication* is made effective through accurate, precise, indexed and searchable documentation of the model refinements. Altogether the ASM refinement method combined with the executable character of the models it produces supports evolutionary approaches to software development. This book illustrates how using ASMs helps to achieve these goals.

Remark on the development process. We summarize by Fig. 1.1 the constituents of an ASM-based development process. Once a ground model is defined and justified, the remaining software development task is that of

---

[14] See the related extension concept to build product lines by stepwise addition of features, recently used [132] to incrementally construct platform independent models of dataflow programs.

refining the ground model to executable code, as explained in Sect. 1.2. But the *process* of developing a ground model and its refinements is by no means linear. It usually happens that during some refinement step, some missing elements are discovered in the requirements which (under the guidance of the domain experts) have to be introduced into the ground model, triggering corresponding corrections or additions in the already performed refinement steps. One can be sure about the completeness of the ground model once its refinement to executable code has been obtained. What is important is that the refinement-correctness-relation between the ground model and the executable code is maintained and fully documented; in other words maintenance must be performed on the models and the code to avoid creating inconsistencies between the code and the software specification.

At this point, the reader may wonder whether using modeling—starting with ground models and turning them by stepwise refinements into software—unnecessarily complicates the code development process. In fact, direct code development instead of accurate modeling is currently still the prevailing practice in software engineering—the negative consequences, including the enormous cost of late testing and bad quality of the delivered software, are well known. This is an issue not only for safety critical systems but concerns the professionality of software development. The modeling method this book is about supports and requires to 'think a lot before coding' [2, p. 11]. It proposes to combine two concerns:

- Give the needed attention, prior to coding, to the description and analysis of the real-world problem until it is fully explained and understood by the parties involved—the *Ground Model Concern* (Sect. 1.1) which is advocated (though not under this name) also in [155].
- Document, for system explanation and maintenance reasons, the relevant design decisions, taken to transform the ground model into code—the *Model Refinement Concern*.

As a result, system software can gain in reliability, by being well understood and effectively documented, and in the cost for its development and maintenance, due to saving the cost of reacting to software (or even software project) failures.

Caveat. Using ASMs for modeling is not suggested as a stand-alone (sort of universal) software engineering method. In the contrary, due to the flexibility of the ASM concept, using ASMs is compatible with and can be integrated at various stages into numerous existing software development environments and validation and verification frameworks, as can be seen from the large variety of successful applications of the ASM method reported in the literature. For some surveys, see [38, 43]. See also the Epilogue on page 317.

Chapter 2
Seven Constructs for Modeling Single-Agent Behavior

In this chapter we introduce the seven behavioral (action describing) constructs which constitute the building blocks for Abstract State Machines (ASMs). We do this in small steps.

Here is the roadmap:

- abstract assignment (update operation :=), **if then else**, parallel execution (**par**) (Sect. 2.1, 2.2).

  – What is introduced here are ASMs M which consist of finitely many rules of the form **if** *condition* **then** *Updates*, where *condition* is any Boolean-valued (abstract) expression and *Updates* a set of assignments $f(t_1, \ldots, t_n) := t$ with any (abstract) terms t_i, t. Here one step of M, in any state S, consists in *simultaneously* applying to S, for *each* rule of M whose *condition* is true in S, *each* update $f(t_1, \ldots, t_n) := t$ in the set of *Updates* of the rule, with the values of t_i, t computed in S. Obviously such a step is possible only if no inconsistent updates appear.

- **forall, let** (Sect. 2.3).

  – Here the synchronous parallelism is strengthened, by permitting, for an already defined ASM M, to write rules of the form **forall** x **with** *condition* **do** $M(x)$. These rules, in every state S, in one step simultaneously apply to S, for *each* x which satisfies the *condition* in S, *each* update computed by $M(x)$ in S. Permitting to write rules of the form **let** $x = expression$ **in** $M(x)$ integrates a local form of sequentialization into the synchronous parallel execution paradigm of ASMs: in one step, in state S, first the *expression* is computed and then one step of $M(val)$ is performed in S with the computed *value*.

- **call, choose** (Sect. 2.4).

  – This permits to describe non-determinism, by rules of the form **choose** x **with** *condition* **do** M, and submachine calls $N(t_1, \ldots, t_n)$, where M is an already defined ASM and N is defined by $N(x_1, \ldots, x_n) = M$.

Each of these constructs represents a well known and commonly used basic concept to express how a state evolves when under specific conditions some of its elements or some of their properties (attributes) or relations change. We introduce these model building constructs one by one, illustrating by simple case studies how to define, for given requirements, justifiably correct rigorous ground models as characterized in Sect. 1.1. We explain them in intuitive but precise terms, providing a working definition practitioners can apply correctly without need of further training. In addition, several important concepts are introduced rigorously (but not formally) within the narrative of the examples, which should therefore be read slowly and allowing time for reflection. We invite the skeptical reader to check that the formal mathematical definition of the behavior of ASM programs in Chap. 7 (which is the basis for the development of ASM tools) supports the intuitive understanding we explain in this chapter.

Since the examples we use in this chapter are about the control of equipment of some sort, the models are single-agent ASMs called *basic* ASMs.[1] We use in particular a visualizable form called *control state* ASMs. They generalize Finite State Machines (FSMs) and their flowchart representation. Each example is focussed on illustrating specific constructs and how to use them to cope with a particular methodological concern. Among them are the following:

- stepwise model development by what is called *ASM refinement*, a method which supports the separation of concerns and a piecemeal introduction of features to capture the requirements (Sect. 2.1),
- model reuse when requirements change (Sects. 2.1, 2.2, 2.3.1),
- modular composition and decomposition of models (Sects. 2.3.1, 2.4),
- integration of data and control features,
- separation of normal behavior from error or failure handling (Sects. 2.3.1.1, 2.3.1.2, 2.4),
- definition of behavioral interfaces (Sect. 2.4).

In Chap. 3 the reader will see that in multi-agent ASMs which are used to model distributed systems, the single, sequential, components come with basic ASM programs as defined in this chapter.

---

[1] They are also called *sequential* ASMs, though they contain some bounded parallelism, to distinguish them from concurrent ASMs or ASMs with unbounded parallelism. We deviate terminologically from finer distinctions between sequential and synchronous parallel ASMs, distinctions which are made in the literature for reasons concerning the underlying logic.

2.1 Assignment, 'if then else', 'par': Traffic Light Control

In this section we introduce the ASM constructs for assignment, IfThenElse and parallel execution by defining a ground model for a given set of informal requirements concerning a One-Way Traffic Light Control problem.[2] We apply to this ground model three characteristic ASM refinement types: vertical ASM refinements (adding implementation details), horizontal ASM refinements (adding new features) and data refinements (refining only data definitions but no rule). We discuss how such refinements can be combined in practice.

We quote the informal requirements *1WayTrafLightReq* concerning the One-Way Traffic Light Control problem from [155, p. 49], with some naming added to ease their traceability.

PlantReq ... to enforce one-way traffic...the traffic is controlled by a pair of simple portable traffic light units...one unit at each end of the one-way section...connect(ed)...to a small computer that controls the sequence of lights.

UnitReq. Each unit has a Stop light and a Go light.

PulseReq. The computer controls the lights by emitting rPulses and gPulses, to which the units respond by turning the light on and off.

RegimeReq. The regime for the lights repeats a fixed cycle of four phases. First, for 50 seconds, both units show Stop; then, for 120 seconds, one unit shows Stop and the other Go; then for 50 seconds both show Stop again; then for 120 seconds the unit that previously showed Go shows Stop, and the other shows Go. Then the cycle is repeated.

In a first step we abstractly model the functionality of the system—'the sequence of lights' described in the *PlantReq*, the light *RegimeReq*irement and the *UnitReq*irement—by a ground model which abstracts from the computer and its connection to the units (Sect. 2.1.1). To this overall system model 1WAYSTOPGOLIGHTSPEC, we apply a vertical ASM refinement to separate the computer control 1WAYSTOPGOPULSECTL from the actions of the hardware environment, as suggested by the *PulseReq*irement and the *PlantReq*irement (Sect. 2.1.2). On these models, we apply a horizontal ASM refinement to illustrate how to smoothly integrate additional requirements presented later (Sect. 2.1.3). We then illustrate the reuse of ASM models by a data refinement yielding a Two-Way Traffic Light Control (Sect. 2.1.4), to which one can apply again horizontal and vertical ASM refinement steps to incorporate further requirements or to move towards an implementation. The detailed roadmap for the section is given in Fig. 2.1.

---

[2] The section reelaborates an example ASM from [41].

2.1.1 One-Way Traffic Light Ground Model

To build a precise executable model for a system, one first of all has to analyze
what the system elements are and their properties (attributes) and relations.
They are represented in the model by an interpretation of what is called its
signature or *vocabulary*, which consists of names for sets of objects, for their
predicates (i. e. attributes or relations) and for operations which are defined
on them.[3]

Excursus on the naming discipline. To ease the understanding of a
model and to simplify its inspection (in the sense characterized in Sect. 1.1.1),
we usually present the signature elements together with their intended interpretation, paraphrasing the informal descriptions to-be-modeled and using
evocative names. To support this notationally, we often emphasize in the text
the elements which have a direct correspondence in the model signature and
let this correspondence stand out by using in the signature the same names

---

[3] In the literature, the signature is often called 'object model'.

Fig. 2.1 Refinements for Traffic Light ASMs

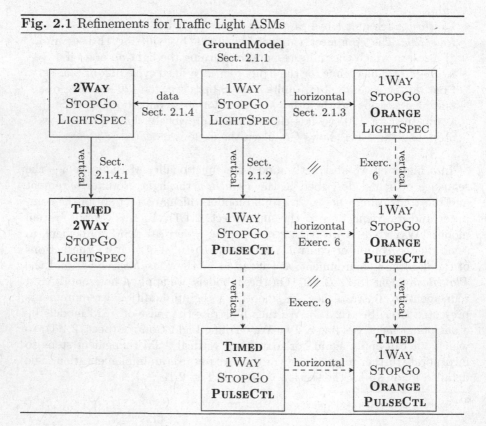

which are used in the informal description or names similar to those. For traceability reasons, we also add some naming to parts of the requirements. **End of excursus.**

The *UnitR*equirement speaks about two units, each with a *StopLight* and a *GoLight*, which we model as parameterized variables to distinguish their instantiations, say $StopLight(i)$ and $GoLight(i)$ for $i = 1, 2$.[4] By the *PulseR*equirement, each of these variables at each moment can take one of two possible values, *on* or *off*:

$$StopLight(i), GoLight(i) \in \{on, off\} \text{ (for } i = 1, 2)$$

The *RegimeReq*, to unambiguously 'show Go' or 'show Stop', seems to suggest that in each phase, the two lights of a unit take always opposite values, i.e. $StopLight(i) = on$ implies $GoLight(i) = off$ and vice versa[5]. We formulate these unit state properties by the following definition for the intended phase representation in the model (for $i = 1, 2$)[6]:

$Stop(i)$ **iff** $StopLight(i) = on$ **and** $GoLight(i) = off$ -- show Stop i
$Go(i)$ **iff** $StopLight(i) = off$ **and** $GoLight(i) = on$ -- show Go i

The *RegimeR*equirement describes the *conditions* and *actions* the model must express. The actions speak in particular about the desired changes of the current *phase* in a cycle. There are four phase values. They are represented as follows by what we call *control states* (names for what in FSMs are called internal states).[7] For mnemonic reason we denote here each control states by one ordered pair of vertically displayed labels *Stopi* and *Goj* with $i, j \in \{1, 2\}$. A label *Stop*1 is used to remind the reader that in any ordered pair where *Stop*1 is one of the two labels the predicate $Stop(1)$ defined above is true; the same for *Stop*2, *Go*1, *Go*2.

*Stop*1	*Go*1	*Stop*2	*Go*2
*Stop*2	*Stop*2	*Stop*1	*Stop*1

The cyclic change of *phase* required by the *RegimeReq* is visualized in Fig. 2.2, a generalization of the well known flowchart representation of FSMs and defined precisely below.

The *condition* in Fig. 2.2 is similar for each *phase* value and therefore denoted in a parameterized form, *Passed*(*phase*), expressing when the time frame required for a *phase* expired. In this case, *Passed*(*phase*) means that the

---

[4] In the object oriented programming world, one would write $i.StopLight$ and $i.GoLight$, where i represents the traffic light with number i. The object-oriented notation is a specific form of parametrization, which is widely used in ASM models (see Chap. 4).

[5] A different interpretation is given in Sect. 2.1.3

[6] **iff** stands for 'if and only if'.

[7] We use the wording 'control state' to distinguish this bit from the more comprehensive notion of 'state' of an ASM explained below.

characteristic *period(phase)* has *Elapsed* since the *phase* was entered.[8] The function *period(phase)* assumes the value 50 or 120 seconds as stipulated by *RegimeReq*. Since these values do not depend on the system states, we declare the function *period*[9] as *static*, as distinguished from functions (or variables)[10] like *phase* and the Boolean valued function *Passed*, whose values depend on the current system state and therefore are declared as *dynamic*.

To abstract in this model from how timers are set, we define the *Passed* predicate by the following equation:

$$Passed(phase) = Elapsed(period(phase))$$

with *Elapsed* treated as an *input function*, meaning that its values are determined by the environment. *Elapsed* is assumed to provide an external clock signal, say the Boolean value *true*, each time *period(ctlstate)* has elapsed since *phase* has been updated to (read: since the ASM entered) *ctlstate*. We document this as an explicit assumption on the runs, explained and analyzed below, of the machine 1WAYSTOPGOLIGHTSPEC with program defined by Fig. 2.2.

- *TimerAssumption.* If in a run (of 1WAYSTOPGOLIGHTSPEC as defined in Fig. 2.2), *phase* is updated by a rule to a *ctlstate*, then after *period(ctlstate)*,

---

[8] Its meaning may also refer to other constraints, for an example see Sect. 2.1.4.

[9] For notational convenience but without loss of generality, we treat predicates as characteristic Boolean-valued functions of their arguments.

[10] To simplify the notation, we consider variables as 0-ary functions.

Fig. 2.2 1Way Traffic Light Ground Model 1WAYSTOPGOLIGHTSPEC [41] © 2010 Springer-Verlag Berlin Heidelberg, reprinted with permission

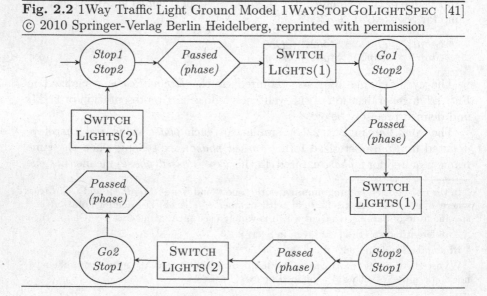

the timeout signal $Elapsed(period(ctlstate))$ is set in the environment by an external timer (to $true$). It is reset (to $false$) when the rule it triggers is executed.[11]

Also the action requested by the $RegimeReq$ is similar for each $phase$ value, namely to SWITCHLIGHTS(i) of the involved unit i from their current values to those required for the next phase. Abstracting from the computer and its connection to the light units one can specify SWITCHLIGHTS(i) for $i = 1, 2$ at the functional level of abstraction as updating the light values of unit i to their opposite values. For pragmatic reasons we use the **where** notation, to mark the auxiliary (usually local) character of the definition in the **where** clause, and shading for intuitive comments.

> SWITCHLIGHTS(i) = [12]
> SWITCH($StopLight(i)$)
> SWITCH($GoLight(i)$)
> **where**
> SWITCH(l) = ($l := l'$)   --$'$ denotes the opposite value

Fig. 2.2 together with the above definitions of its constituents is our first example of a ground model ASM which we call 1WAYSTOPGOLIGHTSPEC. For the sake of illustration we rephrase its rules also in an equivalent textual form. For layout reasons, in the text we display control states horizontally in the form $Move_i Move_j$.

> 1WAYSTOPGOLIGHTSPEC =
> **if** $phase \in \{Stop1Stop2, Go1Stop2\}$ **and** $Passed(phase)$ **then**
>   SWITCHLIGHTS(1)   -- from $Stop(1)$ to $Go(1)$ or viceversa
>   **if** $phase = Stop1Stop2$ **then** $phase := Go1Stop2$
>   **else** $phase := Stop2Stop1$
> **if** $phase \in \{Stop2Stop1, Go2Stop1\}$ **and** $Passed(phase)$ **then**
>   SWITCHLIGHTS(2)   -- from $Stop(2)$ to $Go(2)$ or viceversa
>   **if** $phase = Stop2Stop1$ **then** $phase := Go2Stop1$
>   **else** $phase := Stop1Stop2$
> **where**
>   SWITCHLIGHTS(i) =
>   SWITCH($StopLight(i)$)
>   SWITCH($GoLight(i)$)
>   SWITCH(l) = ($l := l'$)   --$'$ denotes the opposite value
> $Passed(phase) = Elapsed(period(phase))$

---

[11] This magic looking external timer assumption can be easily modeled by an explicit timing mechanism, see Sect. 2.1.4.1.

[12] For notational simplicity we use the equality symbol = not only for comparison, but also for equality by definition, avoiding to introduce a special symbol $=_{def}$ for definitions. The context makes it clear whether = denotes an equality by definition.

The states of 1WAYSTOPGOLIGHTSPEC consist, besides the static function *period* and the input function *Elapsed*, of an interpretation of the dynamic predicate symbol *Passed* and of the five variables (dynamic 0-ary function symbols) *phase*, *StopLight*(i), *GoLight*(i) for $i = 1, 2$. The interpretation of *Passed* is given by the above definition, the interpretation of *Elapsed* is constrained by the above *TimerAssumption*. The interpretation of the three functions *phase*, *StopLight*(i), *GoLight*(i) reflects the requested evolution of the state of the lights and is controlled by the steps of 1WAYSTOPGOLIGHTSPEC. Therefore such functions are also called *controlled functions* (see the function classification below). The transition rules of the ground model are called the ASM *program*.

Before we analyze how running the 1WAYSTOPGOLIGHTSPEC program satisfies the requirements, we characterize in their full generality the first three basic ASM constituents we have introduced in the model, namely *assignment* and *if then else* rules and their *parallel* execution.

Excursus on flowcharts and ASM rules. Control states are pictorially represented in flowcharts by circles labeled with the control state name. The system state changes are represented by transitions which are pictorially represented by arrows leading from a control state, the *phase = source*, to a rhombus labeled by a transition guard *condition*, from there to a rectangle labeled by an *action* and from there to a control state, the *target*. The behavioral meaning is defined in intuitive terms as follows. In Chap. 7 we provide a precise definition, in terms of ASMs, which supports this natural language description. It extends FSM flowcharts to ASMs diagrams, which we call Control State Diagrams (CSDs).

• if the system is in the control state *source* and the *condition* is true in the current system state, then the *action* is performed changing the system state and the system enters the next control state *target*.

Often instead of *phase* also *mode* or *stage* are used to name the control state.

Textually ASM transitions are formulated by rules of the following form (and therefore also called *ASM rules*):

    if *condition* **then** *action*

where an action is typically a finite number of *assignment statements* $s := t$. They denote, as usual, that the value of t is computed and assigned as new value to s, in other words that the value of s is updated to the value computed for t. The ASM language admits any kind of value to appear here, no a priori type restriction is imposed. The expressions s are allowed to be parameterized so that one can specify functional dependencies of the form $f(s_1, \ldots, s_n)$ for any natural number n.

In the specific case of flowchart transitions like in Fig. 2.2, the corresponding textual ASM rules include the *phase* updates and therefore have the following special form:[13]

> **if** *phase* = *source* **and** *condition* **then**
> *action*
> *phase* := *target*

Each pair of a function symbol f and of a list of arguments $(val_1, \ldots, val_n)$ is called a *location*. We invite the reader to view a location as abstract container—a place in memory—where a value is stored. A pair (loc, val) of a location and a value to be stored there is called an *update*. To perform (we also say execute or apply) an update means to assign *val* as value to *loc*, whereby the current value of *loc* may be changed to *val*. A set of updates is called an *update set*. It is called *consistent* if it contains no two pairs with same *loc* and different *val*. We also say that two updates u_1, u_2 are consistent resp. inconsistent if the set $\{u_1, u_2\}$ is consistent resp. inconsistent. We denote for an ASM rule R and an ASM state S by $Upd(R, S)$ the set of updates R requires to execute in state S; we also say that R generates in state S the update set $Upd(R, S)$. To execute (we also say apply) rule R in state S means to *simultaneously* perform in S all updates which are in the update set $Upd(R, S)$. Clearly this can be done only if the update set is consistent. If $Upd(R, S)$ is inconsistent the rule cannot be applied in state S so that no next state is defined.

One step of an ASM M in a given state S **consists in applying simultaneously each rule** R of M in this state S, producing a successor state S'. This means to simultaneously perform in S each update which is in at least one update set $Upd(R, S)$ generated by the rule R of M in state S. Simultaneous execution of all rules implies that the resulting state S' can be obtained by executing the single updates in any order. Technically speaking, we define the update set $Upd(M, S)$ of the machine as the union of all $Upd(R, S)$ for every rule R of M:

$$Upd(M, S) = \bigcup\nolimits_{R \text{ is a rule of } M} Upd(R, S).$$

If this update set $Upd(M, S)$ is inconsistent, it is because either for some rule R of M already $Upd(R, S)$ is inconsistent or because there are two inconsistent updates u_i $(i = 1, 2)$ with u_i belonging to the update set $Upd(R_i, S)$ of two rules R_i of M. In this case the machine cannot execute its step in state S and no next state S' is defined.[14]

---

[13] This scheme is a direct generalization of FSM instructions: checking whether there is still a symbol (or word) on the input tape and reading it (the rule guard *input* = *a*) is replaced by an arbitrary *condition*, writing a symbol (or word) on the output tape (the update *output* := *b*) is replaced by an arbitrary state changing *action*. Note that an FSM performs *output* := *b* in parallel with the control state update of *phase*, a parallelism ASMs generalize to finitely many simultaneous updates.

[14] There are no side effects. Every update in $Upd(M, S)$ and only those are executed in a step.

This **synchronous parallelism** for executing (the rules of) a given single ASM is not to be confused with concurrency, as we will explain in detail in Chap. 3 when introducing multi-agent ASMs. The synchronous parallelism invites to avoid, where conceptually possible at the given level of abstraction, any premature sequentialization that belongs only to the implementation by code in a language which is based upon the sequential execution paradigm. This helps to model and use orthogonal system features independently of each other, a seemingly small detail which however can simplify models and their understanding considerably. In the ASM framework sequential execution has to be specified explicitly where needed. Using the *mode* function of a control state ASM is one way to impose sequencing; two alternatives which hide the FSM-like control states are defined in Sect. 4.5.

A sequence of successive steps is called an ASM *run* (or computation or execution). Thus ASMs are what in the literature is called a *reactive* system, i. e. a system that does not terminate but executes continuously. If termination is a concern, this has to be modeled explicitly, for example by introducing terminal control states or by defining the ASM in such a way that eventually no rule is applicable any more or such that no rule execution changes the state any more.

Since in one step, an ASM can perform finitely many updates, we also allow already defined machines $M_1, \ldots, M_n$ to appear as *action*s. Their effect is to contribute their updates, in each step, to the updates of the other rules. Rules or machines which are executed in parallel are usually displayed vertically. The following equivalent notations are used:

$$\textbf{if } cond \textbf{ then } M_1 \qquad \textbf{if } cond \textbf{ then } M_1 \qquad \textbf{if } cond \textbf{ then par } (M_1, \ldots, M_n)$$
$$\vdots \qquad\qquad\qquad \vdots$$
$$M_n \qquad \textbf{if } cond \textbf{ then } M_n$$

The keyword **par** is used only rarely because the synchronous parallelism is the default execution mechanism of ASMs. Also common notational abbreviations are used, for example one rule **if** *cond* **then** M **else** N instead of the equivalent two rules **if** *cond* **then** M and **if not** *cond* **then** N, etc.
End of excursus.

Coming back to the ASM 1WAYSTOPGOLIGHTSPEC we still need to know how the initial states are defined. One initial state is implicitly mentioned in the *RegimeReq*, but for the sake of traceability we describe and document it explicitly as a requirement:

InitReq. The light regime initiates with both units showing Stop.

Correspondingly we define the initial state in the ASM model by the following condition:

$$\left(phase = \frac{Stop1}{Stop2} \right) \textbf{ and } Stop(1) \textbf{ and } Stop(2)$$

Here the two conjuncts $Stop(i)$ for $i = 1, 2$ initialize the meaning we invite the reader to associate with the ordered pair of labels which constitutes the initial control state.

By model inspection, given the above explained intended interpretation of the functions of 1WAYSTOPGOLIGHTSPEC, it is easy to show the following model property, where we call a run of 1WAYSTOPGOLIGHTSPEC *legal* if it is started in the initial state and satisfies the *TimerAssumption*:

Correctness Property: each legal run of 1WAYSTOPGOLIGHTSPEC satisfies the *RegimeReq*.[15]

Remark on legal runs. Frequently one has to consider runs under certain constraints on their initialization, on timing, on fairness of selection mechanisms, etc. This implies each time a corresponding notion of *legal runs* and an obligation to verify, as part of a correctness argument, that their implementation yields legal executions.

Exercise 1. Define a ground model ASM for the following Lift Control requirements (Davis 1984, rephrased from [1, Chap. 8.3]).

Design the logic to move n lifts between m floors satisfying the following requirements:

1. Each lift has for each floor one button which, if pressed, illuminates and causes the lift to visit (read: move to and stop at) that floor. The illumination is canceled when the floor is visited by the lift.
2. Each floor (except ground and top) has two buttons to request an up-lift and a down-lift. They are canceled when a lift visits the floor and is either traveling in the desired direction, or visits the floor with no requests outstanding. In the latter case, if both floor request buttons are illuminated, only one should be canceled.
3. A lift without requests should remain in its final destination and await further requests.
4. Each lift has an emergency button which, if pressed, causes a warning to be sent to the site manager. The lift is then deemed "out of service". Each lift has a mechanism to cancel its "out of service" status.

Prove its well functioning ('correctness') in the following sense:

1. All requests for floors within lifts must be serviced eventually, with floors being serviced sequentially in the direction of travel.
2. All requests for lifts from floors must be serviced eventually, with all floors given equal priority.

For an ASM solution, see [76, Chap. 2.3]. For a machine-supported, verification-driven solution using the B-method, see [1, Chap. 8.3].

---

[15] A detailed justification can be mathematically supported by an induction on the runs of the ASM.

In the ASM framework the distinction of locations and functions with respect to the associated read/write permissions is known under the name of *function classification*. We describe it briefly for use in the following sections.

Excursus on function classification. A *static* function is a function f whose values $f(x)$ depend only on x. A function f used in an ASM M is called *dynamic* if its values $f(x)$ depend on x and the current state of M in which x is presented as argument to compute $f()$. The description of a static function can often be given by purely functional means, separated as component from the dynamic system behavior for whose description it is used. ASMs allow the designer to introduce into a model any static function whatsoever which may be useful. Static functions are used in particular to separate descriptions of what is called the *background* of a model, for example fixed data structures upon which runs are based, from the description of the dynamic model behavior. Such functions are also called *external* or background functions.

We distinguish five groups of dynamic functions (and analogously locations) of an ASM M, depending on the rights M has to read and/or update values of the functions for given arguments. To which group a function belongs has to be declared as part of the machine definition.

- A *controlled function* of M, also called a local or private function of M, is a function f whose value $f(t_1, \ldots, t_n)$ for any given argument $(t_1, \ldots, t_n)$ can be read by M and also updated ('written') by steps of M and only of M. The write privilege implies that f appears in some transition rule of M as function symbol on the left hand side of an assignment statement $f(t_1, \ldots, t_n) := t$ (where for 0-ary functions $n = 0$), but that neither the environment nor any other machine can change any value of f.[16] Typical examples are the 0-ary function (variable) *phase* in 1WAYSTOPGOLIGHTSPEC and the *mode* function in Exerc. 2.

- A *monitored function* (also called input function) of M is a function f whose value $f(t_1, \ldots, t_n)$ for any given argument $(t_1, \ldots, t_n)$ can only be read but not updated (written) in steps of M. This is the case if f appears in some term in some transition rule of M but nowhere as function symbol on the left hand side of an assignment statement $f(t_1, \ldots, t_n) := t$. Such functions are dynamic functions which are assumed to be updated by some other machine or the environment of M. Examples are the functions *Elapsed* in 1WAYSTOPGOLIGHTSPEC and *input* in Exerc. 2.

- A function is called *output function* of M if its value for any given argument can be updated by some rule of M but not read by M. This implies that f appears in M only as function symbol on the left hand side of assignment statements $f(t_1, \ldots, t_n) := t$. Examples are the *out* functions in Exerc. 2. Such functions are typically read but not updated by the environment or other machines.

---

[16] These functions are not procedures, they are just mathematical functions whose values at some arguments may be updated during a computation.

- A function is *shared* by M and another ASM (or the environment) if its value for any given argument can be read and updated by both. Obviously, for consistency reasons, a protocol is needed to guarantee the uniqueness of the values of shared functions. We will see a first example in the next section.

- A function f is called a *derived function* of M if the definition of M comes with a fixed computation scheme for f (for example by an equation $f(t_1, \ldots, t_n) = exp$) in which some dynamic function appears. Since the computation scheme is fixed and independent of the program of M, M cannot update any of its derived functions, but it can read them. An example is the time signal *Passed* in 1WAYSTOPGOLIGHTSPEC.

End of excursus.

Exercise 2. Classify the functions in the following three interpreter ASMs for 2-way Finite State Machines (FSMs), Turing machines (TMs) and their extension by interactive TMs. Interactive TMs in each step may receive input from the environment and yield output to the environment [241].

> TWOWAYFSM(*nextMode, write, move*) =
> *mode* := *nextMode*(*mode, input*(*head*))   -- update internal state
> *out* := *write*(*mode, input*(*head*))   -- print output
> *head* := *head*+*move*(*mode, input*(*head*))-- move reading head by 1,-1,0
> TURINGMACHINE(*nextMode, write, move*) =
> *mode* := *nextMode*(*mode, tape*(*head*))
> *tape*(*head*) := *write*(*mode, tape*(*head*))   -- update *tape* cell
> *head* := *head* + *move*(*mode, tape*(*head*))
> INTERACTIVETURINGMACHINE(*nextMode, write, move*) =
> *mode* := *nextMode*(*mode, tape*(*head*), *input*)
> *tape*(*head*) := *write*(*mode, tape*(*head*), *input*)
> *head* := *head* + *move*(*mode, tape*(*head*), *input*)
> *out* := *output*(*mode, tape*(*head*), *input*)

Explain the role the functions *input, out, tape* play for the difference in expressivity and computational complexity of FSMs, TMs, interactive TMs.

Exercise 3. (Role of initialization) Explain why the TURINGMACHINE in Exerc. 2 defines a universal Turing machine.

2.1.2 Refining One-Way Traffic Light Control

In this section we apply to 1WAYSTOPGOLIGHTSPEC what is called a *vertical ASM refinement*. The abstract model expresses a functional system view, treating the lights as elements of the model which can be 'switched directly' to realize the desired 'sequence of lights'. The domain knowledge presented in the *PulseReq* leads us to **separate the pulse emitting computer actions from the resulting actions of the** light equipment, which represents the **environment** of the software model we ultimately have to define. It comes up to split the one ('atomic') SWITCHLIGHTS step of the system model into two (at the more detailed level of abstraction, 'atomic') steps, a computer action EMIT($pulse$) and a corresponding environment action which SWITCHes the lights. The splitting must be done in such a way that the interaction of the two detailed steps—here by their 'sequential control'—is a correct refinement of the abstract 1WAYSTOPGOLIGHTSPEC step, meaning that it preserves the correctness property of the abstract model (Sect. 2.1.2.1). The environment actions can be described declaratively by appropriate axioms or by an abstract model. To simplify their formulation, as well as the later refinement to a mechanically executable model, we define the environment actions abstractly by an ASM LIGHTUNITRESPONSE.

Therefore, to model *PulseReq*, we transform 1WAYSTOPGOLIGHTSPEC into a control software specification 1WAYSTOPGOPULSECTL by simply changing the definition of the SWITCHLIGHTS component (for $i = 1, 2$) to emit pulses, defined as setting them to, say, *high* (from *low*).

> SWITCHLIGHTS(i) =
>   EMIT($rPulse(i)$)   -- trigger SWITCH($StopLight(i)$)
>   EMIT($gPulse(i)$)   -- trigger SWITCH($GoLight(i)$)
> **where** EMIT(p) = ($p := high$)

Due to the *PulseReq*, the requested LIGHTUNITRESPONSE to such pulses can be formulated by an environment ASM with two rules, one per unit:

> LIGHTUNITRESPONSE =
>   **forall** $i \in \{1, 2\}$ **do** LIGHTUNITRESPONSE(i)[17]
> **where**
>   LIGHTUNITRESPONSE(i) =
>   REACTTO($rPulse(i)$)   -- switch $StopLight(i)$
>   REACTTO($gPulse(i)$)   -- switch $GoLight(i)$
>   REACTTO($rPulse(i)$) =
>   **if** $Event(rPulse(i))$ **then**
>   SWITCH($StopLight(i)$)
>   CONSUME($rPulse(i)$)
>   REACTTO($gPulse(i)$) =
>   **if** $Event(gPulse(i))$ **then**
>   SWITCH($GoLight(i)$)
>   CONSUME($gPulse(i)$)
> $Event(p)$ **iff** [18] $p = high$
>   CONSUME(p) = ($p := low$)

---

[17] The quantifier **forall** is used here to avoid writing the same text twice with different parameters. In Sect. 2.3.1 we explain the wider use of the quantifier to define ASMs.
[18] **iff** abbreviates 'if and only if'.

As a consequence one has to extend the initialization conditions by:

InitPulseReq. Initially no pulses have been emitted.

and correspondingly the initialization for 1WAYSTOPGOPULSECTL and PULSES by:

forall $i \in \{1, 2\}$ $rPulse(i) = gPulse(i) = low$.

The link between pulse emission and unit reaction indicated in *PulseReq* has to be made more precise to describe the compatibility condition of the light unit response time with the above *TimerAssumption*. We formulate this assumption as follows:

- *LightUnitResponseAssumption.* Every SWITCHLIGHTS(i) step of the software component 1WAYSTOPGOPULSECTL in any phase triggers in the environment the execution of the LIGHTUNITRESPONSE(i) rule to happen shortly after. Here shortly later means that the light unit response time is negligible with respect to the beginning of the *Passed* count when 1WAYSTOPGOPULSECTL enters its next phase.

Thus $rPulse(i)$ and $gPulse(i)$ are variables that are shared by the software component 1WAYSTOPGOPULSECTL and the environment component LIGHTUNITRESPONSE. The consistency of their updates is guaranteed by the *LightUnitResponseAssumption*.

Be aware of the synchronous parallelism in ASMs. A flowchart and its textual formulation by a set of rules are two presentations of the same ASM. Due to the strictly sequential nature of 1WAYSTOPGOLIGHTSPEC requested by the requirements, in every state only one of its four rules can be applied, each performing simultaneously two updates in its SWITCHLIGHTS(i) component. However, the parallel execution paradigm of ASMs explained on page 23 supports the simultaneous execution not only of multiple updates, but also of more than one rule, abstracting from irrelevant sequentialization of steps. Here irrelevant means that the update sets computed by the rules in question are independent of each other except for sharing the same state in which they are computed (and applied to yield the successor state).

- In an ASM step all *enabled rules* (i. e. rules whose guard is true) are applied simultaneously.

In other words, in every state S, an ASM M performs atomically every action (read: all updates) of every rule whose guard is true in S. Obviously the resulting state is only defined if the simultaneously executed actions (the updates to be performed in $Upd(M, S)$) are consistent; in the case of inconsistency S has no successor state and the computation stops with failure. For example, when LIGHTUNITRESPONSE(i) is enabled, its two rules are executed simultaneously. Another typical example is the SWAP operator where the parallel computation model avoids to invoke the use of intermediate storage:

$$\text{SWAP}(x, y) =$$
$$x := y$$
$$y := x$$

Even the classical Finite State Machine and Turing Machine computation models are usually explained using (though implicitly) the parallel execution of multiple updates (see Exerc. 2).

The consistency condition for synchronous parallel execution rules out conflicting updates. But note that for example a monitored location of M can be read by M in state S and simultaneously be updated by the environment; analogously an output location can simultaneously be updated by M and read by the environment. In the ASM framework, to simultaneously read and write a same location does not represent a race condition. What is read is always the current value (in state S), the updated value will become available only in the successor state of S. The reader will see in the following chapters, where we present some less elementary examples, that by this seemingly minor technical detail, **ASMs avoid conceptually irrelevant sequentialization, which helps enormously to keep models small and understandable at a single blow.**[19]

2.1.2.1 Analysis of the Refinement

Each software step $\text{SWITCHLIGHTS}(i)$ is linked sequentially to an environment step $\text{LIGHTUNITRESPONSE}(i)$ by the *LightUnitResponseAssumption*. For the sake of comparison to $M = 1\text{WAYSTOPGOLIGHTSPEC}$ steps, we therefore view the two ASM software and environment components as one ASM called the refined model, say M^*, where a pair of sequentially linked (we say *successive*) steps is called a *segment of interest* in a run of M^*. To verify the correctness of the refinement, we now relate each such segment to a corresponding segment of interest—in this case, consisting of only one step—of the given abstract model M (here $1\text{WAYSTOPGOLIGHTSPEC}$) and formulate and prove their equivalence with respect to the correctness property of M to be preserved.

Since the property to be preserved is the desired sequence of lights, two states S^* of the refined model M^* and S of the abstract model M are called equivalent if they have the same *phase* value and satisfy the same light combination. Satisfying the same light combination means that in the states the same conjunction *showLight*(i) **and** *showLight*(j) with $i \neq j$ is true; here *showLight*(k) is one of the predicates *Stop*(k) or *Go*(k) defined in Sect. 2.1.1.

We call a run of the refined model M^* *legal* if it is started in its initial state and satisfies the *TimerAssumption* and *LightUnitResponseAssumption*.

---

[19] The major practical examples we know of for the positive effect of avoiding irrelevant sequentialization are the ASM models to interpret Java programs (10 pages in [232, Appendix B1]) and JVM code (16 pages for three stepwise refined models in [232, Appendix C3]).

By inspecting the rules in the two models M, M^*, it is easy to prove the following:

Refinement Correctness Property. For each legal run R^* of the refined model M^* there is a legal run R of the abstract model M such that for every natural number n, the state S^* which is reached in the run R^* at the end of the n-th segment [SWITCHLIGHTS(i), LIGHTUNITRESPONSE(i)] of interest is equivalent to the state S reached in the run R after the n-th step SWITCHLIGHTS(i) (a one-element run segment) of M.

Excursus on the ASM refinement concept. The above refinement refines objects and data—in 1WAYSTOPGOPULSECTL, the lights are replaced by pulses—and the set of operations performed on them; that is, the refinement concerns both the states and how they are changed. The ASM refinement notion offers the designer to freely choose the level of abstraction of refined states and state changing operations—to fit whatever underlying idea for a detailed design one wants to apply (here the domain-knowledge-expressing *PlantReq* and *PulseReq*). **ASM refinement supports the piecemeal realization of orthogonal or successive design ideas by separate refinement steps and thus facilitates a modular management of design** ideas and design changes.

An intermediate segment state in the refined model—here the state reached by the first step in a segment—usually has nothing it would correspond to in the abstract model. This is the reason why the Refinement Correctness Property stipulates the equivalence only for what we call *corresponding states of interest*. They are pairs S^*, S of states at the end of a segment which are also the states with which the next segment in the refined, respectively abstract, run begins. The **practicality of the ASM refinement method** results from this possibility, which exploits the state-based character of the ASM method, **to hide implementation details that are specific to the refined level of abstraction** and cannot (or need not) be related to anything in the abstract model or vice versa. It also simplifies the task to understand, formulate and justify the Refinement Correctness Property. In the present example, one step of $M = $ 1WAYSTOPGOLIGHTSPEC is refined to two steps in the refined model M^* of the software component and the environment ASM. We call this a refinement of type $(1, 2)$. In general, ASM refinements can be of type (m, n), for any natural numbers m, n, but also of type $(m, *)$ which indicates that m abstract steps correspond to a finite number n of concrete steps where the relation between m and n is not fixed. It often is a function of m and some other parameters, as for example in the refinement of the one UNIFY(s, t) step in the model for Prolog [68] to its implementation by the WAM code model [69] where the length of the refined computation segment depends on the length of the terms s, t. For an example in this book see Exerc. 18. Refinements with $m > n$ often appear with optimizations where some steps can be saved.

Furthermore the notion of equivalence of states can be tailored to the way the targeted detailed refined level of abstraction reflects the correctness property of the abstract model. In general, in an ASM refinement, it can be any precise (not necessarily functional) relation between parts of the abstract and the refined model. This considerably reduces the complexity of a precise intuition-guided formulation of the design details introduced in an ASM refinement and the degree of difficulty of its verification.

Since the ASM refinement in this section leads from an abstract level to a more detailed one, possibly closer to the desired implementation, it is called a *vertical ASM refinement*.

The correctness property relates two mathematically precise models so that it can be justified not only by model inspection (as for ground models) but also by mathematical means (here by an induction on runs), including machine supported verification.[20] It implies that the ground model correctness established by model inspection in Sect. 2.1.1 (i. e. 'the sequence of lights' requested by the *RegimeReq*) is preserved in the refined model.
End of excursus.

2.1.3 Adding Requirements by Horizontal Refinement

In this section we show how by modular refinement steps, called *horizontal ASM refinement*, one can smoothly integrate additional requirements into a model for previously given requirements.[21] Consider the following addition to the requirements in Sect. 2.1.

> *OrangeLightReq.* Use simultaneous Stop and Go lights to indicate 'Stop, but be prepared to Go'.
> *OrangeLightRegimeReq.* The simultaneous Stop and Go lights period is 10 seconds and is inserted into the cycle between the Stop period and the Go period of the corresponding light.

First we show how to refine the ground model 1WAYSTOPGOLIGHTSPEC to include the new requirements. To reflect in the model the additional phases requested by *OrangeLightReq*, two new corresponding control states *prepareToGo*1 and *prepareToGo*2 are added to the signature with the following definition for the intended orange light phase representation in the model:

$\quad$ *PrepareToGo(i)* iff
$\quad\quad$ *StopLight(i) = on* **and** *GoLight(i) = on* **and** *Stop(j)* for $j \neq i$

---

[20] The theorem proving system KIV [161] provides machine support for the verification of ASM refinements covering the full generality of the concept (Fig. 2.30), see [212, 213, 214, 216, 215, 217].

[21] For another example of 'modeling for change' with ASMs, see Sect. 5.2.2.

Fig. 2.3 Refined SWITCHLIGHTS(i) in 1WAYSTOPGOORANGELIGHTSPEC [41] © 2010 Springer-Verlag Berlin Heidelberg, reprinted with permission

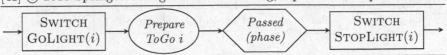

The condition $Stop(j)$ for $j \neq i$ is crucial; it reflects the safety concern that two units never simultaneously 'show Go'.

To model the *OrangeLightRegimeReq*, a) the *period* function is extended to take as value 10 seconds for the new phases (a data refinement with corresponding extension of the *TimerAssumption*) and b) the upper and lower occurrences of the SWITCHLIGHTS component in Fig. 2.2 are replaced by the corresponding refined control state ASM defined in Fig. 2.3. This is an operation refinement of type (1,2). The refined component is obviously equivalent to the replaced one in the sense that both lead to the same final light unit state. We invite the reader to formulate the Refinement Correctness Property for the resulting 1WAYSTOPGOORANGELIGHTSPEC model.

Similarly, we can refine the software model 1WAYSTOPGOPULSECTL by refining its two SWITCHLIGHTS components in question as in Fig. 2.3 using EMIT($gPulse(i)$) instead of SWITCH($GoLight(i)$) and EMIT($rPulse(i)$) instead of SWITCH($StopLight(i)$). The LIGHTUNITRESPONSE environment ASM remains unchanged.[22] The resulting 1WAYSTOPGOORANGEPULSECTL ASM is shown in Fig. 2.4, where the refined components are highlighted. We invite the reader to formulate the corresponding Refinement Correctness Property.

Exercise 4. Introduce the complementary additional requirement to 'Stop unless it is unsafe not to Go' for 20 seconds when the phase switches from Go to Stop.

Exercise 5. Refine the ground model ASM from Exerc. 1. For various refinements that model later added requirements, see [76, Chap. 2.3] and compare them to the Petri net model in [127, Chap. 5.5.3.2].

Remark on combining vertical and horizontal refinements. The model transformation in this subsection is called *horizontal ASM refinement* because it adds new features to the given models 1WAYSTOPGOLIGHTSPEC resp. 1WAYSTOPGOPULSECTL without changing their level of abstraction. In fact, for both models, the behavior of the new component is defined using the same terms, here SWITCH($Go/StopLight(i)$), EMIT($gPulse(i)/rPulse(i)$) and *Passed*. Thus 1WAYSTOPGOORANGEPULSECTL, the horizontal refinement of the vertical refinement 1WAYSTOPGOPULSECTL, is also a correct

---

[22] We invite the reader to check why this is the case.

Fig. 2.4 1WAYSTOPGOORANGEPULSECTL by added read & green lights

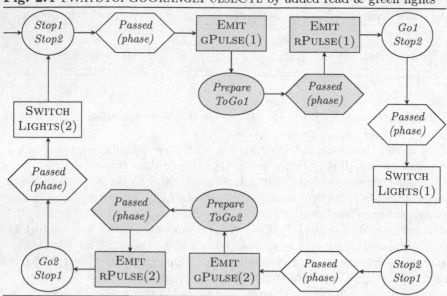

vertical refinement of 1WAYSTOPGOORANGELIGHTSPEC, the horizontal refinement of the ground model 1WAYSTOPGOLIGHTSPEC (commutativity of the vertical and the horizontal refinements of the ground model, see Fig. 2.1 and Exerc. 6). Also horizontal refinements can be of any type (n, m), like vertical refinements. The component-wise ASM refinement technique supports modular feature-based design, combining horizontal and vertical ASM refinements to piecemeal introduce component-wise modeled desired features or ideas about how to further detail the design. We illustrate this by another simple example in the following section. Be aware however that if there is what is called (possibly conflicting) feature interaction between the given and the added requirements, corresponding work has to be put into the refinement to care about conflict resolution.

Exercise 6. Show that 1WAYSTOPGOORANGEPULSECTL is a correct vertical refinement of 1WAYSTOPGOORANGELIGHTSPEC. Conclude that the refinement diagram for the ground model in Fig. 2.1 is commutative, meaning that the models obtained by applying to the ground model first the horizontal and then the vertical refinement resp. vice versa have an equivalent behavior.

Excursus on the flowchart representation of atomic steps and their refinement by sequential sub-steps. The hurried reader may skip this excursus on a technical detail concerning the graphical flowchart representation of atomic steps and their refinement. We will come back to it only in Sect. 4.5.2.

Rectangular boxes in the flowchart representation of control state ASMs represent a level of abstraction. They realize an advice formulated by Knuth in [162, p. 72] that

> ... we should give meaningful names for the larger constructs in our program that correspond to meaningful levels of abstraction, and we should define those levels of abstraction in one place, and merely use their names (instead of including the detailed code) when they are used to build larger concepts.

A rectangle in a flowchart with an inscribed ASM name represents such an abstraction. When an atomic step, like a step of SWITCHLIGHTS(I), is refined into two or more successive steps, the control state values must follow the intended refined sequential execution. In the flowchart representation, this means that the corresponding black box in the abstract model Fig. 2.2, in the example the rectangle named SWITCHLIGHTS(I), is 'opened' in the refined model Fig. 2.4 to make the intermediate steps visible, including the new intermediate updates of the control state location *phase*. Therefore the atomic flowchart view of a step of a machine **if** *Cond* **then** N, passing from *phase* $= i$ to *phase* $= j$, namely

> **if** *phase* $= i$ **then**
>   **if** *Cond* **then** N
>   *phase* $:= j$

is behaviorally different from its refined view where the machine is 'opened' to make its internal guard-structure visible:

> **if** *phase* $= i$ **and** *Cond* **then**
> N
>   *phase* $:= j$

In Sect. 4.5.2 we define and analyze a different notion for an ASM refinement of atomic steps which offers sequential control inside the refinement of the abstract machine M but hides it at the outside view of M, at the level of abstraction where M is executed in parallel with other machines. In Sect. 5.2, a sequential refinement pattern is investigated which offers an explicit notion of completion for the execution of a refined machine.

2.1.4 Model Reuse: Two-Way Traffic Light Control

In this section we show how by a *data refinement* the models built in the preceding sections of this chapter can be reused to define Two-Way Traffic Light Controllers as refined One-Way Traffic Light Controllers. The reuse consists in re-interpreting the concept of 1-way control. The 'permission to pass on the road in direction i' for two opposite directions $i = 1, 2$ is now interpreted as 'permission to pass on road i' where 1 stands for a main and 2 for a secondary road which cross each other.

Fig. 2.5 Different interpretations of 'permission to go'

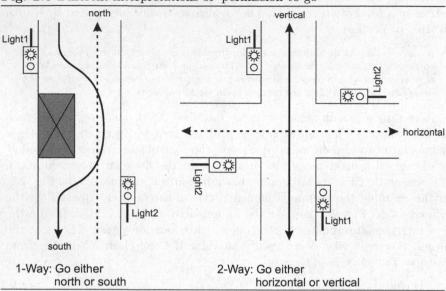

1-Way: Go either   2-Way: Go either
    north or south   horizontal or vertical

In other words, the idea is to interpret the lights for the two exclusive directions as lights for the two directions of the main road and of the small road, respectively (see Fig. 2.5). We exemplify the reuse for the 1WAYSTOPGOLIGHTSPEC ground model by refining it to a ground model 2WAYSTOPGOLIGHTSPEC. One can proceed analogously for the component-wise vertical and/or horizontal refinements illustrated in Sect. 2.1.3.

We quote the informal requirements *2WayTrafLightReq* from [2, Sect. 8.4.1] with our naming.

PlantReq. We intend to install a traffic light at the crossing between a main road and a small road ... in such a way that the traffic on the main road is somehow given a certain advantage over that on the small road. *MainRoadPriority.* When the light controlling the main road is green, it only turns ... red ... when some cars are present on the small road (the presence of such cars is detected by appropriate sensors) ... provided that [the main] road has already kept the priority for at least a certain (long) fixed delay.

SmallRoadAllowance. ... the small road, when given priority, keeps it as long as there are cars willing to cross the main road ... provided a (long) delay (the same delay as for the main road) has not passed. When the delay is over, the priority systematically returns back to the main road.

To reuse 1WAYSTOPGOLIGHTSPEC, we interpret $Go(1)$ as 'the main road is green' (vertical permission to go, see Fig. 2.5), $Go(2)$ as 'the small road is green' (horizontal permission to go, see Fig. 2.5), analogously for $Stop(1)$ and

$Stop(2)$. To incorporate the *MainRoadPriority* and the *SmallRoadAllowance*, it suffices to refine the monitored *Passed* predicate, namely by adding the car presence conditions to the time constraints for the two relevant *phases*, but not for the other two. In the new definition, the sensor detecting the presence of cars on the small road is represented by a monitored Boolean-valued function *CarsOnSmallRoad*.

if $phase = \begin{matrix} Go1 \\ Stop2 \end{matrix}$ **then**   -- we are in main road Go phase

$\quad$ *Passed(phase)* **iff** *Elapsed(period(phase))* **and** *CarsOnSmallRoad*

if $phase = \begin{matrix} Go2 \\ Stop1 \end{matrix}$ **then**   -- we are in small road Go phase

$\quad$ *Passed(phase)* **iff** *Elapsed(period(phase))* **or** *NoCarsOnSmallRoad*
$\quad$ **where**
$\qquad$ *NoCarsOnSmallRoad* = **not** *CarsOnSmallRoad*

The delays mentioned in *MainRoadPriority* and *SmallRoadAllowance* are represented by the value of *period(phase)*, for the two phases in question.[23] We use this example to illustrate how the needed link—between the sensor actions in the environment and the effect they produce in the model—can be described by a run constraint. This constraint is added to the assumptions made for legal runs of 1WAYSTOPGOLIGHTSPEC, instead of being formulated by an environment ASM, as shown with LIGHTUNITRESPONSE in Sect. 2.1.2:

- *SensorAssumption.* Whenever the sensor detects a car on the small road, the environment sets *CarsOnSmallRoad* immediately to true; the value remains unchanged until the sensor detects that there is no car on the small road. This is the moment in which the environment resets *CarsOnSmallRoad* to false.

We leave it to the reader to justify the correctness claim for the resulting refined model 2WAYSTOPGOLIGHTSPEC by combining the already justified 1WAYSTOPGOLIGHTSPEC correctness property (Sect. 2.1.1) with model inspection for the new Two-Way Traffic Light features:

Correctness Property: each legal run of 2WAYSTOPGOLIGHTSPEC satisfies the above *2WayTrafLightRe*quirements.

Exercise 7. Apply to 2WAYSTOPGOLIGHTSPEC the vertical and horizontal refinements as introduced for 1WAYSTOPGOLIGHTSPEC in Sects. 2.1.2, 2.1.3 and prove their correctness.

---

[23] The informal requirements above do not mention any Stop phase delay, but for the sake of illustration we keep it unchanged from the *RegimeReq* in Sect. 2.1.1, which is integrated into 1WAYSTOPGOLIGHTSPEC.

Remark on separation of concerns. The model reuse we have explained here shows that there are two different concerns involved.

One is to reuse the one-way controller to control the two-way traffic lights, which involves only a reinterpretation of the meaning of *dir*ection. In the one-way controller, *dir*ection means one of two opposite directions (north or south) on the same road, that is elements of the set

$$\{dir(road), dir'(road)\} = \{north, south\}.$$

In the two-way controller, it means a pair of two opposite directions ($\{north, south\}$ or $\{east, west\}$) of the vertical resp. horizontal direction of the two crossing roads, i.e. one of the following two pairs:

$$\{dir(main), dir'(main)\} = \{north, south\} \qquad \text{-- vertical direction}$$
$$\{dir(small), dir'(small)\}\} = \{east, west\} \qquad \text{-- horizontal direction}$$

In other words, the one-way controller is linked to two traffic lights, one for each of the two opposite directions north/south. The two-way controller is linked to two pairs of traffic lights, for each road its vertical resp. horizontal pair north/south resp. east/west, where the components of each pair show the same light behavior for the two opposite directions of the road. (This is a requirement on how the software triggered pulses are linked to the equipment in the real environment.) The reader will have noticed this from exercise 7.

There are numerous examples of such a model reuse. Imagine we want to allow the cars in a crossing to also turn left or right, but respecting the right of pedestrians to pass, as illustrated in Fig. 2.6. No new software model is needed if the requirements allow us to rely upon the usual traffic law regulations. One probably would sugggest to install for each Light two more synchronized copies for the pedestrians. That suffices to make our model appropriate to regulate the traffic as illustrated in Fig. 2.6. Assume that Light1 shows Go (so that Light2 shows Stop). Then the pedestrians who move in a vertical direction (A or B) can go (due to their priority over cars), whereas pedestrians and cars wishing to move in a horizontal direction must wait (since Light2 shows Stop); cars moving in direction A or B can go too (since going straight on has priority over turning left), cars moving to the right (A-right or B-right) can go too, but only if there are no pedestrians left (as required by the priority given to pedestrians), cars turning left (A-left or B-left) can go too, but only after the cars moving in direction B or B-right resp. A or A-right have left (as required by the priority given to a) going straight on over turning left or right, and b) to a right turn over a left turn).

The second concern we have considered in our refinement is the priority policy, which needed a changed definition for two *Passed*(*phase*) predicates. It can be further modified by just redefining the *Passed* predicate, without changing the realization of the corresponding light sequence by the ASM program. This is a typical way in which abstraction and refinement can be exploited by ASMs to support the separation of concerns.

Fig. 2.6 Two-way traffic lights extended by traffic law regulation

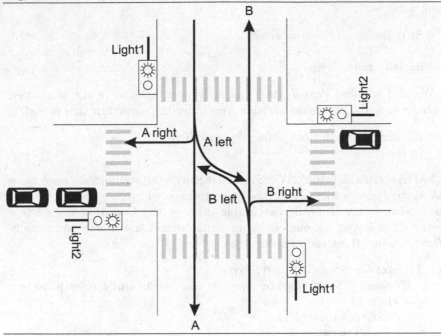

Remark on data refinement. The refinement in this section changed only the interpretation of some data in 1WAYSTOPGOLIGHTSPEC, not the operations (rules). See Sect. 2.4.9 for more on this rather simple, though frequently used, type of refinement, called *data refinement*.

2.1.4.1 Timer Refinement

In this section we show how by a vertical refinement, one can replace the external timer assumptions by an internal timing mechanism. As an example, we refine 2WAYSTOPGOLIGHTSPEC to a TIMED2WAYSTOPGOLIGHTSPEC.

In the *TimerAssumption* in Sect. 2.1.1 an external clock emits a signal. We implement this signal emission by an internal action that updates a local *timer* function. The *timer* is SET to the current value of the monitored system clock *now* upon entering every to-be-timed *ctlstate*. It is used to check, by the refined *Passed* predicate, whether the delay *time* in question has *Elapsed*, i. e. whether $now - timer \geq time$. The system *clock* is assumed to be monotonically increasing and measured in terms which are compatible with the terms used to formulate the length of *period* for the *phases* in question.

To refine 2WAYSTOPGOLIGHTSPEC to TIMED2WAYSTOPGOLIGHTSPEC, we add to each SWITCHLIGHTS machine a timer component SET(*timer*).

Usually it is assumed to be initialized by the current value of the system clock *now*.

$\text{SET}(timer) = (timer := now)$
-- also written SETTIMER if *timer* is clear from context
Initially *timer = now*   -- initialization condition

We also redefine *Passed(phase)* as a derived function of the monitored variable *now*, the controlled variable *timer* and the static function *period*.

$Elapsed(phase)$ **iff** $now - timer \geq period(phase)$

We recapitulate TIMED2WAYSTOPGOLIGHTSPEC to illustrate once more the textual description of ASMs, descriptions which are used to refine the models to mechanically executable ones by the CoreASM engine (see Sect. 8). For layout reasons, we again write control states here horizontally $Move(i)\ Move'(j)$ instead of vertically.

TIMED2WAYSTOPGOLIGHTSPEC =
    if $(phase = Stop1\ Stop2$ **or** $phase = Go1\ Stop2)$ **and** $Passed(phase)$
        then
            SWITCHLIGHTS(1)
            SETTIMER
            if $phase = Stop1\ Stop2$ **then** $phase := Go1\ Stop2$
                else $phase := Stop2\ Stop1$
    if $(phase = Stop2\ Stop1$ **or** $phase = Go2\ Stop1)$ **and** $Passed(phase)$
        then
            SWITCHLIGHTS(2)
            SETTIMER
            if $phase = Stop2\ Stop1$ **then** $phase := Go2\ Stop1$
                else $phase := Stop1\ Stop2$
    where
        SWITCHLIGHTS$(i) =$
            SWITCH$(StopLight(i))$
            SWITCH$(GoLight(i))$
        SWITCH$(l) = (l := l')$ --$'$ denotes the opposite value
        SETTIMER $= (timer := now)$
        $Elapsed(period(phase))$ iff $now - timer \geq period(phase)$
        $Passed(phase)$ defined as above for 2WAYSTOPGOLIGHTSPEC

Exercise 8. Formulate in which sense TIMED2WAYSTOPGOLIGHTSPEC is a correct refinement of 2WAYSTOPGOLIGHTSPEC and prove this property.

Remark on combining vertical refinements. In Exerc. 6 it has been observed that the considered vertical and horizontal refinement steps can be applied in any order, resulting in equivalent model behavior. This was

expressed by saying that the two refinements commute. If there is no conflicting feature interaction of the design ideas which underly two vertical
refinements, then also different vertical refinements may commute. For example, the pulse emission control refinement in Sect. 2.1.2 and the timer
refinement in Sect. 2.1.4.1 commute (see Exerc. 9).

Exercise 9. Apply to 1WAYSTOPGOPULSECTL the vertical timer refinement (the one which has been applied to transform 2WAYSTOPGOLIGHT-
SPEC to TIMED2WAYSTOPGOLIGHTSPEC). Apply the vertical timer refinement also to 1WAYSTOPGOORANGEPULSECTL. Apply the orange light refinement to TIMED1WAYSTOPGOPULSECTL and then show that the resulting diagram in Fig. 2.1 commutes.

2.1.4.2 TIMERPATTERN

The timing mechanism above (Sect. 2.1.4.1) is often used to abstractly model
the eventual completion within real-time constraints of a time consuming operation. We capture this by an abstract TIMERPATTERN which comes with
two time setting operations and a *Timeout* predicate. It provides *timer*s parameterized by *timedOp*s and equipped with *deltaTime*(*timedOp*), which determine the *Timeout*(*timedOp*) predicate. As usual, the monitored location
now describes the current system time, for TIMERPATTERN it is a monitored variable governed by appropriate *TimerAssumptions* on its evolution
and whatever unit assumptions.

$$\text{SETTIMER}(timedOp) = (timer(timedOp) := now)$$
$$Timeout(timedOp) = (now - timer(timedOp) > deltaTime(timedOp))$$
$$\text{RESETTIMER}(timedOp) = (timer(timedOp) := \infty)$$
$$\text{-- falsifies } Timeout(timedOp)$$

2.2 Model Reuse via Refinement: Sluice Gate Control

In this section we illustrate model refinement and reuse by another device
control example. The reader will see how the concern to keep the ground
model components and definitions as abstract as possible, driven by the desire
to reflect the requirements without adding anything concerning behaviorally
irrelevant implementation features, paves the way for reuse and refinements.

After the definition of a ground model SLUICEGATESPEC for an automatically controlled sluice gate, we apply to this model two vertical
(Sect. 2.2.1, 2.2.2) and two data refinements (Sect. 2.2.3), proceeding in
analogy to what has been introduced already for the traffic light ASMs in
Sect. 2.1. Then we show how to *reuse* the ground model to build a model that
satisfies a similar set of requirements, namely for a SLUICEGATEOPERATOR

Fig. 2.7 Refinements for Sluice Gate ASMs

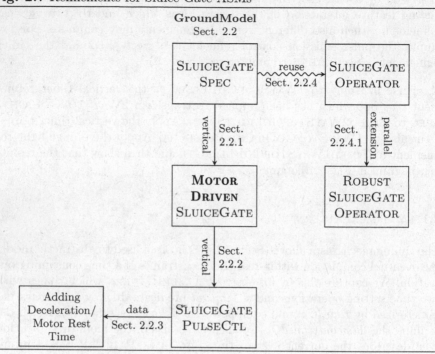

(Sect. 2.2.4). By a parallel extension we refine this machine to satisfy additional robustness requirements (Sect. 2.2.4.1). Figure 2.7 guides through the refinement steps.[24]

We start with listing the informal requirements *SluiceGateReq* which are quoted once more from [155, p. 87] with our naming.

PlantReq A small sluice, with a rising and falling gate, is used in a simple irrigation system. A computer system is needed to control the sluice gate.
FunctionalReq. The requirement is that the gate should be held in the fully open position for ten minutes in every three hours and otherwise kept in the fully closed position.
MotorReq. The gate is opened and closed by rotating vertical screws. The screws are driven by a small motor, which can be controlled by clockwise, anticlockwise, on and off pulses.
SensorReq. There are sensors at the top and bottom of the gate travel; at the top it's fully open, at the bottom it's fully shut.
PulseReq. The connection to the computer consists of four pulse lines for motor control and two status lines for the gate sensors.

---

[24] The section reelaborates an example ASM from [41].

Fig. 2.8 Sluice Gate Ground Model SLUICEGATESPEC [41]
© 2010 Springer-Verlag Berlin Heidelberg, reprinted with permission

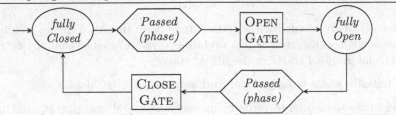

We first define a control state ASM ground model SLUICEGATESPEC which satisfies the *FunctionalReq*, as done for 1WAYSTOPGOLIGHTSPEC in Sect. 2.1.1. The signature of SLUICEGATESPEC to represent the elements that appear in the *FunctionalReq*uirements is similar to that of 1WAYSTOPGOLIGHTSPEC and consists of the following elements:

- a controlled variable (0-ary function) *phase* indicating the current phase with possible values *fullyOpen*, *fullyClosed*,
- a controlled variable *gatePos* ∈ {*fullyOpen*, *fullyClosed*} indicating the current gate position,[25]
- the same derived time signal *Passed*(*phase*) = *Elapsed*(*period*(*phase*)) and monitored timer function *Elapsed* coming with the *TimerAssumption* as for 1WAYSTOPGOLIGHTSPEC,
- static functions *interval* = 3 *h* and *period*(*phase*) with value 10 *min* and 170 *min*, respectively, as defined by the *FunctionalReq*.

The state changing actions of SLUICEGATESPEC requested by the *FunctionalReq* are defined by Fig. 2.8. Here to open or close the gate simply means to change its position, abstracting from the motor, the screws, the sensors and the connection between the computer and the gate in the real-world. This abstraction is analogous to the one we made in Fig. 2.2. [26]

OPENGATE = (*gatePos* := *fullyOpen*)
CLOSEGATE = (*gatePos* := *fullyClosed*)

Presumably some initialization condition is present, for example the following:

---

[25] *gatePos* ∈ {*fullyOpen*, *fullyClosed*} implies that in this functional ground model we consider no intermediate gate position
[26] This definition interprets 'held in *pos* for time *period* in every *interval* of time' as meaning 'held consecutively in *pos* for time *period* in successive *intervals* of time'. To convey a general character to the specification, we introduce *interval* and *period* as configurable system constants.

InitReq. The sluice gate initially (say at time 0) is in the fully closed position.

Correspondingly, we define the initial state S_0 in the ASM model as follows, where *phase* is considered as just updated to *fullyClosed* so that the external time count *Elapsed* starts in the initial state:

Initially *phase = fullyClosed* **and** *gatePos = fullyClosed*.

We invite the reader to verify by inspection of legal runs (i. e. started in the initial state and satisfying the *TimerAssumption*) that SLUICEGATESPEC is a correct ground model (considering the atomic machine actions as 0-time actions):

Correctness Property: each legal run of SLUICEGATESPEC satisfies the *FunctionalReq.*

2.2.1 *Refinement to* MOTORDRIVENSLUICEGATE

We vertically refine SLUICEGATESPEC to MOTORDRIVENSLUICEGATE which also satisfies *MotorReq* and *SensorReq*. These requirements express domain knowledge of how the gate is moved by a motor with the help of screws and sensors. To represent this, corresponding signature elements have to be added: controlled variables to indicate the current *motorStatus* $\in \{on, off\}$ and the current *moveDir* $\in \{clockwise, anticlockwise\}$ and two monitored (parameterized) variables *Event(top)*, *Event(bottom)*, assumed to signal that the gate in the real world did reach its top/bottom position.

Still abstracting from how the computer is connected to the motor, one can then define MOTORDRIVENSLUICEGATE by the SLUICEGATESPEC flowchart in Fig. 2.8 but with refined components OPENGATE and CLOSEGATE as defined by Fig. 2.9. We assume that our customer informed us that the move up is done by turning the screw clockwise and down with anticlockwise.

STARTTORAISE =
    moveDir := clockwise
    motorStatus := on
STARTTOLOWER =
    moveDir := anticlockwise
    motorStatus := on
STOPMOTOR = (*motorStatus := off*)

Correspondingly one has to add *motorStatus = off* to the initial state condition.

The refinement type is (1,2): every OPEN/CLOSEGATE step in the abstract model SLUICEGATESPEC is refined by two steps STARTTORAISE/LOWER followed by STOPMOTOR. For mnemonic reasons, we use the same name

Fig. 2.9 Refined OPENGATE, CLOSEGATE in MOTORDRIVENSLUICEGATE [41] © 2010 Springer-Verlag Berlin Heidelberg, reprinted with permission

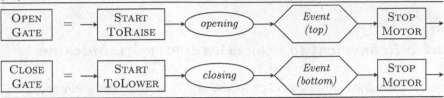

gatePos for the related variable in the two ASMs. However, we remind the reader that in the abstract model this variable is controlled. in the refined model it belongs to the environment where it indicates the current position of the gate in the real world. To make the refinement correct, legal MOTORDRIVENSLUICEGATE runs, in addition to the *TimerAssumption*, need an assumption about how the environment, via detection of the real-world *gatePos* by the sensors, updates the monitored variables *Event*(*top/bottom*):

- *GateMotorAssumption.* If after any STARTTORAISE/LOWER step the motor remains on for some *opening/closingTime* in the corresponding direction, then the *Event*(*top/bottom*) happens, namely when the gate has reached its final position *gatePos = fullyOpen/Closed*.

The (say constant system) time the motor must remain on to bring the gate into the final position in question concerns the *opening/closingTime*s. The question remains how they are related to the condition *interval = period*(*fullyClosed*) + *period*(*fullyOpen*) stated in the *FunctionalReq*. The equation, and correspondingly the *FunctionalReq*, have to be corrected[27] to include these moving time periods:

$$interval = period(fullyClosed) + period(fullyOpen)$$
$$+ openingTime + closingTime$$

Correctness Property. MOTORDRIVENSLUICEGATE correctly refines SLUICEGATESPEC and each of its legal runs satisfies the *MotorReq* and *SensorReq*.

It follows that for each MOTORDRIVENSLUICEGATE run $S_0, S_1, \ldots$ (i.e. sequence of states reached by successive steps) in which the *TimerAssumption* and the *GateMotorAssumption* hold and which is started in the initial state S_0, the gate, in every *interval*, stays for *period*(*fullyClosed*) time in the *fullyClosed* position, then it moves in *openingTime* to the *fullyOpen* position, stays for *period*(*fullyOpen*) time in that position and finally in *closingTime* moves back to *fullyClosed*.

---

[27] The correction concerns the meaning of 'otherwise' in the *FunctionalReq*. For the ground model it did not create any problem due to the fact that atomic machine actions are considered as 0-time actions.

Exercise 10. Prove the refinement correctness and justify by model inspection that *MotorReq* and *SensorReq* are correctly captured.

2.2.2 Refinement to SLUICEGATEPULSECTL Machine

The MOTORDRIVENSLUICEGATE model still directly updates motor status and direction, something the computer cannot do. The domain knowledge *PulseReq* provides the necessary information for the next (again a vertical) ASM refinement step, separating the software control from the physical motor reaction. The transformation is similar to the one explained in Sect. 2.1.2 so that we formulate here only the refinement of the components STARTTORAISE/LOWER and MOTORSTOP for the resulting software model SLUICEGATEPULSECTL whose flowchart definition is the same as in the unfolding of Fig. 2.8 by Fig. 2.9.

> STARTTORAISE =
>   EMIT(*Pulse*(*clockwise*))
>   EMIT(*Pulse*(*motorOn*))
> STARTTOLOWER =
>   EMIT(*Pulse*(*anticlockwise*))
>   EMIT(*Pulse*(*motorOn*))
> STOPMOTOR = EMIT(*Pulse*(*motorOff*))
> **where** EMIT(p) = ($p := high$)

Exercise 11. Define the corresponding MOTORRESPONSE environment machine, formulate the *MotorResponseAssumption* relating the actions of the software machine SLUICEGATEPULSECTL to the triggered physical motor actions, prove the correctness of the resulting refinement and justify by model inspection that SLUICEGATEPULSECTL satisfies also the *PulseReq*. Hint: see Sects. 2.1.2, 2.1.2.1.

Exercise 12. Apply the timer refinement defined in Sect. 2.1.4.1 to SLUICEGATEPULSECONTROL.

2.2.3 Adding Requirements to SLUICEGATEPULSECTL

In this section, we show how to incorporate by a simple data refinement two typical additional requirements discussed in [156]. One is to consider that the gate may still move during a *motorDecelerationTime*, a time period in which the gate is decelerated when the motor is turned off. A way to reflect this is to add the *motorDecelerationTime* twice to *interval* (one for stopping moving up and one for stopping moving down) and to consider it as included in *period(fullyOpen/Closed)*.[28]

We maintain as *fullyOpen/Closed* position the position that is reached in *opening/closingTime*. This means that we consider the difference to the 'real' *gatePosition*, which is reached by deceleration, as negligible. Obviously this decision has to be documented and to be confirmed by the domain experts as correct, since easily a scenario can be imagined where neglecting the difference may create serious problems.

$$interval = period(fullyClosed) + period(fullyOpen)$$
$$+ openingTime + closingTime + 2 \times motorDecelerationTime$$

In the ASM framework, this is a pure (and obviously correct) data refinement. The domain experts have to decide whether this refinement reflects the real-world phenomenon or whether a different representation in the model is needed, e. g. by an operation refinement based upon additional sensors which report the completion of the gate movement to the software component.

Another additional requirement suggested in op.cit is the breakage concern:

SwitchDirectionReq. For any period over which the gate is moved, the direction must be constant—the reason being that the motor will be damaged if it is switched between directions without being brought to rest in between.

Again a pure data refinement seems to work to incorporate this requirement. Let *motorRestTime* be the amount of time the motor must be kept in *motorStatus = off* before switching to another direction. One can consider it as included in (i. e. ≤) *period(fullyOpen/Closed)*. Here too, an operational refinement could be used, guarding the STARTTORAISE/LOWER by an additional timer condition *safeToSwitchDirection*. The domain experts have to judge what is appropriate.

2.2.4 Model Reuse for SLUICEGATEOPERATOR

In this section we reuse MOTORDRIVENSLUICEGATE, adapting the program appropriately, to define a machine SLUICEGATEOPERATOR which satisfies *SluiceGateOperatorReq*uirements requesting 'to raise and lower the sluice gate in response to the commands of an operator' [155, p. 90/1]. *MotorReq*, *SensorReq* from *SluiceGateReq* in Sect. 2.2 are identical, for the other requirements we quote here only the additions and changes.

---

[28] The second condition serves to avoid that the motor is triggered to start an opposite gate movement before the current movement has come to a complete stop.

PlantReq. ... to raise and lower the sluice gate in response to the commands of an operator.

FunctionalReq. ... the operator can position the gate as desired by issuing Raise, Lower and Stop commands: the machine should respond to a Raise by putting the gate and motor into a Rising state, and so on ... The Rising and Falling states are mutually exclusive.

PulseReq. ... and a status line for each class of operator command.

The reuse idea is to replace the time-triggered raise/lower transitions by operator command triggered ones. Since the new requirements explicitly speak about *Rising* and *Falling* control states (phases), we start the reuse with MOTORDRIVENSLUICEGATE, where these concepts appear and where we perform the following changes:

- replacing the time events *Passed(fullyClosed/Open)* by command events *Event(Raise/Lower)*,
- renaming phases *opening/closing* to *rising/falling*.

Each time *Elapsed(time)* is checked there is a well-defined answer *true* or *false* and how fast *Elapsed(period(phase))* switches from one to its opposite value is determined by the definition of *period(phase)*. If we replace this by checking whether a command has been issued, we must clarify how multiple, simultaneously or successively issued commands are to be treated. This leads to a general question discussed in [155]:

- How to discipline command issuing by the operator?
- How to prevent the machine from executing some in a given context undesired but issued command?

Declaratively, this is easily achieved by constraining runs to exclude certain command sequences which may be impossible to realize or not be reasonable or not desired. Modeling operational solutions allows one to experiment prior to coding with various options to fully understand the issues involved. For the sake of illustration, we consider the following, simple example (referring to [155] for a more detailed classification of commands as sensible, viable, overrunnable, etc.):

CommandSequenceReq. At each moment, at most one command is issued and in command sequences only successive command pairs (*Raise,Stop*), (*Lower,Stop*),(*Stop,Raise*) or (*Stop,Lower*) make sense.

The one-command-per-step assumption is captured by the single-agent ASM run notion where actions of the agent (affecting the agent's controlled, shared and output locations) alternate with environment actions (affecting the agent's monitored and shared locations). Here it also abstracts from a FIFO command queue so that one can represent an issued but not yet executed command by a variable *currCmd*. This location is shared by the operator and the control program. Its values in the set of possible commands (here Raise, Lower, Stop), including **undef**, standing for $NoCmd$. Inconsistent updates of $currCmd$ are excluded by the strict alternation of operator and environment actions which is assumed in the model.

Remark on undef. In general we use **undef** to denote an undefined value, writing $f(arg) = $ **undef** instead of stating that f is a partial function which for this $argument$ is undefined (has no value). [29]

Applying this reinterpretation of Fig. 2.8 and its refinement by Fig. 2.9 yields for $SluiceGateOperatorReq$ and $CommandSequenceReq$ the ground model SLUICEGATEOPERATOR defined by Fig. 2.10, where each rule is of the following form:

> if $phase = p$ **then**
>   REACTTO($command, proceedTo(q)$)
> **where**
>   REACTTO($cmd, proceedTo(q)$) =
>   **if** $Event(cmd)$ **then**
>   PERFORM(cmd)
>   CONSUME(cmd)
> $phase := q$
> $Event(cmd) = (currCmd = cmd)$
>   CONSUME(cmd) = ($currCmd := $ **undef**)[30]

In this model the machine can execute only certain specific command sequences. For example, if in $phase = rising$ another $Event(raise)$ happens, the machine has no rule to execute it so that it makes no step; hopefully the environment will make the event disappear eventually. It is possible that the physical machinery in the real world guarantees such a robustness feature, thus realizing the $CmdSequenceRe$quirement also in practice. If however one wants to let the software reject and report to the user undesired but issued commands, one has to add robustness or more generally speaking exception handling rules. We illustrate an example in the next Sect. 2.2.4.1.

Exercise 13. Refine the machine in Fig. 2.10 to satisfy also the $InertialEffectRe$quirement: if a Raise or Lower command is immediately followed by a Stop command, then the gate movement may not yet have started. Hint: Abstract from timing issues and interpret 'immediately' as 'detecting via the sensors that the gate is still in its top/bottom position'.

---

[29] As a consequence, we can consider functions as total with value **undef** where intuitively the function is undefined. This simplifies the underlying logic.

[30] We set $currCmd$ to **undef** because of the assumption that at each moment, at most one command is issued. The operator decides whether there will be a next command event and which one it is.

Fig. 2.10 SLUICEGATEOPERATOR

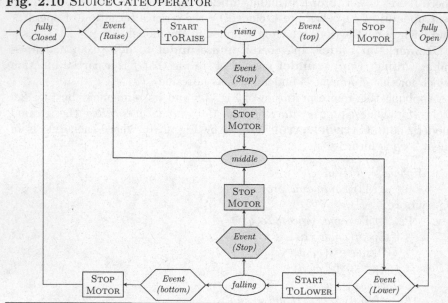

2.2.4.1 Refinement by Failure Detection and Robustness

In this section we refine the SLUICEGATEOPERATOR by a *parallel extension* so that it 'rejects' as insensible (as defined by the *CommandSequenceRe*quirement) the second command in any of the following command pairs, should one of them be issued:

- Raise, Lower: possibly not viable for physical reasons,
- Raise, Raise: not viable, including 'no Raise in top position',
- Lower, Raise: possibly not viable for physical reasons,
- Lower, Lower: not viable, includes 'no Lower in bottom position',
- Stop, Stop: Stop when Stopped not reasonable. Note that both the operator and the machine can trigger STOP.

For robustness concerns, let us add to this the case of a Lower command issued when the gate is in its bottom position, and of a Raise command issued when the gate is at its top position.

For the sake of illustration, we interpret here rejection as a) 'canceling' the issued command that has to-be-rejected, so that it will not be executed, and b) 'notifying' to the user the insensible command which occurred. The natural idea is to add to the SLUICEGATEOPERATOR machine a component DETECTINSENSIBLECMD that handles this new feature. This component must check, for each *phase*, whether a command issued in this *phase* is insensible and in case report and cancel it.

DETECTINSENSIBLECMD =
  if *phase* ∈ {*fullyClosed, fullyOpen, middle*} then
    REJECT(*Stop, phase*) .   -- no Stop Stop
  if *phase* = *fullyClosed* then   -- no Lower at bottom
    REJECT(*Lower, phase*)
  if *phase* = *fullyOpen* then   -- no Raise at top
    REJECT(*Raise, phase*)
  if *phase* ∈ {*rising, falling*} then
    REJECT(*Lower, phase*)   -- no Raise Lower, no Lower Lower
    REJECT(*Raise, phase*)   -- no Raise Raise, no Lower Raise
  where REJECT(*command, phase*) =
  if *Event*(*command*) then
    REPORT(*command, phase*)
    CONSUME(*command*)

Before placing the new machine in parallel with SLUICEGATEOPERATOR, we must check whether there is a feature interaction between the two which could create a conflict. Here it means that we must guarantee two properties: a) in case an insensible command is issued, the command must be CONSUMEd by DETECTINSENSIBLECMD before SLUICEGATEOPERATOR could try to execute it, and b) if a sensible command is issued, it must be executed by SLUICEGATEOPERATOR and not be touched by DETECTINSENSIBLECMD. In the special case we have here, b) results directly from the definitions of the two machines. For a) it holds that whenever an insensible command *cmd* ∈ *Raise, Lower, Stop* appears in a given *phase*, SLUICEGATEOPERATOR has no rule to react to this *Event*(*cmd*) in that *phase*. Therefore no feature interaction conflict can derive from refining SLUICEGATEOPERATOR by adding in parallel the DETECTINSENSIBLECMD component. Thus we define:

ROBUSTSLUICEGATEOPERATOR =
  SLUICEGATEOPERATOR   -- defined by Fig. 2.10
  DETECTINSENSIBLECMD

What is to be reported depends on the *phase* and can be described independently case by case, directly realizing the above stipulations about rejection:

REPORT(*cmd, phase*) =
  if *cmd* = *Stop* and *phase* ∈ {*fullyClosed, fullyOpen, middle*}
    then NOTIFY(*StopStop*)
  if *cmd* = *Lower* then
    if *phase* = *fullyClosed* then NOTIFY(*LowerAtBottom*)
    if *phase* = *rising* then NOTIFY(*RaiseLower*)
    if *phase* = *falling* then NOTIFY(*LowerLower*)
  if *cmd* = *Raise* then
    if *phase* = *fullyOpen* then NOTIFY(*RaiseAtTop*)
    if *phase* = *rising* then NOTIFY(*RaiseRaise*)
    if *phase* = *falling* then NOTIFY(*LowerRaise*)

Remark on the parallel extension refinement. The frequently used refinement scheme we have applied here is called *parallel extension*. It can be applied in case there is no feature interaction conflict between the components which are put in parallel to build one machine. In case of possibly conflicting feature interaction one can apply instead the conservative refinement pattern which is explained in Sect. 2.3.1.2. It resolves possible conflicts by separating normal from exceptional behavior as follows:

if *NormalCase* **then** NORMALBEHAVIOR **else** EXCEPTIONHANDLER

Exercise 14. Apply to ROBUSTSLUICEGATEOPERATOR the refinement of Sect. 2.2.2.

2.3 Synchronous Parallelism ('forall') and 'let'

The synchronous parallelism of ASM executions is supported by two related constructs, **par** to express bounded parallelism and **forall** to express potentially unbounded parallelism. In this section, we illustrate their use by a simple PACKAGEROUTER example.[31]

2.3.1 PACKAGEROUTER *Ground Model (with 'new', 'self')*

We slightly simplify the informal *PackageRouterRe*quirements in [145, Sect. 1] and use the occasion to illustrate how application-domain-driven decisions steer the formulation of the ground model.

PlantReq. A package router sorts packages according to their destination into *destination bins*. Packages arriving in the *entry station* carry code indicating their *destination* which they can reach sliding down a path formed by two-position *switches* equipped with entry and exit *sensors* and connected by *pipes* (see Fig. 2.11).

FunctionalReq. The controller reads the destination code and steers, for each package, its path to the destination bin by appropriately positioning the switches on this path.

EntryStationReq. The entry station processes one entering package per round. First it reads the package code, then it lets the package slide down while blocking the entry of other packages until the entered package has left the entry station.

SensorReq. The sensors of switches are guaranteed to detect each package separately.

---

[31] The section reelaborates an example ASM from [41].

Fig. 2.11 The background structure of PACKAGEROUTER [41]
© 2010 Springer-Verlag Berlin Heidelberg, reprinted with permission

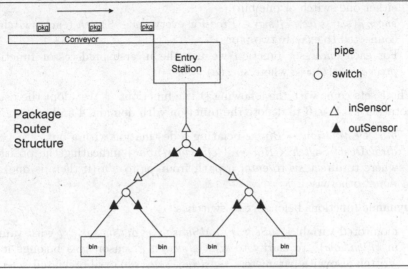

SwitchReq. A switch must be free when its position is flipped, i. e. there must not be any package between the two sensors.

MisroutingReq. When a package arrives at the entry sensor of a switch that has to be flipped to correctly route this package before the preceding package has passed the exit sensor of the switch, then the switch is not flipped and the arriving package is misrouted. Since this can happen repeatedly, a misrouted package may be routed to any bin and an appropriate report should be issued.

PkgSlidingReq. Packages may slide down at different speeds so that more than one package may be in a pipe or switch. No package can overtake another, neither in a pipe nor in a switch.

The signature for PACKAGEROUTER is extracted from the *PlantReq.* The data structure of the problem is determined by the elements which we have emphasized there and are represented by homonymous signature elements to simplify model inspection. Most of this structure is static background structure whose description can be separated from (but must be documented for) the behavioral description where it is used.

- Static sets *Bin*, *Pipe*, *Switch* with static tree structure (see Fig. 2.11) represented by the root *EntryStation*[32] and static *successor* functions satisfying the following:

---

[32] The conveyor belt appears in the model only as bringing packages to the router through an external event which triggers the entry station to process the package.

- $succ(EntryStation) \in Pipe$ (the $EntryStation$ is connected to one pipe),
- $succ(p) \in Switch \cup Bin$ for every $p \in Pipe$ (each pipe is connected to either one switch or one bin),
- $succ_{left}(sw), succ_{right}(sw) \in Pipe$ for every $sw \in Switch$ (each switch is connected to exactly two pipes).
- For each $succ$essor function we use the inverse predecessor function $predecessor(b) = a$ where $succ(a) = b$.

These sets come with the following static functions.[33] We adopt the usual notation $f\colon A \to B$ to denote the function with domain A and range B:

- $bin\colon Destination \to Bin$ associating a destination with a bin.
- $dirToDest\colon Switch \times Bin \to \{left, right, none\}$ indicating the position where to direct sw to enter a path from sw to bin (if there is one) or $none$ (otherwise).

- Dynamic functions belonging to switches:

  - monitored variables $inSensor$, $outSensor_{left}$, $outSensor_{right}$ with values in $\{high, low\}$. To clarify to which switch a sensor $sens$ belongs it is written also with parameters $sens(sw)$, $sens(sw)$ or abbreviated $sens_{sw}$, $sens_{sw}$,
  - a controlled variable pos with values in $\{right, left\}$ indicating the current position of the switch, also written $pos(sw)$ or pos_{sw}.

- Two monitored predicates of the entry station:

  - $PkgArrival$ signaling to the reader component the arrival of a package that can be read,
  - $PkgLeftEntry$ signaling that the package has left the entry station.

These monitored predicates represent sensor events. The link of a real-word phenomenon to its sensor predicate is typically expressed by a $Sensor$ $Assumption$ like the $PkgArrival/ExitAssumption$ below.
- A controlled variable $pkgId$ updated by the reader component of the entry station to a new value in a dynamic set $PkgId$, a value which internally represents the entering package. The set $PkgId$ is dynamic because it has to be extended for each newly arriving package.
- A function $dest(id)$ controlled by the entry station to record the value it reads from the package code associated with id, provided by an external reader function $pkgDest$ which extracts from the currently read package code $currPkgCode$ the destination of the encoded package. $currPkgCode$ is a monitored variable.

---

[33] For a system reconfiguration model, the tree structure would become modifiable and thus dynamic, but to satisfy the $PackageRouterReq$ behavior, the background is static.

The *PkgSlidingReq* together with *SwitchReq* and *MisroutingReq* indicate that pipes and switches may contain a sequence of packages, represented in the model by a FIFO (First In First Out) *queue* structure:[34]

- $queue_{pipe}$ representing the packages in the *pipe* $\in$ *Pipe*,
- for each *sw* $\in$ *Switch* a $queue_{sw}$ to contain *pkgid*s which

  - entered into *switch* at its entry point *inSensor*,
  - did not yet exit the *switch* at one of its exit points $outSensor_{left}$ or $outSensor_{right}$.

In [145, Sect. 1], a monoprocessor solution is asked for. We satisfy this by specifying the controller by one ASM, not involving any synchronous or asynchronous multi-agent execution mechanism. However, we exploit the independence of the various components (*EntryStation*, switches, pipes and bins) by defining PACKAGEROUTER using the bounded parallelism of ASMs. The new construct introduced here comes in the following form (or commonly used notational variations thereof):

> **forall** x **with** *cond* **do** $M(x)$

and means to execute simultaneously, as one step, all instances $M(x)$ of M for which the parameter x satisfies the *cond*ition.

Excursus on (un-) bounded parallelism. Bounded parallelism is expressed in ASMs by the **par** construct (see p. 24) or also the **forall** construct, applied to a finite number of machines. The meaning is to let them execute their steps in parallel, simultaneously, to change the current state to the successor state. In terms of update sets, it means that one step of **forall** x **with** *cond* **do** $M(x)$ in state S generates the union of all $Upd(M(x), S)$ for each interpretation of the logical variable x satisfying *cond*.[35] The parallelism is called unbounded if **forall** is applied to an infinite (or dynamically growing finite) set. During the specification phase, it is often useful to abstract from whether a set is finite or infinite; ASMs allow one to do so. The synchronous parallelism in ASMs defines a frame for a variety of alternative sequential implementations.

End of excursus.

---

[34] Using such a data structure means that its typical operations and functions (here ENQUEUE at the end of the queue), DEQUEUE (the *head* of the queue) and *tail* denoting the part of the queue without the *head*) are used in the model as background operations whose meaning is defined separately from the rules of the model. The freedom of *abstract*ion that is characteristic for ASMs permits to use as given any data structure whatsoever whose operations are unambiguously defined. Their implementation in CoreASM can be provided by adding corresponding plug-ins.

[35] The interpretation of logical (read-only) variables is usually described separately from the state by a function ζ which assigns values to free occurrences of variables. Where possible without risking ambiguity, we suppress this function notationally.

PACKAGEROUTER =
　ENTRYENGINE
　forall $sw \in Switch$ SWITCH$(sw)^{36}$
　forall $bin \in Bin$ ENTERPKGINTO(bin)

The component machines SWITCH(sw) (for any sw in the set $Switch$) and
ENTERPKGINTO(bin) (for any $bin \in Bin$) are defined below. Not surprisingly,
the pipes turn out to be inactive components, representing only queues which
record the current position of packages. A simultaneous access to these queues
by their predecessors and successors in the package router structure is conceptually consistent, given that the former operate on them by ENQUEUing
at the head and the latter by DEQUEUing at the tail of the queue.

To satisfy the *EntryStationReq*, the ENTRYENGINE comes with a sequential control structure as defined in Fig. 2.12. The machine uses two submachines, OPENEXIT (used in SLIDEDOWNPKG) and OPENENTRY, which we
leave abstract here, extracting from their description in [145, Sect. 1] the following (and assuming appropriate initialization conditions which we do not
state here):

- *SingleEntryAssumption.* Once the destination of the currently examined
  package has been decoded, OPENEXIT opens the entry station to let this
  package slide down by gravity, while blocking the entry of the next package. OPENENTRY reopens the entry station to read a next package, once
  the just examined package has left the entry station and enters the successor pipe.
- *PkgArrival/ExitAssumption.* When a package arrives at the reader component of the entry station, the predicate *PkgArrival* becomes true and
  switches back to false when the entry station is opened to let the package slide down. When a package has left the entry station, the predicate
  PkgLeftEntry becomes true and switches back to false when the entry station is reopened to let the next package enter the reader component.

Using the technique explained in Sect. 2.1.2, these two components can
be refined to emit pulses, which trigger the corresponding physical device in
the reader station described in [145, Sect. 1]. The other two entry station
components are defined as follows.

READPKG =
　let $id = $ **new** $(PkgId)$
　　$pkgId := id$
　　$dest(id) := pkgDest(currPkgCode)$

---

[36] The parameter sw is used here to denote an instance of SWITCH; each instance comes
with its own dynamic state functions. This is a form of machine call, similarly for
ENTERPKGINTO(bin). See Sect. 2.4.2 for details.

[37] The dashed rectangle marks a region that will be refined in Fig. 2.14. For more
information see Sect. 9.5.

Fig. 2.12 The sequential ENTRYENGINE[37]

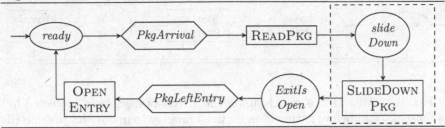

SLIDEDOWNPKG =
   ENQUEUE($pkgId$, $queue(succ(EntryStation))$)
   OPENEXIT

Excursus on 'new' and 'let'. These two constructs are used in the ASM expression language. The **new** construct applied to a set X provides a completely fresh element (from what is called the *Reserve* set which stands for fresh memory) and places it into X by updating the characteristic function of X for the new element to 'true'.

In case an *exp*ression appears more than once in an ASM, it can be abbreviated by **let** $x = exp$ to a name x which is then used to represent exp; one also says that x is bound to exp. In this way, **let** $x = exp$ **in** M also incorporates a local form of sequentialization: first exp is evaluated and for the execution of M, this value holds wherever x appears in M (called the *scope* of this occurrence of **let**).[38] For a systematic use of **let** to define sophisticated binding mechanisms, see Chap. 4 on ambient ASMs. We use also other self explanatory forms like **let** x **with** *cond* **in** M. The keyword **in** may be omitted if the scope M becomes clear by other means, like indentation. **End of excursus.**

The *FunctionalReq* and the *SwitchReq* imply that the switch control performs two actions, a SWITCHENTRY to update the switch *position* where needed to correctly route an incoming package and a SWITCHEXIT when a package slides down to the successor pipe. Since these two actions are conceptually independent of each other, one operating at the head and one at the tail of the switch queue, we abstract here from their sequentialization and put them in parallel.[39]

   SWITCH(sw) = **par** (SWITCHENTRY(sw), SWITCHEXIT(sw))

---

[38] Technically speaking, **let** represents parameter call by value.

[39] Formally speaking, this abstraction from sequential execution of queue operations treats the two operations ENQUEUE and DEQUEUE involved here as what are called *update instructions* for queues. This is a technical issue concerning simultaneous queue operations discussed at the end of Sect. 8.1.2.

Fig. 2.13 SWITCHENTRY component of SWITCH in PACKAGEROUTER

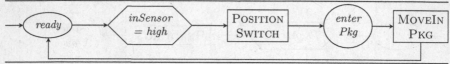

For SWITCHENTRY, a *switch*, upon the arrival of a *package* (detected by *inSensor$_{sw}$*) and before letting it enter, must first try to update its *position* (if needed) to the direction *dirToDest*(sw, db). This is needed to correctly route the *package* from this *switch* to its destination bin $db = bin(dest(p))$ (unless the package is already misrouted, in which case *dirToDest*(sw, db) = *none*). This is expressed by the definition of SWITCHENTRY in Fig. 2.13. For the definition of the POSITIONSWITCH component below, we use the practical **self** notation.

Excursus on self. Since all switches execute the same program, we prefer to write this program and its components only once. To distribute an ASM to multiple instances, we either parameterize it by an instance name (here by switch) or by **self** wherever it is needed to clarify that a function in question is not global but belongs to the currently considered instance **self** (here of a switch). For systematic treatment of parameterization as a means to partition states, see Chap. 4.
End of excursus.

> POSITIONSWITCH =
>   **let** *pipe* = *predecessor*(**self**)   -- the pipe before the considered switch
>   **let** *pkg* = *head*(*queue*(*pipe*))   -- the package arriving from *pipe*
>   **if** *NeededToSwitch*(*pos*, *pkg*) **and** *Free*(**self**) **then** FLIP(*pos*)
> MOVEINPKG =
>   **let** *pipe* = *predecessor*(**self**)
>   **let** *pkg* = *head*(*queue*(*pipe*)) **in**
>   DEQUEUE(*queue*(*pipe*))   -- move package out of *pipe*
>   ENQUEUE(*pkg*, *queue*(**self**))   -- move package into switch

The auxiliary concepts are defined as follows:

> *NeededToSwitch*(*pos*, *p*) **iff** *pos* ≠ *dirToDest*(**self**, *bin*(*dest*(*p*)))
>   -- NB. current switch *position* would lead to misrouting of p[40]
> *Free*(*sw*) **iff** *queue*(*sw*) = [ ]   -- there is no pkg in the switch
> FLIP(*pos*) = (*pos* := *pos′*)   -- *pos′* denotes the opposite *position*
> *pos′* = the opposite value of *pos*

SWITCHEXIT means to simply move a package from the switch into its successor pipe.

---

[40] This implies that *pos* is FLIPped also in case *dirToDest*(**self**, *bin*(*dest*(*p*))) = *none* holds, case in which both directions of the switch lead to misrouting.

SWITCHEXIT =
   if $outSensor_{left} = high$ **or** $outSensor_{right} = high$ **then**
     MOVEOUTPKG
where
  MOVEOUTPKG =
    let $pkg = head(queue(\textbf{self}))$
     ENQUEUE(pkg, $queue(succ(\textbf{self}))$)
     DEQUEUE($queue(\textbf{self})$)

The controller must ENTERPKGINTO(bin) when a package slides from a pipe into a *bin*. This includes checking whether a misrouting has to be reported. The *MisroutingReq* does not indicate at which point the misrouting report should be issued, though it makes a difference whether it is done along the way of a package or upon its arrival in a bin. For such issues, a decision by the customer or by a domain expert is needed to figure out what should be specified. In fact, a later addition to the *PackageRouterReq*uirements in [145, p. 1/5] has clarified that the report should be issued when a misrouted package arrives in a bin. This explains the following definition, where we use an abstract operation INSERT to denote insertion of a package into the container of a bin.

ENTERPKGINTO(bin) =
  let $pipe = predecessor(bin)$
   if $queue(pipe) \neq [\,]$ **then**
    let $pkg = head(pipe)$
     DEQUEUE($queue(pipe)$)   -- move pkg out of $pipe$
     INSERT(pkg, bin)   -- move pkg into bin
     REPORTMISROUTING(pkg, bin)
where
  REPORTMISROUTING(p, b) =
   if $bin(dest(p)) \neq b$ **then**
    DISPLAY('p has been misrouted to b instead of $dest(p)$')

It is straightforward to formulate the PACKAGEROUTER correctness condition and to establish it by model inspection. The real problem is that from the way the *PackageRouterReq*uirements are formulated, they would still be satisfied even if every package is misrouted! Clearly a major concern has not been expressed yet in those requirements, namely that most packages should be routed correctly. We use this issue to illustrate in the next section how to adapt an ASM by exploiting its component structure when additional requirements (here the throughput concern) are introduced at a later stage.

Putting everything together we obtain the following complete program PACKAGEROUTER, where for the sake of illustration we write SWITCH(sw) and ENTERPKGINTO(bin) in textual form. We do not repeat the signature and the various assumptions described in the above text.

PACKAGEROUTER =
  ENTRYENGINE   -- defined by Fig. 2.12
  forall $sw \in Switch$
    SWITCH(sw)
  forall $bin \in Bin$
    ENTERPKGINTO(bin)

The submachines are defined as follows:

SWITCH(sw) =
  SWITCHENTRY(sw)
  SWITCHEXIT(sw)
SWITCHEXIT(sw) =   -- move package from $switch$ to pipe
  if $outSensor_{left,sw} = high$ **or** $outSensor_{right,sw} = high$ **then**
    MOVEOUTPKG(sw)
SWITCHENTRY(sw) =   -- textual version of Fig. 2.13
  if $mode_{sw,entry} = ready$ **and** $inSensor_{sw} = high$ **then**
    POSITIONSWITCH(sw)
    $mode_{sw,entry} := enterPkg$
  if $mode_{sw,entry} = enterPkg$ **then**
    MOVEINPKG(sw)
    $mode_{sw,entry} := ready$
POSITIONSWITCH(sw) =
  let $pipe = predecessor(sw)$ -- the pipe before the $switch$
    let $pkg = head(queue(pipe))$ -- the package arriving from $pipe$
      if $NeededToSwitch(pos_{sw}, pkg)$ **and** $Free(sw)$ **then**
        FLIP(pos_{sw})   -- $pos := pos'$ with pos' the opposite value of pos
$NeededToSwitch(pos_{sw}, p)$ **iff** $pos_{sw} \neq dirToDest(sw, bin(dest(p)))$
               -- NB. current switch $position$ would lead to misroute p
$Free(sw)$ **iff** $queue(sw) = [\,]$ -- there is no pkg in the switch
MOVEINPKG(sw) =
  let $pipe = predecessor(sw)$
    let $pkg = head(queue(pipe))$
      DEQUEUE($queue(pipe)$)   -- move package out of $pipe$
      ENQUEUE($pkg, queue(sw)$)   -- move package into switch
MOVEOUTPKG(sw) =
  let $pkg = head(queue(sw))$
    DEQUEUE($queue(sw)$)   -- move package out of $switch$
    ENQUEUE($pkg, queue(succ(sw))$)   -- move pkg into $successor$ pipe
ENTERPKGINTO(bin) =
  let $pipe = predecessor(bin)$
    if $queue(pipe) \neq [\,]$ **then**
      let $pkg = head(pipe)$
        DEQUEUE($queue(pipe)$)   -- move pkg out of $pipe$
        INSERT(pkg, bin)   -- move pkg into bin
        REPORTMISROUTING(pkg, bin)

REPORTMISROUTING$(p, b) =$
    if $bin(dest(p)) \neq b$ **then**
        DISPLAY('p has been misrouted to b instead of $dest(p)$')

2.3.1.1 Conservative Refinement of PACKAGEROUTER

Due to the *MisroutingRe*quirement, the throughput concern that 'most packages will be routed correctly' is an issue of how often it happens that in a switch, packages meet which need opposite switch positions to be routed correctly. Since by *PkgSlidingReq* it is an issue of how fast packages slide down, the software alone cannot solve the problem. Some domain expertise is needed. In fact, in [145, Sect. 1], an additional condition is expressed to guarantee the desired throughput ratio:

> *EntryStationDelayReq.* The entry station checks whether the destination of the currently entering package is the same as for the previously entered one. If this is not the case, then sliding down the currently entering package must be delayed such that the switches the package has to pass can be flipped in time where needed for a correct routing.

To satisfy this additional requirement, we exploit the component-wise definition of ENTRYENGINE in Fig. 2.12. It allows us to directly insert the new requirements into the two affected machine components READPKG and SLIDEDOWNPKG and to replace these components in ENTRYENGINE by their refined versions, thus obtaining a DELAYREFINEDPACKAGEROUTER.

For the reader component it suffices to record in a new controlled, appropriately initialized, variable *previousPkgDest* the destination of the previous package, before *pkgId* is updated for the newly entered package.

DELAYREFINEDREADPKG $=$
    previousPkgDest $:= dest(pkgId)$ -- record the previous destination[41]
    READPKG

---

[41] The value of *pkgId* on the right hand side of the assignment is the *id* of the previously entered package.

Fig. 2.14 DELAYEDSLIDEDOWNPKG component of ENTRYENGINE

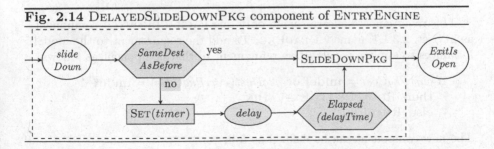

The refined machine DELAYEDSLIDEDOWNPKG is obtained by applying to SLIDEDOWNPKG what is called a *conservative ASM refinement*, a special form of horizontal refinement. A new guard is introduced—here checking whether the reader has read the same destination as before for the preceding package—and the given component is executed without change if the guard is true. Otherwise a new component is executed, here consisting in delaying the execution of SLIDEDOWNPKG by a domain-specific *delayTime* value, using the timer refinement technique explained in Sect. 2.1.4.1. This explains the definition of DELAYEDSLIDEDOWNPKG in Fig. 2.14 where we have highlighted the new component and use the following predicates:

$$SameDestAsBefore \text{ iff } dest(pkgId) = previousPkgDest$$
$$Passed(delayTime) \text{ iff } now - timer \geq delayTime$$

2.3.1.2 Refining Normal Behavior by Error Handling

In this section we illustrate how conservative ASM refinements allow the designer to define normal and error handling behavior component-wise. Here is one simple but frequently used structural schema:

- **Conservative ASM Refinement Pattern**. A conservative refinement of an ASM M has the form

  CONSERVATIVEREFINED(M, *NormalCase*, NEWBEHAVIOR) =
     if *NormalCase* **then** M **else** NEWBEHAVIOR

Expressed the other way round, it reads

   if *NewCase* **then** NEWBEHAVIOR **else** M

where *NormalCase* and *NewCase* are new guards and NEWBEHAVIOR is a new ASM to handle an additional (e. g. error or failure) case.

Consider the following failure case formulated in [145, p. 1/5] as an addition to the *PackageRouterReq*uirements for the normal behavior:

CodeFailureReq. If a package enters without code or if there is no bin for its destination, then the package is routed to an extra bin.

This requirement concerns again only one PACKAGEROUTER component, as in Sect. 2.3.1.1, namely READPKG. To add the requirement to the model, it suffices to apply a conservative refinement to that component as follows.

   if *currPkgCode* = **undef or** *pkgDest*(*currPkgCode*) = **undef**
     then ROUTEPKGTOEXTRABIN
     else READPKG

The new component can be defined as follows:

RoutePkgToExtraBin =
  let id = **new** ($PkgId$)
    $pkgId := id$
    $dest(id) := extraBin$

Remark on conservative refinements. The conservative ASM refinement pattern supports the separation of different concerns not only for system design, but also for verification. This is well known from mathematical logic, where the term 'conservative model extension' has been coined. One can split the verification of a ConservativeRefined(M, $cond$, M') property into two independent parts, namely an analysis of the behavior of M under the assumption that $cond$ is true and an analysis of the behavior of M' under the assumption that $cond$ is false. Numerous challenging examples of conservative ASM refinements can be found in the literature. To mention one, see [232], where conservative ASM refinements have been used to specify and verify Java and the JVM component-by-component. This turned out to be easily adaptable to a complete model of C# (see [54]) and can be brought even to the level of instruction-by-instruction language extension (see [22]).

Exercise 15. Use unbounded parallelism to define an ASM which executes Conway's GameOfLife [123, 240] in the plane where any cell a) dies if it has less than two or more than three live neighbors, b) regains life if it has exactly three live neighbors and c) survives with exactly two live neighbors.

Exercise 16. Prove that for a directed graph and a distinguished *source* node the following GraphTraversal machine, if started with $Visited = \{source\}$, a) marks every node that is reachable from *source* just once as *Visited* and b) terminates if the graph is finite.

GraphTraversal =
  forall $u \in Visited$ **do** PropagateVisitToNeighb(u)
where
  PropagateVisitToNeighb(u) =
    forall $v \in neighb(u)$ **do** MakeVisited(v)
  MakeVisited(v) =
    if not $Visited(v)$ **then** $Visited(v) := true$

Formulate in which sense it is correctly $(1,1)$-refined by the following ASM GraphTraversal₁, started with $JustVisited = \{source\}$, and prove the refinement correctness.

GraphTraversal₁ =
  forall $u \in JustVisited$
    PropagateFreshVisitToNeighb(u)
    Delete(u, $JustVisited$)

The submachine is defined as follows:

PROPAGATEFRESHVISITTONEIGHB(u) =
  forall $v \in neighb(u)$ **do** MAKEJUSTVISITED(v)
MAKEJUSTVISITED(v) =
  MAKEVISITED(v)
  if not *Visited*(v) **then** INSERT(v, *JustVisited*)

Here the static set *neighb*(u) denotes the set of nodes v for which in the graph there is an edge that connects u to v.

2.4 Machine 'call' and Nondeterminism ('choose'): ATM

In this section we illustrate how component-wise definition (supported by horizontal ASM refinement) and stepwise detailing of abstract components to their implementation (by vertical ASM refinement) can be combined to smoothly integrate data and control features. We also illustrate how ASMs allow one to define not only declarative (functional or axiomatic) interface constraints, but also behavioral interface conditions by calling machines declared at the needed level of abstraction.

We use the Automatic Teller Machine (ATM) case study and paraphrase the informal *AtmRe*quirements proposed in [90]. They give us the opportunity to illustrate that during the construction of a ground model, one often has to ask the domain experts for additional information on the intended requirements to make the model complete ('complete' in the sense explained in Sect. 1.1).

PlantReq. There are many tills which can access a central resource (CR) containing the detailed records of customers' bank accounts.
TillAccessReq. A till is used by inserting a card and typing in a PIN which is encoded by the till and compared with a code stored on the card.
FunctionalReq. After successfully identifying themselves to the system, customers may try to:

1. view the balance of their accounts,
2. make a withdrawal of cash,
3. ask for a statement of their account to be sent by post.

Information on accounts is held in a central database and may be unavailable. If the database is available, any amount up to the total in the account may be withdrawn, subject to a fixed daily limit on withdrawals.
CardReq. The fixed daily limit on withdrawals means that the amount withdrawn within the day must be stored on the card. "Illegal" cards are kept by the till.

Fig. 2.15 Interaction structure of a generic ATM

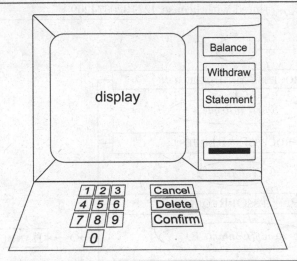

InterruptReq. A till or the Central Resource can be interrupted and the connection between them can fail.

CustomerInterruptReq. Customers can change or cancel their request at any time, e. g. abort the session, change the amount they want to withdraw.

ConcurrencyReq. Concurrent access to the database from two or more different tills is allowed, in particular concurrent attempts from two card holders who are authorized to use the same account.

TransactionalReq. Once a user has initiated a transaction, the transaction is completed eventually, and preferably within some real time constraint.

ReliabilityReq. Minimize the possibility of the use of stolen cards to gain access to an account.

Fig. 2.15 visualizes an abstract ATM interface one can extract from the requirements. The card slot is on the right and above are buttons for the selection of the requested functions "Balance", "Withdraw", and "Statements". At the front, the number pad enables to enter the PIN or the amount of money to withdraw. "Cancel" cancels the complete transaction and ejects the card. "Delete" and "Confirm" can be used during input. Finally, in the center, the display shows current information and error messages.

We follow [79] to develop a ground model (software specification) for these *AtmRe*quirements. For validation purposes it has been refined further to a CoreASM executable program [244].

The sequence of actions, requested by the *TillAccessReq* and *Functional-Req*, is directly reflected by the sequential composition of the ground model

Fig. 2.16 Architecture of ATM machine (Component Structure View) [79]
© 2015 ACM, reprinted with license 4271320674209

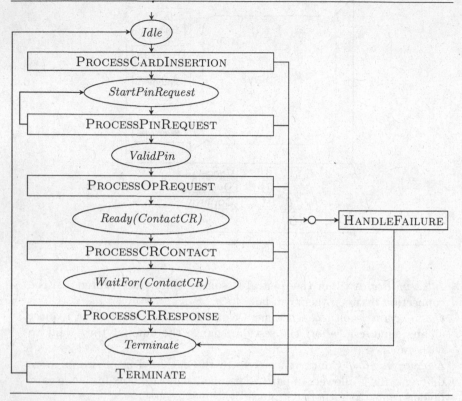

out of components which correspond to the successive session phases. Since, in each phase, the component M executing the 'normal' behavior expected in this phase can encounter various failures (which are not formulated in the given *AtmRe*quirements but will come out during the analysis below), each component has one exit connected to the entry of the component for the next phase and other exits to a HANDLEFAILURE(M) component. This explains the architectural overview of the control state ATM in Fig. 2.16.

Since by *CustomerInterruptReq* and *InterruptReq*, at any moment in parallel to the normal execution, some INTERRUPTTRIGGER may occur that has to be handled, the structure of the ATM ground model is defined as follows:

GROUNDATM =
  INTERRUPTTRIGGER
  if *ThereAreInterrupts*
    then HANDLEINTERRUPT
    else par (ATM, HANDLEFAILURE)

Fig. 2.17 Procedural (type $(1, n+1)$) refinement of control state ASMs

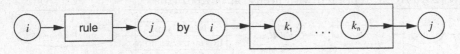

We now refine each component of GROUNDATM to capture the corresponding *AtmRequirements* and start with the ATM-components as depicted in Fig. 2.16.

Excursus on procedural refinement. Many of the refinements defined below for the components of GROUNDATM illustrate what we call *procedural* or submachine refinement, a special form of vertical refinement. In general, in a procedural refinement, an entire machine M (in a given ASM) is replaced by some other, usually more detailed, machine N. In the case of a control state ASM, a rule of form **if** *phase = entry* **then par** (*BlackBox, phase := exit*) may be replaced by a fixed number $n \geq 1$ of successive steps of a control state ASM with the same *entry* and the same *exit*. Such a refinement is called of type $(1, n)$ and graphically represented by Fig. 2.17. Usually, the interesting cases are where $n > 1$. We saw an example of type $(1, 2)$ in Fig. 2.9. The refinement type $(1, 1)$ is the special case where $n = 1$ upon which many other refinement concepts in the literature are focussed. In ASM refinements, multiple entries/exits are allowed, the refinement type may be (m, n) with arbitrary m, n and the relation between m and n can be not only static (as in Fig. 2.17), but also run-time determined. In the last case m abstract steps may result in a finite number of refined steps, where this number depends on values of some parameters in the state where the steps are executed. This is indicated by writing $n = f(m, params)$ or $(m, *)$. In a procedural refinement, the refined machine is treated as ONE machine, there is no 'outer' (abstract) machine which 'calls' an 'inner' (detailed) submachine.

Control state ASMs allow one to handle the problem that

> ... we rapidly lose our ability to understand larger and larger flowcharts; some intermediate levels of abstraction are necessary. [162]

In fact, the needed abstractions can be defined as submachines which appear in flowchart nodes as black boxes ('names for larger constructs') but have their details defined by refinement:

> ... we should give meaningful names for the larger constructs in our program that correspond to meaningful levels of abstraction, and we should define those levels of abstraction in one place, and merely use their names (instead of including the detailed code) when they are used to build larger concepts. [162]

End of excursus.

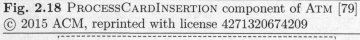

Fig. 2.18 PROCESSCARDINSERTION component of ATM [79]
© 2015 ACM, reprinted with license 4271320674209

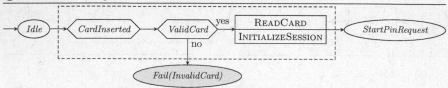

2.4.1 PROCESSCARDINSERTION *Component*

This component describes the start of an ATM session, when a user physically inserts a card. We reflect the card insertion by a monitored event *CardInserted* which is assumed to become true when a card is physically inserted and false when it is physically removed.

There is more one has to ask the domain experts than what is formulated as *TillAccessReq*. Certainly, at any time, the till is assumed to be used only by one user, implying that a new session can be started only when the till is in an *Idle* control state. Probably the till should also check whether an *insertedCard* is a *ValidCard*: only if *Readable(insertedCard)* is true, the machine can and must READCARD for retrieval of the data, INITIALIZESESSION and *StartPinRequest*; otherwise, the till should (enter a *Fail(InvalidCard)* mode to) call the corresponding HANDLEFAILURE component.

The meaning of *ValidCard* has to be decided by the domain experts. For the sake of illustration we use it as meaning that the *insertedCard* is *Readable* and belongs to a *circuit* the till does accept. Being *Readable* is a robustness concern, whether the card is corrupted or not an ATM card at all.

$$ValidCard = Readable(insertedCard) \textbf{ and } circuit(currCard) \in Circuit$$

Also the meaning of READCARD must be clarified with the domain experts to know which are the attributes the reader can retrieve from a card so that the till can manage the session. Again, for the sake of illustration, we consider the following functions:

- *circuit(card)* describing the card type, *pinCode(card)*, *account(card)*,
- *centralResource(card)* where the *account(card)* is managed,
- *dailyLimit(card)*,
- *alreadyWithdrawn(day, card)* indicating the total amount of money withdrawn this *day* (as a date) in previous sessions at some tills using *card*,
- *dayOfLastWithdrawal(card)*.

It is an implementation issue how READCARD records card attributes. In Sect. 2.3, we have modeled real-life objects internally by *Id*s. Since, in this example, in every session, only one card is involved, one can use a more abstract modeling alternative by copying *insertedCard* into an ATM-controlled variable *currCard := insertedCard*. This allows one to use any *attribute(currCard)* as derived function, thereby abstracting from how the value *attributeValReadFrom(insertedCard)* is stored by the reader.

Some card attributes may need an update when the card is inserted. *dayOfLastWithdrawal(card)*, for example, has to be updated to *today* upon a withdrawal. Functions like *alreadyWithdrawn(today, card)* should probably be updated in yet another component INITIALIZESESSION, here by a rule of the following form:

> **if** *dayOfLastWithdrawal(card) < today* **then**
> *alreadyWithdrawn(today, card) := 0*

Consequently one should assume that *today*, which is monitored for PROCESSCARDINSERTION, is updated at midnight by a CALENDAR component of the ATM.

This leads to the definition of PROCESSCARDINSERTION in Fig. 2.18. Note that, formally, this procedural refinement is of type $(1, 1)$, given that in the step count, reading the guard goes together with writing the updates. We still call it a refinement because the refined machine provides more detail than the abstract one.

2.4.2 PROCESSPINREQUEST *Component*

The formulation of the *TillAccessReq* does not mention that 'typing in a PIN' is a non-atomic time-constrained user activity where the till has a) to ASKFOR(*Pin*) and b) to check whether the user input produced a *ValidPin*. For other interactions of this kind during a session, we make ASKFOR reusable by parameterizing it, indicating the type of things asked for. This is an application of the ASM call construct which supports modularity.

The detailed definition of this component involves processing keywise-provided input streams, see the refinement in Sect. 2.4.9. We separate it from the following abstract specification of its interface behavior: ASKFOR stores the monitored *userInput* value it asks for in a location, say *valFor(param)*, and enters mode *Ready(param)* (such that it can RESETTIMER(ASKFOR (*param*)), see the timer pattern in Sect. 2.1.4.2). The *Timeout* of *param* is checked in the INTERRUPTTRIGGER component (see Sect. 2.4.7).

> ASKFOR(*param*) =
> *valFor(param) := userInput*
> *mode := Ready(param)*
> RESETTIMER(ASKFOR(*param*))[42]

---

[42] The ASM modeling language allows us to use the rule with its parameters directly as identifier for the timed operation.

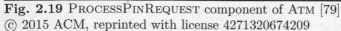

Fig. 2.19 PROCESSPINREQUEST component of ATM [79]
© 2015 ACM, reprinted with license 4271320674209

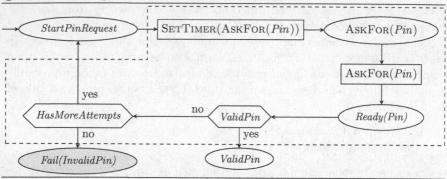

For the sake of illustration, we discuss another feature not mentioned in *TillAccessReq*, namely that if the user input did not produce a *ValidPin*, the user probably *HasMoreAttempts* so that the pin requests can be repeated. But for how long? Say until *Fail(InvalidPin)* or *ValidPin* is reached—unless a timeout event triggers an interrupt. This is captured by the definition of PROCESSPINREQUEST in Fig. 2.19. The *TillAccessReq* guides the definition of the *ValidPin* predicate where the reader function *pinCode* extracts the 'code stored on the card' and the external $encode_{Pin}$ function performs the 'encoding by the till':

$$ValidPin = (pinCode(currCard) = encode_{Pin}(valFor(Pin)))$$

Excursus on the call ASM construct. ASMs can be used in parameterized form $N(params)$ if a definition (called *declaration* for N) of the form

$$N(x_1, \ldots, x_n) = M$$

is given where the body M of the declaration is an (already defined) ASM and its free variables all occur in the parameter list $x_1, \ldots, x_n$; the parameters in the head of the declaration are called *formal parameters*. Such a machine is called a *named* ASM. When $N(exp_1, \ldots, exp_n)$ is called, the body M of the machine declaration is executed with the variables x_i substituted by the call parameters exp_i (not by their values).[43] Therefore executing a submachine call is treated as one atomic step; it yields a defined result only if the execution of the machine body yields a defined result. This call mechanism generalizes the use of a parameterized version of the SWITCH machine in Sect. 2.3.1. **End of excursus.**

---

[43] This is *call by name* because the call parameters are evaluated only in the state in which the body is executed; if there are some sequential steps (see Sect. 4.5), this may not be the state in which the machine was called. *call by value* is definable by
$N(exp_1, \ldots, exp_n) = \textbf{let } (x_1 = exp_1, \ldots, x_n = exp_n) \textbf{ in } M.$

Fig. 2.20 PROCESSOPREQUEST component of ATM [79]
© 2015 ACM, reprinted with license 4271320674209

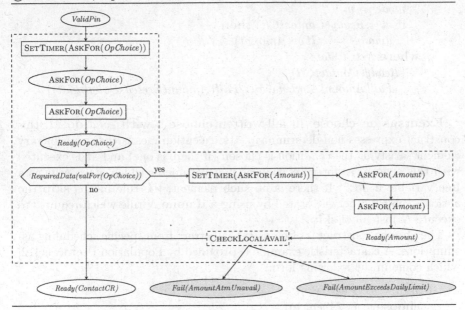

2.4.3 PROCESSOPREQUEST *Component*

The way PROCESSPINREQUEST used ASKFOR(*Pin*) to interact with the
user can be repeated in using ASKFOR(*OpChoice*) in PROCESSOPREQUEST,
to capture the user's choice described in *FunctionalReq*. If, for the chosen
operation, the till needs further *RequiredData*, it has to ASKFOR them too,
here only in case of *op = Withdrawal* for the requested *amount* of money.
By *FunctionalReq*, it must be checked whether *AmountExceedsDailyLimit*, to
which we add a local *AmountATMUnavail*ability check. This is captured by
the definition in Fig. 2.20.

The definition of the CHECKLOCALAVAILability component is an occasion to illustrate how to seamlessly combine its mere control flow view
with a description of the underlying data. Here it suffices to specify only
its interface behavior, namely to which next control state the component
may proceed depending on the underlying data, here either the normal exit
Ready(*ContactCR*) or one of the two possible parameterized *Fail*ure exits.
For the behavioral interface, only the next control state is relevant, not the
reason why it has been chosen, which depends on the data. This can be
expressed by a nondeterministic choice, for which we introduce the **choose**
construct. The detailed refinement in Sect. 2.4.9 replaces the nondeterminism
by giving the reasons why a particular next control state is entered.

CHECKLOCALAVAIL =
   choose $m \in NxtCtlState$
   $mode := m$
   if $m = Ready(ContactCR)$ **then**
     $amount := valFor(Amount)$
   where $NxtCtlState =$
   $\{Ready(ContactCR),$
     $Fail(AmountAtmUnavail), Fail(AmountExceedsDailyLimit)\}$

Excursus on choose. In full written **choose** x **with** *cond* **do** M, this construct expresses non-determinism. Its execution means that an arbitrary element satisfying the *cond*ition is chosen (if there is one) and M is executed with this element as interpretation of x, a parameter which may occur as a free variable in M.[44] If there is no such element, the rule means **skip** (no action)—unless otherwise stated by using a **if none** N rule which requires to execute N instead of **skip**.

The **choose** construct is often used to abstract from specific scheduling assumptions. A characteristic example is provided by Population Protocols [12] which come in the following form:

POPULATIONPROTOCOL =
   choose $a, b \in Agent$ **in**
     INTERACT(a, b)[45]

For such protocols different sets of constraints on **choose** (read: usually probabilistic schedules which implement the choice) are described and analyzed with respect to the effect they have on the behavior and computational power of the resulting protocol.

Analogously **choose** can be used to implement parallelism without introducing any specific execution order (so that as a later refinement step any convenient optimized execution order can be introduced). For an example see the iterative refinements of machines built with the **forall** construct in Exerc. 18.

Another widespread use of **choose** to abstract from specific schedulers is encountered when modeling sets of computational *Process*es with the *InterleavingPattern* in mind. With interleaving at each moment, only one process

---

[44] Due to this non-deterministic choice, the update set $Upd(M, S)$ generated in a state S by executing M also depends on the chosen value for x, so that Upd is really not a function of only M and S but a relation involving also the interpretation ζ of freely occurring (logical) variables. Whenever possible without risking ambiguity, we notationally suppress the dependence of the chosen value and write $Upd(\textbf{choose } x \textbf{ with } cond \textbf{ do } M, S)$.

[45] Usually in such protocols INTERACTion uses a local Mealy automata state transition function $\delta\colon Q \times Q \to Q \times Q$ to update for $Agent = \{a_1, \ldots, a_n\}$ the global current state

$$mode = (mode(a_1), \ldots, mode(a_n))$$

by updating the local internal state pair $(mode(a), mode(b))$ to $\delta(mode(a), mode(b))$.

(say among the *Enabled* ones) is active, so that it can be executed without any risk of read/write or resource conflicts with other processes:

INTERLEAVINGPATTERN(*Process*) =
　one of ({$p \in Process$) | $Enabled(p)$})
　　where
　　　one of (*Rules*) = **choose** $R \in Rules$ **do** R^{46}

In a more sophisticated concurrency model, in every step a process may decide to either *globally* interact with its environment, which is constituted by the other concurrently working processes, or to perform a *local* computation.

- In *mode* = *global*, the reads and/or updates of globally visible (i. e. shared, monitored or output) locations are synchronized with the corresponding ones performed by any other process which simultaneously performs a global step. The consistency condition constrains the simultaneous application of the updates which are computed by any of the processes interacting in a global mode step. In global mode, a process may also decide to switch to a local subcomputation; in this case its interaction with the environment consists only in a READGLOBALDATA step.
- In *mode* = *local*, if the process decides to perform a local step, its updates affect only private memory locations; if in a local step the process makes use of globally visible locations, it uses only their local copies which have been updated by the last READGLOBALDATA step. If the process decides to interact again with other processes, it will switch to *global mode* and WRITEBACK to perform updates of globally visible locations. By switching to *mode* = *global*, the process in its next step will listen again to the environment for meanwhile possibly changed values of monitored and shared locations.

This implies three global process steps which are to-be-synchronized:

- READGLOBALDATA, typically with locally recording the values retrieved from monitored or shared locations,
- WRITEBACK to shared and output locations,
- their combined version GLOBALEXECution, a simultaneous atomic read and write of all concerned locations, like in a traditional ASM step.

The separation of these global steps from the asynchronously executable local steps LOCALEXECution can be expressed follows:[47]

CONCURRENCYPATTERN(*Process*) =
　forall $p \in Process$
　　CONCURSTEP(p)

---

[46] We also write **one of**　*Rules* and similar with vertical notation of *Rules* (without braces).

[47] Viewed as a single-agent ASM, CONCURRENCYPATTERN(P) generates all the concurrent ASM runs of the machines in P as defined in [70], see Sect. 3.4.

where
   $\text{CONCURSTEP}(p) =$
     if $mode = global$ **then**
       choose $step \in \{globalStep, globalRead\}$
         if $step = globalStep$ **then**
           $\text{GLOBALEXEC}(p)$ -- read/write interaction
         else
           $\text{READGLOBALDATA}(p)$ -- read interaction
           $mode := local$ -- switch to local step
     if $mode = local$ **then**
       choose $step \in \{localStep, globalWrite\}$
         if $step = localStep$ **then**
           $\text{LOCALEXEC}(p)$ -- local step
         else
           $\text{WRITEBACK}(p)$ -- write interaction
           $mode := global$ -- switch to next global read

Instead of **choose** x **with** $cond$ **in** M, we often use $M(x/select_{cond})$ where x is substituted by $select_{cond}$, a (static or dynamic) *selection function* (often also called *choice function*) which when called provides an element satisfying the selection criterion $cond$. Using selection functions offers more flexibility than **choose** to steer specifications and implementations of the choice criteria. Another (not always equivalent) form we sometimes use is **let** $x = select_{cond}$ **in** M.

End of excursus.

Exercise 17. (Implementing parallelism by a queue.) Formulate in which respect the following ASM GRAPHTRAVERSAL_2 is a correct $(1, *)$-refinement of the machine GRAPHTRAVERSAL_1 from Exerc. 16 with *JustVisited* refined to a queue.[48] Prove the refinement correctness.

   $\text{GRAPHTRAVERSAL}_2 =$
     let $u = head(JustVisited)$
     $\text{PROPAGATEFRESHVISITTONEIGHB}(u)$
     $\text{DEQUEUE}(u, JustVisited)$

Exercise 18. (Implementing parallelism by **choose**.) Formulate in which respect the following machine GRAPHTRAVERSAL_3, initialized with $mode = startPropagationToNeighb$, $JustVisited = [source]$ and $ToVisit = \emptyset$, is a correct $(1, *)$-refinement of the machine GRAPHTRAVERSAL_2 from the preceding Exerc. 17.

---

[48] Thus INSERTION of elements into *JustVisited* is refined to ENQUEUE where simultaneous ENQUEUEs for multiple elements are performed in any order.

GRAPHTRAVERSAL$_3$ =
 if $mode = startPropagationToNeighb$ **then**
  if $JustVisited \neq [\,]$ **then**
   let $u = head(JustVisited)$
    INITIALIZEPROPAGATIONTONEIGHB(u)
    DEQUEUE($u, JustVisited$)
    $mode := propagate$ --switch to iterate through $neighb(u)$
 if $mode = propagate$ **then**
  if $ToVisit \neq \emptyset$
   then choose $v \in ToVisit$
    MAKEJUSTVISITED(v)
    DELETE($v, ToVisit$)
   else $mode := startPropagationToNeighb$
 where
  INITIALIZEPROPAGATIONTONEIGHB(u) =
   $ToVisit := neighb(u)$

GRAPHTRAVERSAL$_3$ can be refined in a provably correct way to an algorithm SHORTESTPATH as defined in [92] or [190] and to an implementation in C^{++} [235], for more details see [76, Sect. 3.2.2].

2.4.4 PROCESSCRCONTACT *Component*

The PROCESSCRCONTACT component describes how the till a) triggers the physical process to forward through the communication medium a request and b) makes the till $WaitFor(ContactCR)$ until a response is received—unless a timeout or contact failure happen as contemplated in the *InterruptReq*. This is captured by Fig. 2.21.

Fig. 2.21 PROCESSCRCONTACT component of ATM [79]
© 2015 ACM, reprinted with license 4271320674209

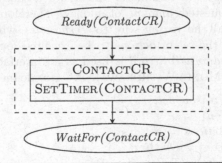

Reflecting the absence of detailed *AtmReq*uirements on the communication mechanism, we formulate communication rather abstractly using a) a component which we assume to SEND messages with the indicated content to a receiver and b) a monitored location *CRresp* where response messages from the Central Resource (assumed to be different from some *defaultValue*) are received. For a detailed treatment of communicating ASMs, we refer the reader to Sect. 3.3. Messages from the till to CR encode, besides the sender and the receiver, the information on the *currCard*, the user's operation choice *valFor(OpChoice)* and, for a *Withdrawal* operation, also the requested *amount*.

> CONTACTCR =
> SEND($encode_{till}(Atm, CR, RequestData)$)
> DISPLAY(*WaitingForCentralResourceContact*)

Here we use the following abbreviations:

> $Atm = address(till(\textbf{self}))$
> $CR = address(centralResource(currCard))$
> $RequestData = opChoiceData(currCard, valFor(OpChoice))$
> $opChoiceData(card, op) =$
> $\begin{cases} (card, op) & \textbf{if } op \in \{Balance, Statement\} \\ (card, op, amount) & \textbf{if } op = Withdrawal \end{cases}$

2.4.5 PROCESSCRRESPONSE *Component*

By *InterruptReq*, a *ConnectionRefused* response may arrive from CR and lead to the corresponding *Fail*ure mode. Other *CentralResourceresp*onses lead the till to normally PROCESSRESPONSE. This is what is defined by Fig. 2.22.

PROCESSRESPONSE, defined by Fig. 2.23, triggers the appropriate termination actions (displaying information, card ejection or withdrawal, money ejection) when a response message *CRresp* from the CR is received.

In *Terminate* mode, the till must a) EJECT or KEEP the *currCard*, depending on the given *reason* to terminate, and b) for a successful *Withdrawal*, also EJECT the requested *amount* of money. Therefore we parametrize TERMINATEOP by a) the *reason* why to *Terminate*—which is DISPLAYed to the user—and b) the set of *actions* to be executed for that *reason*. The location *MoneyWithdrawalToRecord* is used as an interface to the separate component RECORDMONEYWITHDRAWALONCARD defined below.

> TERMINATEOP(*reason, actions*) =
> DISPLAY(*reason*)
> *TerminationActions* := *actions*
> **if** $answer(reason) = Ok$ **then**
> *MoneyWithdrawalToRecord* := *true*

Fig. 2.22 PROCESSCRRESPONSE component of ATM

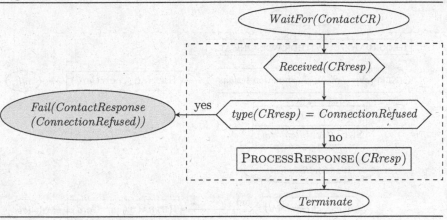

Fig. 2.23 PROCESSRESPONSE(r) component of ATM

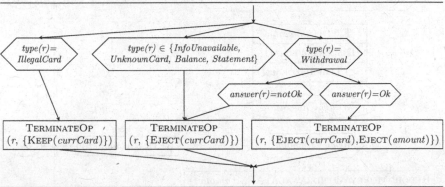

2.4.6 Termination Actions: TERMINATE *Component*

We assume that, as usual with ATMs, first the card and then the money is ejected in case of a granted amount ($answer(response) = Ok$). Therefore, to satisfy the *dailyLimit* requirement stated in *CardReq*, the TERMINATE component must

- RECORDMONEYWITHDRAWALONCARD for *today* before the *currCard* is EJECTed,
- RECORDMONEYWITHDRAWALATATM after the successful removal of the money.

In the spirit of the *ReliabilityReq*, the TERMINATE action should also take care of the case in which a card or the money is not withdrawn within *deltaTime(Removal)* (see Sect. 2.1.4.2 for the timer pattern). This leads to define TERMINATE by Fig. 2.24 using the following submachines:

Fig. 2.24 TERMINATE component

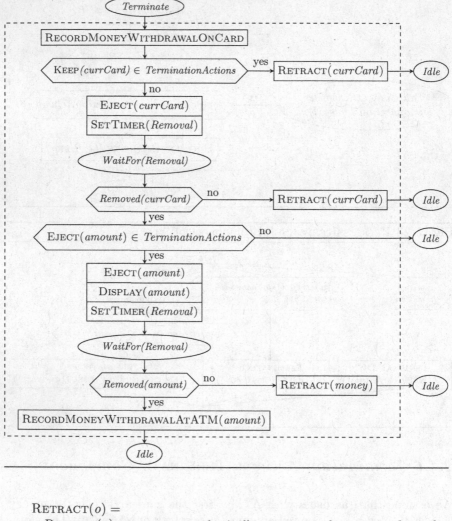

RETRACT(o) =
   REMOVE(o)   -- physically remove card or money from slot
   LOGMISSEDWITHDRAWAL(o)   -- if applicable
RECORDMONEYWITHDRAWALONCARD =
   if *MoneyWithdrawalToRecord* **then**   -- only if amount was granted
     alreadyWithdrawn(today, currCard) :=
       amount + alreadyWithdrawn(today, currCard)
     dayOfLastWithdrawal(currCard) := *today*
     MoneyWithdrawalToRecord := *false*
RECORDMONEYWITHDRAWALATATM(o) =
   money(Atm) := *money(Atm) − o*
              -- called only after successful money withdrawal

EJECT(o) is assumed to trigger a physical action of a hardware component which passes the card or money to the slot where the user can fetch it.

Exercise 19. Refine the abstract REMOVE machine to trigger the physical environment action (see Sect. 2.1.2).

Exercise 20. Think about how to solve the problem that the till, after having EJECTed the card, may not EJECT the due *amount* of money, though the *amount* has been added already to *alreadyWithdrawn*(*today*, *currCard*), thus possibly affecting the next *WithinDailyLimit* check (see Fig. 2.26).

2.4.7 HANDLEFAILURE *and* INTERRUPT *Components*

When the ATM enters a failure mode *Fail*(*param*), the HANDLEFAILURE component is called. The kind of *Fail*ure is extracted from the current mode so that for each exception case, a separate definition can be given to support modularity and ease of definitional changes.[49] We show it for the *Fail*(*InvalidPin*) case, where the *CardReq* requests to KEEP(*currCard*) as "Illegal", in the other *Fail*ure cases an ATM typically will EJECT the card. We decided not to keep but to immediately EJECT *InvalidCards*, i. e. unreadable cards or cards which do not belong to the circuits the till accepts. Cards the CR declares as *IllegalCard* are kept by the corresponding TERMINATEOPeration (see Fig. 2.23).

HANDLEFAILURE =
    if *mode* = *Fail*(*InvalidPin*) **then**
        TERMINATEOP(*InvalidPin*, {KEEP(*currCard*)})
    else TERMINATEOP(*mode*, {EJECT(*currCard*)})
    CLOSECONNECTIONTOCENTRALRESOURCE

We illustrate modeling interrupts for timeouts and cancel commands by the customer. For the sake of generality, we include modeling the possibility to define a region where such interrupts should produce an effect. If the user has *Pressed* the *CancelKey* when the ATM *IsInCancelRegion*, or if automatically a *Timeout*(*timedOp*) happens when the ATM *IsInTimerRegion* for the *timedOp*, then INTERRUPTTRIGGER activates HANDLEINTERRUPT, e. g. by inserting these events into *InterruptEvent*.

INTERRUPTTRIGGER[50] =
    INTERRUPTBY(*Cancel*)
    INTERRUPTBY(*Time*)

---

[49] The reader will have noticed that this encoding of the failure *reason* into the *mode* value *Fail*(*reason*) refines the blank *mode* circle in Fig. 2.16 to a set of circles, one for each possible failure *mode* value. This becomes explicit in the refined flowchart in Fig. 2.28.
[50] For running ATM scenarios in CoreASM with an input providing user, in [244] 'any time' is interpreted as 'any user input time'.

where
  $\text{INTERRUPTBy}(\textit{Cancel}) =$
    if $Pressed(\textit{CancelKey})$ **and** $IsInCancelRegion(\text{ATM})$ **then**
      $\text{INSERT}(\textit{Cancel}, \textit{InterruptEvent})$
  $\text{INTERRUPTBy}(\textit{Time}) =$
    forall $timedOp \in \{AskFor(param), ContactCR, Removal\}$
      if $Timeout(timedOp)$ **and** $IsInTimerRegion(timedOp)$ **then**
        $\text{INSERT}(timer(timedOp), \textit{InterruptEvent})$
        $\text{RESETTIMER}(timedOp)$

For the sake of illustration, we include, into the model, a priority mechanism for interrupts so that one could, for example, declare *Cancel* commands to be of higher priority than *Timeouts*. For reasons of modularity, we separate the definition of the priority scheme from its use by a function *highPriority* which can be defined independently. Therefore HANDLEINTERRUPT chooses a *highPriority* interrupt event e to HANDLE(e). For *Cancel* events e occurring when $IsInCancelRegion(\text{ATM})$ and for *Timeout* events e concerning a *timedOp* occurring when $IsInTimerRegion(timedOp)$, HANDLE(e) means to TERMINATESESSION with EJECTing the card.

  $\text{HANDLEINTERRUPT} =$
    let $e = highPriority(\textit{InterruptEvent})$
      $\text{HANDLE}(e)$
      $\text{DELETE}(e, \textit{InterruptEvent})$
  where
    $\text{HANDLE}(\textit{Cancel}) =$
      if $IsInCancelRegion(\text{ATM})$ **then** $\text{TERMINATESESSION}(\textit{Cancel})$
    $\text{HANDLE}(timer(timedOperation)) =$
      if $IsInTimerRegion(timedOperation)$ **then**
        $\text{TERMINATESESSION}(Timeout(timedOperation))$
    $\text{TERMINATESESSION}(p) =$
      $\text{DISCONNECTATMFROMCR}$
      $\text{TERMINATEOP}(p, \text{EJECT}(currCard))$
      $mode := Terminate$

Using control state ASMs, one can define interrupt regions by referring to the *mode*s in which an interrupt event should take effect. The following definition expresses that no *Cancel* command has any effect outside a user session (when $mode = Idle$) or when the ATM is performing automatically its final stage to TERMINATE the session.[51]

  $IsInCancelRegion(\text{ATM}) = mode \notin \{Idle, Terminate\})$
  $IsInTimerRegion(AskFor(param)) =$
    $mode \in \{AskFor(param), WaitFor(param)\}$

---

[51] One could include into HANDLEINTERRUPT to discard interrupt events which happen outside their region. This is a garbage collection concern we do not pursue further here.

$$IsInTimerRegion(ContactCR) =$$
$$mode = WaitFor(ContactCR)$$
$$IsInTimerRegion(RemovalCard) =$$
$$(mode \in \{WaitFor(RemovalCard), WaitFor(RemovalMoney)\})$$

Exercise 21. Define an interrupt refinement that reflects the *CustomerInterruptReq* that customers can change, at any time, the amount they want to withdraw.

2.4.8 Assumptions for the Central Resource

ATM behaves correctly only under appropriate assumptions on its interaction with its environment, here represented by the communication medium and the Central Resource where the database with account information is kept. We formulate the assumptions on the CR by a behavioral model CENTRALRESOURCE which asynchronously works together with the ATM. Given the abstraction level at which we treat the communication medium, it suffices to stipulate for CR that an ACCEPTREQUESTS component moves request messages (in whatever order, expressed by using **choose**) from a $Mailbox_{CR}$ into an internal *Request* set, from where a HANDLEREQUESTS component asynchronously fetches requests to handle them. For the sake of illustration, we include that when moving requests from the $Mailbox_{CR}$, they are *decoded* into a format the CR works with.

CENTRALRESOURCE =
   one of (ACCEPTREQUESTS, HANDLEREQUESTS)

The ACCEPTREQUESTS component is defined as follows:

ACCEPTREQUESTS =
  if $Mailbox_{CR} \neq \emptyset$ **then**
    choose $R \subseteq Mailbox_{CR}$ **with** $R \neq \emptyset$
      forall $msg \in R$
        INSERT($decode_{CR}(msg)$, *Request*)
        DELETE(msg, $Mailbox_{CR}$)

We assume requests to have a unique identity so that it is consistent to permit simultaneous access to the *Request* set by the two CR components, even for multiple messages or (under certain constraints, see below) multiple requests at a time. This way, the ASM parallelism offers the greatest possible freedom to satisfy the *ConcurrencyReq* and to separate its two different concerns, namely to a) allow for flexible priority resp. scheduling policies when implementing concurrent database accesses for different accounts and b) guarantee exclusive access to one account upon 'concurrent access to the database from two or more different tills' concerning that account, so that two simultaneously present requests cannot violate the *FunctionalReq* that only 'any amount up to the total in the account may be withdrawn'.

In the same spirit, we define HANDLEREQUESTS, using a *select$_{CR}$* function which each time it is applied to the dynamic set *Request* chooses a *Consistent* non-empty subset $R \subseteq Request$[52] where *Consistent(R)* means that R contains no multiple Withdraw requests concerning a same account. This way all requests in R can be HANDLEd in parallel.[53]

> HANDLEREQUESTS =
> **if** *Request* $\neq \emptyset$ **then**
>   **let** $R = select_{CR}(Request)$ -- NB. R is assumed to be *Consistent*
>   **forall** $r \in R \begin{cases} \text{HANDLE}(r) \\ \text{DELETE}(r, Request) \end{cases}$
> **where** *Consistent(R)* **iff**
>   **thereisno** $r, r' \in R$ **with** $r \neq r'$ **and**
> $account(r) = account(r')$ **and** $op(r) = op(r') = Withdrawal$

It remains to define the assumptions to be made for the ATM on the behavioral effect of HANDLE(*request*) when performed by CR, that is, we have to refine HANDLE(*req*) to trigger CR to SEND a correct *CRresp*onse of type *op(req)* to the *sender(req)*, where *op(req)* is one of *Withdrawal, Statement* or *Balance*. The definition is given in Fig. 2.25.

---

[52] This is a typical example for a function belonging to the signature of the ASM which is used only under the assumption of a specific constraint. In case of a refinement, one has to take care of the satisfaction of this constraint.

[53] An alternative approach to guarantee transactional behavior of the CR is to define HANDLEREQUESTS(*request*) for single *request*s and then to harness a set of its instances by the transaction control operator pattern defined in terms of ASMs in [72].

Fig. 2.25 HANDLE(*req*) component of ATM

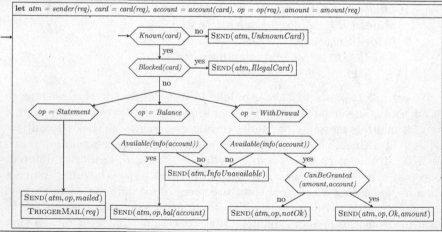

Fig. 2.26 Refined CHECKLOCALAVAIL component of ATM [79]
© 2015 ACM, reprinted with license 4271320674209

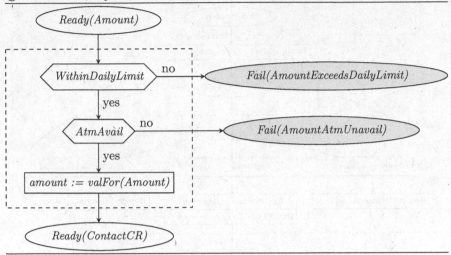

2.4.9 Refinements of Auxiliary ATM Components

To illustrate some more refinement step which prepares the ground for the CoreASM executable model in [244] we define in this section refinements of two major auxiliary components.

The first example is a data refinement of CHECKLOCALAVAIL by Fig. 2.26. It refines the abstract interface defined in Sect. 2.4.3, directing the (in the abstract interface nondeterministic) control state update by the exact local availability reasons for which the machine may become *Ready* to contact the Central Resource or not.

Excursus on ASM data refinement. An ASM *data refinement* is an (m, n) refinement where the correspondence between abstract and refined operations is one-to-one (i.e. $m = n = 1$) so that usually we do not even change the names of the operations but only their definition. This is the most frequent refinement type used in the literature, but from the modeling perspective it is only a special instance of the more general ASM refinement concept. **End of excursus.**

The next example is a combined data and operation refinement of the behavioral interface ASKFOR defined in Sect. 2.4.2. Allowing such *procedural refinements* supports stepwise modular introduction of design ideas and characterizes the ASM refinement method. The very refinement of ASKFOR is defined by components.

The idea is to introduce stepwise reading and processing of input key values. The machine starts with an INITIALIZEINPUTELABORATION which

Fig. 2.27 Refined AskFor(*param*) component of ATM [79]
© 2015 ACM, reprinted with license 4271320674209

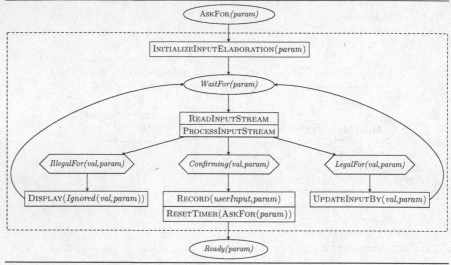

serves to DISPLAY the request to the user and to guarantee a robustness property—keys pressed before the ATM begins to *WaitFor(param)* should yield no input—by taking user input only during the execution of ASKFOR. Then the machine will READINPUTSTREAM and PROCESSINPUTSTREAM until by a *Confirm* it moves to *Ready(param)*, see Fig. 2.27.

Into INITIALIZEINPUTELABORATION we insert a COUNTDOWN which serves to control multiple *attemptsFor(Pin)*-insertion, assuming an initialization of *attemptsFor(Pin)* to a positive value (say in INITIALIZESESSION). Consequently the abstract predicate *HasMoreAttempts* used in Fig. 2.19 is detailed to *attemptsFor(Pin)* > 0.

> INITIALIZEINPUTELABORATION(*param*) =
>   INITIALIZE(*inputStream*)   -- Start listening to user input
>   INITIALIZE(*userInput*)   -- Start processing user input
>   DISPLAY(*AskFor(param)*)   -- Ask user to input *param*
>   **if** *param* = *Pin* **then** COUNTDOWN(*attemptsFor(Pin)*)
> **where**
>   INITIALIZE(*Stream*) = (*Stream* := [ ])
>   INITIALIZE(*userInput*) = (*userInput* := [ ])
>   COUNTDOWN(*attemptsFor(Pin)*) =
>   *attemptsFor(Pin)* := *attemptsFor(Pin)* − 1

Exercise 22. Change the model to introduce a *dailyPinRequestLimit(card)* to help prevent repeated successive sessions attempting to find out the correct pin. Analyze the feature interaction with *dailyLimit* in case a user on one day makes numerous *Withdrawals* without exceeding the *dailyLimit* and without inserting an invalid pin.

To define READINPUTSTREAM one has to clarify what should happen if a user hits simultaneously multiple keys. Since usually the hardware transforms this into a randomly ordered *inputStream* we make this explicit by introducing a function *randomOrder* which randomly yields for any *set* a sequence *randomOrder(set)* that is ADDed to the current *inputStream*. Usually the hardware before applying *randomOrder* to a *set* will also *truncate(set)* in a device-dependent manner to a subset. The function *inputVal* yields element-wise·for every pressed key in a given sequence its input value. These are the external functions used in the following definition.

READINPUTSTREAM =
  let *PressedKeys* = {*key* | *Pressed(key)*}
  let *Newinput* = *inputval(randomOrder(truncate(PressedKeys)))*
    ADDATTHELEFT(*Newinput, inputStream*) -- Insert at the left end
PROCESSINPUTSTREAM =
  if *inputStream* ≠ [ ] **then**
    let *val* = *fstOut(inputStream)*
    REMOVEATTHERIGHT(*val, inputStream*)

Placing READINPUTSTREAM and PROCESSINPUTSTREAM in parallel is consistent since ADDATTHELEFT and REMOVEATTHERIGHT concern different occurrences of the *inputval*ue of pressed keys.

The UPDATEINPUTBY component in Fig. 2.27 writes one by one (say from right to left) the *inputStream* values that are *LegalFor param* into *userInput* until a *Confirming* value is encountered which triggers a normal *Ready(param)* exit (unless an INTERRUPTTRIGGER occurs). By the *CustomerInterruptReq* the user can change the input any time so that the *Delete* key must be considered as *LegalFor* every *parame*ter. How to HANDLEILLEGALINPUT(*val, param*) is not considered in the *AtmReq* so that to make the ASM CoreASM executable we decided to ignore such input, but to inform the user about it by a DISPLAY.

UPDATEINPUTBY(*val, param*) =
  if *val* ≠ *Delete* **then** ADDTOINPUT(*val, param*)
  if *val* = *Delete* **then** REMOVEFROMINPUT(*param*)
ADDTOINPUT(*val, param*) =
  userInput := *concatenateAtTheRight(userInput, val)*
  DISPLAY(*concatenateAtTheRight(userInput, val), param*)
REMOVEFROMINPUT(*param*) =
  userInput := *removeLast(userInput)*
  DISPLAY(*removeLast(userInput), param*)
Confirming(val, param) if and only if
  $\begin{cases} param \in \{Pin, Amount\} \text{ \textbf{and} } val = Confirm \\ param = OpChoice \text{ \textbf{and} } val \in \{Balance, Statement, Withdrawal\} \end{cases}$

Fig. 2.28 ATM Unfolded Refined View [79]
© 2015 ACM, reprinted with license 4271320674209

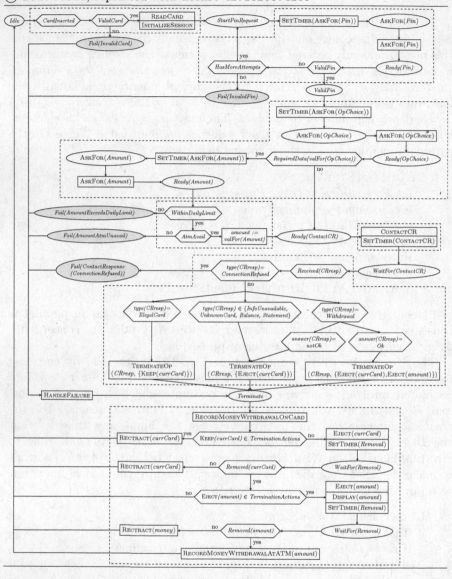

$$\text{RECORD}(input, param) =$$
$$valFor(param) := input \ \textbf{if} \ param \in \{Pin, Amount\}$$
$$valFor(param) := param \ \textbf{if}$$
$$\quad param \in \{Balance, Statement, Withdrawal\}$$

Final consideration. The final result is the software specification in Fig. 2.28, an unfolded view of the control state ASM in Fig. 2.16. For each components its exit from a normal to an exception phase is highlighted by darker control states. The figure shows the limits of printing graphical representations (not of computer supported zooming techniques one can use in digitalized documentations): the relevant point is that the inspection, justifying that the ATM satisfies the *AtmReq*, can be done component-wise, using the small component flowcharts above, given their simple sequential connection, here by identifying the exit control state of one with the entry control state of its successor.

The specification in Fig. 2.28 satisfies the initially given requirements. These requirements do not address however the security-critical aspect of a service, like money withdrawal at an ATM dealing with which involves the use of to-be-verified cryptographic protocols. In [35] a method is presented which integrates interactive theorem-proving verification of application-specific security properties into the development process: together with an ASM, serving as software specification, executable code is generated which is shown to be correct and secure with respect to the specification; the application-specific security properties of interest are mechanically verified for the ASM.

Exercise 23. Formulate the correctness statement for the ATM components and justify by model inspection the correctness of the components and how this implies the correctness of the GROUNDATM. Show how the timer properties imply the *TransactionalReq*uirement.

2.5 Recap: Single-Agent ASM Constructs/Refinements

We recapitulate the working definition of ASMs which has been introduced piecemeal by elementary examples in this chapter. For the technical reader, a systematic and more detailed mathematical definition is provided in Chap. 7.

Definition 1. An ASM program (or also simply called an ASM) is a finite set of rules, each of one of the following five forms:

> **if** *condition* **then** *updates*
> **forall** x **with** *condition* **do** M -- NB. with abbreviates 'satisfying'
> **choose** x **with** *condition* **do** M
> $N(exp_1, \ldots, exp_n)$ given a declaration $N(x_1, \ldots, x_n) = M$
> **let** $x = exp$ **in** M

where M is an already defined ASM program, the variables x, x_i may occur as free variable in *condition* and M resp. N, and *updates* denotes finitely many assignment instructions of the following form:

$f(exp_1, \ldots, exp_n) := exp$

Here f is an n-ary function symbol and *condition* a Boolean-valued expression, called rule guard. We usually omit the **do** when using vertical rule layout.

In *expressions* one can use any term that can be built

- starting with *constants* (fixed names or symbols for concrete objects) and
- *variables* (names or symbols where the context decides upon which concrete objects they denote)
- applying finitely often function symbols f of any arity $n > 0$ to already built terms $t_1, \ldots, t_n$, obtaining $f(t_1, \ldots, t_n)$.

In particular, it is allowed to use the following expressions:

- **new** (D), denoting a fresh element to be added to a domain (set) D,
- **self** which parameterizes an expression by the current ASM instance,[54]
- **undef** to denote an undefined value in cases where no (default) value is specified.

Sometimes we use as a placeholder for later refinements an empty assignment instruction denoted **skip**. Its effect is to do nothing (perform no change).

To distinguish this class of ASMs from its various extensions these ASMs are also called *basic* ASMs. In the literature they are also called *sequential* ASMs because their semantics (read: behavior) is defined as execution of a sequence of steps.

Semantics of basic ASMs. A *state* of an ASM is an interpretation of all its function *symbols* (those which occur in its *signature*) by functions over some domain. In an abstract memory perspective an ASM state can be viewed in two ways:

- as a flat set of memory *locations*, denoted by pairs (f, v) of some label (function name) f and a sequence v of parameter values, containing a unique value of whatever type, denoted $f(v)$, or
- as a structured set of function tables, one per function symbol f in the signature, associating arguments with values.

To simplify the notation we treat predicates (attributes and relations) in terms of their characteristic functions so that ASM states in the abstract structured memory perspective are arbitrary mathematical *structures* (objects/elements in some sets with operations on and relations among them). In logic they are called Tarski structures, in computing they are known as data structures.

An execution *step* of an ASM P consists in applying in a given state S simultaneously all the rules of P whose guard evaluates to true in this state. This comes up to perform simultaneously the set $Upd(P, S)$ of all the updates in the body of those rules thus yielding (in one step!) the next state which

---

[54] See Chap. 4 for a systematic treatment of state partitioning by parameterization.

we denote $S + U$ and call the *sequel* of S where $U = Upd(P, S)$—if that set U is consistent, otherwise the sequel $S + U$ is undefined.[55] In the literature $Upd(P, S)$ is also written $\Delta(P, S)$. Pairs (loc, val) of a *location* and a *value* to which the *location* has to be updated are called *updates*;[56] a set U of updates is called an *update set*. It is called *consistent* if it does not contain two updates with the same location and different values, otherwise it is called inconsistent. $Locs(U)$ denotes the set of locations of updates in U.

A *run* or *execution* is a sequence of states reached by successive steps of the machine, where in case of an active environment after each step of the ASM the environment may perform a step, elaborating the output (and possibly also shared) locations of the machine and updating the machine's monitored (and possibly also shared) locations for the next machine step. Thus ASMs are *reactive* machines which at each moment may perform a (just one) step. Defining the semantics of ASMs only by the one-step relation (and runs as its transitive closure) is intended. It frees applications of ASMs from the burden to have to think about fixpoint technicalities which are relegated to the metatheory the practitioner has not to worry about.

Usually runs of interest are started in states belonging to a particular class of states, called *initial* states; where termination is of interest usually also the termination states are states belonging to a specific class of states called *final* states. Initial/final states can be defined declaratively, but for execution initial states often are the result of an initialization program which is usually defined independently of the program for the run behavior. The reader who wants to see how this intuitive understanding of ASM runs is supported by a mathematically precise definition is referred to Chap. 7.

Control state ASMs. These machines come with a top-level FSM-like control-state structure so that all their rules are of the form defined in Fig. 2.29 (or of commonly used similar graphical forms representing precisely defined behavior, see Sect. 4.5.1). The guards are supposed to be disjoint to guarantee rule consistency. We call this extension of FSM flowcharts to ASMs *Control State Diagrams* (CSDs). In Chap. 9 we use ASMs to provide a systematic definition of the syntax and the semantics of such diagrams, which supports their intuitive understanding and makes them ready for machine processing.

The **combination of graphical** CSD notation **with textual definitions** of components is characteristic for how we use control state ASMs and CSDs. It allows one to smoothly but accurately integrate into the control-flow view via refinement also the state, read: data ('information model'), environ-

---

[55] We notationally suppress where possible without risking ambiguity that $U = Upd(P, S)$ also depends on the interpretation ζ of the logical variables by values of some domain and represents not a function but only a relation 'yields' in case a P-step involves choices by the **choose** operator. Correctly one should write yields(P, S, ζ, U). See Chap. 7 for the technical details.

[56] Sometimes we use the word 'update' also for 'assignment statement'; the context prevents possible ambiguity.

Fig. 2.29 Flowchart for control state ASM rules with disjoint $cond_i$ [76]
© 2003 Springer-Verlag Berlin Heidelberg, reprinted with permission

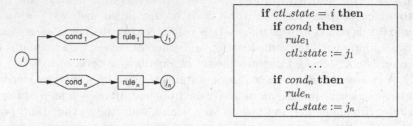

ment and resource concerns. This makes ASMs particularly useful to accurately model complex business processes (see Chap. 5). In fact they "allow propagating the information from a value chain perspective to a software-development perspective in a coherent and consistent way" and provide the business process expert with an effective "end-to-end control ... to build process-managed enterprise" [110, Sect. 2, pp. 3–4]. This is advocated by the S-BPM [109] approach (see Sect. 5.2.2) and IBM's recent Guard-State-Milestone approach [148] (see Sect. 5.2.1).

ASM refinements. The concept is illustrated by Fig. 2.30. It illustrates the freedom the ASM refinement notion offers the designer to decide, without being restricted by the straitjacket of a formal framework, upon when to apply which design ideas to implement an abstract model:

- concerning the data:

  - how to define the *refined* states, guided by the design ideas which determine the details to be introduced to refine given abstractions,
  - which pairs of (abstract,concrete) locations of interest or otherwise corresponding locations in states of interest to compare,
  - which notion of 'equivalence' (refinement correctness) to stipulate,

- concerning the flow of operations (control structure):

  - which (abstract,concrete) state pairs (S, S^*) and computation segments $(\tau_1 \ldots \tau_m, \sigma_1 \ldots \sigma_n)$ of interest to relate (suppressing the details of intermediate states to ease the comparison). n can be a function of m and other parameters; type $(m, *)$ indicates that m abstract steps correspond to finitely many refined steps.

If one has chosen an equivalence notion (for data in corresponding locations of interest in corresponding states of interest), a refinement M^* of M is called *correct* if each M^*-run $S_0^*, S_1^*, \ldots$ simulates an M-run $S_0, S_1, \ldots$ in the sense that the two runs can be partitioned into corresponding segments $segm_{i_0}^*, segm_{i_1}^*, \ldots$ resp. $segm_{j_0}, segm_{j_1}, \ldots$ of interest whose first states $(S_{i_k}^*, S_{j_k})$ are corresponding states of interest and equivalent, including the

Fig. 2.30 The ASM refinement scheme [76, p. 45]
© 2003 Springer-Verlag Berlin Heidelberg, reprinted with permission

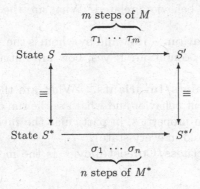

With an equivalence relation ≡, between data in locations of
interest in corresponding states, which is typically not the identity.

pairs of initial and (if any) final states (i. e. the two runs either both terminate or both are infinite).

This scheme describes the refinement of single-agent ASMs. For multi-
agent ASMs more complex refinement patterns appear. However often the
analysis of the relation between an abstract and a more detailed behavior of
a concurrent system can be performed by an analysis of refinements of single
components M, M^*, comparing corresponding segments of computation of
M and M^* in the abstract resp. refined concurrent runs. For examples see
Sect. 3.3.1.2, 3.3.2.

The theorem proving system KIV [161] provides machine support for the
verification of fully general ASM refinements [212, 213, 214, 216, 215, 217]. It
has been used with success in challenging verification projects where ASMs
were adopted to specify the system behavior, see for example [141, 140, 142,
139, 218].

Six fundamental modeling concerns. We extract from the model developments in this chapter six issues one has to care about when defining a
system model, in particular when building a ground model to capture given
requirements. We anticipate the role of multiple actors in distributed systems
we deal with in the following chapters.

Actors. Who are the *agents* of the system and how are they *related*? In
particular, what is the relation between the *system* and its *environment*?

States.   What are the system's (domains of) objects with their attributes, relations and function types (system *signature*)?

Transitions.   When (under which internal or external conditions) and how do system states *evolve* (behavioral *rules*)? How are normal, exceptional and erroneous system behaviors related? What are the robustness conditions?

Initialization/Termination.   How and by whom is the system initialized? Is there a termination condition? If yes, how are initial/final states and input/output related?

Assumptions/Constraints/Invariants.   What are the assumptions on system and environment behavior and what are the run constraints? What are the desired system properties, in particular the *invariants*(properties which for every run hold in every state)?

Completeness/Correctness/Consistency.   Is the model correct, complete and consistent?

Chapter 3
Modeling Concurrent Systems

In nowadays ubiquitous multi-agent systems, components typically run concurrently and largely independently, working at different speeds and reacting to independent inputs from different sources. They interact via shared memory or message exchange and possibly compete for resources. To understand such systems requires an understanding not only of the behavior of the single components, which was the subject of Chap. 2, but also of the underlying models of time and of interprocess communication, which influence the interaction behavior.

In the synchronous computational interaction model, a global system clock determines a system step as consisting of simultaneous lock-step executions of all components. This can be easily described exploiting the parallelism of single-agent ASMs. The function classification in Sect. 2.1.1 appropriately captures the synchronous component interaction, essentially via shared memory. Interaction via shared memory is easier to understand and analyze than message exchange where delivery, delivery order and/or delivery time may be uncertain.

However, if component processes work asynchronously, each at its own pace (read: with its own notion of step) and interacting via a possibly unreliable message exchange medium, this results in hard to control and difficult to analyze orderings of single component steps in 'system steps' and therefore needs a definition of what are 'system runs'. An additional complication derives from the typical system requirement that, if some component fails, the desired overall system behavior should not be 'affected too much', and the system should 'adapt' somehow to possible failures.

In this chapter we address the question how to model and analyze such multi-agent and in particular distributed software intensive systems. We introduce multi-agent ASMs as systems whose components are the single-agent ASMs defined in Chap. 2. We illustrate how to use them, building upon what has been explained in Chap. 2 on modeling sequential system components, proceeding by abstraction and refinement. We provide examples for synchronous (Sect. 3.1) and for concurrent (asynchronous) multi-agent sys-

© Springer-Verlag GmbH Germany, part of Springer Nature 2018
E. Börger, A. Raschke, *Modeling Companion for Software Practitioners*,
https://doi.org/10.1007/978-3-662-56641-1_3

tems (Sect. 3.2), including the outstanding class of communicating ASMs (Sect. 3.3), which instead of shared functions use message passing operations. We illustrate the use of communicating ASMs by two examples. As first example we construct a precise model for monitoring asynchronous network system runs with respect to their termination (Sect. 3.3.1). Then we model a local synchronization operator which permits to asynchronously execute, with equivalent local behavior, components which have been defined with the synchronous computation model in mind (Sect. 3.3.2). The local synchronizer refinement illustrates particularly well the flexibility and generality of the ASM refinement concept. That refinement involves not only a program transformation for the communicating agents, but also the introduction of a refined network structure and of additional agents, which monitor the asynchronous component steps with respect to the desired synchronization property.

One crucial issue for the analysis of multi-agent systems is what are their states, and how the global system view relates to the local single-agent views. Since ASMs allow one to define precise *behavioral interfaces*, not restricted to structural or mere signature terms, often a local analysis of the behavior of single components suffices to derive some global system properties of interest.

This happens in particular when the 'global' property comes as quantification of component behavior in the form 'In each run, for each component machine m, after each step (or sequence of steps) of m property $P(m)$ holds'. Such properties typically describe the effect of steps of m in reaction to the behavior of other machines in some well defined neighborhood, which appears as environment of m and in this form enters the 'local' analysis.

We will use the examples in this chapter to demonstrate how this feature of the ASM method allows the designer to analyze and reason about the global system behavior in intuitive but precise run-time terms, focussed on component behavior.

Definition 2. A *multi-agent* ASM $\mathcal{M}$ is a family

$$(ag(p), pgm(p))_{p \in Process}$$

of single-agent ASMs consisting of a set of *Process*es p viewed as

- agents $ag(p)$ which execute step by step ('sequentially')
- each its program $pgm(p)$, a finite set of ASM rules as defined in Chap. 2,
- interacting with each other via reading/writing in designated (shared or input/output) locations.

Both functions $ag : Process \rightarrow Agent$ and $pgm : Process \rightarrow AsmRule$ may be dynamic so that one can easily describe run-time creation and deletion of agents as well as run-time program changes. The sequential component machines interact with each other via reading/writing values of input/output or shared locations using appropriate protocols to guarantee update consistency.

The agent concept provides the following technically simple, but due to its abstraction level rather general, *model instantiation* mechanism.[1]

Definition 3. A set *Instance*(M) of instances of a basic ASM program M is a multi-agent ASM $(ag_i, M)_{i \in Process}$ created by introducing a set of agents ag_i ($i \in Process$ for some index set *Process*) with same signature, same program text M, maybe even same initialization but possibly different evolution of their state, their current interpretation of the signature.

The different state evolution of model instances is typically due to possibly different timing/order of single-agent steps which may encounter different values provided by the environment on which the reaction of each instance depends. In ASM models the agents could be simply names, but they can also be equipped with their own structure, which is determined by the corresponding agent model. An equivalent notation parameterizes directly the program in the form M_{a_i} or $M(a_i)$ as introduced already in Sect. 2.3.1, 2.4.2 and supported by the **self** notation explained there.

This form of parameterization provides also a technically simple but rather general mechanism to pass, in a modular way, from single-agent sequential to concurrent multi-agent models, as will be illustrated in this chapter by necessarily modest but characteristic examples.[2]

Multi-agent ASMs come in two forms. One is a *synchronous* ASM, where the agents execute their sequential steps simultaneously ('lock-step parallelism'), synchronized by a global system clock. For synchronous multi-agent ASMs a run is behaviorally equivalent to the lock-step parallel execution

forall $p \in Process\ pgm(p)$

of all involved programs. Conceptually this can be understood as single-agent program execution.

The other form of multi-agent ASMs is a *concurrent* (*asynchronous*) ASM where each agent executes its steps sequentially, at its own pace, following its own clock. The difference between the two forms is in the corresponding notion of run. In this chapter we work with an intuitive understanding of concurrency and make no specific assumptions on asynchronous (concurrent) runs of multi-agent ASMs. In particular we do not assume interleaving of component actions. Where necessary to be precise, we state what is assumed. We state in Sect. 3.4 the underlying detailed definition of truly *concurrent ASM runs*, which captures an arguably most general class of concurrent computation concepts.

---

[1] This abstracts from the particularities of, but is compatible with, any concrete underlying class concept, as encountered in object-oriented programming languages.

[2] For a more challenging application see Sect. 4.2.2.1.

3.1 From Synchronous to Asynchronous Models

In this section we illustrate how multi-agent ASMs allow one to pass, by an ASM refinement step, from a synchronous (easy to grasp) understanding to an asynchronous (harder to check) view, and from there to a CoreASM executable version.

As example we use Franklin's well-known leader election algorithm. By this algorithm, finitely many processes, arranged in a bidirectional ring, find out who is the largest among them—efficiently, without any central control and passing information only to the respective two neighbors. We quote the *ExtremaFindingReq*uirements from [113], adding names for traceability reasons, and follow [226] to turn them first into a synchronous ground model EXTREMAFINDING, and then into a refined (behaviorally, but not complexity equivalent) concurrent (asynchronous) ASM CONCUREXTREMAFINDING. Both models come with an ASM refinement into a CoreASM [84] executable program.

Remarkably, the CoreASM programs can be executed and their behavior visualized via any web browser, using the embedding of the CoreASM engine in a web page presented in [248].

Plant&FunctionalReq. Finding without a central controller the largest element in a bidirectional ring of processes whose size N is not known in advance.

BeingActiveReq. We will define an inactive process as one that knows that it is not the largest; the other processes are active.

ActiveNeighbReq. The two neighbors of an active process are those active processes closest to it in each direction along the ring. In the degenerate case of a ring with only two active processes, each becomes the two neighbors of the other; similarly, if there is only one active process, it becomes both of its neighbors.

ExchangeInfoReq. Each active process sends a message with its value to each of its neighbors and receives such messages from its two active neighbors. If either of the messages it receives is larger than its value, then it makes itself inactive.

ForwardInfoReq. The process of sending a message to an active neighbor is apparently complicated by the fact that a given process does not know the exact locations of its active neighbors. This is, in fact, no problem if we pass messages by the convention that inactive processes simply pass on received messages from either direction in the same direction, while active processes do not.

StepReq. Thus, during each step every inactive process receives and forwards two messages, while each active process transmits and receives two messages.

TerminationReq. The repetition of steps terminates when in some step a process receives a message from itself; this implies that it is the only active process left and that its value is the largest of the set. As a final action, that process announces that fact to all the other processes in N message passes.

3.1.1 *Synchronous* EXTREMAFINDING *Ground Model*

The *Plant&FunctionalReq* describes, besides the desired functionality, also the background structure which is assumed to be static. It is represented in the model by a set of *Process*es of any cardinality N, coming with a linear order $<$ and arranged in a ring structure. We represent this structure by two left/right ring neighbor functions $l, r : Process \rightarrow Process$, that is satisfying $l(p_i) = p_{i-1} \bmod N$ and $r(m_i) = p_{i+1} \bmod N$ for $Process = \{p_o, \ldots, p_{N-1}\}$.

The *BeingActiveReq* is represented for each process p by a controlled function $mode_p$ whose values can be *active*, *inactive* or *terminated*. It is initialized for each process p by $mode_p = active$, since initially all processes are reasonably assumed not to know who is the largest.

The notion of *active neighbor* mentioned in *ActiveNeighbReq* can be defined as a derived function (using the two ring functions l, r and the current value of *mode*), for use in the analysis of the model. For the specification itself it is not needed due to the *ForwardInfoReq*.

We formulate the information exchange requirements at the level of abstraction the informal *ExtremaFindingReq*uirements use for the underlying communication mechanism, which is characterized in *StepReq* by the following assumptions:[3]

- All processes perform their 'steps' synchronized in rounds.
- In each round every process reads two messages, one it received from the right neighbor and one it received from the left neighbor, and sends one message to both neighbors.
- Message delivery is reliable (no message gets lost or corrupted) and immediate: each message, sent in a round by a process to its left or right neighbor, is received and read by them in the next round.

To capture this functional send/receive behavior, we equip each process p with two variables $fromRightMsg_p$, $fromLeftMsg_p$ (abstract 'mailboxes') where, in each round, p reads the unique message 'received' there (due to the neighbor's send action in the previous round) and 'receives' the unique

---

[3] Some of these assumptions are implicit in *ExtremaFindingReq* and therefore are subject to interpretation. In real-life modeling situations every such doubt must be checked with the domain expert who is responsible for the requirements. This crucial issue to make ground models 'correct' (as explained in Sect. 1.1.1) is illustrated further in Sect. 3.2.

new message sent by the neighbor in this round.[4] Initially these locations are assumed to contain no message.[5]

Thus *ExchangeInfoReq* is expressed by the following rule, whose parallelism makes the independence of the read/write actions of neighboring processes explicit. **self** denotes the process instance in question which executes the rule, more precisely the executing process agent.

$$\text{EXCHANGEINFO} =$$
$$\quad \textbf{if } mode = active \textbf{ then}$$
$$\quad\quad \text{TRANSMITINFO}(\textbf{self})$$
$$\quad\quad \text{CHECKFORLARGERMSG}(\textbf{self})$$
$$\textbf{where}$$
$$\quad \text{TRANSMITINFO}(p) =$$
$$\quad\quad fromRightMsg_{l(p)} := p \qquad\qquad\qquad \text{-- } p \text{ sends 'its value'}$$
$$\quad\quad fromLeftMsg_{r(p)} := p$$
$$\quad \text{CHECKFORLARGERMSG}(p) = \qquad \text{-- } p \text{ reads \& checks received msgs}$$
$$\quad\quad \text{CHECKWHETHERLARGER}(p, fromLeftMsg_p)$$
$$\quad\quad \text{CHECKWHETHERLARGER}(p, fromRightMsg_p)$$
$$\quad \text{CHECKWHETHERLARGER}(p, m) =$$
$$\quad\quad \textbf{if } m > p \textbf{ then } mode_p := inactive$$

The following rule captures the *ForwardInfoReq*, which for the sake of illustration we formulate using an explicit process parameter p instead of the equivalent **self** notation:

$$\text{FORWARDINFO} =$$
$$\quad \textbf{if } mode = inactive \textbf{ then } \text{PASSMSGS}(\textbf{self})$$
$$\textbf{where}$$
$$\quad \text{PASSMSGS}(p) =$$
$$\quad\quad fromRightMsg_{l(p)} := fromRightMsg_p \qquad \text{-- from right to left}$$
$$\quad\quad fromLeftMsg_{r(p)} := fromLeftMsg_p \qquad\quad \text{-- from left to right}$$

The *TerminationReq* is reflected by two additional rules. One rule concerns an active process p which detects the leader, namely by receiving a message which was initially sent by p itself. When that happens, the process is *recognizedAsLargest* so that it can proceed as follows:

1. set this location, which initially is false for each process q, to true for itself,[6]

---

[4] Characteristically, in an ASM, one can express two such read-current-value/write-next-value actions concerning one location as one parallel step, abstracting from their conceptually unnecessary explicit sequentialization.

[5] In the model this means that they do not satisfy the rule guard of NOTIFYLEADER-DETECTED or CHECKFORLARGERMSG; in the ASM language this can be expressed by assigning as initial value **undef**.

[6] This interprets the informal clause 'its value is the largest of the set' in *TerminationReq*, which is certainly not meant to express the static property 'to be' the largest, but the dynamic 'discovery that it is'.

2. start 'as a final action' a round to notify the other processes, and
3. stop.

$$\text{CHECKNOTIFYLEADERDETECTED}(p) =$$
$$\quad \text{NOTIFYLEADERDETECTED}(fromLeftMsg_p)$$
$$\quad \text{NOTIFYLEADERDETECTED}(fromRightMsg_p)$$
where
$$\quad \text{NOTIFYLEADERDETECTED}(msg) =\ ^7$$
$$\quad\quad \textbf{if self} = msg\ \textbf{then} \qquad \text{-- process receives a } msg \text{ from itself}$$
$$\quad\quad\quad recognizedAsLargest_{\textbf{self}} := true$$
$$\quad\quad\quad notified_{r(\textbf{self})} := true$$
$$\quad\quad\quad mode_{\textbf{self}} := terminated$$

The other rule is for the remaining (the inactive) processes, to pass the notification. To illustrate how instead of message passing one can use shared locations (here among neighbors), we let each notified process set a location *notified* of its right ring neighbor to true. All instances of the variable *notified* are assumed to be initially false.

$$\textbf{if } notified_p = true\ \textbf{then}\ \text{FORWARDNOTIFY}(p)$$
$$\quad \textbf{where}$$
$$\quad\quad \text{FORWARDNOTIFY}(p) =$$
$$\quad\quad\quad notified_{r(p)} := true$$
$$\quad\quad\quad mode_p := terminated$$

Since the *TerminationReq* requests to stop the 'repetition of steps' once a process has been *recognizedAsLargest*, for each inactive process we disable its FORWARDINFO rule when the process gets *notified*. For this it suffices to guard the rule by *notified = false*. For the same reason the TRANSMITINFO rule for active processes is guarded additionally by **not** *recognizedAsLargest*(p). Thus, the resulting EXTREMAFINDING ground model is defined as follows (with the components defined above):

$$\text{EXTREMAFINDING} =$$
$$\quad \textbf{forall } p \in Process$$
$$\quad\quad \textbf{if } mode_p = active\ \textbf{then}$$
$$\quad\quad\quad \textbf{if not } recognizedAsLargest_p\ \textbf{then}\ \text{TRANSMITINFO}(p)$$
$$\quad\quad\quad \text{CHECKFORLARGERMSG}(p)$$
$$\quad\quad\quad \text{CHECKNOTIFYLEADERDETECTED}(p)$$
$$\quad\quad \textbf{if } mode_p = inactive\ \textbf{then}$$
$$\quad\quad\quad \textbf{if } notified_p = true$$
$$\quad\quad\quad\quad \textbf{then}\ \text{FORWARDNOTIFY}(p)$$
$$\quad\quad\quad\quad \textbf{else}\ \text{PASSMSGS}(p)$$

---

[7] This formulates one possible interpretation of the meaning of 'announce' in *TerminationReq*. Should announcing be intended to mean letting each process know the identity of the leader, it would suffice to change the function *Notified* to yield, not a truth value, but the leaders identity (initially **undef**), and to correspondingly refine FORWARDNOTIFY.

We invite the reader to inspect the refinement·of EXTREMAFINDING to the CoreASM executable model EXTREMAFINDING.*casm* in [226]. One reason is to realize that essentially only data refinements are needed to transform the 'abstract' view of data in EXTREMAFINDING into CoreASM data structures. The model structure is preserved, a property which supports the traceability of requirements in the code. A second reason is to realize how one can run experiments to (in-) validate model (not only code) properties.

Remark on parameter notation. For parameterizing ASMs, when dealing with single-agent ASMs we usually index 0-ary functions, in other cases we normally use explicit parameters.

Exercise 24. Inspect EXTREMAFINDING to formulate and show its correctness property with respect to the algorithmic *ExtremaFindingReq*uirements quoted from [113].

Exercise 25. Change EXTREMAFINDING by modeling the notification process via message passing, instead of using shared variables.

3.1.2 Refined Concurrent CONCUREXTREMAFINDING

The *StepReq* eases the complexity analysis of the EXTREMAFINDING algorithm in [113]. However, from the point of view of distributed algorithms expressed in *Plant&FunctionalReq*—the algorithm should work 'without a central controller'—an asynchronous model without synchronous **forall**-parallelism seems to be appropriate, so that each sequential component process can perform its steps of the algorithm at its own pace. This means that sending a message by a sender (via TRANSMITINFO or PASSMSGS), and receiving that message by the receiver (to CHECKFORLARGERMSG or to check the leader detection in NOTIFYLEADERDETECTED), happen without synchronization.

To turn the synchronous EXTREMAFINDING ASM into an asynchronous truly multi-agent CONCUREXTREMAFINDING machine, it suffices to refine the locations *fromRightMsg* and *fromLeftMsg* to mailboxes *FromRightMsgs* resp. *FromLeftMsgs*, where sent messages are stored and received messages fetched to be checked. Since we want to preserve the correctness of the algorithm, we make the following assumptions on process fairness and on the reliability of message passing, assumptions which were implicit already in the *ExtremaFindingReq*. The message passing mechanism which is still kept at a rather high behavioral direct-mailbox-handling level of abstraction.

Assumptions for Concurrent Extrema Finding Runs.

- Every process which is enabled will eventually perform a step.
- No messages are lost or corrupted and messages arrive in the order they are sent.

Accordingly we treat the mailboxes *FromRightMsgs*, *FromLeftMsgs* as queues and refine read and write operations involving *fromRightMsg* or *fromLeftMsg* as follows:

- Updates *fromRightMsg* := q are refined to ENQUEUE(q, *FromRightMsgs*) (the same with *Left*) resulting in the refined ASM ASYNCTRANSMITINFO. For the refinement correctness analysis below, we call such a pair of an update and its refined ENQUEUE operation corresponding send actions of interest.

- Readings of *fromRightMsg* are refined to readings of *head*(*FromRightMsgs*) (the same with *Left*), namely in the guards of CHECKFORLARGERMSG, NOTIFYLEADERDETECTED and in the refinement of ASYNCPASSMSGS. For the refinement correctness analysis below, we call such a pair of abstract and refined location a pair of corresponding locations of interest.

As a consequence, the implicit overwriting of *fromRight/LeftMsg* when these locations are updated in EXTREMAFINDING must be formulated by an explicit action to delete a read message, that is a DEQUEUE operation on the mailboxes (if they are not empty).

This refinement leads to a family of asynchronous multi-agent ASMs

$$M_p = (p, \text{CONCUREXTREMAFINDING}_p)$$

where we use $p \in Process$ as agent name and equip each of them with an instance of the following program. The instantiation means that all the local functions are private for p, determining the local state of p. For this reason we suppress p notationally.

CONCUREXTREMAFINDING =
  if *mode* = *active* **then**
    if not *recognizedAsLargest* **then** ASYNCTRANSMITINFO
    forall $q \in \{$*FromLeftMsgs*, *FromRightMsgs*$\}$ -- for both queues
      if $q \neq []$ **then**
        CHECKWHETHERLARGER(**self**, *head*(q))
        NOTIFYLEADERDETECTED(*head*(q))
        DEQUEUE(q)   -- remove *head*(q)
  if *mode* = *inactive* **then**
    if *notified* = *true*
    then FORWARDNOTIFY
    else ASYNCPASSMSGS

The submachines are defined as follows:

ASYNCTRANSMITINFO =
  ENQUEUE(**self**, *FromRightMsgs*$_{l(\textbf{self})}$)   -- **self** sends 'its value'
  ENQUEUE(**self**, *FromLeftMsgs*$_{r(\textbf{self})}$)
FORWARDNOTIFY = FORWARDNOTIFY(**self**)

$\text{AsyncPassMsgs} =$
   if $FromRightMsgs \neq [\,]$ **then**
      $\text{Enqueue}(head(FromRightMsgs), FromRightMsgs(l(\textbf{self})))$
      $\text{Dequeue}(FromRightMsgs)$
   if $FromLeftMsgs \neq [\,]$ **then**
      $\text{Enqueue}(head(FromLeftMsgs), FromLeftMsgs(r(\textbf{self})))$
      $\text{Dequeue}(FromLeftMsgs)$
   $\text{CheckWhetherLarger}(p, m) =$
      if $m > p$ **then** $mode_p := inactive$
   $\text{NotifyLeaderDetected}(msg) =$
      if self $= msg$ **then**   -- process receives a msg from itself
         $recognizedAsLargest_{\textbf{self}} := true$
         $notified_{r(\textbf{self})} := true$
         $mode_{\textbf{self}} := terminated$

For a CoreASM executable $\text{ExtremaFindingRefined}.casm$ model (with some notational differences) see [226].

Refinement Correctness Proof. Remember that in the abstract resp. in the refined model the read/write actions of neighboring processes follow a simple producer/consumer protocol. Each process performs in each step two kinds of action:

- 'write' to each corresponding neighbors' mailbox by placing one message there, namely via an abstract update resp. a refined Enqueue operation,
- 'read' in each of the two own mailboxes one received message, where the corresponding neighbor has sent it, and consume the message, namely by an abstract overwrite resp. a refined Dequeue action.

As a result, the correspondence of to-be-compared actions and locations of interest in the abstract and the refined model is so simple that, for this proof, we need no detailed definition of the underlying concept of concurrent ASM run for $\text{ConcurExtremaFinding}$; the skeptical reader can find the definition in Sect. 3.4. Here the analysis of corresponding single-process actions and corresponding locations of interest in the abstract and the refined model suffices.

In any pair of ExtremaFinding and of $\text{ConcurExtremaFinding}$ runs, which are started in equivalent initial states, the corresponding actions of interest are the following ones (we disregard the trivial final, purely sequential notification subprocess):

- for active processes a) the pairs of corresponding send actions in the abstract rule TransmitInfo resp. its refinement AsyncTransmitInfo, and b) the pairs of corresponding checks in $\text{CheckWhetherLarger}(msg)$ (the same for $\text{NotifyLeaderDetected}(msg)$) concerning corresponding locations of interest with related updates;

- for inactive processes, pairs of an abstract send action (with implicit overwrite) and the corresponding refined ENQUEUE, together with the explicit DEQUEUE.

Since messages are not lost, arrive in order and with their original content, the update effects of corresponding actions on the corresponding locations of interest are equivalent. One abstract double-check action CHECKFORLARGERMSG may split in the refined model into two separate check-actions CHECKWHETHERLARGER($head(q)$) for each neighbor's mailbox q. However, this does not affect neither that in the refined model (by the concurrent run assumption) the check is done for both mailboxes in question (as in the abstract model), nor the check result. Similarly for NOTIFYLEADERDETECTED.

The correctness of the refinement preserves the correctness of the abstract machine. By the concurrent run assumption each process will perform its send and check actions (though at its pace) until it becomes inactive (because recognized as smaller than some other process)—except the largest process, which eventually will be *RecognizedAsLargest*. □

3.2 Role of Model Validation: Termination Detection

In this section we emphasize the *importance of machine-supported validation besides model inspection* for getting the ground model of a distributed system complete and correct. As example we use the 'algorithm for the detection of the termination of a distributed computation', proposed in [95] with the goal 'to demonstrate how the algorithm can be derived in a number of steps'. We focus our attention here on formulating an accurate model for the algorithm such that

- the model exhibits various implicit assumptions, apparently made by the authors of the algorithm, resolves potential conflicts in the requirements, and completes the requirements by missing elements which are needed to achieve the purpose of the algorithm,
- the model can be shown to be consistent, to adequately represent the completed requirements (ground model correctness) and to satisfy the purpose of the algorithm (functional correctness).

Therefore, we rephrase the requirements stated in [95], grouping them differently, slightly abbreviating the wording and introducing evocative names. We extend the analysis in [126] where the authors carefully illustrate 'the virtuous circle where difficulties with the formal specification prompt further elicitation of the requirements', difficulties revealed by combining model inspection and model execution in CoreASM [84].

We begin with describing the *TerminationDetectVerbalRe*quirements.

Plant&FunctionalReq. We consider N machines arranged in a ring. Each machine is either active or passive. The state in which all machines are passive is stable: the distributed computation is said to have terminated. The purpose of the algorithm to be designed is to enable one of the machines, machine nr. 0 say, to detect that this stable state has been reached.

ProbeSignatureReq. Denote the process by which termination is to be detected by the "probe". We assume the availability of communication facilities such that (i) machine nr. 0 can initiate the probe by sending a signal to machine nr. $N-1$ (ii) machine nr. $i+1$ can propagate the probe around the ring by sending a signal to machine nr. i. The propagation of the probe around the ring allows us to describe that probe as sending a token around the ring. The probe ends with machine nr. 0 being the machine at which the token resides. The token being returned to machine nr. 0 will be an essential component of the justification of the conclusion that all machines are passive.

TokenProgressReq. When active, machine nr. $i+1$ keeps the token; when passive, it hands over the token to machine nr. i. For each machine, the transition from the active to the passive state may occur "spontaneously".

ActivationReq. Only active machines send "messages" to other machines; message transmission is considered instantaneous. After having received a message, a machine is active; the receipt of a message is the only mechanism that triggers for a passive machine its transition to activity.

Since a machine can be (re-) activated after having handed over the token to its left ring neighbor, some mechanism is needed to inform the token owner about the probe failure resulting from such an activation, so that this information is available when the token comes back to the master. The information is provided by black coloring of activators and of tokens they forward: a token, once colored black, remains black until the end of the probe, where the *master* recognizes this as probe failure.

RecordActivationEventReq. Machines and tokens are postulated to be either black or white. A machine sending a message to a recipient with a number higher than its own makes itself black.

ForwardActivationEventInfoReq. When machine nr. $i+1$ propagates the probe, it hands over a black token to machine nr. i if it is black itself, whereas while being white it leaves the color of the token unchanged. Upon transmission of the token to machine nr. i, machine nr. $i+1$ becomes white. (Note that its original color may have influenced the color of the token).

EvalActivityInfoReq. When a black token is returned to machine nr. 0 or the token is returned to a black machine nr. 0, the conclusion of termination cannot be drawn.

Fig. 3.1 Example situation during Termination Detection

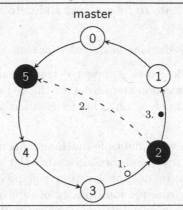

<table>
</table>

> *ProbeStartReq.* Machine nr. 0 initiates the probe by making itself white and sending a white token to machine nr. $N - 1$. After the completion of an unsuccessful probe, machine nr. 0 initiates the next probe.
> *InitializationReq.* It is furthermore required that the detection algorithm can cope with any distribution of the activity at the moment machine nr. 0 initiates the detection algorithm.

Figure 3.1 shows a possible situation during an example run of the termination detection algorithm for six machines. It illustrates the situation where

1. machine nr. 2 got a white token from machine nr. 3,
2. the active machine nr. 2 sent a message to nr. 5, thus making this node active (black) again,
3. nr. 2 sends a black token to nr. 1, because it has sent a message to a machine with a higher number than itself.

We now analyze these rather precise requirements—to discover a certain number of implicit assumptions and missing stipulations, which have to be added to let the algorithm achieve its goal.

3.2.1 *The Signature of* TERMINATIONDETECTION

First we extract from the *TerminationDetectVerbalReq*uirements the model signature. The *Plant&FunctionalReq* present the domain of discourse, a finite set $Machine = \{m_0, \ldots, m_{N-1}\}$ of machines with a designated $master = m_0$ and arranged in a ring, a static background structure represented by a function $pred : Machine \rightarrow Machine$ with $pred(m_{i+1}) = m_{i \bmod N}$.

Each machine has a controlled *mode* variable with two possible values *active* or *passive*. The state to be reached and detected by the protocol is called *stable* and is defined by:

Stable iff **forall** $m \in$ *Machine mode*$(m) =$ *passive.*

The *ActivationReq* describes a message transmission mechanism which triggers the following question the owner of the requirements (domain expert, customer) has to decide upon. The decision has to be included into the requirements.

- What should happen when multiple machines concurrently send messages to a same receiver? Are these messages stored at the receiver's site and elaborated there, one by one, or are they collapsed into a single trigger element, abstracting from the multiplicity of received messages and from their not furthermore specified content? Since in [95] messages are specified only as 'transition-to-activity'-trigger, we assume in the following the second alternative.[8] One way to formulate this interpretation is to let machines update an activation predicate *hasMessage* at the *dest*ination machine to *true*, 'instantaneously' when they send a message there. In the parallel ASM execution model different machines are allowed to simultaneously update a same location—if they do it consistently, i. e. to the same value. Such a definition SENDMSG$(dest) = (hasMessage_{dest} := true)$ has a 'cumulative' effect. It would also answer the question what is the meaning of 'instantaneous' transmission of sent messages, which, by the way, is presumably also understood as happening without message loss or corruption. In Sect. 3.2.2 we will however have to change this definition, due to yet another (a behavioral) problem with the *ActivationRe*quirement.
- There is also the minor issue, namely how to interpret the restriction to 'only active machines' in the *ActivationReq*. It seems reasonable to consider it as requesting to verify this property for the algorithm.[9]

The *ProbeSignatureReq* states that, during a probe, precisely one machine has a (for the probe unique) token and can FORWARDTOKEN to and only to its *pred*ecessor in the ring. To formulate the 'presence of the token at a machine' by an evocative easy-to-remember name, we use a controlled Boolean-valued variable *hasToken* to express the token forwarding:[10]

---

[8] The first alternative is considered in [94] for a variation of the original algorithm where message transmission is no longer instantaneous, see the ASM-model based analysis of this variation in [102].

[9] This issue is relevant for *declarative* specifications of the algorithm because, for logical reasons, when using axiomatic descriptions one must formulate not only what does change, but also explicitly exclude what does not change. This is called the *frame problem* of declarative formalizations, which contributes to their complexity and size. In the operational ASM framework it suffices to state the desired changes, because the underlying semantics guarantees that nothing changes unless explicitly described by an update to change.

[10] In [95] a variable 't denotes the number of the machine at which the token resides'.

FORWARDTOKEN =
  $hasToken(\textbf{self}) := false$ -- forward token from machine nr. $i+1$
  $hasToken(pred(\textbf{self})) := true$ --... to predecessor machine nr. i

The *EvalActivityInfoReq* defines in terms of token and machine coloring when a probe is evaluated as unsuccessful. For the formulation of the colors introduced in *RecordActivationEventReq* we use controlled functions $color(m), tokenColor$ with values in $\{black, white\}$.

  ProbeNotSuccessful iff
    $hasToken(master)$ **and**
      $(tokenColor = black$ **or** $color(master) = black)$

3.2.2 *The Behavior of* TERMINATIONDETECTION

The *ActivationReq* expresses that if $hasMessage(m)$ then $mode(m) := active$. Three questions remain to be answered by the requirements owner: a) whether 'after having received a message' this message is consumed and if yes when, b) whether 'transition to activity' is meant to imply that being passive is a condition for receiving a message, c) whether the 'only' clause is a property of the algorithm that is to-be-proved. Concerning c) one can statically check this property for TERMINATIONDETECTION (Exerc. 26). For b) we consider the more liberal interpretation that also active machines can receive messages. For a) it seems to be necessary to stipulate that a message is consumed by a machine, since otherwise the message would stay forever and could trigger again and again the 'transition-to-activity'. Furthermore, it seems to be reasonable to consume the received message upon the 'transition to activity'. This would lead to a rule stating that if $hasMessage(m)$ then $mode(m) := active$ and $hasMessage(m) := false$.

But if a machine *dest* executes this rule concurrently with other machines which simultaneously SENDMSG(*dest*), a requirements conflict shows up. In the ASM execution it shows up as an inconsistent update set, so that no next state is defined. To resolve this conflict—in a real-world situation after consultation with the domain expert who has to decide how to solve the conflict—we introduce an appropriate data structure, to model an amended conflict-free version of the requirements. We stipulate that, to not loose any trigger, the sending wins over consuming. More precisely, let for each machine $Triggered(m)$ be a Boolean-valued variable shared by all machines. We introduce two *update instructions* ACTIVATE(*trigger*) and DEACTIVATE(*trigger*). Their interpretation is that simultaneously executed ACTIVATE(*trigger*) actions, even if in presence of a simultaneously executed DEACTIVATE(*trigger*) action, produce the single update $trigger := true$,

whereas DEACTIVATE(*trigger*) executed alone updates *trigger* to *false*.[11]
Then *hasMessage* becomes a derived function and we have the following rule
expressing the 'receive-message' part of the *ActivationReq* (for the changed
SENDMSG see the next rule).

> BECOMEACTIVE =
>   **if** *hasMessage* **then**
>   *mode*(**self**) := *active*
>   DEACTIVATE(*Triggered*(**self**))
>   **where**
>   *hasMessage* iff *Triggered*(**self**) = *true*

The message sending part of the *ActivationReq* is interpreted as stating
that a machine may spontaneously decide to send a message to any predecessor machine (with larger number). *RecordActivationEventReq* adds to
this the blackening of the message sender. This blackening is in potential
conflict with machine whitening, required by *ForwardActivationEventInfoReq*
and *ProbeStartReq*, namely when the machine simultaneously forwards the
token (see PASSTOKEN below). One possible way to resolve this conflict is to
allow a machine to SENDMESSAGE only when it does not have the token.[12]

The spontaneous decision of a machine to send a message must be reflected
in the model by an equally spontaneous decision to apply the corresponding
ASM rule. Since this situation appears frequently, we formulate it as an
instance of the *Spontaneous Execution Pattern*, to spontaneously choose a
machine in a set $\mathcal{M}$ of machines:

> SPONTANEOUSLYDO($\mathcal{M}$) =
>   **choose** $R \in \mathcal{M} \cup \{$**skip**$\}$ **do** R

We write SPONTANEOUSLYDO(M) if M is a single machine. We also use the
vertical notation:

> SPONTANEOUSLYDO
> $\mathcal{M}$

This leads to the following rule to trigger the activation of a machine by
sending a message there:

> TRIGGERACTIVATION =
>   **if** *mode* = *active* **then** SPONTANEOUSLYDO(TRIGGERACT)

---

[11] The definition of such appropriately tailored update instructions is supported by
CoreASM, see Sect. 8.

[12] This conflict disappears in an interleaved interpretation of single machine actions
the authors of [95] may have had in mind (without stating it!), so that a machine is
assumed to perform in each step either a COLOR&FORWARDTOKEN or a SENDMESSAGE
step. Given the declarative spirit in which [95] is written, we exclude a purely sequential
interpretation which too would let the conflict disappear. This is a typical situation
where the modeler, before proceeding, must ask the requirements owner to decide about
the issue.

The TRIGGERACTIVATION components are defined as follows:

> TRIGGERACT =
>   **if not** *hasToken* **then**
>   **choose** *dest* ∈ *Machine* **do** SENDMESSAGE(*dest*)
> SENDMESSAGE(*m*) =
>   ACTIVATE(*Triggered*(*m*))
>   **if** $number(m) > number(\textbf{self})$ **then** $color(\textbf{self}) := black$
> **where**
> $number(m_i) = i \bmod N$

Looking at the *TokenProgressReq* one discovers another potential requirements conflict, namely with *ActivationReq*. If in some state a machine *hasMessage* and in this state decides to also 'spontaneously' transition (say from active) to passive, that contradicts the *ActivationReq*, whereby the machine should become (in the considered case remain) active. We avoid this requirements conflict by stipulating additionally (and documenting the amended requirement) that a machine can become passive only when there is no trigger from the environment (i.e. when it has no message)[13], thus privileging active *mode*.[14]

> BECOMEPASSIVE =
>   **if not** *hasMessage* **then**
>   SPONTANEOUSLYDO(**if** *mode* = *active* **then** *mode* := *passive*)

Now we come to the rules which govern the probe requirements. In the *TokenProgressReq* we interpret '$i + 1$ keeps the token' as implying that $hasToken(i + 1)$. We recognize the informal formulation of this rule for $i + 1$ to mean that it holds not for the master machine with nr. 0. In a real-world situation we would add this annotation to *TokenProgressReq* in the documentation. If one wants to explicitly express that nothing happens if the machine is in *mode* = *active*, the language of ASMs offers to describe this as follows, using the **skip** machine.

---

[13] This assumption appears mutatis mutandis as an explicit run constraint C1 in [102], where an abstract ASM model for a slight variation of the algorithm (the one published in [94]) is defined and refined to a detailed ASM, coming with a refinement correctness proof. For the ground model (and consequently also for the refinement), for each single machine interleaving of its basic actions SendMsg, ReceiveMsg, TransmitToken, InitiateProbe, NextProbe is assumed and claimed to be justifiable with respect to the given requirements. Concurrent runs are considered as given by interleaving steps of single machines.

[14] As above, this conflict disappears in an interleaved interpretation of single machine actions the authors of [95] may have had in mind, here assuming a machine to perform in each step at most one transition among those requested to become passive and to become active. When asking the requirements owner about the issue, the modeler may point out that making the assumption would allow a machine to not react to an environment trigger, but instead choose in splendid isolation to get passive.

PASSTOKEN' =
   if *hasToken* **then**
     if *mode* = *active* **then skip**
      else if self $\neq$ *master* **then** FORWARDTOKEN

ForwardActivationEventInfoReq requests FORWARDTOKEN to perform also color updates. In extending the definition correspondingly, we have to take into account the exceptional case of the *master* machine, the one with nr. 0. In fact *ProbeStartReq* states that the *master* when initiating a probe sends a white token, never a black one. Therefore we define:[15]

COLOR&FORWARDTOKEN =
   COLORTOKEN
   FORWARDTOKEN
   GETWHITE
where
   COLORTOKEN =
     if self = *master* **then** *tokenColor* := *white*
      else if *color*(**self**) = *black* **then** *tokenColor* := *black*[16]
   GETWHITE = (*color*(**self**) := *white*)

Thus, we extend the above PASSTOKEN' rule to also include the coloring effect, using the occasion to eliminate the skip clause.

PASSTOKEN =
   if *hasToken* **and** *mode* = *passive* **then**
     if self $\neq$ *master* **then** COLOR&FORWARDTOKEN

It remains to formulate the initialization and probe start conditions. The *InitializationReq* can be expressed by an initialization rule which, for every $m \in$ *Machine*, non-deterministically sets *mode*(m) to *active* or *passive* (see below the definition of *initial* states). By condition (i) in *ProbeSignatureReq* and by *ProbeStartReq*, to start a probe (including the first one which presumably starts the computation of the algorithm), the *master* must execute COLOR&FORWARDTOKEN. Therefore, to (re-) start a probe is expressed by the following rule:

STARTPROBE =
   if *ProbeNotSuccessful* **and self** = *master* **then**
     COLOR&FORWARDTOKEN

---

[15] As an alternative one could define two versions of COLOR&FORWARDTOKEN, one for the *master* and one for the other machines.

[16] An ASM rule explicitly yields all locations which have to be updated in applying the rule. Therefore, no rule is needed to state that some location does not change its value, as is the case here for the token color in case the token forwarding machine is white. In this way, the ASM framework avoids what is known as *frame problem* descriptions by logical formulae come with.

It remains to express initialization (and where needed also termination) of the distributed computation. There are two ways to express them:

1. either by defining the set of initial (resp. also final) states and considering only runs which are started in an initial state (and in case reach a final state), or
2. by explicit initialization and stop rules.

We choose the first alternative. Thus, we define as *initial state* any state which satisfies the following conditions. They are used for an initialization rule in CoreASM executable refinements, see the two programs reported in [126]. As we explain in Sect. 3.2.3, it should be added that initially there are *NoMsgsAround*.[17] Once more we see a case where the decision, about in which states legal computations are assumed to start, is to be taken by the owner of the requirements, long before coding, and not by the programmer. We say that a run is *properly initialized* if it is started in an initial state.

A state is an *initial* state iff it satisfies the following:
> **forall** $m \in Machine$
> $mode(m) \in \{active, passive\}$ *-- InitializationReq*
> $color(m) \in \{black, white\}$ -- any initial machine coloring[18]
> $hasToken(master) = true$ -- the master *hasToken*
> **if** $m \neq master$ **then** $hasToken(m) = false$ -- ... and nobody else
> $Triggered(m) = false$ -- meaning: NoMsgsAround
> $tokenColor = black$ -- triggers *master* to start a probe

Concerning the termination detection, how does 'the token being returned' to the *master* in *ProbeSignatureReq* permit to 'draw the conclusion' that all machines have $mode = passive$? From the formulation of the *EvalActivityInfoReq* we infer that it is defined as follows :[19]

> *TerminationDetected* iff
> $hasToken(master)$ **and** $mode(master) = passive$
> **and** $color(master) = white$ **and** $tokenColor = white$

This characterizes the *final* states of the distributed computation. An explicit STOPRULE, expressing that if *TerminationDetected* becomes true then the *master* stops the computation, has been defined in the CoreASM executable versions reported in [126]. To justify the functional correctness of the

---

[17] In [94] the condition that 'no messages are on their way' is explicitly added. It is assumed in the analysis in [102].

[18] In [102] it is assumed that initially all machines have white color. In [126] only the *master* is initially colored white. In [95] it is noted that the algorithm works correctly independently of the initial machine colors (as can be proved for our model).

[19] In [102] it is added that there is *NoMsgsAround* at the *master*. But this is a global predicate one should not assume in a concurrent context as part of the definition of a single-agent property or action. For our model this property can be proved however, see Sect. 3.2.3.

model (read: of the algorithm), it has to be shown (see the proof in Sect. 3.2.3) that, starting from an initial state, if *TerminationDetected* becomes true in some state then this state is *stable*.

Putting the above rules and component definitions together we arrive at the following ground model ASM program.[20]

> TERMINATIONDETECTION =
> > STARTPROBE   -- done by *master* if *ProbeNotSuccessful*
> > TRIGGERACTIVATION   -- spontaneously if *active* without token
> > BECOMEACTIVE   -- if *hasMessage*
> > BECOMEPASSIVE   -- spontaneously if not *hasMessage*
> > PASSTOKEN   -- if *passive* and not the *master*

Then we can define the distributed multi-agent system, which executes the termination detection algorithm, as family of machines $m \in Machine$, each equipped with the properly initialized sequential TERMINATIONDETECTION ASM program:

> DISTRTERMINATIONDETECT =
> > $(m, \text{TERMINATIONDETECTION}_m)_{m \in Machine}$

Exercise 26. Check by inspection of the rules of TERMINATIONDETECTION that during any legal run 'the receipt of a message is the only mechanism that triggers for a passive machine its transition to activity' (*BecomeActiveReq*).

3.2.3 Correctness after Requirements Completion

On the way from the original requirements in [95] to a correct, consistent and complete rigorous behavioral specification by DISTRTERMINATIONDETECT, various open questions have been encountered which led to complete (i. e. restrict or add to) the initially given *TerminationDetectVerbalRe*quirements. It usually requires domain knowledge to confirm implicit assumptions which were detected, to figure out how to resolve conflicting requirements, which requirements to add, etc. As reported in [126], the critical issues for defining a correct DISTRTERMINATIONDETECT model were discovered by combining model inspection with validation experiments, executing runs in CoreASM.[21]

---

[20] One could define two programs, one for the *master* and one for the other machines, defining two versions of COLORTOKEN and thereby COLOR&FORWARDTOKEN, one for the *master* and one for the other machines. They all have the two TRIGGERACTIVATION and BECOMEACTIVE rules, but only the *master* has the STARTPROBE rule and only the other machines have the PASSTOKEN rule. Which way to go depends on how the *master* is declared upon initializing executions of the algorithm. We stick here to the abstractions chosen in [95].

[21] We invite the reader to inspect and run the code for the CoreASM and Asmeta executable refinements. They can be downloaded from `https://sourceforge.net/p/asmeta/code/HEAD/tree/asm_examples/dagstuhl2013/DijkstraTermination/`.

This illustrates how important it is to be able to execute abstract models long before the coding starts, as CoreASM [84] and Asmeta [16] allow the modeler to do. If for mathematical or computer-assisted *verification* it can be a necessity or a technical advantage to consider an interleaving model of computation (as for example in [102]), the *validation* of distributed algorithms must be exposed to concurrent executions. In this respect, the asynchronous (concurrent) runs of multi-agent ASMs—notion we examine more closely in Sect. 3.4—is rather helpful. It is also the experience reported in [126, p. 6], namely that

> ... many of these problematic issues are exposed by the fully parallel and concurrent nature of distributed ASMs. Any purely sequential or interleaving model would not reveal many of these problems, but would also not be faithful to the kind of distributed system imagined by the authors of the original text.

The analysis of concurrent runs of DISTRTERMINATIONDETECT to show its 'functional correctness', namely to detect 'the termination of a distributed computation', reveals yet another assumption which remained hidden in [95] but influences the correctness of the algorithm. We show this in the next section.

3.2.3.1 A Counterexample unless Eagerness is Assumed

If instantaneous message transmission is assumed (as explicitly stated in the *ActivationReq*), a corresponding eagerness assumption for the component machines is needed to make the algorithm correct. Eagerness means that each component machine, when enabled, immediately executes its step ('instantaneous machine activation' assumption).

Here is a simple counterexample, if the eagerness assumption is not made. Let two machines $master = 0, m = 1$ be given where m is initially *passive* and *white*, *master* is initially *active*, starts a probe and then sends a message to m. Then $hasMessage(m)$, but imagine m does not apply the BECOMEACTIVE(m) rule until the end of the unsuccessful first probe (unsuccessful because the *master* as message sender to $m > master$ became *black*). This will trigger a new probe, starting with *white* token and *white master*, where m is still *passive* and *white* and passes the *white* token. Imagine m still does not apply the BECOMEACTIVE(m) rule until the end of this new probe, where the *white* token reaches the *white* and meantime *passive master* so that *TerminationDetected* holds. But in the next state, m could apply the BECOMEACTIVE(m) rule and invalidate the termination property.

The eagerness assumption is not mentioned in [95], but assuming it one can show that the algorithms correctly solves the termination detection problem; see Sect. 3.2.3.2 where we sketch a correctness proof to illustrate how runtime analysis can make simple intuition-based proofs of behavioral properties possible.[22] The instantaneous message transmission assumption is abandoned in the variation of the algorithm in [94]. As a consequence no eagerness assumption is needed, a fairness assumption suffices (see [102]). In fact, the level of abstraction of a concurrent computation of asynchronously interacting (a fortiori if also distributed) components is in general not faithfully reflected if one assumes that a sender of a message by the very send action can alter a receiver location. This is what the instantaneous message transmission requirement allowed and forced us to do, namely with the *Triggered* predicate in SENDMESSAGE. Similarly, assuming the eagerness of the component machines would in general not be faithful to that level of abstraction. This leads us to define in Sect. 3.3 *communicating ASMs*. They can adequately reflect such concurrent message-passing based interactions.

3.2.3.2 Correctness Proof by Run-Time Analysis

Correctness Property of DISTRTERMINATIONDETECT. Let any run R of DISTRTERMINATIONDETECT be given which is started in an initial state. If in this run a state is reached where *TerminationDetected* holds, then in this state all machines are *passive*.

We first prove for any such run R the following lemmata, which are easily verified by an inspection of the corresponding TERMINATIONDETECTION rules.

Lemma 1 (Token Progress). Except the case when the master executes STARTPROBE, in every probe the token is forwarded only by machines in passive mode. After having forwarded the token these machines remain passive—unless they are reactivated by a successor machine before a white and passive master has the white token.

Proof. The definition of PASSTOKEN, the only rule (except STARTPROBE) which can pass the token, implies the first statement. The second statement follows in view of the definition of *TerminationDetected* from the definition of the rules TRIGGERACTIVATION and BECOMEACTIVE, the only rules through whose application a machine can become active. □

Lemma 2 (Token Color Evolution). In every probe the token is originally white and becomes black only if it is forwarded by a black machine, whereafter it remains black until it returns to the master.

Proof. The first statement follows from the definition of STARTPROBE. The second and third statements follow from the definition of the only rule COLORTOKEN by which a token can change color. □

---

[22] This is contrary to a widely held view, namely that *operational* as opposed to *declarative* models make proofs of model properties difficult. Our working experience is that it is not a question of operational versus declarative, but a question of the level of abstraction, and that an operational intuitive understanding of appropriate abstractions is a helpful guide to direct a proof of behavioral (read: runtime) properties.

Lemma 3 (Machine Color Evolution). For every machine, its color is initially arbitrary. During any probe it gets a) black only by applying TRIGGERACTIVATION(*dest*) for some ring predecessor machine *dest* (with larger number), b) white for the master upon starting a probe and for all the other machines when they COLOR&FORWARDTOKEN in passive mode.

Proof. The first statement follows from the initialization condition. The other statements follow from the definition of the corresponding rules.   □

Proof of the correctness of DISTRTERMINATIONDETECT. Consider any probe in R which ends in a *finalState* where *TerminationDetected* holds. We distinguish two cases and show the second one to be impossible.

Case 1. If during this probe the token encounters no black machine (including the master), it remains white (by the token color evolution lemma), and the master remains white (by the machine color evolution lemma). Therefore, when the token reaches the master, all machines preceding the master are passive (by the token progress lemma), and the claim follows when the master gets passive so that *TerminationDetected* holds (since by assumption of this case the master does not turn black).

Case 2. Let *fstBlack* be the first black machine which in this case the token is assumed to encounter during the probe.

Case 2.1. *fstBlack* > *master*. Then the token gets black when forwarded by *fstBlack* and remains black until the final state of this probe (by the token color evolution lemma), contradicting that *TerminationDetected* holds in this probe's *finalState*.

Case 2.2. *fstBlack* = *master*. Then the master must have turned black in this probe, by triggering the activation of a predecessor machine. Then it stays black until the end of the probe (by the machine color evolution lemma), contradicting that *TerminationDetected* holds in this probe's *finalState*.   □

Remark. This proof shows that the algorithm works correctly independently of the initial machine coloring, as remarked in [95].

Exercise 27. Prove that, under the eagerness assumption, for each properly initialized run of DISTRTERMINATIONDETECT (i. e. where *NoMsgsAround* holds initially), in every state satisfying *TerminationDetected* also the property *NoMsgsAround* holds.

3.3 Communicating ASMs

In Sects. 3.2, 3.1 shared functions have been used to model the requested 'immediate' message transmission. However, to model distributed systems, the shared memory approach becomes quickly inadequate, so that in this section we follow [71] to introduce *communicating ASMs*. These are multi-agent ASMs which have disjoint states and perform only local actions (i. e. updates of controlled locations), besides inter-process communication. We keep the communication concept abstract so that the communicating ASM models can be instantiated to any concrete communication pattern. We illustrate the expressiveness and the flexibility of communicating ASMs by two examples.

As first example we define an ASM operator for monitoring asynchronous network system runs (Sect. 3.3.1.2), which we apply to a distributed leader election model over connected graphs (Sect. 3.3.1.1). As second example we define a scheme (Sect. 3.3.2) to transform multi-agent programs designed for synchronous execution into programs one can run concurrently in an asynchronous network, with provably equivalent behavior. This generalizes the transformation we applied in Sect. 3.1.2 to turn the synchronous multi-agent EXTREMAFINDING algorithm of Sect. 3.1.1 into an equivalent concurrent program.

Definition 4. A system of *communicating* ASMs is defined as multi-agent ASM of components $p = (ag(p), pgm(p), mailbox(p))$ for $p \in Process$ where *Process* is assumed to be finite (unless otherwise stated) and:

- the signatures are pairwise disjoint so that each agent has its own private, also called *internal state* or *local state*,
- each agent is enriched by a mailbox for incoming messages,
- each program $pgm(p)$ may contain, besides the usual ASM constructs, the abstract communication actions SEND(*message*), CONSUME(*message*) and the *Received*(*message*) predicate.

These communication constructs deliberately abstract from communication channels and are used with the following intended interpretation, to be furthermore specified where needed:[23]

> SEND(m, **to** q)
>   -- transfer the message (m, **from self**, **to** q) to the communication medium which should deliver it to $mailbox(q)$
> $Received(msg) = (msg \in mailbox(\textbf{self}))$ -- msg has been delivered
> CONSUME(msg) = DELETE($msg, mailbox(\textbf{self})$)

The message content m (also called payload) together with *sender* and *receiver* form a complete message $(m, \textbf{from}\ p, \textbf{to}\ q)$. We use functions $payload(msg)$, $sender(msg)$ and $receiver(msg)$ to extract the components from a message. When it is clear from the context, we omit notationally the sender or receiver of messages or write (m, p, q) instead of $(m, \textbf{from}\ p, \textbf{to}\ q)$. But we assume that, when $(m, \textbf{to}\ q)$ sent by p is delivered to q, it is delivered as $(m, \textbf{from}\ p)$, i.e. containing the sender information. Often we omit mentioning agents and mailboxes, focusing on the ASM program.

For notational brevity we use parameterized messages and abbreviate by **if** $Received(msg(params))$ **then** $M(msg(params))$ the following rule:

---

[23] These abstract communication actions can be viewed as typical examples of update instructions.

if thereissome $msg(params) \in mailbox$ **then**
  choose $m \in \{msg(params) \mid msg(params) \in mailbox\}$ **in** $M(m)$

When the order of messages is relevant, we still may use parameterized messages and abstract notationally from the order-reflecting $next$ function, which retrieves the next message from the $mailbox$. In that case we let
if $Received(msg(params))$ **then** $M(msg(params))$ stand for the following rule:

  if $m = next(mailbox)$ **and forsome** $params$ $m = msg(params)$
  then $M(m)$

The disjoint signature assumption does not exclude that two ASMs $(a, M, mailbox(a)), (b, N, mailbox(b))$ have the same program $M = N$, with the same function symbols. We assume all function symbols f as implicitly parameterized ('instantiated') by the executing agents a, b in the form f_a, f_b, thus guaranteeing disjoint locations (read: local states).[24] It is also possible that communicating ASMs have input or output locations, but those are used only for providing input or output from/to the environment (if any) and not for interprocess communication (in case the environment is not seen as an additional process).

Mailbox, Receive, Delivery abstractions. Unless otherwise stated, we treat $mailbox$ as a set where $Received$ messages are stored, but it could be a multiset (to distinguish among multiple occurrences of identical messages; a set will do if sender timestamps are added to messages) or a FIFO-queue or a priority queue, etc. Sometimes, a separate mailbox for outgoing messages is considered; to distinguish the two mailboxes we use the names $inbox$ (instead of $mailbox$) and $outbox$.

One can interpret $Received(msg)$ as signaling that a RECEIVE(msg) action has been performed by the receiver, see for example [169, 184]. The predicate notation allows one to consider RECEIVE as an action of the communication medium, affecting the receiver's mailbox, and to independently specify a receiver's RECEIVE action. A receiver's RECEIVE action details when and how the receiver retrieves messages from its mailbox, for example using pattern matching or allowing to ignore or defer certain messages by configurable RECEIVE actions, etc.[25] We define in this book various such receiver's RECEIVE actions (Sect. 4.4, 5.1.1).

The delivery can happen in various ways, depending on the case by case to-be-specified properties of the communication medium. Here are some examples:

- *Immediate reliable communication*: every message sent in one 'step' (e. g. in a synchronous round) is in the receiver's mailbox at the beginning of

---

[24] For a systematic treatment of parameterization as a means to partition states see Chap. 4 on ambient ASMs.

[25] For a characteristic example see the input pools in S-BPM [109, p. 335-337].

the next step (e. g. in the next synchronous round). This has been modeled in Sect. 3.2, 3.1 using shared locations.

- *Reliable communication*: every message sent in one 'step' eventually arrives in the receiver's mailbox.
- *Eventually reliable communication* (asynchronous computation model) where either no message is lost or where multiple delivery attempts (message repetition) are performed, assuming that at least one of them eventually succeeds.
- *Lossy uncorrupted communication* (in the asynchronous model), where messages can get lost but not corrupted.
- *Lossy corrupted communication* (in the asynchronous computation model), where messages can get lost or be delivered corrupted.

In Sect. 4.4 we model some high-level interaction patterns for concurrent processes which refine the abstract SEND and RECEIVE communication machines.

3.3.1 Monitoring Asynchronous Network System Runs

In this section we illustrate the use of communicating ASMs, in comparison to ASM models with shared memory. For the sake of an instructive comparison of the advantages and disadvantages of the two modeling approaches, we consider once more distributed leader election (Sect. 3.1.2) and termination detection (Sect. 3.2.2). However, to avoid repetition, we

1. generalize the two algorithms for a more comprehensive background structure for the placement of machines, namely connected graphs instead of rings, which yields some new challenges (Sect. 3.3.1.1), and
2. define an operator which, when applied to what is known as 'diffusing concurrent multi-agent systems', yields a conservative extension that monitors the asynchronous runs to detect their termination (Sect. 3.3.1.2).

The operator definition illustrates how to rigorously define the composition of network machines out of components with precisely defined *behavioral interfaces*, not restricted to purely structural or signature descriptions.

We call *network of processes* each set of processes which are located at the nodes of a graph. For simplicity, we often identify the nodes with the processes, writing (*Process*, *Edge*) for the network. Unless otherwise stated, in such networks every process communicates only with processes it is connected to by an *edge* ∈ *Edge* in the graph. We write *Neighb*(*p*) to denote the set of 'neighbors' to which *p* can send messages, that is of those nodes to which there is an edge in the graph with source *p*. Think about edges as communication channels. Usually directed edges represent unidirectional communication and undirected edges bidirectional communication. Where we need to distinguish between neighbors to which to send and neighbors from which to receive messages, we write $OutNeighb(p)$ respectively $InNeighb(p)$.

3.3.1.1 Concurrent Leader Election in Connected Graphs

In this section we illustrate communicating ASMs to model an asynchronous leader election algorithm for a network of machines, distributed at the nodes of a connected directed graph, thus generalizing the ring structure based version in Sect. 3.1.2. Here is a formulation of the verbal *LeaderElection-Requirements*:

> *PlantReq.* Consider a network of finitely many linearly ordered *Processes* without shared memory, located at the nodes of a directed connected graph and communicating asynchronously with their neighbors (only).
> *FunctionalReq.* Design and verify a distributed algorithm whose execution lets every process know the leader.

Here is a typical idea to design such an algorithm [184, Sect. 15.2]:

> *StepReq.* Every process maintains a record, say *cand*, of the greatest process it has seen so far, initially its own. It alternates between a) sending *cand* to all its neighbors and b) updating *cand* in case its knowledge has been improved by receiving a message with larger value from some neighbor.

Exercise 28. Define the signature to represent the data (objects and functions) mentioned in the *LeaderElectionRe*quirements.

To satisfy the requirements we define a system GRAPHLEADELECT of communicating ASMs:

$$M_p = (p, \text{LEADELECT}_p, mailbox_p)$$

We use process names $p \in Process$ as agent name and equip each of them with an instance of the LEADELECT program, defined by Fig. 3.2, with the following components and predicates:

Initially $mode = send$ **and** $cand = \textbf{self}$ **and** $mailbox = \emptyset$
PROPOSE = **forall** $q \in Neighb$ SEND$(cand, q)$
RECEIVEMSG =
    choose $(c, \textbf{from } q) \in mailbox$
        $curMsg := c$
        CONSUME$(c, \textbf{from } q)$
KnowledgeImproved **iff** $curMsg > \textbf{self}$
UPDATEKNOWL = $(cand := curMsg)$

Fig. 3.2 LEADELECT program of GRAPHLEADELECT component ASMs [76]
© 2003 Springer-Verlag Berlin Heidelberg, reprinted with permission

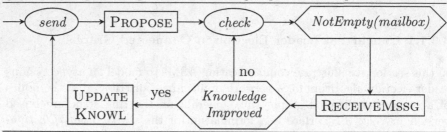

GRAPHLEADELECT **Behavior Property**: In properly initialized concurrent GRAPHLEADELECT runs with reliable communication and without infinitely lazy components—i. e. every enabled process will eventually make a move—eventually for every $p \in Process$ holds:

- $cand = max(Process)$ (everybody 'knows' the leader w. r. t. their order $<$)
- $mailbox = \emptyset$ (there is no more communication)
- $mode = check$

Proof. Index the elements of *Process* with order-reflecting increasing indices $p_0 < p_1 < \ldots < p_{Max}$. Consider any run and any $p \in Process$. Each UPDATEKNOWL-step of p in the run decreases the discrepancy $Max - index(cand_p)$ between the real *leader* and the leader knowledge $cand_p$ of p. When the discrepancy becomes 0 for every $p \in Process$, the claim follows. □

We do not call this a correctness property, because the interpretation of 'every process knows the leader' as 'eventually $cand = max(Process)$' is not a satisfactory solution of the problem. In fact, due to the asynchrony of the computation, the processes do not know when they know the leader, in other words, they do not know when the algorithm they execute terminates. We saw above that a ring background structure helps to detect termination by a master receiving its own description (Sect. 3.1.2) or recognizing that a probe was successful (Sect. 3.2). We leave it as exercise 29 to refine LEADELECT with the graph background structure to a machine which also detects the termination of the asynchronous run in case the number of participating processes (i. e. the size of the graph) is known to each process. Observe also that, without additional help, non-leader processes can recognize that they are not the leader (see exercise 30), but not whether their leader knowledge *cand* is the right one. Since this problem is of a more general nature we deal with it in the next Sect. 3.3.1.2.

Exercise 29. Refine LEADELECT to also detect termination in case the size of the graph is known, that is the number of processes or the diameter of the graph (maximum distance between two nodes).

Exercise 30. Refine LEADELECT to let processes which are smaller than the leader know that they are not the leader.

Exercise 31. Data refine LEADELECT to a CoreASM executable version. See https://github.com/CoreASM/coreasm.core/wiki/Examples (for a slightly different ground model).

3.3.1.2 Termination Detector for Diffusing Computations

Definition 5. Following [96], a multi-agent system is called *diffusing* if each of its runs

- is started in a state where all components are quiescent (read: no step is enabled so that no local action can happen),
- is started by the environment which enables exactly one system component by sending a message to this component—only once until the run terminates (if it terminates at all).

Thus a system run starts by sending messages to other components. These may be activated and later return quiescent, repeatedly, until all components return quiescent (if at all) with no more messages any more in the system.

An example of a diffusing system is GRAPHLEADELECT if initial states are defined by *mode* = *check* (instead of the initialization *mode* = *send* used above), together with *cand* = **self** and *mailbox* = $\emptyset$. Observe that, once at least one component of GRAPHLEADELECT is started by changing its *mode* to *send*, by the connectivity of the graph, eventually all components will change their mode at least once to *mode* = *send*. Therefore the GRAPHLEADELECT Behavior Property of Sect. 3.3.1.1 remains true also with the modified diffusing initialization.

We now define a program transformer TERMINATIONDETECTOR for communicating ASMs, using the idea from [96] how to detect the termination of diffusing system runs without any central controller.

The operator, applied to a diffusing system $\mathcal{M}$, transforms it into a multi-agent system TERMINATIONDETECTOR($\mathcal{M}$) which conservatively refines $\mathcal{M}$ by monitoring its termination. More precisely, the concurrent (asynchronous) runs of TERMINATIONDETECTOR($\mathcal{M}$), started in an initial state, are runs of $\mathcal{M}$ but additionally monitored to report the termination of $\mathcal{M}$ should it terminate.

The *environment* component has the program BEGINENDSHELL($\mathcal{M}$) defined in Fig. 3.3.[26] It provides the environment trigger for a diffusing computation by starting one component machine m of $\mathcal{M} = (m)_{m \in Machine}$, and then waiting, before it becomes ready again to receive the termination message from m, for the elaboration of the result of the diffusing computation.

---

[26] In [96] the environment is treated as a special graph node without incoming edges.

Fig. 3.3 BEGINENDSHELL for monitored diffusing computations

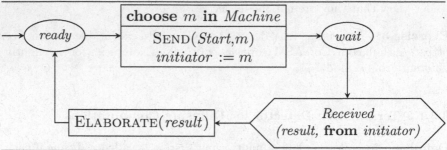

The transformed component programs need two rules whereby a component, when triggered by the *env*ironment in *idle* mode, becomes the master of a diffusing computation. Remember that all components are assumed to be initially quiescent and in *idle* mode. The master, besides executing its own rules (including their additional monitoring rules defined below), will a) START$_{Diffuse}$ and b) when it becomes again idle REPORTRESULT$_{Diffuse}$ to the *env*ironment. We use an interface name *computationResult* for the computed payload of the result message to the *env*ironment. START(**self**) is assumed to enable some rule of **self** to initiate the diffusing computation.

> START$_{Diffuse}$ =
>   **if** *status*(**self**) = *idle* **and** *Received*(*Start*, **from** *env*) **then**
>   *status*(**self**) := *master*
>   START(**self**)   -- assumed to enable self
>   CONSUME(*Start*, **from** *env*)
> REPORTRESULT$_{Diffuse}$ =
>   **if** *status*(**self**) = *master* **and** *quiescent*(**self**) **then**
>   *status*(**self**) := *idle*
>   SEND(*computationResult*, *env*)

The TERMINATIONDETECTOR idea is to use reliable message sending (i. e. no message is corrupted or lost) as mechanism to awaken idle components which, once activated by a 'parent' component, may send further messages to other components, etc. This requires an acknowledgment of each message to figure out when a component can return to *idle* status and report termination to its parent; this situation occurs once the component has become quiescent and all its messages have been acknowledged. As result, a spanning tree of the activated components is built, starting at the master. The tree may also shrink (but also grow again later), using what is called a 'convergecast' procedure to report termination back to the source process.

To be specific the procedure proposed in [96] requires the following:

SpanningTreeBuildReq. Each non-master component designates the neighbor from which it first receives a non-acknowledgment message as its parent in the spanning tree. Any subsequent non-acknowledgment message is immediately acknowledged (also by the master).

ConvergeCastReq. When a component becomes quiescent and has received an acknowledgment for every non-acknowledgment message it had sent out, then it exits the spanning tree and sends an acknowledgment message to its parent.

TerminationReportReq. When the master becomes quiescent and all the non-acknowledgment messages it had sent have been acknowledged, then it will report to the environment that the computation did terminate.

This leads to define TERMINATIONDETECTOR($\mathcal{M}$) for $\mathcal{M} = (m)_{m \in Machine}$ as system of BEGINENDSHELL($\mathcal{M}$) together with a transformation $\mathcal{M}^*$ of $\mathcal{M}$. The transformation is obtained by adding to the $pgm(m)$ of every $m \in Machine$ the following monitoring components, to form the transformed program $pgm(m)^*$ of m, an extension (conservative refinement) of $pgm(m)$. We use msg for messages in $\mathcal{M}$, to be distinguished from the *Start* and the *ack*nowledgment messages introduced for monitoring. Each machine m has, for each possible receiver m' of messages sent by m, a counter $msgToBeAckBy(m')_m$ indicating the number of messages sent (by m) to but not yet acknowledged by m'.

TERMINATIONDETECTOR($\mathcal{M}$) =
  BEGINENDSHELL($\mathcal{M}$)
  $\mathcal{M}^*$

For each $m \in Machine$ its transformed $pgm(m)^*$ is obtained by adding to $pgm(m)$ the following rules:

START$_{Diffuse}$ -- just once if triggered by the environment
MONITORSENTMSG(msg, **to** $receiver$)   -- record expected acks
  in parallel to any occurrence of SEND(msg, **to** $receiver$) in $pgm(m)$
MONITORACKMSG   -- upon ack arrival decrease expected acks
MONITORRECEIVEDMSG(msg, **from** $sender$)   -- wake up or do ack
  in parallel to each occurrence of RECEIVE(msg, **from** $sender$)
  or action triggered by *Received*(msg, **from** $sender$) in $pgm(m)$
EXITSPANNINGTREE   -- only quiescent tree nodes if *AllAcksArrived*
REPORTRESULT$_{Diffuse}$ -- only master if quiescent & *AllAcksArrived*

The submachines are defined as follows:

MONITORSENTMSG(msg, **to** $receiver$) =
  INCREASE($msgToBeAckBy(receiver)$)   -- expected acks counter
MONITORACKMSG =   -- decrease counter of expected acks
  if *Received*(ack, **from** $receiver$) **then**
    DECREASE($msgToBeAckBy(receiver)$)
    CONSUME(ack, **from** $receiver$)

MONITORRECEIVEDMSG(msg, **from** $sender$) =
  if $status$(**self**) = $idle$
    then ENTERSPANNINGTREE($sender$)   -- get started
    else SEND(ack, $sender$)   -- immediate ack if already woken up
    CONSUME(msg, **from** $sender$)[27]
ENTERSPANNINGTREE($sender$) =
  $status$(**self**) := $treeNode$
  $parent$(**self**) := $sender$
EXITSPANNINGTREE =
  if $status$(**self**) = $treeNode$ **and** $quiescent$(**self**) **and**
    $AllAcksArrived$(**self**) **then**
      SEND(ack, $parent$(**self**))
      $parent$(**self**) := **undef**
      $status$(**self**) := $idle$
$AllAcksArrived$(**self**) **iff**
  forall $m \in Machine$ $msgToBeAckBy_{\textbf{self}}(m) = 0$

The initial states of TERMINATIONDETECTOR($\mathcal{M}$) are defined by initial mode *ready* and each $m \in Machine$ being quiescent in $status = idle$, with no parent defined ($parent = $ **undef**), empty *mailbox*, without sent but not yet received messages around in the communication medium and without messages to be acknowledged (i. e. for each $m' \in Machine$ holds $msgToBeAckBy(m')_m = 0$).

TERMINATIONDETECTOR($\mathcal{M}$) **Behavior Lemma.** In every properly initialized TERMINATIONDETECTOR($\mathcal{M}$) run in every state the following holds:

- For every machine $m \neq initiator$: $status = idle$ iff $parent = $ **undef** and in that case (read: if m is not a node of the spanning tree) m has not to wait for any message to be acknowledged (formally expressed $msgToBeAckBy(m')_m = 0$ for each $m' \in Machine$).
- The machines linked by a *parent* path to the root *initiator* form a spanning tree of all machines with $status \neq idle$.

Exercise 32. Prove the lemma by analyzing TERMINATIONDETECTOR($\mathcal{M}$) runs.

Instantiation to leader election. We only have to define the START and ELABORATE($result$) components left abstract in START$_{Diffuse}$ (see p. 122) respectively BEGINENDSHELL. For the latter, define $computationResult = cand$ in REPORTRESULT$_{Diffuse}$, whereby the *initiator* machine upon termination of GRAPHLEADELECT sends the information on the leader to the environment:

---

[27] Without this CONSUME action the transformation would be incorrect. Presumably the authors of [96] assumed it to be performed by the receive action (RECEIVE or the action triggered by $Received(msg, \textbf{from } sender)$) in $pgm(m)$.

$\text{START}(m) = (mode(m)^{28} := send)$ -- this enables PROPOSE
$\text{ELABORATE}(result)_{Diffuse} = \text{NOTIFY}(leader = result)$

Correctness of TERMINATIONDETECTOR(GRAPHLEADELECT):
Consider runs with reliable message passing and without infinitely lazy components. Then TERMINATIONDETECTOR(GRAPHLEADELECT), started in an initial state, does NOTIFY(*leader = result*) correctly when and only when the GRAPHLEADELECT machine started by the *initiator* enters a state where all components have *status = idle*.

Proof. Assume GRAPHLEADELECT has been started by the *initiator* entering *mode = send* and enters a state where all components have *status = idle*. Then they are all quiescent by the definition of EXITSPANNINGTREE and REPORTRESULT$_{Diffuse}$. Thus, by the GRAPHLEADELECT Behavior Property of Sect. 3.3.1.1, every component including the *initiator* has correct *cand = max(Process)* knowledge. Therefore, when the *initiator* executes its last action REPORTRESULT$_{Diffuse}$, it passes the correct *computationResult* which the environment will NOTIFY.

Inversely, assume the computation ends with NOTIFY(*leader = result*). This notification, by definition of the environment actions (Fig. 3.3), is executed only when the environment *Received*(*result*, **from** *initiator*). This happens by definition of REPORTRESULT$_{Diffuse}$ only after the *initiator* has become quiescent and received acknowledgments to all messages it had sent out. But this implies, by the definition of rule EXITSPANNINGTREE, that every neighbor of the *initiator*—which has been activated by a message from the *initiator* and by the GRAPHLEADELECT Behavior Property of Sect. 3.3.1.1 eventually returned to quiescent with all other received messages acknowledged—eventually entered *status = idle*. By an induction on the growing and shrinking spanning tree the claim follows.   □

Exercise 33. Define a system of communicating ASMs which are located at the nodes of a connected graph and communicate only with their neighbors in the graph. Assume the graph to be undirected, for bi-directional reliable communication. An initiator's message can be broadcast to all machines (building a spanning tree) and be acknowledged by all machines. Justify the correctness of the defined system. For a solution see [44, Sect. 2.3] (where also other simple communicating ASM network examples can be found) and [184, Sect. 4.2.2].

3.3.2 Local Synchronization Operator

It is usually easier to design and verify machines for execution in rounds of a synchronous network than in asynchronous networks without rounds. Hence

---

[28] This is the *mode* from the GRAPHLEADELECT machine in Fig. 3.2.

the interest to transform, in a provably correct way, machines which have been designed to run in synchronous rounds to machines which can be executed also asynchronously, but with unchanged or equivalent local component behavior. In this section we use communicating ASMs to model and verify for the sake of illustration one such transformation scheme described in [184, Sect. 16.2], where the communication is assumed to be reliable. We present here its generalization in [71], from an interleaving computation model to truly concurrent communicating ASMs.

In this section let (*Process*, *Edge*) be a network of communicating ASMs and assume the communication medium to be reliable. Its *synchronous execution model* is characterized by the runs of the following single-agent ASM, which is also written SYNCNET(*Process*) if the underlying graph structure is clear from the context:

SYNCNET(*Process*, *Edge*) =
   forall $p \in Process$
    $pgm(p)$
   INCREASEROUND   -- i. e. $curRound := curRound + 1$

In fact, its (appropriately initialized) runs are sequences $(State_r)_{r=0,1,...}$ of states in 'round' r, each one comprising the local states of all processes in round r, including all messages sent resp. received in 'round' r by any component process. The SEND actions are assumed to be reliable and to have immediate effect. This means that messages that are sent in round r are *Received* and thereby in the mailbox of their receiver in the next round. For simplicity of exposition, it is assumed that in SYNCNET(*Process*, *Edge*), in each round, each process sends exactly one (possibly empty) message to each of its neighbors.[29]

In concurrent runs $(S_0, P_0), (S_1, P_1), \ldots$ of the (syntactically identical) network ASYNCNET(*Process*, *Edge*) there is no round concept. Both the steps of any single process (including their send/receive actions) and the message transfer and delivery action of the communication medium happen asynchronously. Since the component states are assumed to be disjoint there are no update conflicts, including the communication actions of processes and of the communication medium. Therefore, in a concurrent run $S_0, S_1, \ldots$ let P_n be the subset of those $p \in Process$ which perform a step in state S_n (restricted to the signature of p) together with a step of the communication medium (to transfer or deliver some messages) resulting in state S_{n+1}. Observe that, due to asynchrony, the messages a process p finds in its *mailbox* in state S_n are

---

[29] This is without loss of generality. In fact one can treat a set of messages sent in round r to the same receiver as bundled into one round-r message. The assumption corresponds to treating a round as constituted by one atomic step for each component. This atomicity abstracts from the possible sequence $S_0, S_1, \ldots$ of successive steps of a component p in round r, in which p performs no other RECEIVE step than reading the *mailbox* in the initial round state S_0. In other words, after state S_0, process p does not read newly arriving messages until the initial state of the next round.

assumed to have been sent in a preceding state S_j ($j < n$), in accordance with [169], so that there is no conflict between the delivery of a new message in $mailbox(p)$ and a CONSUME action by p.[30] The interleaving model is characterized by the restriction of P_n to one-element sets.

We define now a LOCALSYNCTRANSFORMER. Applied to ($Process, Edge$) it builds an asynchronous network which emulates each global round-r-step of the synchronized network SYNCNET($Process, Edge$), for each $r = 0, 1, \ldots$. The given network ($Process, Edge$) will be a subnet of the asynchronous network, but with $pgm(p)$ transformed into SYNCSHELL(p). A global round-r-step of the network consists of the local round-r-steps by each network component. Therefore, the asynchronous network synchronizes for each process p the asynchronous emulation of p's round-r-step with the asynchronous emulation of the round-r-steps of all its neighbors it communicates with. Hence the name 'local synchronization'.

The extension the transformer provides for the behavior of each process p is a particularly interesting form of ASM refinement. It implies not only a program change for the agent $ag(p)$, namely from $pgm(p)$ to SYNCSHELL(p), but also introduces new processes which are located at new graph nodes and execute a SYNCHRONIZER(p)) machine to monitor and steer the emulation of each p-step by SYNCSHELL(p).

More precisely, the given graph $Edge$ is changed to a graph $Edge^*$ by replacing edges between processes p and q as illustrated in Fig. 3.4 by the following two kinds of edges:

• Edges between each node p resp. q and its communication monitoring process, which is executed by a dedicated agent $synchronizer(p)$ resp. $synchronizer(q)$ equipped with an instance of the SYNCHRONIZER program. The agents which are equipped with an instance of the transformation of $pgm(p)$ into SYNCSHELL(p) are also called $syncshell(p)$ agent.
• Edges between the two communication monitoring processes.

In a LOCALSYNCTRANSFORMER($Process$) run, to emulate a round-r-step of SYNCNET($Process$), each process p executes its original $pgm(m)$ step, but instead of sending a message msg to a neighbor q it performs two steps:

• p sends the msg enriched by the information on the currently emulated $curRound_p = r$ to its $synchronizer(p)$ process,
• p SUSPENDs itself until it becomes $ReadyForNextRound$.

The $synchronizer(p)$ process collects and forwards the received message to the $synchronizer(q)$. Process p becomes $ReadyForNextRound$ once it has received a) a $resume$ message from its $synchronizer(p)$ and b) also all messages sent to it in this round by its neighbors (via the synchronizers). The

---

[30] In the general case of concurrent ASMs with shared locations, the generation of all concurrent ASM runs described at the end of Sect. 2.4.3 must also take the update consistency into account.

Fig. 3.4 LOCALSYNCTRANSFORMER graph structure

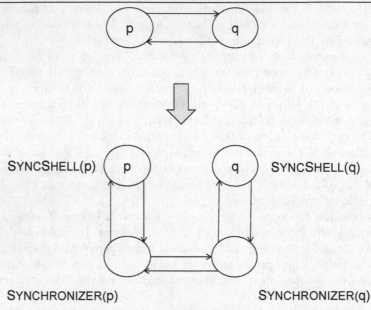

monitor process sends this *resume* message only after it has seen that to-gether with p also all its neighbors q have *MadeOneStep*(q, r), to emulate their part in the round-r-step of SYNCNET(*Process*). Therefore, just before p SUSPENDs itself (after the execution of its round-r-step), it informs via its *synchronizer* the *synchronizer* of each neighbor by a *stepInfo*(p) message that it has *MadeOneStep* in the *curRound*$_p$.

Therefore, we define two programs: a) SYNCSHELL each p is equipped with and b) SYNCHRONIZER each *synchronizer* agent is equipped with in the transformed network over *Edge** such that:

LOCALSYNCTRANSFORMER(*Process*, *Edge*) = (*Process**, *Edge**)
where *Process** = $(ag(p), \text{SYNCSHELL}(p), mailbox(p))_{p \in Process}$
    $\cup (synchronizer(p), \text{SYNCHRONIZER}(p), mailbox(synchronizer(p)))_{p \in Process}$

It remains to define these two programs. The above explanations motivate the following transformation of $pgm(p)$:

SYNCSHELL(p) =
    if *ReadyForNextRound*$_p$ **then**
        $pgm(p)^*$
        SUSPEND(p)
    else
        if *Received*(*resume*, **from** *synchronizer*(p)) **then**
            RESUME(p)

The SYNCSHELL submachines are defined as follows.

$ReadyForNextRound_p$ iff
   $Resumed(p)$ **and** $ReceivedAllMsgsFor(curRound_p, p)$
$pgm(p)^* = pgm(p)$ with
   SEND(m, **to** q) replaced by
       SEND(($m, curRound_p$, **to** q), **to** $synchronizer(p)$)
   RECEIVED(m, **from** q) replaced by
       RECEIVED(($m, curRound_p - 1$, **from** q), **from** $synchronizer(p)$)
$ReceivedAllMsgsFor(r + 1, p)$ iff[31]
   forall $q \in Neighb(p)$ **forsome** m --some msg sent in round r
   $Received((m, r, \textbf{from } q), \textbf{from } synchronizer(p))$
SUSPEND(p) =
   $WaitingForNextRoundTick(p) := true$
   INFORMABOUTSTEP(p)
   INCREASE($curRound_p$)
INFORMABOUTSTEP(p) =
   SEND($stepInfo(p, curRound_p)$, **to** $synchronizer(p)$)
INCREASE(l) = ($l := l + 1$)
RESUME(p) =
   $WaitingForNextRoundTick(p) := false$
   CONSUME(($resume$, **from** $synchronizer(p)$))
$Resumed(p)$ iff $WaitingForNextRoundTick(p) = false$

Therefore, the $synchronizer(p)$ process must FORWARDMSGSSENTBY(p, r) to $synchronizer(q)$ for each message destination neighbor q of p, including $stepInfo$ messages received from p.[32] The main role of $synchronizer(p)$ is to CLOSEROUND(r, p), meaning to WAKEUP(p) for the next round when two conditions are satisfied:

1. p and each $q \in Neighb(p)$ has $MadeOneStep$ in the to be emulated $curRound$, and
2. the messages sent in this round, which must be passed to p for its next round step, have all been received.

The monitor recognizes this situation when it has received these messages and a $stepInfo$ message with payload $curRound(\textbf{self})$ from each neighbor $synchronizer(q)$. This explains the following definition:

SYNCHRONIZER(p) =
   let $r = curRound(\textbf{self})$
   FORWARDMSGSSENTBY(p, r)
   CLOSEROUND(r, p)

---

[31] $ReceivedAllMsgsFor(0, p)$ is assumed to be true by initialization.

[32] For notational convenience, we assume the set of $stepInfo$ messages to be disjoint from the set $ProcessMsg$ of messages in mailboxes of synchronizers, which record messages exchanged between $Processes$, e. g. appearing in a SEND(msg) of some $pgm(p)$ with $p \in Process$.

The SYNCHRONIZER submachines are defined as follows:

FORWARDMSGSSENTBY$(p, r) =$
  if $Received((m, r, \textbf{to } q), \textbf{from } p)$ **then**
    SEND$((m, r, \textbf{from } p), \textbf{to } synchronizer(q))$
    CONSUME$(m, r, \textbf{to } q)$
  if $Received(stepInfo(p, r), \textbf{from } p)$ **then**
    forall $q \in Neighb(p)$
      SEND$(stepInfo(p, r), \textbf{to } synchronizer(q))$
CLOSEROUND$(r, p) =$
  if $Received(stepInfo(p, r), \textbf{from } p)$ -- p made a round-r-step
    and (**forall** $q \in Neighb(p)$ $MadeOneStep(q, r)$)
    and $ReceivedAllMsgsToPassTo(p, r)$ **then**
      PASSMSGSSENTTO(p, r)
      WAKEUP(p)
      INCREASE$(curRound(\textbf{self}))^{33}$
$MadeOneStep(q, r)$ **iff**   -- NB. $r = curRound_q$
  $Received(stepInfo(q, r), \textbf{from } synchronizer(q))$
$ReceivedAllMsgsToPassTo(p, r)$ **iff**
  forall $q \in Neighb(p)$
  forsome m $Received((m, r, \textbf{to } p), \textbf{from } synchronizer(q))$
PASSMSGSSENTTO$(p, r) =$ -- msgs to-be-received in round $r + 1$
  forall $q \in Neighb(p)$ **forall**   -- all msgs of type $ProcessMsg$
  $((m, r, \textbf{to } p), \textbf{from } synchronizer(q)) \in mailbox \cap ProcessMsg$
    SEND$((m, r, \textbf{from } q), \textbf{to } p)$
    CONSUME$(m, r, \textbf{from } q)^{34}$
WAKEUP$(p) = $ SEND$(resume, \textbf{to } syncShell(p))$

In Sect. 3.3.2.1 we formulate and prove the correctness of the emulation.

3.3.2.1 Local Synchronization Correctness

Initial states of runs of SYNCNET$(Process, Edge)$ satisfy $curRound = 0$ and $mailbox = \emptyset$ for each $p \in Process$. LOCALSYNCTRANSFORMER$(Process, Edge)$ has initial states which satisfy, for each component c (including the synchronizers), $curRound_c = 0$, $mailbox_c = \emptyset$ and for each $p \in Process$ both predicates $ReadyForNextRound_p$ and $ReceivedAllMsgsToPassTo(p)$ being true.

In properly initialized runs R_s of SYNCNET$(Process, Edge)$, for each round number r and each process p, the round-r-step of p consists of the one step p performs when $curRound = r$. The emulation in properly initialized runs R_a of LOCALSYNCTRANSFORMER$(Process, Edge)$ refines each such p-step into a

---

[33] One could add here a garbage collector CLEARSYNCMAILBOX$(p, curRound)$ to delete from $mailbox_{synchronizer(p)}$ all round messages $((m, r, \textbf{to } p), \textbf{from } q) \in ProcessMsg$ and all step info messages $(r, \textbf{from } q)$ it contains.

[34] This is only a garbage collection action.

first SYNCSHELL(p) step, followed by message forwarding steps performed by its *synchronizer*(p) and the *synchronizers* of its neighbors q, concluded by a final CLOSEROUND(r, p) step that enables the second SYNCSHELL(p) step:

- SYNCSHELL(p) is enabled when *ReadyForNextRound$_p$* = *true*,
- when all neighbors of p made a step and the messages sent in this step to p have been received by the *synchronizer*(p), CLOSEROUND(r, p) is enabled to PASSMSGSSENTTO(p, r) and to WAKEUP(p),
- the RESUME(p) step in SYNCSHELL(p) is enabled after having *Received* both the (*resume,* **from** *synchronizer*(p)) message and all messages sent to p in round r.

Local Synchronization Correctness Property. Let R_s, R_a be any properly initialized runs of SYNCNET(*Process, Edge*) and of its transformation LOCALSYNCTRANSFORMER(*Process, Edge*), started with equal values in same-named locations. For every process p and every round number r the following holds: when $ag(p)$ starts its round r in R_s resp. in R_a, in the two runs the values of same-named p-locations are the same and also the payload and process destination of corresponding messages (m, **to** q) and (m, *curRound$_p$*, **to** q), sent by $ag(p)$ in round r to (and similarly *Received* from) its neighbor processes.

The equality of values of same-named p-locations at the beginning of round r = *curRound*$_{\text{SYNCNET}(Process, Edge)}$ = *curRound$_p$* can be expressed as *StateEquality*(p, r):

$$state_{R_s}(r) \downarrow \Sigma_p = state_{R_a}(p, r) \downarrow \Sigma_p$$

where $state_{R_s}(r)$ denotes the state of SYNCNET(*Process, Edge*) in which p starts its r-th round in R_s, $state_{R_a}(p, r)$ denotes the state in which p starts its round r in R_a, $S \downarrow \Sigma_p$ denotes the restriction of state S to the signature Σ_p of p.

Proof (by induction on r). For round 0 the claim is true due to the initialization condition. For $r > 0$ from *StateEquality*(p, r) and the definition of *pgm*(p)*, executed in the first SYNCSHELL(p)-step for round r, it follows that the p-locations are updated the same way in both runs. There are no further updates for them until p becomes again *ReadyForNextRound*, this time for round $r + 1$, namely when it has been *Resumed* and did receive all messages its neighbors have sent to p in round r. The pairs of corresponding messages (m, **from** p, **to** q) in R_s and ((m, r, **to** q), *synchronizer*(p)) or ((m, r, **from** p), **to** *synchronizer*(q))in R_a, sent in round r to neighbor processes resp. synchronizers, do not change neither the original payload m nor the original process source p or destination q. □

Exercise 34. Show that the *stepInfo* related updates and checks (which we used to ease the explanation) can be eliminated in SYNCSHELL and SYNCHRONIZER.

3.4 Recap: Sequential versus Concurrent ASMs

Concurrent ASMs are families $\mathcal{M}$ of single-agent sequential ASMs $p = (ag(p), pgm(p))$ ($p \in Process$ for some set $Process$) running asynchronously. Each process executes its program following its own clock and interacting with other processes via input/output or shared locations (mailboxes in the case of communicating ASMs).[35] The intuitive understanding of concurrent runs as sequences of observable snapshots of the states when some sequential agents interact is captured by the following definition of concurrent ASM runs. It is taken from [70].

Definition 6. A *concurrent run* of a multi-agent ASM $\mathcal{M}$ is a sequence $(S_0, P_0), (S_1, P_1), \ldots$ of states S_n and subsets $P_n \subseteq Process$ such that each state S_{n+1} is obtained from S_n by applying to it the updates computed by the processes $p \in P_n$. Here each $p \in P_n$ started an internal computation segment by reading (and maybe recording internally the values read of) its input and shared locations in some preceding state S_{j_p} ($j_p \leq n$), depending on p, and terminates this internal computation segment by a write-back step in state S_n. A write-back step is a step which may update also output and shared locations, whereby it becomes observable by other agents. In an internal computation segment, a process works only with its controlled locations and does neither read nor write its monitored, output or shared locations.[36] The run terminates in state S_n if the updates computed by the agents in P_n are inconsistent.

This definition generalizes the notion of concurrent runs of communicating ASMs explained in Sect. 3.3.2. It also generalizes the definition of runs of sequential ASMs whose moves alternate with environment moves (see Sect. 7.2).[37]

The ASM CONCURRENCYPATTERN(*Process*) in Sect. 2.4.3 (p. 73) generates all concurrent runs of $\mathcal{M}$. It explicitly expresses the separation of asynchronous steps from steps that are to-be-synchronized:

- Interaction steps that are to-be-synchronized. These steps directly contribute to building S_{n+1}. Each such a step can be a WRITEBACK(p) to output or shared locations, but also a direct EXECUTE(p) step. The result of these steps becomes observable by other processes so that these steps are also called 'global'.

---

[35] We consider here synchronously running multi-agent ASMs as a special form of single-agent parallel ASM, see SYNCNET(*Process, Edge*) in Sect. 3.3.2.

[36] If for some process $j = n$ holds, the internal computation segment is empty since the process performs in S_n both its external reads and writes.

[37] The definition has been introduced for practical purposes. It replaces the purely axiomatic, mathematically very elegant but impractical notion of so-called distributed (partial order) ASM runs [136]. It also generalizes Lamport's concept of sequentially consistent runs. See [70] for a detailed analysis.

- Asynchronously executable internal steps LOCALEXECUTE(p), also called 'local' steps. They are based upon an initial reading of input and shared locations in mode *listenToEnv* in some preceding state S_{j_p} ($j_p \leq n$).

This satisfies the *read-cleanness* requirement that even when in a run reading and writing of a location by two processes are overlapping, the reading provides a clear value, either taken before the writings start or after both operations are terminated (see [168, 171]). For this reason our definition abstracts from possibly overlapping reads/writes.

One can describe the above definition also by the following equation. $S_{lastExternalRead(p,n)}$ denotes the state in which process p performed its reads of all monitored and shared locations it uses for the internal computation segment it completes with a write-back step in state S_n (so that $lastExternalRead(p, n) \leq n$).

$$S_{n+1} = S_n + \bigcup_{p \in P_n} Upd(pgm(p), S_{lastExternalRead(p,n)})$$

We say that p starts its j-th globally observable step in state S_j with $j = lastExternalRead(p, n)$ and completes it in state S_n. Remember that $S + U$ is not defined if U is an inconsistent update set.

Chapter 4
Modeling Context Awareness

Modeling context-aware systems is intimately related to parameterization. Parameterized ASMs have been used in various ways in Chaps. 2 and 3. They were crucial for a) building succinct complete behavioral models of Java and C#, at the level of abstraction of those languages, and for b) the proven to be correct refinement of those models to equally succinct models at the level of compiled code execution by the corresponding Virtual Machines [232, 54, 117, 119, 120]. In this chapter we analyze the ASM parameterization mechanism systematically. We show how it permits to gently model context-aware behavior. This leads to the concept of *ambient* ASMs. They support a rather general form of partitioning of states and of distributed computations, which can be instantiated to various forms of information hiding (encapsulation of memory and concurrent computations).

In Sect. 4.1 we define *ambient* ASMs by bootstrapping, defining them in terms of basic ASMs. Then we apply them to model various state and run hiding disciplines (Sect. 4.2), programming patterns (Sect. 4.3), communication patterns (Sect. 4.4) and some common control flow schemes (Sect. 4.5). For an application of ambient ASMs to model typical Ambient Calculus operations [83] see [47, 80].

Also in this chapter we avoid a formalization and provide a *precise* explanation, using *intuitive* terms, of the concept of environment-sensitive computations. For a detailed mathematical description which captures the underlying intuition we refer to Sect. 7.2.1. The concept of ambient ASMs and its applications is taken from [47, 247].

4.1 Definition of Ambient ASMs

The basic idea of context-sensitive computations is to offer capabilities to specify and manage 'program environments' which influence the behavioral meaning of the program, i. e. determine the result of its execution in depen-

© Springer-Verlag GmbH Germany, part of Springer Nature 2018

E. Börger, A. Raschke, *Modeling Companion for Software Practitioners*,

https://doi.org/10.1007/978-3-662-56641-1_4

dence of a given environment. Exploiting the abstraction capabilities of ASMs one can formulate such dependencies and their management in a most general way, to create, modify, delete environments, also at run time. It suffices to a) enrich ASM executions by an abstract environment parameter, with respect to which the terms involved in a step are evaluated, and b) to add to the language of ASM rules a dedicated construct, which permits to define such program-instantiating environments at whatever level of abstraction.

Definition 7. The ambient construct for ASMs is syntactically defined as **amb** *exp* **in** P where, to achieve generality in the widest terms, *exp* is any expression and P any (already defined) ASM program.

ASMs where this construct occurs are called *ambient* ASMs. The behavioral effect of **amb** *exp* **in** P is defined as updating the current *environment* for the execution of P. More precisely, this means to PUSH the evaluation *eval*(*exp*, *env*) of the newly declared environment to the given *environment* and to execute P in the updated *environment*. In this way environments are passed by value and can be nested, providing the means for hierarchical state partitioning.

To make this description precise, it remains to explain how the set of updates a machine P yields in a given state is determined depending on the current *environment* as additional parameter. Essentially this comes up to rigorously explain how the update set yielded by an assignment statement $f(s_1, \ldots, s_n) := s$ depends not only on the given state $\mathcal{A}$ and the given assignment ζ of values to each free variable occurrence, but maybe also on the current *environment*.

However, not all functions will be environment dependent. Therefore, we extend the ASM classification of functions by the concept of *environment independent functions*. These are functions for which $f(e, x) = f(e', x)$ holds for all environments e, e' and all arguments x. For such functions, the *evaluation* of terms (in state $\mathcal{A}$ with variable interpretation ζ) remains unchanged, the same as without environment parameter.

Definition 8. For environment dependent functions f, for every state S and every variable interpretation ζ (i. e. assignment of values to each free variable occurrence), the *evaluation* of terms $t = f(t_1, \ldots, t_n)$ in state S is defined inductively by the following clause. It parameterizes f, passing the given *environment* by value as parameter to evaluate t. When the parameters are clear from the context we write *eval* instead of $eval_\zeta^S$.

$$eval(f(t_1, \ldots, t_n), env) = f^S(env, eval(t_1, env), \ldots, eval(t_n, env))$$

where f^S denotes the interpretation of the parameterized function symbol f in state S.

Formally, the parameterization of the *evaluation* function replaces $eval(t)$ by $eval(t, env)$. This is notationally displayed also by indexing $eval_{env}$, fully written out $eval^S_{\zeta,env}$. In the literature often the notation $[\![t]\!]^S_{\zeta,env}$ is used for $eval^S_{\zeta,env}(t)$.

The parameterization implies that each environment dependent n-ary function $f^{(n)}$ is turned into a family of possibly different functions $f^{(n)}_{env}$, each distinguished ('isolated', separated from the others) by its env. The memory locations $(f_{env}, args)$ are 'isolated' from the memory locations $(f_{env'}, args)$ of other functions $f^{(n)}_{env'}$ of the same family. To avoid signature blow up that could result from dynamic environment nesting we treat env as a sequence, in fact as a stack of single environment values (since we pass environments by value). Thereby the function $f^{(n)}$ of terms t is replaced by an $n+1$-ary function of t and the current env. We denote this by writing $f_{env}(t) = f(env, t)$, using the same function name (but with different arity which is usually clear from the context). We interpret $eval(t, [\,])$ as $eval(t)$ (evaluation in the empty environment).

This ends the intuitive explanation of the behavior of ambient ASMs. Before illustrating in the next section some typical usage we mention one frequently used special case (which is the one introduced in [47]).

Flat-ambient ASMs. Consider the case where, instead of an environment stack to which each newly declared environment is PUSHed, only the last declared (most recent) environment is kept. This can be done by binding its *value* (computed in the current environment) to a logical variable, say *curamb*,[1] which is reused in case of nested ambients. Essentially this interpretation of ambient ASMs is equivalent to a syntactic transformation to basic ASMs, defined as follows. We write **amb$_{\text{flat}}$** to distinguish the *flat-ambient* ASM version from the more general structured *hierarchical-ambient* ASMs, defined in [247] and explained above.

Definition 9. $(\text{amb}_{\text{flat}}\ exp\ \text{in}\ P)^* = (\text{let}\ curamb = exp^*\ \text{in}\ P^*)$
where exp^* is obtained from exp by replacing the names f of ambient dependent functions in exp by f_{curamb}. Logical variables r and names r of parameterized rules (with declaration $r(params) = Q$) are classified as ambient independent, so that their calls are transformed by $(r(t_1, \ldots, t_n))^* = r(t_1^*, \ldots, t_n^*)$. The rest goes by induction. Worth mentioning is the case of **let**, where the property $(\zeta[x \mapsto v])[x \mapsto v'] = \zeta[x \mapsto v']$ of variable interpretations is used:

$$(\text{let}\ x = t\ \text{in}\ P)^* = (\text{let}\ x = t^*\ \text{in}\ P^*).$$

Exercise 35. Consider the following flat-ambient behavioral ASM model of the object-oriented State Pattern, which is required to 'allow an object to alter its behavior when its internal state changes. The object will appear to change its class' [122, p. 305]. The class ('internal state') change is modeled by entering a nested environment:

---

[1] This binding is technically done by the variable interpretation function $\zeta[curamb \mapsto val]$, which is the modification of ζ by assigning val to $curamb$. Reuse is supported by the fact that $(\zeta[x \mapsto v])[x \mapsto v'] = \zeta[x \mapsto v']$, i.e. the last binding for x counts.

STATEPATTERN($Operation$) =
  amb$_{\text{flat}}$ $abstractClass$ **in**

                              -- enter state of $abstractClass$
  $Operation$
                          -- execute $Operation$ defined in $abstractClass$
  amb$_{\text{flat}}$ $concreteClass$ **in** $Operation$
                      -- due to 'internal state change alter behavior' to
                            execution of $Operation$ defined in $concreteClass$
  where
  $Operation = (f(a) := b)$ -- for the sake of illustration

Show that the behavior of $Operation$ changes depending on the class where it
is called to execute, e. g. by the 'object' $this = $ **self**. The first call of $Operation$
computes an update for the function f interpreted as $f_{abstractClass}$, the second
one for the function f interpreted as $f_{concreteClass}$ (assuming for the sake of
illustration the two class names to be environment independent). Show that
with the hierarchical-ambient interpretation, the pattern can be generalized
by making the execution of $Operation$ in the $conreteClass$ dependent also on
the $abstractClass$, from where the execution in the $concreteClass$ was called.

4.2 Encapsulating States and Runs by Ambient ASMs

In this section we illustrate the use of ambient ASMs by simple models for
some common name space disciplines, which *isolate states* by name bindings
(Sect. 4.2.1), and for ways to *encapsulate computations* of multiple processes
(Sect. 4.2.2).

4.2.1 Encapsulating State: Scoping Disciplines

Programming languages come with a great variety of static and dynamic
scoping disciplines. A common feature is that the value of a name *id* in a
state depends on the *pos*ition where the *id*entifier occurs and on a for each
case to-be-determined environment, among those *Env*ironments which have
a binding for the *id*entifier, i. e. a defined associated value, and whose *scope*
(program part where its bindings are valid) includes *pos*. *Env* is a dynamic
set because a) entering a new scope resp. leaving a scope adds resp. deletes
an environment, and b) declarations establishing new bindings in a scope
change environments. We formulate this commonality as ENVSENSITIVEEVAL
pattern, where we use an abstract machine GETVALUE which retrieves the
value of an *id*entifier, once the environment is given. To express the choice,
we apply here a *select*ion function to environment sets. This function can be
static or dynamic, depending on the language.

ENVSENSITIVEEVAL($id, pos, state$) =
  if $Occurs(id, pos, state)$ **then**
    let $E = Env \cap \{e \mid InScope(pos, e, state) \wedge HasBinding(e, id)\}$
      let $env = select(E)$ -- stands for **choose** $env \in E$
        amb env **in** GETVALUE(id)

Variations of this pattern result from refining the *selection* mechanism and the meaning of the *InScope* predicate.

A well-known example for a refinement of *InScope* is *lexical scoping*, also called static scoping. It is used in many languages, for example in Pascal, Modula-2, C where *InScope(pos, e, state)* is refined to a compiler-definable predicate *InLexicalScope(pos, e)*. Other examples for *InScope* refinements are *dynamic scoping* (as in Logo) and combinations of the two (as in Java).

A refinement of the *selection* function appears with mechanisms to shadow bindings, in case an *identifier* is bound in multiple environments all of which are valid at a given *position*. A frequent policy uses the stack-based last-in/first-out (LIFO) scope selection. For its description we use $\sqsubseteq$ to express the particular nesting order specified by the programming language:

ENVSENSITIVELIFOEVAL($id, pos, state$) =
  ENVSENSITIVEEVAL($id, pos, state$)
where $select(E)$ is constrained to yield an env satisfying
  forall $e \in E$ $env \sqsubseteq e$

A different policy appears in the TCL language [199], which allows the programmer to select any binding of names established in any enclosing scope (and possibly hidden by a nearer scope). Denote by *Env(state)* the list of scopes in the current state (below the state is suppressed notationally). The list is updated when a procedure is entered or left. Let **global** *id* refer to the global scope *Env*[0] (the outermost with index 0), *id* to the current (the last created) scope $Env[n]$ where $n = length(Env)$. A declaration **upvar** k *id* v binds the local variable v to the identifier *id* as bound in the k-th scope "up" from the current scope, the same for **upvar** #k *id* v with the k-th scope "down" from the global one. Then the TCL environment-sensitive evaluation policy can be modeled as follows:

TCLEVAL($id, pos, state$) =
  if $Occurs(id, pos, state)$ **then**
    let $e = selectenv(pos, state)$
      amb e **in** GETVALUE(id)
where
  let $n = length(Env)$

$$selectenv(pos, s) = \begin{cases} Env[0] & \text{if } pos \text{ is in } \textbf{global } id \\ Env[n-k] & \text{if } pos \text{ is in } \textbf{upvar } k \; id \; v \\ Env[k] & \text{if } pos \text{ is in } \textbf{upvar } \#k \; id \; v \\ Env[n] & \text{otherwise} \end{cases}$$

4.2.2 Encapsulating Computations: Thread Handling

Encapsulation of computations is needed for distributed processes to isolate the execution of various tasks by different threads. In this section we illustrate how to gently pass with ambient ASMs from a sequential single-agent to a concurrent model, using as example the Java interpreter ASM defined in [232] (Sect. 4.2.2.1). Then we use ambient ASMs to separate the description of thread management handling for concurrent processes from application-logic-programming of single processes, using as example the THREADPOOLEXECUTOR of J2SE 5.0 [193] (Sect. 4.2.2.2); the idea is taken from [47].

4.2.2.1 Multi-Thread Java Interpreter

Let SINGLETHREADJAVAINTERPRETER be a single-thread Java interpreter, for definiteness say the one defined in terms of ASMs in [232] from where we borrow the terminology for this example. To separate scheduling from the association of threads with a to-be-executed Java program, we use an abstract predicate *Scheduled*. It is assumed to select *Runnable* threads out of the current *Thread* class instances in the *heap*. A *Runnable* thread can be *Active* or *Synchronizing* or *Notified*. In case it is not yet *active* but *Synchronizing* or *Notified* and chosen for execution, it should first SYNCHRONIZE respectively WAKEUP—whereby it becomes *Active*, so that it can then RUN to execute its associated program. Once running, it is not any more *Scheduled*. This explains the following ambient ASM; the flat ambient version suffices because threads are not nested and have a unique context.

$$
\begin{aligned}
&\text{MULTITHREADJAVAINTERPRETER} = \\
&\quad \textbf{choose } q \textbf{ with } Scheduled(q) \\
&\qquad \textbf{if } Active(q) \textbf{ then} \\
&\qquad\quad \text{RUN}(q) \\
&\qquad\quad \text{DESCHEDULE}(q) \\
&\qquad \textbf{else} \\
&\qquad\quad \textbf{if } Synchronizing(q) \textbf{ then } \text{SYNCHRONIZE}(q) \\
&\qquad\quad \textbf{if } Notified(q) \textbf{ then } \text{WAKEUP}(q) \\
&\qquad\quad Active(q) := true \\
&\quad \textbf{where} \\
&\qquad \text{RUN}(q) = \textbf{amb}_{\text{flat}} \; q \textbf{ in } \text{SINGLETHREADJAVAINTERPRETER} \\
&\qquad \text{DESCHEDULE}(q) = (Scheduled(q) := false)
\end{aligned}
$$

We do not describe here how a thread becomes passive. The *Scheduled* predicate abstracts in particular from how many threads the scheduler can support. Exerc. 36 considers the case of a multi-thread interpreter with a bounded number of threads.

Remark on process instantiation. MULTITHREADJAVAINTERPRETER is a concrete example for the instantiation of a process P by an executing agent **self** which carries its own environment, a special case of Def. 3. This instantiation technique has often been used in the literature when dealing with multi-agent ASMs. It offers a conceptually simple but general mechanism to uniformly define *process instantiation*. It has been applied in [75] to provide a clean separation of business process models and their instances.[2] The process instantiation scheme underlies also the object-oriented notation *this.P*, which corresponds to **amb** *this* **in** P.

Remark on support of modular verification by ambient ASMs. Ambient separation in behavioral interfaces supports modular verification methods. For concrete examples we refer to the literature, in particular to the ASM-based analysis of the C# thread model in [229, 228] and the stepwise extended proofs for incremental Java model extensions in [23].

4.2.2.2 Thread Pool Management

In this section we illustrate how ambient ASMs support the separation of concerns, taking as example a thread pool manager. One of the pragmatic values of thread pool handlers consists in separating the specification of thread management—creation, deletion and scheduling of threads to concurrently run tasks—from the application-logic-level description of tasks. For the sake of definiteness we illustrate this here for Java programs, but the principles can be applied also to other concurrent request management systems, e. g. web servers.

We start with a natural language description of the J2SE 5.0 thread pool which is based upon [193, Chap. 10].

corePoolSizeReq. The thread pool should be kept as much as possible within *corePoolSize*. When a new task is submitted and fewer than *corePoolSize* threads are running, a new thread is created to handle the request, even if there are idle threads. If when the task is submitted the pool has reached or exceeds the *corePoolSize* but not the *maxPoolSize* and there are idle threads in the pool, one of them is assigned to run the task.

maxPoolSizeReq. If a task is submitted for execution when the pool is full and all threads in the pool are running, the task is inserted into a *queue*. If the *queue* is full the task is rejected.

QueuePriorityReq. If a task is submitted for execution when *corePoolSize* or more threads are running but the pool is not yet full and no idle thread

---

[2] For the problem statement see [242] and the OMG business process modeling notation standard BPMN [196].

is available, then a new thread is created and assigned to run the task
only if the task cannot be placed to the *queue* without blocking it.
RunCompletionReq. If when a thread has completed its current run there
are tasks in the queue, the thread is assigned to run one of them. Otherwise it becomes idle.
IdleThreadReuseReq. When there is a task in the queue, an idle thread,
if there is one, is assigned to run the task.
IdleThreadExitReq If there are more than *corePoolSize* threads in the
pool, excess threads will be terminated if they have been idle for more
than the *keepAliveTime*.

The first three requirements ask to HANDLENEWTASKs, the last three concern idle threads and describe how to HANDLEQUEUEDTASKs. Both groups
foresee that an idle thread may be assigned to run the task in question, but
only one task per thread. Therefore, if one wants to split the specification of
the THREADPOOLEXECUTOR into two components, one must either schedule
(sequentialize) them, avoiding conflicting task assignments to a single thread,
or provide some exclusive access to the set of idle threads when selecting an
element. Since our purpose is to illustrate the use of ambient ASMs, we abstract here from this scheduling issue by letting the THREADPOOLEXECUTOR
execute in each step one of the two components:

> THREADPOOLEXECUTOR =
>   **one of** ({HANDLENEWTASK, HANDLEQUEUEDTASK})

HANDLENEWTASK is triggered by a task submitted for execution. For
simplicity we express this by a monitored predicate *Submitted*(*task*).[3] The
first two clauses reflect the *corePoolSizeRequirement*. The **ifnone** clause reflects the *QueuePriorityRequirement*. The final clause reflects the *maxPool-
SizeRequirement*. We use two abstract machines, one to REJECT a task and
one to EXECUTE as task 'interpreter' the program of a task, in analogy to
the SINGLETHREADJAVAINTERPRETER in Sect. 4.2.2.1. We make crucial use
of the flat ambient construct in the RUN definition. In this definition, the
program(*task*), which is to be EXECUTEed, is assumed to be retrievable by
the threads from the *task* environment, e. g. by *pgm*(*thread*) := **amb** *task* **in**
EXECUTE(*thread*). The described rule is laid out on the next page.

For the HANDLEQUEUEDTASK component we use a monitored predicate *Terminated*(*thread*) to express that a *thread* has completed the run
for the assigned task, the condition which appears in the *RunComple-
tionRequirement*. This requirement seems to establish a reuse priority of
Terminated threads over idle ones. Therefore, first an attempt is made to
FINDTASKFORTERMINATED threads satisfying *RunCompletionReq*, then to
FINDTASKFORIDLE threads satisfying the two idle thread requirements. If
there is no task in the queue, a terminated *thread* becomes idle. An idle

---

[3] In a communication based model one could define *Submitted*(*task*) as receiving an
execution request for the *task*.

thread may be killed, namely if the pool grew over the *corePoolSize* and the *keepAliveTime*(*thread*) has expired. This explains the definition below.

HANDLENEWTASK(*task*) = **if** *Submitted*(*task*) **then**
   if | *Pool* |< *corePoolSize* **then**
    let $t =$ **new** (*Pool*) **in** RUN(*t*, *task*)
                   -- first create *corePoolSize* many threads
   else
    if | *Pool* |< *maxPoolSize* **then**   -- first use *Idle* threads
      choose $t \in Pool$ **with** *Idle*(*t*)
        RUN(*t*, *task*)
      ifnone
        if *BlockingFreePlaceable*(*task*, *queue*)
          then INSERT(*task*, *queue*)
                -- first fill *queue* before creating new threads
          else let $t =$ **new** (*Pool*) **in**
             RUN(*t*, *task*)
    else
      if forall $t \in Pool$ *Running*(*t*) **then**
        if | *queue* |< *maxQueuesize*
        then INSERT(*task*, *queue*)
        else REJECT(*task*)
   where
    RUN(*thread*, *task*) =
      mode(*thread*) := *running*
    amb$_{\text{flat}}$ *task* **in** EXECUTE
    Idle(*thread*) **iff** *mode*(*thread*) = *idle*

HANDLEQUEUEDTASK =
  choose *thread* $\in$ *Pool* **with** *Terminated*(*thread*)
    FINDTASKFORTERMINATED(*thread*)
  if none
  choose *thread* $\in$ *Pool* **with** *Idle*(*thread*)
    FINDTASKFORIDLE(*thread*)

The HANDLEQUEUEDTASK predicates and submachines are defined as follows:

  Terminated(*thread*) **iff** *mode*(*thread*) = *terminated*
  FINDTASKFORTERMINATED(*thread*) =
  choose *task* $\in$ *queue*
    RUN(*thread*, *task*)
    DELETE(*task*, *queue*)
  ifnone
    MAKEIDLE(*thread*)

$\text{FindTaskForIdle}(\textit{thread}) =$
 choose $\textit{task} \in \textit{queue}$
  $\text{Run}(\textit{thread}, \textit{task})$
  $\text{Delete}(\textit{task}, \textit{queue})$
 ifnone $\text{TryToKill}(\textit{thread})$
$\text{MakeIdle}(\textit{thread}) =$
 $\textit{mode}(\textit{thread}) := \textit{idle}$
 $\textit{terminationTime}(\textit{thread}) := \textit{now}$
$\text{TryToKill}(t) =$
 if $|\textit{ Pool }| > \textit{corePoolSize}$ **then**
  if $\textit{Expired}(\textit{aliveTime}(t))$ **then**
   $\text{Delete}(t, \textit{Pool})$
$\textit{Expired}(\textit{aliveTime}(t))$ iff
 $\textit{now} - \textit{terminationTime}(t) > \textit{keepAliveTime}(t)$

Exercise 36. Setting *maxPoolSize* to $\textit{max}_{int}$ accommodates a to all practical purposes unlimited number of threads, as considered in Sect. 4.2.2.1 for the MultiThreadJavaInterpreter. Refine it to a machine with a bounded number of threads, combining it with ThreadPoolExecutor.

4.3 Modeling Behavioral Programming Patterns

In this section we illustrate the use of ambient ASMs by deriving some well-known patterns from object-oriented programming as instances of a few simple behavioral ambient ASM models.

In a sense every 'abstract' machine expresses a scheme for the structure and the behavior of a family of possible process instances. Whereas a particular ASM represents the class of its possible implementations, a pattern names the parameters which constitute the schematic nature of the machine and are subject to ASM (data or operation) refinements.

A characteristic scheme for the (static or dynamic) instantiation of programs by specific execution environments is the *Delegation* pattern of object-oriented programming. The ambient ASM model we define for it explicitly and precisely exhibits its abstract computational behavior. Furthermore, it allows us to specialize it to some of its variations, which are known under the names *Template*, *Responsibility* (together with its deterministic instance *ChainOfResponsibility*), *Proxy* (together with its remote, virtual and protection versions), *Strategy*, *State* and *Bridge* patterns.

Delegation 'separates' instantiations of an OPERATION, read: it decouples an interface in an *AbstractClass* from its implementations. It does it in such a way that at run-time, for a call of OPERATION(x) with input x, one can determine an environment *delegate* (read: an object in an appropriate *classOf(delegate)*) to carry out the call, namely by executing the

Fig. 4.1 Delegation Class Structure

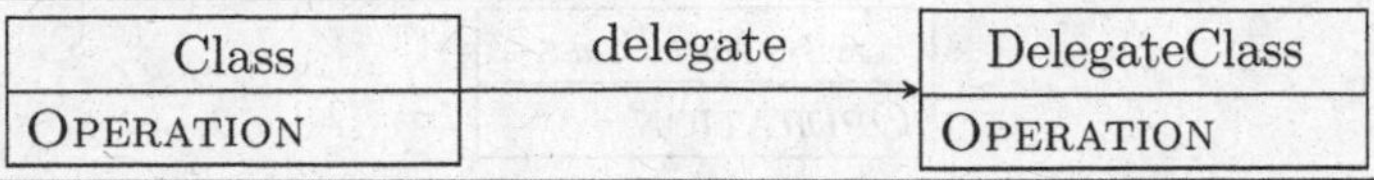

Class	delegate	DelegateClass
OPERATION	→	OPERATION

corresponding OPERATION instance (read: the implementation provided in *classOf(delegate)*). This is expressed by the following definition of an ASM delegation pattern. The hierarchical ambient ASM version covers nested delegation.

$$\text{DELEGATE}(\text{OPERATION}, delegate)(x)^4 =$$
$$\textbf{amb } delegate \textbf{ in } \text{OPERATION}(x)$$

In the object-oriented interpretation (see the visualization of the class structure in Fig. 4.1), the parameterization of OPERATION by *delegate* implies that what is executed in the *delegate* context is the OPERATION as implemented in the *classOf(delegate)*.

Variations of this pattern result from different ways to define the *delegate* environment parameter. Referring to the object-oriented class structure, this can be done in various ways we are going to explain below:

- *internally* by having *delegate* as a location
  - in the *AbstractClass*, like in the *Bridge* pattern, or
  - in some dedicated subclass, like in the *Proxy*, *Strategy* and *State* patterns,

- *externally*, which can be done in two ways:
  - statically, either determined by the class structure (like in the *Template* pattern) or by a data-structure related function (like the chain traversal function in the *ChainOfResponsibility* pattern), or
  - dynamically, for example via some run-time determined *selection* function as in the *Responsibility* pattern.

Template Pattern. In [122, p. 325] this pattern is described as follows:

Define the skeleton of an algorithm in an operation, deferring some steps to subclasses. Template Method lets subclasses redefine certain steps of an algorithm without changing the algorithm's structure.

This means that *delegate* denotes one of the subclasses *ConcreteClass*, which are determined by the static subclass structure of the *AbstractClass* (see Fig. 4.2).

Since in ambient ASMs there is no restriction on environment expressions, we can simply replace the *delegate* parameter in the above defined DELEGATE

---

[4] DELEGATE(OPERATION, *delegate*) defines a machine which is called with x as parameter

Fig. 4.2 Template Pattern Class Structure

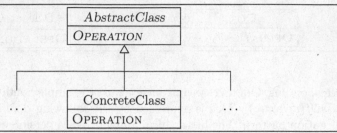

ASM by the name of the *ConcreteClass*. This yields the following instance of the ASM DELEGATE pattern:

TEMPLATE = DELEGATE **where** *delegate = ConcreteClass*

Following [122], OPERATION stands here for 'the skeleton of an algorithm' which may call some abstract *PrimitiveOperations*, i.e. interfaces provided by the *AbstractClass* for which an implementation is provided by the ambient parameter *ConcreteClass*. *AbstractClass* stands for an 'Application'; every subclass *ConcreteClass* stands for an individual 'MyApplication', which provides its interpretation *op(ConcreteClass, x)* of the abstract *PrimitiveOperations op(x)* 'to carry out subclass-specific steps of the algorithm'. One can restrict these subclass-specific operations by declaring only those operations as the class ambient dependent ones. This is an example of ASM refinement of type $(1, 1)$.

Chain of Responsibility Pattern. Following [122, p. 223] this pattern serves to

> avoid coupling the sender of a request to its receiver by giving more than one object a chance to handle the request

in particular when a static association of the caller with a delegate is impossible. This can be defined as a pure data refinement of DELEGATE as follows: *delegate* is determined by applying a *selection* function to the set of *Receivers* in subclasses *ConcreteClass* which *CanHandle* the input $x = request$ (using their implementation of OPERATION). The underlying class structure is visualized in Fig. 4.3.

RESPONSIBILITY = DELEGATE
   where *delegate = select(PossibleHandler(x))*
PossibleHandler(request) = Receiver(request) ∩ Handler(request)
Handler(request) = {o | CanHandle(o, OPERATION)(request)}

In the *Chain of Responsibility* pattern the *selection* mechanism is further detailed in op.cit. by the stipulation to 'chain the receiving objects and pass the request along the chain until an object handles it' because 'the handler

Fig. 4.3 Responsibility Pattern Class Structure

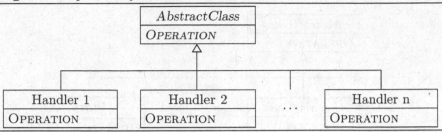

should be ascertained automatically'. This means to data refine the non-deterministic choice function *select* to a deterministic function which provides the *first* element that *CanHandle* the input *request*, with respect to an order < ('chain') of *Receiver(request)*:

$$select(PossibleHandler(x)) = first(PossibleHandler(x))$$

To ascertain the handler automatically means to program this function.

 CHAINOFRESPONSIBILITY = DELEGATE
  where *delegate* = *first(PossibleHandler(x))*

Proxy Pattern. Following [122, p. 207] the *Proxy* pattern is intended to

provide a surrogate or placeholder for another object to control access to it.

This refines *delegate* to 'the real object that the proxy represents' and thus is renamed in op.cit. to *RealSubject*. More precisely, the value of the *delegate* expression is a *ConcreteClass* instance (of one of the subclasses of *AbstractClass*), kept in a placeholder location of a dedicated subclass of *AbstractClass* called *Proxy*. This makes it possible 'that a Proxy can be used anywhere a RealSubject is expected' [122, p. 210]. See Fig. 4.4 for the underlying class structure.

In this way, via *Proxy*, client calls of OPERATION are forwarded for execution to the *delegate*, which is passed as ambient parameter to the ASM refinement of OPERATION (read: to its implementation in the *classOf(delegate)*). Thus the PROXY ASM is another data refinement of DELEGATE.

 PROXY = DELEGATE
  where *delegate* denotes a location of *Proxy*
   with values in any subclass of *AbstractClass*

Various instances of the *Proxy* pattern represent data or operation refinements of PROXY, essentially imposing some constraints on where the values of *delegate* are stored or the access to *delegate*. For example,

- in a REMOTEPROXY the *delegate* location is required to be in a different address space,

Fig. 4.4 Proxy Pattern Class Structure

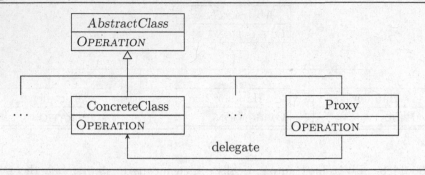

- in a VIRTUALPROXY the *delegate* value is cached via some operation CACHE(*delegate*, *request*) so that its access can be postponed,
- in a PROTECTIONPROXY it is checked whether the caller has the permission to access the OPERATION in the *delegate* environment (read: in *classOf*(*delegate*)).

Remark on refinements. From the behavioral point of view, the *Strategy* and *State* patterns are two more variations of the PROXY pattern to make different implementations 'interchangeable' [122, p. 315]. The difference is only in how the concrete implementations are selected, which is a question of how *delegate* is determined. The literature contains various examples of such refinement variations. See the LEADELECTection ASM in Sect. 3.3.1.1, which is built out of three abstract components PROPOSE, RECEIVEMSG, and UPDATEKNOWLedge. One can refine them to compute either only the leader, or the leader plus notification of the termination (see Exerc. 29) or the leader together with a shortest path to it (see [76, Sect. 6.1.5]).

Bridge Pattern. In the *Bridge* pattern [122, p. 151] *delegate* is declared as a location of the *AbstractClass*, which takes as values instances of the implementing subclasses. These subclasses are outsourced as (renamed) subclasses *ConcreteImplementor* of another class, called *Implementor*. A link relates the OPERATION parameter of BRIDGE (read: the interface in the *AbstractClass*) to the OPERATIONIMPL parameter (read: the interface in the *Implementor* class). In this way OPERATION is refined to **amb** *delegate* in OPERATIONIMPL. See Fig. 4.5 for the underlying class structure.[5]

> BRIDGE(OPERATION, *delegate*) =
>   DELEGATE(OPERATIONIMPL, *delegate*)

---

[5] The OPERATIONIMPL interface for implementation classes 'doesn't have to correspond exactly to *Abstraction*'s interface; in fact the two interfaces can be quite different. Typically the *Implementor* interface provides only primitive operations, and *Abstraction* defines higher-level operations based on these primitives' [122, p. 154].

Fig. 4.5 Bridge Pattern Class Structure

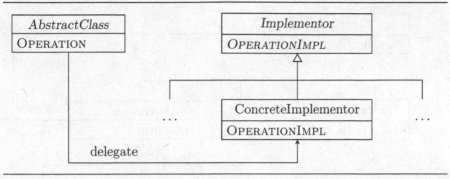

This instantiation of the DELEGATE pattern provides run-time choices between different refinements of abstract machines OPERATION, namely via updates of the *delegate* context parameter which determine the desired refinement. Such a run-time choice may be desirable to replace the static binding of an implementation to its abstraction via class inheritance.

Decorator Pattern. The *Decorator* pattern is focussed on a specific way to 'alter behavior' at run-time, namely by *extending the functionality* of an OPERATION for one object of an abstract class (which for this pattern is renamed to *Component* with subclasses *ConcreteComponent*), leaving the OPERATION behavior of other instances of the same class unchanged. If the pattern use is restricted to functionality extension and not complete overriding, it represents an instance of incremental ('conservative') ASM refinements.

In [122, p. 175] the role of the *Decorator* pattern is declared to

'attach additional responsibilities to an object dynamically' as 'a flexible alternative to subclassing for extending functionality'.

To this purpose 'a reference to a *Component* object' is kept in a location called *component*, an 'interface for objects that can have responsibilities added to them dynamically', which is kept in a dedicated subclass *Decorator*. This subclass comes with multiple subclasses *ConcreteDecorator*, one for each considered ADDEDBEHAVIOR, as visualized in Fig. 4.6. The behavioral definition of the DECORATOR pattern follows the same scheme as the DELEGATE pattern:

DECORATOR(OPERATION, *component*) =
    amb *component* **in** OPERATION

The difference between the two patterns is in how the parameterization of OPERATION by the environment (read here: the implementation of OPERATION in the *classOf*(*component*)) is defined, here as *Component* OPERATION 'extended' by some machine ADDEDBEHAVIOR.

Fig. 4.6 Decorator Pattern Class Structure

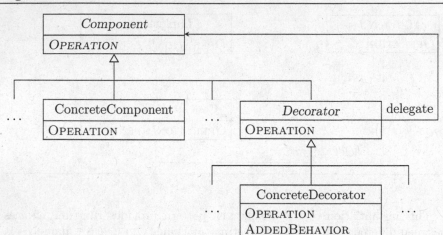

If complete overriding of OPERATION$_{Component}$ is allowed instead of extending, then the OPERATION$_{Component}$ part disappears, but may still be called within the execution of ADDEDBEHAVIOR. ADDEDBEHAVIOR in that case really is new behavior.

4.4 Communication Patterns

Communicating ASMs come with abstract communication actions SEND(msg) and RECEIVE(msg) (see Sect. 3.3). In this section we refine them following [21] to four basic bilateral (Sect. 4.4.1) and four basic multilateral (Sect. 4.4.2) Send/Receive patterns. These patterns can be composed and instantiated to a variety of so-called *process interaction patterns*, used in the fields of business process modeling and service-oriented computing. To show an example from a different area, we explain the ASM model defined in [85] for synchronous message passing (Sect. 4.4.3), a well-known form of communication used in operating systems.

4.4.1 Bilateral Interaction Patterns

Any bilateral (one-to-one) interaction pattern can be composed using the four basic pattern types shown in Fig. 4.7: *Send*, *Receive* and their sequential combinations *SendReceive* (for sending a request followed by receiving a response) and *ReceiveSend* (for receiving a request followed by sending a response). Each of them describes one interaction side, so that the machines which perform them are single-agent machines.

For each basic interaction type four parameters are considered for its variations, namely whether

- an *acknowledgment* is requested,
- the communication action is *blocking*, forcing the agent to wait for a response,
- the communication action *fails*,
- the communication action is *repeated* until an acknowledgment arrives, to be used in case the delivery is not reliable.

4.4.1.1 Send Patterns

We define a basic SENDPATTERN. By refining it appropriately one can capture each of the mentioned interaction types. The pattern definition foresees in particular that various types of failure may happen. In the following definition one may imagine $OkSend(m)$ to mean that there is a channel connecting the sender to the recipient, which is open to send m. SEND(m) is the abstract machine which forwards messages to the communication medium.

> SENDPATTERN(m) =
>   if $ToSend(m)$ then   -- trigger predicate at the sender
>   if $OkSend(m)$ then
>   SEND(m)
>   if $AckRequested(m)$ then SETWAITCOND(m)
>   if $BlockingSend(m)$ then $status := awaitAck(m)$
>   else HANDLESENDFAILURE($m, notOkSend$)
>   DONE(m)
> where
>   DONE(m) = ($readyToSend(m) := false$)
> $ToSend(m)$ iff $readyToSend(m) = true$

The four basic bilateral interaction patterns of Fig. 4.7 can be obtained by refining SENDPATTERN, namely either by adding constraints on the pa-

---

Fig. 4.7 Basic Bilateral Interaction Pattern Types [21]

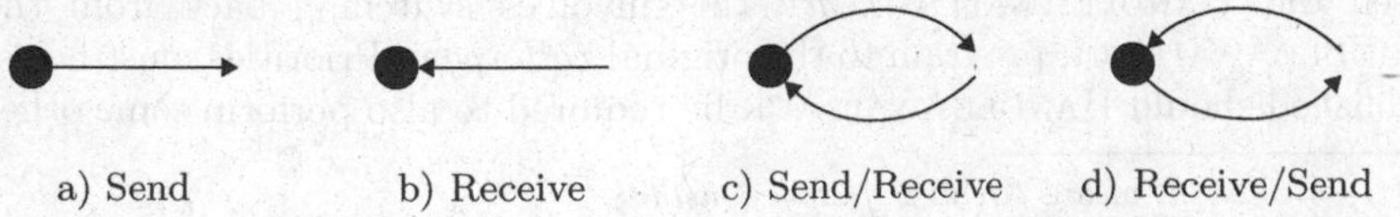

a) Send   b) Receive   c) Send/Receive   d) Receive/Send

rameters or by refining some component. We now define such variations for the following set of *SendTypes*:

$$SendType = \{noAck,\ ack,\ AckAwait,\ UntilAck,\ UntilAckAwait\}$$

The SEND_{noAck} without acknowledgment can be used in case of a reliable communication medium, where messages are neither lost nor corrupted:

$\text{SEND}_{noAck}(m) =$
  $\text{SENDPATTERN}(m)$
where
  $AckRequested(\_) = false^{6}$
  $BlockingSend(\_) = false$

If an acknowledgment is required the sender must SETWAITCONDition for m. Depending on whether the sender should be blocked or not, it means that either itself or some other agent should $\text{BECOMEAWAITHANDLER}$ for m. After an appropriate initialization, which records also the callback data, this agent has to $\text{HANDLEAWAITACK}(m)$. In the non-blocking case, the *status* of the sender is not changed, so that it can continue its program execution while another agent will $\text{HANDLEAWAITACK}(m)$.

$\text{SEND}_{Ack}(m) = \text{SENDPATTERN}(m)$
  where
    $AckRequested(\_) = true$
    $BlockingSend(\_) = false$
    $\text{SETWAITCOND}(m) =$
      let $a = new(Agent)$
        $\text{BECOMEAWAITHANDLER}(a, m)$
    $\text{BECOMEAWAITHANDLER}(a, m) =$
      $caller(a) := \textbf{self}$
      $callerpgm(a) := pgm(\textbf{self})$
      $pgm(a) := \text{HANDLEAWAITACK}(m)$
      $\text{INITIALIZEAWAITPARAMS}(m)$
    $\text{INITIALIZEAWAITPARAMS}(m) =$
      $\text{SET}(waitParams(m))$ -- typically *deadline, resendtime,...*

$\text{HANDLEAWAITACK}(m)$ terminates when an acknowledgment message is received. Then the sender—the *caller* of the agent which executed the $\text{HANDLEAWAITACK}(m)$—is UNBLOCKed (as part of some other possible $\text{PERFORMACTION}(m)$ we leave abstract here, including resetting the *status*) so that it can continue to execute its sender program. In case the sender itself did $\text{HANDLEAWAITACK}(m)$, this involves switching back from the HANDLEAWAITACK program to the original *callerpgm*. Priorities must be established should HANDLEAWAITACK be required to also perform some other

---

[6] $f(\_) = constant$ means **forall** $x\ f(x) = constant$.

wait activities, which are triggered by events that could happen simultaneously, like timeouts, failure notice etc. Since such priorities much depend on the particular application, we leave the further specification of the choice open using the **one of** operator.

This explains the definition of the acknowledgment handler scheme:

$\text{HANDLEAWAITACK}(m) =$
 if $Received(Ack(m))$[7] **then** $\text{TERMINATEAWAITACK}(m)$
  else $\text{PERFORMOTHERWAITACTIVITIES}(m)$
 where
  $\text{TERMINATEAWAITACK}(m) =$
   $\text{PERFORMACTION}(m)$ -- including $\text{UNBLOCK}(status(caller(\textbf{self})))$
   if $\textbf{self} = caller(\textbf{self})$ -- sender itself did HANDLEAWAITACK
   then $pgm(\textbf{self}) := callerpgm(\textbf{self})$
            -- switch back to sender pgm

    else EXIT
   $\text{EXIT} = \text{DELETE}(\textbf{self}, Agent)$
   $\text{PERFORMOTHERWAITACTIVITIES}(m) =$
    one of
     if $Timeout(m, waitingForAck)$ **then**
      $\text{HANDLETIMEOUT}(m, waitingForAck)$
     if $Received(Failed(Ack, m))$ **then**
      $\text{HANDLESENDFAILURE}(m, Ack)$
     $\text{OTHERWAITRULES}(m)$ -- placeholder for extensions

For the blocking variant of SEND_{Ack} it suffices to refine $\text{SETWAITCOND}(m)$ to let the sender itself $\text{BECOMEAWAITHANDLER}(\textbf{self}, m)$. As a consequence, the sender is blocked by setting its $status$ to $awaitAck(m)$:

$\text{SEND}_{AckAwait}(m) = \text{SENDPATTERN}(m)$
 where
  $AckRequested(\_) = true$
  $BlockingSend(\_) = true$[8]
  $\text{SETWAITCOND}(m) =$
   $\text{BECOMEAWAITHANDLER}(\textbf{self}, m)$

For the case of unreliable message passing it is foreseen to resend messages until an acknowledgment arrives. This is an ASM refinement of SEND_{Ack} resp. $\text{SEND}_{AckAwait}$, obtained by including a $\text{RESEND}(m)$ rule into the OTHERWAITRULES considered in $\text{PERFORMOTHERWAITACTIVITIES}(m)$. To determine the time when to $\text{RESEND}(m)$, we reuse the timer model of Sect. 2.1.4.1.

---

[7] Here it is assumed that the executing agent has reading access to the mailbox where the acknowledgment message is assumed to arrive. Correspondingly, one may assume that $\text{PERFORMACTION}(m)$ deletes the acknowledgment message for message m from the mailbox.

[8] This has the effect that $status(\textbf{self}) := awaitAck(m)$ by $\text{SENDPATTERN}(m)$.

Fig. 4.8 Generalizing Alternating Bit to SENDUNTILACK$_{Await}$

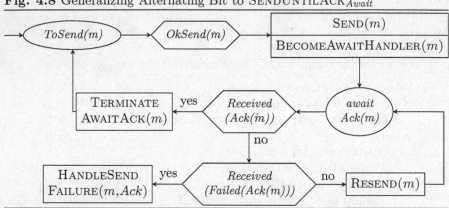

Since message copies may differ from the original (if only by its time attribute), we insert a function *newVersion* into the RESEND(m) rule.

> SENDUNTILACK(m) =   -- non blocking version
>   SEND$_{Ack}$(m)
> SENDUNTILACK$_{Await}$(m) =   -- blocking version
>   SEND$_{AckAwait}$(m)
> **where**
>   PERFORMOTHERWAITACTIVITIES(m) = RESEND(m)
>   RESEND(m) =
>   **if** *Timeout*(*resend*(m)) **then**
>   SEND(*newVersion*(m, *now*))
>   SETTIMER(*resend*(m))

SENDUNTILACK$_{Await}$ (Fig. 4.8) is a generalization of the sender component in the Alternating Bit protocol.[9]

4.4.1.2 Receive Patterns

For receive actions a pattern appears for what a local mailbox handler does when messages arrive. In contrast, what the destination agent of a message does with them is rather application specific and not dealt with here. For a receive action various receive concepts consider whether messages, which cannot be received when *Arriving*, are buffered for further handling or discarded. Abstracting from buffer and mailbox bounds (which could easily be included into the model) leads to the following pattern. We use RECEIVE with the intended interpretation to insert messages into the local *mailbox* of the destination

---

[9] ASMs for the entire protocol and its refinement to the optimized Sliding Window protocol can be found in [76, Sect. 6.3.1], together with a correctness proof.

agent. We assume (but notationally suppress) RECEIVE(m), DISCARD(m) and BUFFER(m) to CONSUME(m) by resetting *Arriving*(m) := *false*.

> RECEIVEPATTERN(m) =
>> **if** *Arriving*(m) **then**
>>> **if** *ReadyToReceive*(m) **then**
>>>> RECEIVE(m)
>>>> **if** *ToBeAcknowledged*(m) **then**
>>>>> SEND($Ack(m), sender(m)$)
>>>
>>> **elseif** *ToBeDiscarded*(m) **then**
>>>> DISCARD(m)
>>>> **if** *ToBeAcknowledged*(m) **then**
>>>>> SEND($Ack(m, discarded), sender(m)$)
>>>
>>> **else**
>>>> BUFFER(m)
>>>> **if** *ToBeAcknowledged*(m) **then**
>>>>> SEND($Ack(m, buffered), sender(m)$)
>>
>> **if** *TimeOut*($insertBuffer(m)$) **then**
>>> RECEIVE(m)
>>> DELETE($m, buffer$)
>
> **where**
>> BUFFER(m) =
>>> **if** *ToBeBuffered*(m) **then**
>>>> INSERT($m, buffer$)
>>>> SETTIMER($insertBuffer(m)$)

Instances of the RECEIVEPATTERN are obtained by constraining the parameters concerning blocking, buffering or discarding. Each of them comes with a default version, without acknowledgment, and a version with acknowledgment, by configuring *ToBeAcknowledged*(m) correspondingly. This yields the following set of *ReceiveTypes* and the corresponding refinements of RECEIVEPATTERN:

> $ReceiveType = \{nonBlocking, blocking, discard, buffer\}$
> $\cup\{nonBlockingAck, blockingAck, discardAck, bufferAck\}$

The non-blocking version (where *ReadyToReceive*(m) is always true) is equivalent to RECEIVE(m) so that we denote it this way.

> RECEIVE$_{nonBlocking}$(m) = RECEIVEPATTERN(m) = RECEIVE(m)
>> **where** *ReadyToReceive*($\_$) = *true*
>
> RECEIVE$_{blocking}$(m) = RECEIVEPATTERN(m)
>> **where** *ToBeDiscarded*($\_$) = *ToBeBuffered*($\_$) = *false*
>
> RECEIVE$_{discard}$(m) = RECEIVEPATTERN(m)
>> **where**
>>> *ToBeBuffered*($\_$) = *false*
>>> *ToBeDiscarded*(m) = **not** *ReadyToReceive*(m)

$\text{RECEIVE}_{buffer}(m) = \text{RECEIVEPATTERN}(m)$
  where
    $ToBeDiscarded(\_) = false$
    $ToBeBuffered(m) = \textbf{not } ReadyToReceive(m)$

4.4.1.3 SENDRECEIVE and RECEIVESEND PATTERN

To constrain an agent a to receive only responses to a previously sent request, as required for the SENDRECEIVE pattern, a relation must be established between request and response and be checked by a when receiving messages. We express it abstractly by a dynamic set $RequestMsg(sender)$ into which the *sender* inserts its request messages, and by a dynamic *responseTag* function. This function is controlled by the *receiver*, to associate its response messages m with the uniquely determined request message $responseTag(m) = m'$ to which m is the response.

Then the before-relation at agent a, between sending a request and receiving the response, can be expressed without directly controlling sequential steps of the sender (as one could alternatively do), simply by refining for the SENDRECEIVE machine the RECEIVE-guard $Arriving(m)$ through the condition that the message which *Arrived* is tagged $responseTag(m) \in RequestMsg(a)$, i.e. to be the response to a request made by a. This implies, by Lamport's ordering of communication events (see [169]), that every sender's $\text{SEND}(m')$ precedes the receiver's $\text{RECEIVE}(m')$, which precedes the receiver's $\text{SEND}(m)$ tagged m', which precedes the sender's $\text{RECEIVE}(m)$. Thus, by transitivity, the Send-precedes-Receive order is established for each pair of request/response messages sent/received by SENDRECEIVE. In the definition we use the **one of** construct because each single agent either sends or receives a message, not both at the same time.

$\text{SENDRECEIVE}_{s,t}(m) = \textbf{one of } (\{\text{SEND}_s(m), \text{RECEIVE}_t(m)\})$
  where
    $Arriving(m)$ iff $Arrived(m)$ **and** $responseTag(m) \in RequestMsg$
    $s \in SendType, t \in ReceiveType$

The symmetric RECEIVESEND pattern is constrained by only sending response messages to received requests. We use an analogous $IsAnswer(m)$ predicate expressing that the message m is a response to a request that has been received.

$\text{RECEIVESEND}_{t,s}(m) = \textbf{one of } (\{\text{RECEIVE}_t(m), \text{SEND}_s(m)\})$
  where
    $ToSend(m)$ iff $readyToSend(m) = true$ **and** $IsAnswer(m)$
    $t \in ReceiveType, s \in SendType$

In [206] the bilateral patterns $\text{SEND}_{noAck,nonBlocking}$, $\text{RECEIVE}_{blocking}$ and $\text{SENDRECEIVE}_{noAck}$, $\text{RECEIVESEND}_{nonBlocking,noAck}$ are refined (and imple-

Fig. 4.9 Basic Multilateral Interaction Pattern Types [21]
© 2005 Springer-Verlag Berlin Heidelberg, reprinted with permission

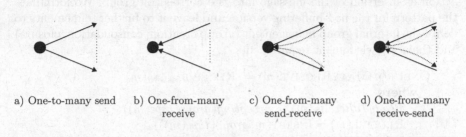

a) One-to-many send   b) One-from-many   c) One-from-many   d) One-from-many
                          receive   send-receive   receive-send

mented to provide validation facilities) to interaction primitives for distributed service-based processes, constructors by which processes request and
provide data concerning service operations. For the web service mediator
model in Sect. 5.1 we use instances of the four bilateral interaction patterns
and of the multilateral ONETOMANYSEND and ONEFROMMANYRECEIVE
patterns.

4.4.2 Multilateral Interaction Patterns

Consider sending requests to and receiving responses from multiple interaction partners instead of one. This turns the four basic bilateral request/re-
sponse interaction types in Fig. 4.7 into four basic multi-party interaction
patterns, see Fig. 4.9.

The ONETOMANYSEND pattern describes broadcasting. It is easily derived from the bilateral Send pattern, using the parallelism of ASMs to send
a message m to all *Recipients* and instantiating the *payload* of the message
template m for each $r \in Recipient$. We consider this here for the non blocking
version SEND$_{noAck}$.

> ONETOMANYSEND$(m) =$ SEND$_{noAck}(m)$
>   **where**
>   SEND(m) is refined to
>   **forall** $r \in Recipient$
>   SEND$(payload(m, r), r)$

The idea of a corresponding ONEFROMMANYRECEIVE pattern conceptually implies correlating somehow arriving messages into correlation *Groups*,
say corresponding to a message *type*.[10] To achieve this, it suffices to refine

---

[10] An example is the S-BPM [109] framework and tool which offer to configure the
mailbox (called input pool) into message groups with respect to a message and receive
type concept. See Sect. 5.2.2.2.

ReadyToReceive(m) in the RECEIVEPATTERN to whether the corresponding message group is *Accepting* messages of that type, and to refine the RECEIVE action as insertion of the message into the correlation group. We formulate the pattern for the non-buffering version and leave it to further refinements to detail the internal group management (group creation, consolidation, closure) and the acknowledgment requirements.

> ONEFROMMANYRECEIVE(m) = RECEIVE$_{discard}$(m)
> **where**
>   *ReadyToReceive*(m) = *Accepting*(*group*(*type*(m))
>   RECEIVE(m) = INSERT(m, *group*(*type*(m)))

A ONETOMANYSENDRECEIVE pattern can be obtained by combining ONETOMANYSEND with ONEFROMMANYRECEIVE, as done for its bilateral analogue. Timing requirements, for example that responses are expected within a given time frame, concern the internal group management, which decides when a group of collected responses is sufficient to be taken for further operation as an answer to the broadcasted request.[11]

> ONETOMANYSENDRECEIVE(m) =
>   ONETOMANYSEND(m)
>   ONEFROMMANYRECEIVE(m)
> **where**
>   *Arriving*(m) iff *Arrived*(m) **and** *responseTag*(m) $\in$ *RequestMsg*

The ONEFROMMANYRECEIVESEND analogue sends to multiple recipients (presumably requestors) a *responseMsg*, formed on the basis of a somehow *Completed* group of received requests. Using *Completed*(g) (group consolidation) and *responseMsg*(g) (forming the response on the basis of the consolidated group of requests) as abstract group management defined functions the pattern can be defined as follows:

> ONEFROMMANYRECEIVESEND(m) =
>   ONEFROMMANYRECEIVE(m)
>   ONETOMANYSEND(m)
> **where**
>   *ToSend*(m) iff *readyToSend*(m) = *true* **and**
> m = *responseMsg*(g) **forsome** $g \in$ *Group* **with** *Completed*(g)

An instance of this pattern is the communication model for distributed systems in [130, Sect. 3.4]. It describes how communicators route messages through a network by forwarding (via ONETOMANYSEND) into the mailboxes of the *Recipient*s the messages found in the communicator's mailbox

----

[11] For an example see the web service mediator model in Sect. 5.1, where FEEDSENDREQ is an instance of ONETOMANYSEND, and RECEIVEANSW is used as a ONEFROMMANYRECEIVE until all expected answers have been received.

(via ONEFROMMANYRECEIVE). The reader who is interested in compositions of the above communication patterns, obtained by ASM refinements of the basic patterns, to form complex interaction patterns used in business process and web service models is referred to [21].

4.4.3 Synchronous Message Passing Pattern

Whereas the concept of communicating ASMs (Sect. 3.3) directly supports asynchronous message passing patterns, we use ASMs in this section to model a synchronous message passing scheme, essentially defining a synchronous version of SEND and RECEIVE actions. We investigate two common ways operating systems deal with synchronous message passing, namely directly controlling the running mode of processes by a scheduler or using a semaphore structure. The two models we explain here are taken from [85]. They provide an occasion to illustrate how the operational character of ASM models supports accurately proving a system property of interest—here the correctness of the two models—by *runtime-based reasoning*, which is directed by the underlying intuitive ideas. In Sect. 4.4.3.1 we define a direct control model SYNCCOMM$_{Ctl}$ for synchronous message passing, in Sect. 4.4.3.2 its refinement SYNCCOMM$_{Sema}$ by semaphores (which has been refined to C-code for testing purposes). The two models exploit the atomicity of ASM steps. This atomicity guarantees the effect of appropriate locking mechanisms [236] from whose specifics we abstract here. See Sect. 4.5 for further discussion of the atomicity issue.

We make only minimal assumptions on the needed scheduler background. To simplify the exposition, we assume a uniprocessor which comes with a notion of currently-executing process, denoted by a function *currp* whose values are *Processes* or the *idleProcess*. The *currp*process is the only one with *status*(*currp*) = *run* (read: instruction pointer *ip* pointing into its code) and is *selected* by the scheduler from a set *readyProc* of processes whose *status* is *ready* to execute.

We leave both the scheduling policy (defined by the function *select*) and the details of the needed scheduler operation SWITCHCURRPROCESS abstract. SWITCHCURRPROCESS plays a double role:

- to suspend *currp*—including to SAVESTATE of *currp*—once this process has started to send a message to a *dest*ination process it wants to synchronize with,
- to select and RESTORESTATE of another process to become the *currp* to run.

We use MAKEREADY(*p*) to INSERT(*p*, *readyProc*) and to update its *status* to *ready*. As a result of executing MAKEREADY(*p*), process *p* becomes a candidate for the scheduler's next choice for updating *currp*. ·

$$\text{MAKEREADY}(p) =$$
$$\quad \text{INSERT}(p, readyProc)$$
$$\quad status(p) := ready$$

4.4.3.1 SyncComm$_{Ctl}$ Ground Model

SyncComm$_{Ctl}$ is defined as a system of communicating ASMs (Sect. 3.3) whose SEND and RECEIVE actions are defined by the machines SyncSend$_{Ctl}$ resp. SyncReceive$_{Ctl}$ explained below. The *SyncMsgPassingReq*uirements for these machines (proved below to be satisfied by our definition) are as follows.

> *SenderWaitReq.* Whenever a process *sender* is scheduled for sending a message, *m*, to a receiver process *dest*, it will record the message for transfer and then wait (without making any further move) until it is synchronized with *dest*; it will wait forever if it cannot be synchronized.
> *ReceiverWaitReq.* Whenever a process, *dest*, is scheduled for receiving a message, it will wait (i.e. not perform any further relevant move) until it is synchronized with a *sender* process.
> *DeliveryReq.* Whenever the *sender* of a message and its receiver *dest* are synchronized, the message is delivered at the receiver process, one at a time and at most once, and the synchronization terminates.

To satisfy the *SenderWaitReq*uirement,

1. the sender will RECORDMSG in its *outbox*,
2. the sender must REGISTERIN a collection called *WaitSndr(dest)* of all senders waiting for their message to be received by the *dest*ination process. This is for the case that the *dest*ination process did already STARTSYNC (by switching to *status = rcvr*),
3. the sender calls the scheduler to MAKEREADY(*dest*),
4. its *status* switches from *run* to *sndr*. Thereby the sender does not execute any more[12] and continues waiting once it is suspended by the next scheduling SWITCHCURRPROCESS step—until the *dest*ination process synchronizes for this message and will MAKEREADY(*sender*).

This explains the following synchronous communication pattern.

$$\text{SYNCSEND}_{Ctl}(m, \textbf{to } dest) =$$
$$\quad \text{RECORDMSG}(m, \textbf{to } dest)$$
$$\quad \text{REGISTERIN}(WaitSndr(dest))$$
$$\quad \textbf{if } status(dest) = rcvr \textbf{ then } \text{MAKEREADY}(dest)$$
$$\quad status(\textbf{self}) := sndr \qquad \text{-- suspend execution of the sender}$$

---

[12] We abstain from an optimization which could include here a message from the *sender* to the scheduler, to inform about being ready for being descheduled.

The two SYNCRECEIVE$_{Ctl}$ submachines are defined as follows:

RECORDMSG(msg) = ($outbox$(**self**) := msg)
REGISTERIN(X) := INSERT(**self**, X)

To satisfy the *ReceiverWaitReq*uirement, in case a *dest*ination process finds no process in its *WaitSndr*(*dest*), it will switch its *status* from *run* to *rcvr* and remain there until a sender will MAKEREADY(*dest*), so that eventually *WaitSndr*(*dest*) will contain some process. When this happens, the *dest*ination process synchronizes with a *sender*, will DELIVERMSGFROMTO from the *sender* (by copying the content of the *outbox*(*sender*) to its *inbox*) and MAKEREADY(*sender*) (to satisfy the *Delivery*Requirement).

It remains to decide whether the protocol permits multiple senders to simultaneously send a message to the same *dest*ination process. If yes, these processes should be ordered in *WaitSndr*(*dest*). We adhere to the usual model of semaphores, which work with queues, so that we treat *WaitSndr*(*dest*) as a (if needed priority) queue.

SYNCRECEIVE$_{Ctl}$ =
  if *WaitSndr*(**self**) = [ ]
    then *status*(**self**) := *rcvr*   -- suspend self
    else let *sender* = *head*(*WaitSndr*(**self**))
      DELIVERMSGFROMTO(*sender*, **self**)
      TERMINATESYNCWITH(*sender*)
  where
    DELIVERMSGFROMTO(*source*, *dest*) =
      (*inbox*(*dest*) := *outbox*(*source*))
    TERMINATESYNCWITH(*sender*) =
      MAKEREADY(*sender*)
      DEQUEUE(*sender*, *WaitSndr*(**self**))

Proof of SyncMsgPassingRequirements. We use an induction on the number of times a process is scheduled in the given run for sending or receiving a message.

The precise meaning of a *sender* being synchronized in the given run with *dest* is that the receiver process *dest* has performed a RECEIVE$_{Ctl}$ move and is scheduled, ready to receive the message sent from *sender*.

The claims of *SenderWaitReq* follow from the execution of the first three updates of SYNCSEND$_{Ctl}$ and the fact that only the *dest* process can MAKEREADY(*sender*) by executing the **else**-clause of SYNCRECEIVE$_{Ctl}$. In fact, being in *status* = *sndr* prevents the *sender* from being scheduled: in order to be scheduled, a process must be in *ready status* and be *selected* by the scheduler.

ReceiverWaitReq follows from the two clauses of SYNCRECEIVE$_{Ctl}$. If the first clause applies, only a SYNCSEND$_{Ctl}$ move can MAKEREADY(*dest*) again so that eventually the second clause applies. *DeliveryReq* follows from the second clause. □

Remark on fairness. We did not mention any fairness assumption. Any fairness property of the scheduler implies a corresponding fairness property of SYNCCOMM$_{Ctl}$. For example, if the scheduler repeatedly schedules every (active) process, every message sent can be proved eventually to be delivered to the receiver. Messages by one *sender* are received in sending order because *WaitSndr* is declared as a queue, preventing overtaking.

4.4.3.2 SYNCCOMM$_{Sema}$ Refinement

The refinement of SYNCCOMM$_{Ctl}$ to SYNCCOMM$_{Sema}$ we define in this section consists in a refinement of the two SYNCSEND$_{Ctl}$ and SYNCRECEIVE$_{Ctl}$ machines by machines which use semaphores. To do this, we borrow the ASM specification of counting semaphores from [49].

A counting semaphore s, in the following called simply semaphore, is characterized by two locations and two atomic operations. A *semaCounter* keeps track of the number of processes which are still allowed to enter the critical section guarded by the semaphore. Unless otherwise stated, its initial value is the number $allowed(s) > 0$ of processes permitted to be simultaneously in the associated critical section. The *semaQueue* contains the processes which are waiting to enter the associated critical section and is initialized by the empty queue.

The operation WAITSEMA is executed when the *currr*process tries to access the critical section. The operation subtracts 1 from the *semaCounter*. If the counter value is non-negative, *currr*process can enter the critical section. Otherwise, at least *allowed* processes are currently in the critical section, so that WAITSEMA adds *currp* to the *semaQueue* and puts it into *status semawait(s)*. The effect is that *currp* is suspended. Only a later SIGNALSEMA move can bring the suspended process back to *ready status*. This explains the following definition, which works under the assumption that the read/write access to *semaCount* is exclusive.

WAITSEMA(s) =
   let $newcount = semaCount(s) - 1$
     $semaCount(s) := newcount$
     if $newcount < 0$ **then**   -- critical section is full
        ENQUEUE(**self**, $semaQueue(s)$)
        $status(\textbf{self}) := semawait(s)$ -- suspend p

In fact, SIGNALSEMA is executed each time a process leaves the critical section. It adds 1 to the *semaCounter*, DEQUEUEs the *head* of the *semaQueue* and applies MAKEREADY to it, so that this process can enter the critical section when it is scheduled next time. This explains the following definition, which works under the assumption that the read/write access to *semaCount* is exclusive.

$\textsc{SignalSema}(s) =$
  $\textbf{let } newcount = semaCount(s) + 1$
    $semaCount(s) := newcount$
    $\textbf{if } newcount \geq 0 \textbf{ then}$ -- still some free place in critical section
      $\textbf{let } h = head(semaQueue(s))$
        $\textsc{Dequeue}(h, semaQueue(s))$
        $\textsc{MakeReady}(h)$ -- to enter critical section

It turns out that to refine $\textsc{SyncSend}_{Ctl}$ and $\textsc{SyncReceive}_{Ctl}$ *binary sema-phores* (often also called *mutual exclusion* or *mutex* semaphores) suffice. They permit at most one process at any time in their critical section (*allowed* = 1). The refinement idea is to replace the *status*-control by binary semaphore moves as follows:

- To synchronize with the *dest*ination process for a message exchange, the sender records the message and throws the ball to the *dest*ination process via a $\textsc{WaitSema}(insema_{dest})$ move for an $insema_{dest}$ semaphore. Via this semaphore the receiver controls the permission, given at any time to at most one process, to write to its $inbox(dest)$.
- The receiver via a $\textsc{SignalSema}(insema_{dest})$ move throws the ball back to the sender. This handshaking is combined with a $\textsc{WaitSema}(outsema_{dest})$ move, which makes the receiver wait for the actual message delivery by the sender.
- The handshaking $\textsc{SignalSema}$ move by the receiver makes the sender ready to deliver the message.
- Simultaneously the sender throws the $outsema_{dest}$-ball back to the receiver by a $\textsc{SignalSema}(outsema_{dest})$ move. This makes also the receiver ready again.

To let this work, differently from the default initial value, both semaphores $insema_{dest}$ and $outsema_{dest}$ are initialized by 0, so that the next $\textsc{WaitSema}$-action blocks the current process.

$\textsc{SyncSend}_{Sema}(m, \textbf{to } dest) =$
  $\textbf{par}$
    $\textsc{RecordMsg}(m, \textbf{to } dest)$
    $\textsc{WaitSema}(insema(dest))$
  $\textbf{step}$
    $\textbf{par}$
      $\textsc{DeliverMsgFromTo}(\textbf{self}, dest)$
      $\textsc{SignalSema}(outsema(dest))$

$\textsc{SyncReceive}_{Sema} =$
  $\textsc{SignalSema}(insema(\textbf{self}))$
  $\textsc{WaitSema}(outsema(\textbf{self}))$

Here we use a new construct **step** which formalizes stepwise execution. It is presented in the next section.

As reported in [85], Iain Craig has implemented the above algorithm for semaphore-based message exchange (in C) to validate by experiments that it correctly realizes synchronous message passing. Such encodings, where the ASM model plays the role of a specification, represent one possibility to make ASM models executable.[13]

Exercise 37. Adapt the proof that SYNCCOMM_{Ctl} satisfies the *SyncMsg-PassingRe*quirements (Sect. 4.4.3.1) to prove that also SYNCCOMM_{Sema} satisfies these requirements.

4.5 Integrating Sequential Control into Parallel Execution

In this section we investigate how to incorporate some common sequential control concepts into the parallel computation model of ASMs. We use basic ASMs to bootstrap two operators, one for an interruptible (Sect. 4.5.1) and one for an atomic (Sect. 4.5.2) execution of a sequence of steps. In Sect. 4.5.3 we bootstrap an **await** construct for use in concurrent ASMs. The reader who is not particularly interested in ASM details may skip the section.

Differently from most programming languages, ASMs offer as explicit basic control construct only **if then** (besides the weak form of sequentialization expressible by **let**). This is motivated by the ground model concern explained in Sect. 1.1 wherefore the modeling language should be at the same time

- *most expressive* (to be usable in the potentially unlimited variety of application domains) but *tiny* (to be easy to define and to implement),
- *precise* (to avoid ambiguities) but *simple* (to be easy to learn, to understand and to work with in practice).

'Most general' expressivity turned out to be a question not of offering a variety of specific control and data types, but of the generality of states and of the actions to manipulate them. Computational states in this general sense have been identified as structures (sets of 'objects' with predicates and functions defined on them) by a variety of state-based specification frameworks.[14] The characteristics of the ASM method is that ASMs not only have structures as states, but also compute structures directly, treating their members (both objects *and* functions f) as first-class citizens, which one can update

---

[13] For two early examples see the C^{++} refinements for the Production Cell ASM in [185] and for the (stepwise developed) constrained shortest path ASM in [235]. Another possibility is to use compilers (see [65] for an example used in an industrial project).

[14] Besides ASMs most notably by B [1], Event-B [2], TLA [173], VDM [152], Z [153].

directly (coding-free) by assignments $f(t_1, \ldots, t_n) := t$ at the given level of abstraction.[15]

On the one side, this generality permits to proceed by bootstrapping to custom-tailor, by appropriate ASM constructs, whatever specific control structures one may wish to use, to simplify the formulation of control-intensive abstract models. On the other side, the introduction of new constructs into the ASM language is a ridge walk between expressivity and simplicity: more features are added more specialistic (and possibly baroque) a system becomes. Furthermore, in particular sequential control reveals a difficult problem related to the question of what is a computational 'step', which is a matter of level of abstraction and refinement. Firing what we call a *BasicRule*—the ASM rules defined in Chap. 2—appears as one atomic step, but when refined its execution may require $n > 1$ steps (see Fig. 2.17). See for example OPENGATE which appears as one step in Fig. 2.8, but represents two steps in the refinement in Fig. 2.9. Breaking down atomic steps into atomic substeps necessitates specifying some execution order, which is not always as easy as in Fig. 2.17. Traditionally, this problem is resolved by complex program counter based techniques (see [176, Chap. 17]) from which we want to abstract.

Therefore, we define here only a small number of additional ASM constructs, which explicitly model some widely used schemes ('patterns') for the ordering of to-be-executed rules. We consider mainly sequential ordering, given that parallelism is the default in the ASM computation model. We specify these control flow schemes in terms of simple ASMs, to illustrate how to custom-tailor ASMs to desired features (bootstrapping). [16]

The $(1, n)$-refinement type triggers the question whether the details of the n refined atomic steps should be hidden, to keep the atomic 1-step view of a *rule*, or whether their stepwise execution at the refine level of abstraction should be made visible. We mentioned this issue already at the end of Sect. 2.1.3, in the context of the flowchart representation of ASMs. The modeling experience with ASMs confirms that both ways can be useful, depending on the context where the *rule* is used and on the purpose of the model it represents. Therefore, we consider two instances for sequential execution, together with the related iteration and guarded iteration ('while') constructs. One instance defines an atomic view of sequential execution (the resulting machines are known as *turbo ASMs*), the other one an interruptible non-atomic one.

For the sequential composition of two ASMs P and Q the first version (Sect. 4.5.2) is denoted P **seq** Q. Its execution is interpreted as *one atomic step* which as a consequence is not interruptible and not reacting to monitored

---

[15] This is theoretically confirmed by the proofs (from corresponding postulates) for various forms of the so-called ASM Thesis, see the extensive bibliography of the rich literature on the subject in the recent paper [220].

[16] For a CoreASM-based specification and implementation of one parameterized generic control construct see [233, 247].

events after the (internally sequentialized) computation started. The second version (Sect. 4.5.1) is denoted $\textbf{stepwise}(P_1, \ldots, P_n)$ and called *StepRule* where P_i are already defined ASMs. In case of two arguments we use also the infix notation $P \textbf{ step } Q$ for $\textbf{stepwise}(P, Q))$. The execution is interpreted as being performed in (at least) n steps, where at each step of the computation an interruption or failure may occur and monitored locations may be read again. Both versions may be displayed also with a vertical notation of their arguments, as for $\textbf{par}$. We now define the behavior of these constructs.

4.5.1 Stepwise Composed Submachines

Obviously we want to define the stepwise composition construct in such a way that the usual properties one expects for sequential execution are satisfied, namely that $\textbf{skip}$ behaves as a neutral element (but counts as a step) and that the operation is associative. Furthermore we want to make the rule-after-rule execution of the arguments of $\textbf{stepwise}(P_1, \ldots, P_n)$ be compatible with the default parallel execution model for ASMs, keeping the atomicity of 'steps' at each considered level of abstraction. Additionally, we want to achieve the *compositionality of stepwise refinement*: if $\textbf{stepwise}(P_1, \ldots, P_m)$ refines P and $\textbf{stepwise}(Q_1, \ldots, Q_n)$ refines Q, then $P \textbf{ step } Q$ should be refined by $\textbf{stepwise}(P_1, \ldots, P_m, Q_1, \ldots, Q_n)$.

Obviously we want to extend ASMs also in a conservative way, implying that a rule P without occurrences of $\textbf{stepwise}$ yields its update set $U = Upd(P, S)$ in a given state S (under a given interpretation ζ of the freely occurring variables we usually suppress notationally) the same way as defined for traditional ASMs.[17]

To ease the definition of yields($\textbf{stepwise}(P_1, \ldots, P_n), \mathfrak{A}, \zeta, U$), we flatten the occurrences of $\textbf{stepwise}$-arguments in an ASM by repeatedly applying the following preprocessing steps as long as possible.

Flattening of nested stepwise occurrences.

- Each call rule occurrence $N(exp_1, \ldots, exp_m)$ with defining body

    $$N(x_1, \ldots, x_m) = \textbf{stepwise}(P_1, \ldots, P_n)$$

    is replaced by an occurrence of

    $$\textbf{stepwise}(P_1(exp_1, \ldots, exp_m), \ldots, P_n(exp_1, \ldots, exp_m))$$

- In each occurrence of $\textbf{stepwise}(P_1, \ldots, P_n)$ each P_i which is of form $\textbf{stepwise}(P_{i,1}, \ldots, P_{i,m_i})$ is replaced by the sequence $P_{i,1}, \ldots, P_{i,m_i}$ of its arguments.

---

[17] We remind the reader that due to the $\textbf{choose}$ construct, P may yield more than one update set $U = Upd(P, S, \zeta)$ in a given state S with given ζ, so that $Upd(P, S, \zeta)$, also written $[\![P]\!]_\zeta^S$, is a function only if P is $\textbf{choose}$-free. See [76] for the detailed definition of the relation yields($P, \mathfrak{A}, \zeta, U$).

As a result, we obtain from a given ASM M a machine $flatten(M)$ in which every $StepRule$ occurrence $\textbf{stepwise}(P_1, \ldots, P_n)$ satisfies that its components P_i (or their defining body in case P_i is a call rule) begin with a construct of an ASM that is not a $StepRule$. We call such machines $Flattened$ (with respect to $\textbf{stepwise}$). For each occurrence of a $Flattened$ $StepRule$ $P = \textbf{stepwise}(P_1, \ldots, P_n)$ (in an ASM M), we define its static $initialStepList(P)$ as $[P_1, \ldots, P_n]$ (with respect to the implicit parameter M we notationally suppress). We use a dynamic function $stepList(P)$ to direct the stepwise control flow in executing a $StepRule$. It is assumed to be initialized by $initialStepList(P)$ as part of the initialization of M.

Bootstrapped interpreter rule for stepwise$(P_1, \ldots, P_n)$. An 'execution round' of a $Flattened$ ASM $P = \textbf{stepwise}(P_1, \ldots, P_n)$ applies the following rule until its $stepList(P)$ becomes empty (in which case it is reinitialized). Due to preprocessing, the arguments P_i of $stepList(P)$ are not $StepRules$, so that by induction their yields-relation is already defined. We extend this relation now inductively to $\textbf{stepwise}(P_1, \ldots, P_n)$.

A sequential execution step in state S yields the update set produced in state S by the $head$ of the current $stepList$-value and an additional singleton update set $StepListUpd$ of the $stepList$, which determines the next sequential execution step. In shorthand notation this reads as follows and is defined more accurately in the STEPEXECRULE rule below:

$$Upd(\textbf{stepwise}(P_1, \ldots, P_n), S) = Upd(head(stepl), S) \cup StepListUpd$$
$$\textbf{where } stepl = eval(stepList(\textbf{stepwise}(P_1, \ldots, P_n)), S)$$

Formally the $StepListUpd$ is a pair of a) the location $(stepList, P)$, where P is the given $StepRule$ occurrence $P = \textbf{stepwise}(P_1, \ldots, P_n)$, and b) the new value for this location. This new value is the $tail$ of the current value of $stepList(P)$, in case this $tail$ is not empty. Otherwise, it is the $initialStepList(P)$, which makes P ready for the next stepwise P-execution round.

> STEPEXECRULE =
>   let $P = \textbf{stepwise}(P_1, \ldots, P_n)$
>   let $stepl = eval(stepList(P), \mathfrak{A}, \zeta)$
>   if yields$(head(stepl), S, \zeta, U)$ then
>   yields$(P, S, \zeta, U \cup StepListUpd)$
>   where
> $$StepListUpd = \begin{cases} \{((stepList, P), tail(stepl))\} & \textbf{if } tail(stepl) \neq [] \\ \{((stepList, P), [P_1, \ldots, P_n])\} & \textbf{else} \end{cases}$$

Correctness of the stepwise refinement pattern. If P is correctly refined by $\textbf{stepwise}(P_1, \ldots, P_{m+1})$ and $\textbf{stepwise}(Q_1, \ldots, Q_{n+1})$ correctly refines Q, then $\textbf{stepwise}(P_1, \ldots, P_{m+1}, Q_1, \ldots, Q_{n+1})$ correctly refines P **step** Q.

Exercise 38. Prove the correctness of the stepwise refinement pattern (see the definition of refinement correctness in Sect. 2.5).

Fig. 4.10 Flowchart for **stepwise**$(M_1, \ldots, M_n)$ with step-free M_i

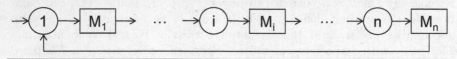

Exercise 39. Rewrite the ASM in Fig. 2.20 using the **stepwise** construct.

Exercise 40. Think about how to refine STEPEXECRULE to include also a break-statement for *StepRules*.

Exercise 41. Formulate in which sense for step-free ASMs M_i, executions of **stepwise**$(M_o, \ldots, M_n)$ are equivalent to executions of the control state machine in Fig. 4.10. Prove the statement.[18]

Exercise 42. Explain why the control state machine in Fig. 4.10 is not equivalent to the control state machine in Fig. 4.11 where $M_i = $ **if** $cond_i$ **then** $rule_i$ (see the explanations at the end of Sect. 2.1.3).

Stepwise iteration pattern. Having the **stepwise** construct available the bounded iteration control construct can be defined as usual inductively:

$$(\textbf{iterate}^n_{stepwise} \ M) = \textbf{stepwise}(\underbrace{M, \ldots, M}_{n \text{ times}})$$

Similarly, one can model the idea underlying the stepwise-execution-interpretation of potentially infinite *guarded iterations*, say by machines $Q = \textbf{while}_{stepwise} \ Cond \ \textbf{do} \ P$ which we call *WhileRules*. When such a machine is called *onceMore*, it must CHECKCONDITION of the iteration. If *Cond* is true, it must EXECUTEBODY and set *onceMore* to false—to prevent a new *Cond* check before the stepwise execution of the body has terminated. Upon termination *onceMore* is reset to check the *Cond*ition once more, etc. The Boolean-valued local functions $onceMore_Q$ are different from each other, there is one for each occurrence Q of **while** $Cond$ **do** P (in a given ASM M). For notation simplicity we write nevertheless only *onceMore*. These functions are assumed to be initialized to *true* (as part of the initialization of M) and

---

[18] This control-state based version of the P **step** Q operator had been defined already in [49, Sect. 1.8].

Fig. 4.11 Flowchart for sequential step-free machines with visible guard

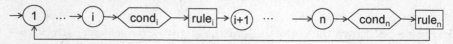

not to be updated in any other place than where indicated in the interpreter rule. We also write MARKEND for the occurrence MARKEND$_Q$. The following ASM bootstraps an interpreter for this behavior.

while$_{stepwise}$ *Cond* **do** $P =$
  if *onceMore* **then** CHECKCONDITION
    else EXECUTEBODY
  where
    CHECKCONDITION =
      if *Cond* **then**
        EXECUTEBODY
        onceMore := *false*
    EXECUTEBODY =
      stepwise(P, MARKEND)
    MARKEND = (*onceMore* := *true*)

To get WhileRules occurring as *stepList* element of a StepRule to be executed in the stepwise manner and not atomically, we must extend the definition of the STEPEXECRULE. Consider the case where, in the current *steplist* of a StepRule, *head*(*stepl*) is a WhileRule $Q =$ **while**$_{stepwise}$ *Cond* **do** P and *onceMore* is true but *Cond* evaluates to false. In this *SkipWhileCase* the execution of Q by STEPEXECRULE yields an empty update set. It terminates the stepwise execution of Q without entering the rule body P any more, so that the *StepListUpd* by STEPEXECRULE works well. Thus, for this case, it suffices to add to the STEPEXECRULE guard the following additional condition:

(**not** *WhileRule*(*head*(*stepl*))) **or** *SkipWhileCase*(*head*(*stepl*)) = *true*)

An additional rule is needed for each of the two cases that the stepwise execution of the WhileRule Q within a StepRule execution either enters or exits the body P.

SkipWhileCase(Q) iff
  $Q =$ **while**$_{stepwise}$ *Cond* **do** P
  and *onceMore* = *true* **and** *Cond* = *false*
EnterWhileCase(Q) iff
  $Q =$ **while**$_{stepwise}$ *Cond* **do** P
  and *onceMore* = *true* **and** *Cond* = *true*
ExitWhileCase(Q, S) iff
  $Q =$ **while**$_{stepwise}$ *Cond* **do** P **and** *StepRule*(S) **and**
  head(*stepList*(S)) = [MARKEND$_Q$]

To ease the definition below of the two refined StepRule interpreter rules, we flatten nested WhileRules by applying the following preprocessing step (to the given ASM M) as long as possible:

- Each occurrence

  $\textbf{while}_{stepwise}\ Cond_1\ \textbf{do}\ (\textbf{while}_{stepwise}\ Cond_2\ \textbf{do}\ R)$

  is replaced by an occurrence of

  $Q = \textbf{while}_{stepwise}\ Cond_1\ \textbf{and}\ Cond_2\ \textbf{do}\ R$

  with $onceMore_Q = (onceMore_1\ \textbf{and}\ onceMore_2)$

We denote the final result of applying the **stepwise** and **while** preprocessing steps to an initially given machine M again by the (refined) function $flatten(M)$. In $flatten(M)$ every WhileRule occurrence **while** $Cond$ **do** P satisfies that P is an ASM that is not a WhileRule, therefore either a BasicRule or a StepRule.[19]

Exercise 43. Show that $flatten(M)$ is a correct refinement of M.

Now we can define the STEPEXECWHILEENTRY rule. Let a WhileRule $Q = \textbf{while}_{stepwise}\ Cond\ \textbf{do}\ R$ be given which shows up in the *head* of the current *steplist* of a StepRule P. To enter its *flattened* body R **step** MARKEND which must be executed, the *initialStepList* is computed. The execution of the body starts with executing the first element in the computed step list. *onceMore* is updated to false, the *stepList(P)* is updated to the tail of the while-body step list (which is *concatenated* with the *tail(stepl)* if this tail is not empty). This is expressed by the following STEPEXECWHILEENTRY rule.

$\begin{aligned}
&\text{STEPEXECWHILEENTRY} = \\
&\quad \textbf{let } P = \textbf{stepwise}(P_1, \ldots, P_n) \\
&\quad \textbf{let } stepl = eval(stepList(P), S, \zeta) \\
&\quad \textbf{if } EnterWhileCase(head(stepl)) \textbf{ then} \\
&\qquad \textbf{let } Q = head(stepl) = \textbf{while}_{stepwise}\ Cond\ \textbf{do}\ R \\
&\qquad \textbf{let } [Q_1, \ldots, Q_m] = initialStepList(flatten(R\ \textbf{step}\ \text{MARKEND})) \\
&\qquad \textbf{if } yields(Q_1, S, \zeta, U) \textbf{ then} \\
&\qquad\quad yields(P, S, \zeta, U \cup \{(onceMore, false), ((stepList, P), val)\}) \\
&\quad \textbf{where } val = \\
&\quad concatenate([Q_2, \ldots, Q_m], tail(stepl)) \textbf{ if } tail(stepl) \neq [\,] \\
&\quad [Q_2, \ldots, Q_m] \textbf{ else}
\end{aligned}$

To exit the body of a WhileRule Q in the current *steplist* of a StepRule P, a MARKEND$_Q$ rule is executed. It updates *onceMore* to *true*, so that *Cond* is checked for another possible while round. For this to work, in the current $stepList(P)$, the head must be reinitialized by the WhileRule Q. This explains the following STEPEXECWHILEEXIT rule.

---

[19] Ambient ASMs can be considered as BasicRules.

STEPEXECWHILEEXIT =
   let $P = $ **stepwise**$(P_1, \ldots, P_n)$, $stepl = eval(stepList(P), S, \zeta)$
     if $head(stepl) = $ MARKEND$_Q$ **then**   -- $ExitWhileCase(Q, P) = true$
         yields$(P, S, \zeta, \{(onceMore, true), ((stepList, P), val)\})$
where
$$val = \begin{cases} concatenate([Q], tail(stepl)) & \text{if } tail(stepl) \neq [\,] \\ [Q] & \textbf{else} \end{cases}$$

4.5.2 Atomic Sequentially-Composed (Turbo) ASMs

The atomic sequential composition construct P **seq** Q for ASMs P, Q has been introduced in [73] to model recursive algorithms in a natural way in the ASM framework (see [45]). It provides a functional black-box view of the composed machine, hiding the internals of executing first P in state S and then Q in the resulting state $S + Upd(P, S)$ (if defined). Thus, the successor state computed by P **seq** Q from state S appears as obtained in one atomic step. To sequentially merge two update sets U and V we write $U \oplus V$, where updates in V may overwrite those of U. Should U be inconsistent, the merge keeps U so that in this case both $S + U$ and $S + (U \oplus V)$ are undefined.

Definition 10. The update set a step of P **seq** Q yields in a state S is defined by:

$$Upd(P \text{ seq } Q, S) = Upd(P, S) \oplus Upd(Q, S + Upd(P, S))$$

The sequential merge $U \oplus V$ of the updates in U followed by those of V is defined by:

$$U \oplus V = \begin{cases} \{(loc, val) \in U \mid loc \notin Locs(V)\} \cup V & \text{if } consistent(U) \\ U, & \text{otherwise} \end{cases}$$

Exercise 44. Show that **seq** is associative, that P **seq skip** and **skip seq** P are equivalent to P and that inconsistency is persistent for **seq**, i.e. if P leads to an inconsistent state, then also P **seq** Q.

Atomic iteration pattern. Finite iterations **iterate**$^n_{atomic}$ have the same definition as **iterate**$^n_{stepwise}$ with 'stepwise' replaced by 'atomic' and **step** by **seq**. For the unbounded **iterate**$^\infty_{atomic}$ it comes natural to consider as fixpoint those states where the update set becomes empty or inconsistent.

Definition 11. Let $R^n = $ **iterate**$^n_{atomic}$ R. $Upd($**iterate**$^\infty_{atomic}$ $R, S)$ is defined as $\lim_{n \to \infty} Upd(R^n, S)$, namely $Upd(R^n, S)$ for the first $n \geq 0$ (if there is some) such that one more application of R yields either $Upd(R, S_n) = \emptyset$ or $Inconsistent(Upd(R, S_n))$ for the state S_n reached by R^n.

In the ASM literature it has become customary to write **iterate** instead of **iterate**$^\infty_{atomic}$.

Exercise 45. Show that **iterate**$^{\infty}_{atomic}$ R is well-defined, i.e. emptiness or inconsistency of $Upd(R, S_n)$ for some state S_n reached by n atomic iterations R^n of R implies that $Upd(R^{n+1}, S) = Upd(R^m, S)$ for all $m \geq n + 1$.

Using unbounded atomic iteration one can define an atomic view of *while* which repeats the execution of its body P as long as it yields a non-empty update set whose application provides a state in which *cond*ition still holds:

$$\textbf{while}_{atomic} \; Cond \; \textbf{do} \; P = \textbf{iterate}^{\infty}_{atomic} \; (\textbf{if} \; Cond \; \textbf{then} \; P).$$

Analogously, calling a named recursive ASM $P(a_1, \ldots, a_n)$—a machine with declaration $P(x_1, \ldots, x_n) = body$ where *body* contains some occurrence(s) of $P(t_1, \ldots, t_n)$—yields a result only if the chain of nested calls of the rule body is finite and its basis yields a well-defined result. This supports the intuitive understanding of recursion.[20]

Definition 12. A *turbo ASM* is any ASM which can be obtained from basic ASMs (including named rules) by applying finitely often the **seq** or **iterate**$^{\infty}_{atomic}$ operator.[21]

Turbo ASMs provide an interesting example of ASM refinement if their black-box view is compared to the micro-steps view. A micro-step is either a basic ASM step (yielding an update set) or a step encapsulated in a **seq** component or a submachine call, see [121]. Turbo ASMs also have an interesting logic tailored for proving their properties, see [230]. We show in Sect. 4.5.3 that control state ASMs whose submachines are turbo ASMs are equivalent to programs in the ^+CAL language [175] for specifying concurrent algorithms.

Exercise 46. (Structured programming theorem [32]) Consider turbo ASMs whose non-controlled functions are one 0-ary input function *in*, one 0-ary output function *out* and the static initial number theoretic functions of recursion theory: $S(x) = x + 1$, $U^n_i(x_1, \ldots, x_n) = x_i$, $C^n_i(x_1, \ldots, x_n) = i$, $notZero(x)$ **iff** $x \neq 0$. Restrict runs to those where initially all dynamic functions except *in* are undefined, where the *in*put is determined by the initial state (i.e. does not change during the run) and where the first update of *out*put determines the final state. Show that every partial recursive (i.e. Turing computable) function can be computed by such runs of these restricted turbo ASMs (also called Böhm-Jacopini machines). See [76, Sect. 4.1.2].

Structured ASM example. Here is an example of a 'structured ASM', i.e. an ASM which uses the sequential constructs **step** (or **seq**) and the

---

[20] See the close correspondence between turbo ASMs and ALGOL60 analyzed in [177].
[21] When using turbo ASMs it is usually assumed that during the execution of any turbo operator component as part of an 'atomic' step, the monitored and shared functions are not updated externally. This is to make the behavioral analysis feasible.

corresponding **while** construct. An instance of this algorithm will be useful in Sect. 9.1, page 300.

Let a finite directed graph $(Node, Edge)$ be given with disjoint union of $Node = PrimaryNode \cup SecondaryNode$. For a primary node p we want to check whether, starting at p, a loop of secondary nodes can be found, i.e. a sequence $n_1, \ldots, n_k$ of connected secondary nodes $n_i \in SecondaryNode$ with $(n_i, n_{i+1}) \in Edge$ (for $1 \leq i < k$), $(p, n_1) \in Edge$ and some $1 \leq l < l' \leq k$ with $n_l = n_{l'}$. Loops among primary nodes are permitted.

The algorithm starts with p as *ToBeChecked* node. For each *ToBeChecked* node it visits all secondary directly connected (called 'secondary successor') nodes *succ* and a) checks whether one of them has been visited already—in that case a loop has been found and the search procedure is *Terminated*—and b) makes all of them *Visited* and *ToBeChecked*, to continue the procedure until it is *Terminated*, either because a loop has been found or because there is no *ToBeChecked* node any more. For termination purposes a *ToBeChecked* node, once it has been chosen, is DELETEd from that set (except if happens to be one of its own *SecondarySuccessors*).

The following ASM is yet another example for how one can 'paraphrase' the verbal explanations of an algorithm line by line by an ASM, thereby establishing a 'direct' correspondence between intuitive and mathematically precise terms which permits a satisfactory justification of ground model 'correctness' (see Sect. 1.1). In the formal definition we write **while** because the algorithm works for both versions, **while**$_{atomic}$ and **while**$_{stepwise}$.

CHECKFORSECONDARYLOOP(p) =   -- for $p \in PrimaryNode$
  INITIALIZEFOR(p) **seq**
    while not *Terminated*
      choose *node* $\in$ *ToBeChecked*   -- initially p is *ToBeChecked*
        forall *succ* $\in$ *SecondarySuccessor*(*node*)
          if *succ* $\in$ *Visited* **then**   -- *succ* appears for the second time
            Terminated := *true*   -- terminates because loop detected
            loopfree(p) := *false*
          INSERT(*succ*, *Visited*)   -- mark *succ* as *Visited*
          INSERT(*succ*, *ToBeChecked*)   -- apply procedure also to *succ*
          if *node* $\notin$ *SecondarySuccessor*(*node*)
            then DELETE(*node*, *ToBeChecked*)
        ifnone *Terminated* := *true*   -- no loop detected
  where
    INITIALIZEFOR(p) =
      ToBeChecked := $\{p\}$ -- start procedure with p
      Visited := $\emptyset$
      Terminated := *false*
      loopfree(p) := *true*   -- will be updated when a loop is found
    SecondarySuccessor(*node*) =
      $\{$*succ* $\in$ *SecondaryNode* $\mid$ (*node*, *succ*) $\in$ *Edge*$\}$

Exercise 47. Justify why CHECKFORSECONDARYLOOP(p) 'correctly' computes the secondary loop freeness property.

Incorporating data and resource concerns into ASM control flow patterns can be done in a uniform way by instantiating the stepwise executed or iterated abstract components P with concrete updates $f(t_1, \ldots, t_n) := t$ and concrete expressions $t_1, \ldots, t_n, t$. For modeling business processes or (web) services, where this is a central concern, we illustrate this further in Chap. 5. It can be seen also from Sect. 4.4 where, to integrate data, it suffices to add considering the content of messages the formulation of communication patterns abstracts from.

4.5.3 Control Construct await in Concurrent ASMs

In this section we define an **await** control construct for ASMs (Sect. 4.5.3.1). We illustrate its use by a definition of the semantics of ^{+}CAL [175] programs in terms of concurrent control state ASMs with turbo ASM submachines (Sect. 4.5.3.2). The section elaborates the definition given in [6].

4.5.3.1 Definition of await for ASMs

In a sequential programming context an **await** *Cond* statement can be programmed as

  (**while not** *Cond* **do skip**) **step** *NextStatement*.

To determine the *NextStatement* in a parallel execution context without a program counter, a more involved definition of the scope of the blocking effect of **await** is needed. The question is whether (and if yes then which) machines that run in parallel with **await** *Cond* should be blocked. There are various options to answer this question. We formulate here three answers to illustrate the flexibility of the ASM modeling method.

The definition in [6] provides a 'global' interpretation which we distinguish by an index g: any **await**$_g$ *Cond* **do** P rule occurring in a machine M may block M. More precisely, in an ASM M the execution of any **await**$_g$ *Cond* **do** P subrule in a state $\mathfrak{A}$ where *Cond* evaluates to false yields an update of a *status* function to value *wait*. In this way, the application of the update set U of the entire machine M to form its next (internal) state $\mathfrak{A} + U$ is blocked until all **await**$_g$ *conditions* in M evaluate again to true (due to changes of monitored or shared locations by actions of concurrently executing agents[22]).

---

[22] As example consider that an **await**$_g$ *Cond* P is one of the rules in the **then** branch M_1 of $M = $ **if** *guard* **then** M_1 **else** M_2, but none in the **else** branch. If in state S the *guard* of M is true, *status* = *run* and *Cond* is false, then executing **await**$_g$ *Cond* P as

Where from the context it is clear which operation is meant, we write the modified $+_{wait} U$ operation again as $+U$. The 0-ary function $status$ is assumed to be initialized by run.

Definition 13 (global await). For the 'global' semantics of **await** we extend the update set yielding relation for the new rules **await** $Cond$ **do** P. For succinctness we use the functional notation. We also extend the next-internal-state operation to $+_{status}$ though we write again $+$ where possible without risking confusion. For any ASM M and every occurrence **await**$_g$ $Cond$ **do** P of a rule in M we define:

$$[\![\textbf{await}_g \ Cond \ \textbf{do} \ P]\!]_\zeta^\mathfrak{A} = \begin{cases} [\![P]\!]_\zeta^\mathfrak{A} & \text{if } eval(Cond, \mathfrak{A}, \zeta) = \text{true} \\ \{(status, wait)\} \ \textbf{else} & \text{-- block the run} \end{cases}$$

if $yield(M, \mathfrak{A}, \zeta, U)$ **then**
    if $(status, wait) \notin U$ **then** $\mathfrak{A} +_{status} U = \mathfrak{A} + U + \{(status, run)\}$
    else $\mathfrak{A} +_{status} U = \mathfrak{A} + \{(status, wait)\}$ -- block the run

A problem with this definition is that its combination with sequential constructs produces undesirable effects, due to the discrepancy of the scoping disciplines. Consider a step of **await**$_g$ $Cond$ **do** $(P$ **step** $Q)$ in a state where $Cond$ is true and where the execution of P makes $Cond$ false. In this case the execution of Q is again blocked by **await**$_g$ $Cond$.

A step-compatible variation of the global interpretation can be obtained by treating **await** $Cond$ as a rule (which we distinguish by an index s), playing the role of an 'instruction' of the language, and composing it sequentially with P:

Definition 14 (step-compatible await). For a **step**-compatible **await** semantics **await**$_s$ $Cond$ is treated as a rule which is composed sequentially with its scope. The definition of $+_{status}$ is taken unchanged from Def. 13.

$$\textbf{await}_s \ Cond \ \textbf{do} \ P = (\textbf{await}_s \ Cond) \ \textbf{step} \ P$$

$$[\![\textbf{await}_s \ Cond]\!]_\zeta^\mathfrak{A} = \begin{cases} \emptyset & \text{if } eval(Cond, \mathfrak{A}, \zeta) = \text{true} \\ \{(status, wait)\} \ \textbf{else} & \text{-- block the run} \end{cases}$$

With this definition, once the execution of **await**$_s$ $Cond$ **do** $(P$ **step** $Q)$ enters P, this occurrence of **await**$_s$ $Cond$ is not executed any more until the execution of Q is terminated. But an **await**$_s$ $Cond$ in another parallel rule can still block the execution of P **step** Q.

The remedy is a 'local' interpretation of **await** $Cond$ **do** P, which blocks only the execution of its scope rule P. To achieve this one needs a) a local function $status_{Cond,P}$ for each occurrence of an **await** $Cond$ and its scope P,

---

part of executing M_1 triggers the blocking effect for M (not only for M_1) by setting $status := wait$. If due to updates made by the environment of M in the next state $guard$ changes to false, then **await**$_g$ $Cond$ P is not called for execution any more, so that the blocking effect disappears by setting $status := run$.

and b) a scope exit mechanism. The function $status_{Cond,P}$ remains with its initial value *wait* if **await** *Cond* is called when *Cond* evaluates to false, it is set to *run* otherwise. Upon scope exit, it is reset to its initial value *wait* by a hidden scope delimiter statement **endawait**, which is inserted at the end of the scope P for the definition of its update set.

Definition 15 (local await). For a scope-determined 'local' **await** semantics, for each occurrence of **await** *Cond* with scope P let $status_{Cond,P}$ be a dedicated 0-ary function (initialized by *wait*). Let **endawait** $_{Cond,P}$ a delimiter statement which is automatically inserted as step after P to signal the termination of P.

$$[\![\textbf{await } Cond \textbf{ do } P]\!]^{\mathfrak{A}}_{\zeta} =$$
$$\begin{cases} \emptyset & \text{if } status_{Cond,P} = wait \text{ and } [\![Cond]\!]^{\mathfrak{A}}_{\zeta} = false \\ \{(status_{Cond,P}, run)\} & \text{if } status_{Cond,P} = wait \text{ and } [\![Cond]\!]^{\mathfrak{A}}_{\zeta} = true \\ [\![P']\!]^{\mathfrak{A}}_{\zeta} & \text{if } status_{Cond,P} = run \end{cases}$$
$$\quad \textbf{where } P' = (P \textbf{ step endawait}_{Cond,P})$$
$$[\![\textbf{endawait}_{Cond,P}]\!]^{\mathfrak{A}}_{\zeta} = \{(status_{Cond,P}, wait)\}$$

With this definition, each **await** *Cond* **do** *P* rule in an ASM M yields in every state $\mathfrak{A}$ an update set it contributes to the update set U of M by which the next (internal) state $\mathfrak{A} + U$ is determined, as usual; no modification $+_{status}$ (as in Def. 13) is needed any more. This update set contains only updates of its local variable $status_{Cond,P}$, in case the *status* control of the construct depending on the evaluation of *Cond* switches to *wait* or *run*. In case of $status = run$ the update set is the one the scope P yields, possibly with sequentially controlled component machines.

Which one of the three versions for the semantics of an **await** construct in the ASM framework to adopt depends on the application. In the next section we rely upon the local version (Def. 15).

4.5.3.2 ASM Interpretation of ^+CAL Programs

^+CAL has been proposed in [175] as a high-level programming notation for defining concurrent processes. In this section we show that the semantics of ^+CAL programs can be defined by control state ASMs with turbo submachines. More precisely, since the considered concurrency model for multiprocesses is interleaving [174, p. 26], using the INTERLEAVINGPATTERN of Sect. 2.4.3 and ambient ASMs (to encapsulate single-process computation as explained in Sect. 4.2.2), one can easily construct an interpreter for concurrent runs of families of ^+CAL programs out of an interpreter for single ^+CAL programs (Exerc. 48).

The ^+CAL language combines sequential control (indicated by the semicolon) with aggregation of sequences of sequential steps into one atomic step. To qualify instruction sequences as atomic they are enclosed by labels. Thus, one can define as *atomic step* each "control path that starts at a label, ends at a label, and passes through no other labels" (op. cit., p. 19). This allows us to associate with each ^{+}CAL program body[23] P a flowchart $dgm(P)$. It represents a control state ASM $asm(P)$ with turbo ASM submachines, which defines the behavior of P. Each label in P is interpreted as a *concurrent control state*, the other control states in $dgm(P)$ (which are linked by semicolons) are called *sequential control states*. The atomic ^{+}CAL program steps are represented by turbo ASM steps.

We leave it as Exerc. 48 to define an interpreter out of such an association of $asm(stm)$ (or equivalently tits flowchart representation $dgm(stm)$) with any ^{+}CAL statement stm.

^{+}CAL statements are composed out of basic *stms*—assign statements or **skip**—applying the following constructs:

- sequencing (denoted by ;),
- the classical structured programming constructs **if then else**, **while**,
- the **await** construct (called **when**),
- two nondeterminism constructs,
- statements to call or return from subprograms.

Since statements can be labeled, also **goto** l statements are included in the language. They correspond to updates of *ctl_state* (to arrows in $dgm(stm)$).

Therefore the association of $dgm(P)$ with any ^{+}CAL program body P can be defined recursively, as we do now.

An **assignment** statement in ^{+}CAL is a finite sequence

$$stm = lhs_1 := exp_1 \ || \ldots || \ lhs_n := exp_n \ ;$$

of assignments, executed by "first evaluating the right-hand sides of all its assignments, and then performing those assignments from left to right". This behavior is that of the following ASM, where the expression evaluation is performed in parallel for all expressions in the current state, whereafter the assignment of the computed values is done in sequence.

$$asm(lhs_1 := exp_1 \ || \ldots || \ lhs_n := exp_n \ ; \ ) =$$
$$\textbf{forall } 1 \leq i \leq n \textbf{ let } x_i = exp_i$$
$$lhs_1 := x_1 \textbf{ seq} \ldots \textbf{ seq } lhs_n := x_n$$

The behavior of **goto** l ; statements is to "end the execution of the current step and causes control to go to the statement labeled l" [174, p. 25], so that one can define $asm(\textbf{goto } l \ ;) = (ctl\_state := l)$.

The **when** *Cond*; statement in ^{+}CAL translates to **await** *Cond* (see Def. 15). As visual representation we use the triangle in Fig. 4.12, the right half ('yes exit') of the traditional rhomb representation for check points in an FSM flowchart.

---

[23] We disregard the declarations in the translation.

Fig. 4.12 Flowchart diagram for **await** *Cond* [6]

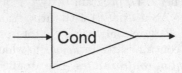

We skip the standard diagrams to translate structured programming constructs.

The non deterministic statement

either M_1 **or** M_2 **or** ... **or** M_n;

means to choose an executable (i. e. *Enabled*) out of finitely many statements. It is defined to be executable if and only if one of M_i is executable so that the execution of this statement has a blocking character. Similarly, the non deterministic statement **with** $id \in S$ **do** M; means to choose an element in a set S if there is one and to execute M for it. The statement is considered as not executable, thus blocking, if the set to choose from is empty. Therefore we use the **await** construct, to execute **choose** only when there is something to choose from.

This leads to the following translation, which is pictorially represented in Fig. 4.13.

$$asm(\textbf{either } M_1 \textbf{ or } M_2 \textbf{ or } ... \textbf{ or } M_n;) =$$
$$\quad \textbf{await forsome } 1 \leq k \leq n \; Enabled(M_k) \textbf{ do}$$
$$\quad\quad \textbf{choose } i \in \{k \mid Enabled(M_k) \textbf{ and } 1 \leq k \leq n\}$$
$$\quad\quad\quad asm(M_i)$$
$$asm(\textbf{with } id \in S \textbf{ do } M;) =$$
$$\quad \textbf{await } S \neq \emptyset \textbf{ do}$$
$$\quad\quad \textbf{choose } x \in S$$
$$\quad\quad\quad asm(M(x))$$

The remaining ^{+}CAL statements deal with procedure call and return in a standard stack machine like manner. For the sake of completeness we provide some details for the translation.

In this context *frames* are quadruples consisting of a control state, the values of the procedure's arguments, the values of its local variables, and the procedure name. We denote the current frame by (*ctl_state, args, locals, proc*). *stack* denotes the frame stack. Executing a call statement $P(expr_1, ..., expr_n)$; "assigns the current values of the expressions $expr_i$ to the corresponding parameters $param_i$, initializes the procedure's local variables, and puts control at the beginning of the procedure body", which "must begin with a labeled statement" [174, p. 27]. As preparation for the return statement one has also to record the current frame on the frame *stack*.

Fig. 4.13 Flowcharts for ^+CAL choice statements [6]
© 2009 Springer-Verlag Berlin Heidelberg, reprinted with permission

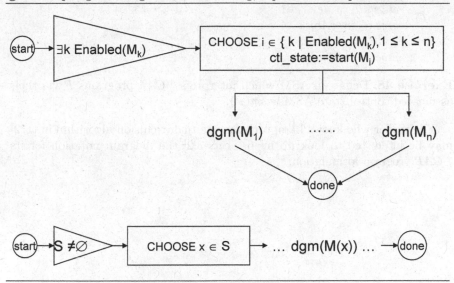

$locVars(P)$ denotes the sequence of local variables of P, $initVal$ their initial values. For the sake of brevity, for sequences $locs$ of locations and $vals$ of values, we write $locs := vals$ for the simultaneous component-wise assignment of the values to the corresponding locations, to be precise for the machine $asm(locs_1 := vals_1 \| \ldots \| locs_n := vals_n\ ;)$ defined above, where $locs = (locs_1, \ldots, locs_n)$ and $vals = (vals_1, \ldots, vals_n)$. Let $start_P$ denote the label of the first statement of P. This explains the following translation.

$asm(P(exps)) =$ -- translation of procedure calls
   PUSHFRAME$(P, exps)$
where
   PUSHFRAME$(P, exps) =$
     $stack :=$ PUSH$(stack, (ctl\_state, args, locals, proc))$
                      -- push current frame on top of the stack
     $ctl\_state := start_P$ -- start execution of the procedure body
     $args := eval(exps, currState)$ -- pass the call parameters
     $locals := initVal(locVars(P))$ -- initialize the local variables
     $proc := P$ -- update the to be executed program

A return statement consists in the inverse machine POPFRAME. If ctl is the point of a call statement in the given program, let $next(ctl)$ denote the point immediately following the call statement. Then one can define the following translation.

$asm(return) =$
   let $(ctl, prevArgs, prevLocs, callingProc) = \text{POP}(stack)$ **in**
      $ctl\_state := next(ctl)$ -- go to next stm after the call stm
      $args := prevArgs$ -- reassign previous values to args
      $locals := prevLocs$ -- reassign previous values to locals
      $proc := callingProc$ -- continue executing the caller program

Exercise 48. Define an ASM which interprets ^{+}CAL programs P via their associated control state ASMs $asm(P)$.

The reader who knows Lamport's fast mutual exclusion algorithm in [172] may be interested to look up in [6, Sect. 3.2] the diagram notation for its ^{+}CAL program formulation.

Chapter 5
Modeling Business Processes

In this chapter we illustrate the use of ASMs in the area of business process modeling (BPM). In the current status of this field a practical method to start the development of business processes (BPs) with accurate, well-understood and fully documented ground models is particularly important, even more than in traditional software engineering. There are two major reasons for this:

- The multitude of stakeholders—BP analysts and operators on the process design and management side, IT technologists and programmers on the implementation side, and last but not least users. They come with rather different background, expertise, language, interest in and understanding of 'processes'.[1]
- The dependency of BP behavior on a multitude of decisions and actions by different kinds of actors. The 'actors' range from software executing computers over technical equipment to communication protocols and human operators whose interactions affect the behavior of the BP.

In Sect. 5.1 we use ASMs to define a web service modeling pattern which emerged from commercial applications at SAP.[2] In Sect. 5.2 we define a business-process-specific class of ASM net diagrams and their execution semantics. These diagrams offer a practical, accurate integration of textual

---

[1] See the two ground model and model refinement concerns (Sect. 1) : a) BPMs should come with a minimal 'semantical distance to human understanding' [110, Sect. 1, p. 1] and 'improve communication among diverse stakeholders about the operations and processes of a business' [148, p. 2]; b) BPMs should be 'actionable, in the sense that there is a relatively direct path from the specification to an implementation of running systems' [148, p. 4], in other words their implementation 'should allow propagating the information from a value chain perspective to a software-development perspective in a coherent and consistent way' to provide an effective "end-to-end control ... to build process-managed enterprise" [110, Sect. 2, pp. 3–4].

[2] For modeling the infrastructure of web applications with ASMs we refer the reader to the literature [125, 48].

(data-oriented) and graphical (control-flow oriented) yet semantically rigorously defined descriptive means. ASM net diagrams can be used to provide a rigorous framework for and to enhance the Guard-State-Milestone approach recently developed for BPM at IBM (Sect. 5.2.1). In Sect. 5.2.2 we use ASM net diagrams to specify the communication scheme of the user-centric Subject-Oriented Business Process Modeling (S-BPM) method [109]. The resulting ground model served as blueprint for the commercial implementation of the S-BPM Workflow Engines [187, 180, 181]. This example offers the occasion to illustrate how ASM refinements support modeling for change in practice. We develop the ground model ASM step by step, each time refining the previously defined model, trying to capture the additional requirements which were presented only piecemeal, each time after the presentation of the preceding model.

5.1 Virtual Provider (Composition of Process Mediators)

We define here an abstract execution model for a compositional mediator pattern VIRTUALPROVIDER (VP), separating in particular internal PROCESSing (Sect. 5.1.2) from the communication interfaces (Sect. 5.1.1). The ASM model has been developed within SAP and became known as a patent [8]. After an example in Sect. 5.1.3, we illustrate in Sect. 5.1.4 that by appropriately composing VIRTUALPROVIDER instances one can specify the behavior of complex web services—including the underlying message-based interaction and standard workflow patterns—succinctly and precisely, building them out of simple, accurately defined service-oriented components.[3] The exposition is an elaboration of [10].

Process mediation plays a central role for the specification (configuration and composition) of web services by communication-based interaction protocols. A mediator stays between the participants of an interaction where a *requestor* sends a *request* to a *provider* which is supposed to return an *answer* (so-called Request-Reply pattern [144]).[4] The role of the VIRTUALPROVIDER is to receive requests, to forward them to potential actual providers, to collect their answers and to construct out of those a final answer that is sent back to the requestor. This explains the architecture of the VIRTUALPROVIDER depicted in Fig. 5.1.

We define the mediator ASM itself out of the five components named in Fig. 5.1, abstracting from how the scheduler calls each time one of the com-

---

[3] For a refinement of the VIRTUALPROVIDER to capture distributed semantic web service discovery with various distribution and semantic matchmaking strategies see [116] and [10, Sect. 5].

[4] The Request-Reply pattern appears also in the web server ASM model in [48].

Fig. 5.1 VIRTUALPROVIDER architecture [7]
© 2006 Springer-Verlag Berlin Heidelberg, reprinted with permission

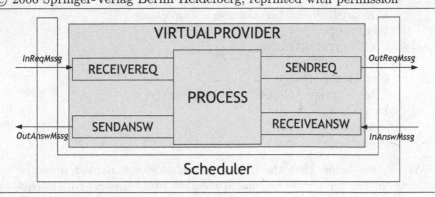

ponents to execute.[5] This leads to the following abstract VIRTUALPROVIDER whose components are defined in the next two sections.

VIRTUALPROVIDER = **one of**
   ({PROCESS, RECEIVEREQ, SENDREQ, RECEIVEANSW, SENDANSW})

5.1.1 VIRTUALPROVIDER *Communication Components*

The four communication components are instances of the communication patterns in Sect. 4.4. We leave it to later design decisions which variation about acknowledgments, discarding or buffering to choose. As a consequence, the send components are unchanged SENDPATTERN instances:

SENDREQ = SENDPATTERN
SENDANSW = SENDPATTERN

For the RECEIVEREQ component we consider a stateless communication model, assuming that a request message, besides sender and receiver address, contains all information that is needed to PROCESS the request. For a 'stateful' refinement see Exerc. 49. Thus, for incoming request messages RECEIVEREQ has only to CREATEREQOBJ, inserting into the set of *ReqObjects* a fresh element, which is INITIALIZEd to represent the request message for the internal PROCESSing. Since RECEIVEREQ and RECEIVEANSW react to different kinds of messages, we stipulate that *ReadyToReceive(m)* filters out messages that are not genuine 'request messages' (read: not elements of the set *InReqMssg*) and messages that are not genuine 'answer messages' (read: not elements of the set *InAnswMssg*).

---

[5] For more on the scheduler background see the explanations at the beginning of Sect. 4.4.3.

RECEIVEREQ = RECEIVEPATTERN
where
  if $ReadyToReceive(m)$ **then** $m \in InReqMssg$
  RECEIVE$(m) =$
    CREATEREQOBJ(m)
    CONSUME(m)
  CREATEREQOBJ$(m) =$
    let $r =$ **new** $(ReqObj)$ **in** INITIALIZE(r, m)
  INITIALIZE$(r, m) =$
    $status(r) := start$
    $reqMsg(r) := m$

We explain below that the mediator PROCESSes a request object r by building an answer to the original $reqMsg(r)$ from answers to subrequests $s \in SubReq(r)$ it sends out to other (typically to some actual) providers. Thus, the RECEIVEANSW component needs a) an $AnswerSet(s)$, where to collect the received answer messages m to each subrequest s, and b) a $subRequestor(m)$ function to identify the subrequest $s = subRequestor(m)$ to which m provides an answer.

RECEIVEANSW = RECEIVEPATTERN
where
  if $ReadyToReceive(m)$ **then** $m \in InAnswMssg$
  RECEIVE$(m) =$
    INSERT$(m, AnswerSet(subRequestor(m)))$
    CONSUME(m)

Exercise 49. Consider a conservative refinement to a 'stateful' communication model where the VIRTUALPROVIDER stores some information from received requests for further processing at a later stage. Hint: use a predicate $NewRequest$ to recognize whether an incoming request message m contains a new request or whether it concerns some previously received request. In the latter case, retrieve the previously created request object $r = prevReqObj(m)$ to REFRESHREQOBJ(r, m) by the additional information provided by m.

5.1.2 PROCESS *Component of* VIRTUAL PROVIDER

To offer means for building, statically or at runtime, whatever needed hierarchical processing structures, the PROCESS component works with the following simple *seq/par tree* request structure, visualized in Fig. 5.2.

- For each request object $req \in ReqObj$ a sequence $seqSubReq(req)$ of subrequests $subreq_i \in SubReq$ $(1 \leq i \leq m)$, which have to be processed one after the other.

Fig. 5.2 Seq-Par-Tree request structure

- For each $subreq_i \in SubReq$ a set $parSubReq(subreq_i) \subseteq ParReq$ of sub-subrequests r_{ij} $(1 \leq j \leq n(i))$, which are sent out in parallel to other providers.

The auxiliary functions $seqSubReq$ and $parSubReq$ may be dynamic and are left abstract, so that they can be tailored for specific service provider instances. It is possible that at runtime the next subrequest, to-be-processed after some $subreq_i$, may not be $subreq_{i+1}$, but another subrequest $subreq_j$ with $j > i + 1$ in $seqSubReq(req)$, depending on the answers received so far in $AnswerSet(subreq_i)$. This is useful in case the information obtained by the answers to $subreq_i$ triggers a case distinction about whether further information is needed and, in case, which one.

We will see in Sect. 5.1.4 that this simple *seq/par tree* structure allows one to accurately model all the standard BPMN [196] workflow patterns.

The VIRTUALPROVIDER kernel PROCESS, when scheduled, chooses a request object r with $status(r) = start$ and delegates to a subrequest $handler(r)$ to HANDLESUBREQ for the sequence $seqSubReq(r)$ of sequential subrequests of r. The $handler(r)$ will accumulate the initially empty $AnswerSet(r)$ out of any $AnswerSet(s)$, consisting of the collected answers to sequential subrequests $s \in seqSubReq(r)$.

PROCESS =
    choose $r \in ReqObj$ **with** $status(r) = start$
        CREATESUBREQHANDLER(r)
        INITIALIZE$(AnswerSet(r))$

The two submachines of PROCESS are defined as follows:

CREATESUBREQHANDLER(r) =
    let $a = $ **new** $(Agent)$
        INITIALIZE(a, r)
        $pgm(a) := $ HANDLESUBREQ

INITIALIZE(a, r) =
    $handler(r) := a$
    $req(a) := r$
    $subReq(a) := head(seqSubReq(r))$ – current subrequest
    $status(r) := handleSubReq$
  INITIALIZE$(Set) = (Set := \emptyset)$

Fig. 5.3 HANDLESUBREQ component of VP PROCESS

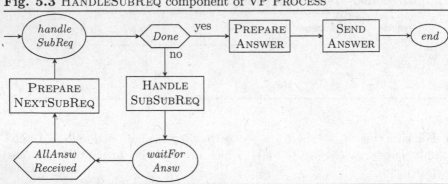

A subrequest $handler(r) = a$ executes the control state ASM program HANDLESUBREQ defined in Fig. 5.3. Here the control states denote the current $status(r)$ for $r = req(a)$. The handler performs an iteration through the subrequest sequence $seqSubReq(r)$. For each $subReq(a) \in SubReq$ it must HANDLESUBSUBREQ, i. e. make the subsubrequests in $parSubReq(subReq(a))$ *readyToSend* for SENDREQ. Then the handler will *waitForAnswer*s, which are inserted upon arrival by RECEIVEANSW into $AnswerSet(subReq(a))$. If *AllAnswReceived*, the handler must PREPARENEXTSUBREQuest and go back to status *handleSubReq*—until it is *Done*. In that case it will PREPAREANSWER, to be sent by SENDANSW to the requestor of the original request r.

The submachines are defined as follows.

> HANDLESUBSUBREQ =
>   PREPAREBROADCAST($parSubReq(subReq)$)
>   INITIALIZE($AnswerSet(subReq)$)

To PREPAREBROADCAST, the subsubrequests must be transformed into the format for an outgoing request message (elements of the set $OutReqMssg$). To make the VIRTUALPROVIDER easily configurable to concrete formats, we use for this purpose an abstract function $outReq2Msg$.

> PREPAREBROADCAST(S) =
>   **forall** $s \in S$ $readyToSend(outReq2Msg(s)) := true$

The definition of *AllAnswReceived* considers that the VP may not need answers for each sent out parallel subsubrequest. We use therefore a function *toBeAnswered*. Using this function the handler can identify those subsubrequests for which an answer is required. A predicate $IsAnswer(m, q)$ expresses the relation between an answer message m and the query q the message is an answer to.

> *AllAnswReceived* iff
>   **forall** $q \in toBeAnswered(parSubReq(subReq))$
>   **thereissome** $m \in AnswerSet(subReq)$ **with** $IsAnswer(m, q)$

As mentioned above, the *next* subrequest is selected by the *handler*$(r) = a$ out of the given *seqSubReq*(*req*(a)) sequence, considering the answers received so far for the current *subReq* value. These answers are added to the *AnswerSet*(*req*(a)).

> *Done* **iff** *subReq* = *done*   -- assuming *done* $\notin$ *SubReq*
> PREPARENEXTSUBREQ =
>   *subReq* := *next*(*subReq*, *seqSubReq*(*req*), *AnswerSet*(*subReq*))
>   ADD(*AnswerSet*(*subReq*), *AnswerSet*(*req*(**self**)))

When the iterated handling of subrequests is *Done*, the *handler*$(r) = a$ must PREPAREANSWER, using the accumulated *AnswerSet*(*req*(a)) to compute the *answer*. Furthermore, it must transform the answer, using a function *outAnsw2Msg*, to a message in the format required for an outgoing answer message (element of the set *OutAnswMssg*). Remember that from the request object $r = req_a$, the *handler*(r) can retrieve the original *reqMsg*(r), which contains the original request and its sender where to send the *answer*.

> PREPAREANSWER =
>   *readyToSend*(*outAnsw2Msg*(*answer*(*req*, *AnswerSet*(*req*)))) := *true*
>   **where** *req* = *req*(**self**)

Exercise 50. Refine for a stateful VIRTUALPROVIDER (Exerc. 49) the definition of PROCESS.

5.1.3 Example: Virtual Internet Service Provider

The example we consider here is taken from [7]. It uses the VIRTUALPROVIDER to adapt a web service to a changed interface. Consider a Virtual Internet Service Provider VISP which serves *InternetDomain* registration requests. Assume that such requests are defined to come with the following four parameters:

- *DomainName* for the new to-be-registered domain,
- *DomainHolderName* of the legal domain owner,
- *AdministrativeContactName* of the domain administrator,
- *TechnicalContactName* of the person to be contacted for technical issues.

Assume that for any request *InternetDomain*(DN, DHN, ACN, TCN) the *answer* $\in$ *OutAnswMssg* contains four so-called RIPE-Handles[6], uniquely identifying the four request message parameters in the RIPE database.

Now imagine this VISP has to be adapted to a domain name registry authority which implements a different interface for registering new domain names, say consisting of four request messages instead of one:

---

[6] RIPE stands for Réseaux IP Européens, see http://ripe.net.

Fig. 5.4 VIRTUALPROVIDER instance adapting VISP [7]
© 2006 Springer-Verlag Berlin Heidelberg, reprinted with permission

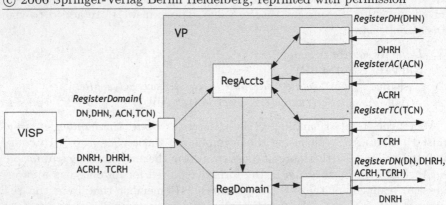

- $RegisterDH(DomainHolderName)$
- $RegisterAC(AdministrativeContactName)$
- $RegisterTC(TechnicalContactName)$
- $RegisterDN(DoName, DHRipeHandle, ACRipeHandle, TCRipeHandle)$

This adaptation can be achieved by linking VISP, without changing its internal structure, to an appropriate VIRTUALPROVIDER instance as indicated in Fig. 5.4.

The VIRTUALPROVIDER instance in Fig. 5.4 serves VISP as subprovider: a *RegisterDomain* request incoming the subprovider is split up into a sequence *seqSubReq(RegisterDomain)* of two subrequests. The first one, *RegAccts*, has a set *parSubReq(RegAccts)* of three parallel subsubrequests, each registering one of the indicated contacts. When *AllAnswReceived* for these parallel subsubrequests, the second sequential subrequest, *RegDomain*, is sent out. Its request message is constructed from the *AnswerSet(RegAccts)* of the first subrequest *RegAccts* and from the *DomainName* parameter *DN* of the original *RegisterDomain* request incoming the subprovider. Finally, PREPAREANSWER triggers the outgoing answer message to be sent by the subprovider back to VISP. By assumption, from the received data VISP can build its answer message to the user who sent the initial *InternetDomain* registration request.

Exercise 51. For the above VIRTUALPROVIDER instance define the instances of its signature elements. See [7].

5.1.4 Workflow Patterns (Composition of VPs)

The compositional communication structure of the VIRTUALPROVIDER together with the *seq/par tree* structure allow one to describe sophisticated web service interaction patterns. We illustrate this here only by one elementary and furthermore pure control flow example. [7]

The composition of VIRTUALPROVIDERs permits to express any control flow structure in a modular fashion, connecting in an appropriate way the communication interfaces visualized in Fig. 5.1. Consider two machines VIRTUALPROVIDER$_i$ and VIRTUALPROVIDER$_j$. To compose them, it suffices to connect their communication interfaces as follows:

- Connect SENDREQ of VP_i with the RECEIVEREQ of VP_j. This requires that the types of the sets $OutReqMssg$ of VP_i and $InReqMssg$ of VP_j are refined to match (via some data mediation).
- Connect SENDANSW of VP_j with the RECEIVEANSW of VP_i. This requires that the types of the sets $OutAnswMssg$ of VP_j and $InAnswMssg$ of VP_i are refined to match (via some data mediation).

Combining this composition scheme with the *seq/par tree* structure, one can configure request processing structures where each sequential subrequest sub_1 (at level 1) of an initial request can trigger a set $parSubReq(sub_1)$ of parallel level-1 subsubrequests $parsub_1$, each of which can trigger a set of further sequential (level-2) subrequests sub_2 of $parsub_1$, each of which again can trigger a set $parSubReq(sub_2)$ of parallel (level-2) subsubrequests, etc.

An illustrative example is the composition of VP1, VP2, VP3 in Fig. 5.6, an instance of Fig. 5.2. It models the PAR-Split/Join workflow of Fig. 5.5 to execute first A, then independently B followed by C resp. D followed by E, and finally F. VP1 has three sequential *subrequests*. $subreq_1$ triggers an execution of A; this may involve a request r_{11} to another VP which sends back an answer $answ_{11}$. $subreq_2$ has two parallel subsubrequests r_{21}, r_{22}. They are sent to providers VP2 and VP3, respectively, which in turn trigger the execution, independently of each other, of B followed by C and of D followed by E, yielding answers $answ_{21}$ and $answ_{22}$, respectively. Once these two answers arrived at VP1, this provider can work on $subreq_3$ to trigger the execution

---

[7] For a critical analysis of the numerous control flow patterns considered by BPMN [196] and their reduction to a few basic ASM patterns we refer the reader to [40, 42].

Fig. 5.5 PAR-Split/Join workflow modeled by Fig. 5.6

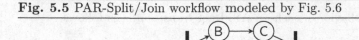

Fig. 5.6 VIRTUALPROVIDER composition for Fig. 5.5

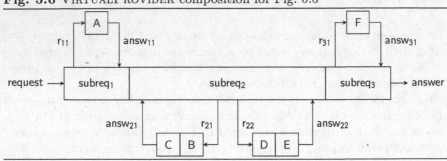

of F (possibly involving yet another provider, via a subsubrequest r_{31} and answer $answ_{31}$), before VP1 can send its *answer* to the original *request*.

Exercise 52. Draw your favorite workflow pattern and model it by a composition of VIRTUALPROVIDER instances.

5.2 ASM Net Diagrams

We enrich in this section the abstract one-step view of control state ASM components (read: of the rectangles in the flowchart representation)[8] by an iterated execution view. It is guided by a completion concept, coming with corresponding entry and exit conditions and actions. This control pattern appears frequently in the area of BPM so that control state ASMs have been tailored in [53] to directly support this scheme.

Definition 16. An *ASM net* N is a (finite) directed graph built from ASM net transitions of the form defined by Fig. 5.7. The transitions are also called ASM net rules with body M. As usual, the circles represent nodes whose labels denote control states, *Entry/ExitCond* are Boolean-valued expressions, M is an ASM (or an already defined ASM net). In the net any *exitnode* of one transition can be connected (read: identified) with one and at most one *entrynode* of another transition. Unless otherwise stated, *EntryCond*itions are required to be pairwise disjoint. Similarly for the *ExitCond*itions, for which it is usually (unless otherwise stated) also required that upon exiting M, at least one of them is true.[9]

The intended behavior of such an ASM net *transition* is as follows.

---

[8] See the discussion at the end of Sect. 2.1.3.

[9] Alternatively, often the first possible entry/exit is declared to be taken, in the order in which their guards appear in the diagram.

Fig. 5.7 ASM Net Transition scheme

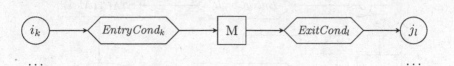

- The execution of (an instance of) the body M begins with executing a START machine and passing control to M, if $mode = i_k'$ and the corresponding $EntryCond_k$ holds for some entry node labeled i_k $(1 \leq k \leq n)$.
- M is executed as long as the body is *active* and not yet *Completed*.
- FINALIZE is executed when M's execution is *Completed*, letting the net computation proceed to $mode = j_l$ for the exit node labeled j_l whose $ExitCond_l$ is satisfied $(1 \leq l \leq m)$.

This behavior can be formalized by the following control state ASM, whose architecture is pictorially represented by Fig. 5.8.[10]

Definition 17. We define the *net transition behavior* for every *transition* as in Fig. 5.7 and for every $i \in \{i_1, \ldots, i_n\}$ by a NETRULE(*transition*, i) ASM.

We parameterize the components of M in NETRULE(*transition*, i) with the current $mode = i$ value; this is for the use cases where the body is instantiated depending on the entry node from which it is called.

We foresee that for the iteration control of the transition body M, an internal location $mode_{M,i}$ may be used. It could (but need not) be different from the external $mode$ location; in that case it is assumed to be initialized by START(M, i).

$\quad$ NETRULE(*transition*, i_k) =
$\quad\quad$ **let** $i = i_k$
$\quad\quad\quad$ **if** $mode = i$ **and** $EntryCond_k$ **then** $\qquad\qquad\qquad$ -- enter M
$\quad\quad\quad\quad$ START(M, i)
$\quad\quad\quad\quad$ $mode := start(M, i)$ $\qquad\qquad\qquad\qquad\qquad$ -- make M active
$\quad\quad\quad$ **if** $active(M, i)$ **then**
$\quad\quad\quad\quad$ **if not** $Completed(M, i)$ **then** M $\qquad\qquad\qquad$ -- iterate M
$\quad\quad\quad\quad$ **if** $Completed(M, i)$ **then**
$\quad\quad\quad\quad\quad$ FINALIZE(M, i)
$\quad\quad\quad\quad\quad$ EXIT$_i$
$\quad\quad$ EXIT$_i$ = **forall** $l \in \{1, \ldots, m\}$ **if** $ExitCond_l$ **then** $mode := j_l$
$\quad\quad$ $active(M, i)$ **iff** $mode_{M,i} \in Mode(M, i)$ **or** $mode = start(M, i)$
$\quad\quad$ $Mode(M, i) =$ set of $mode_{M,i}$ values of M_i

---

[10] In the flowchart we indicate by a line, connecting M to the $Completed(M, i)$ predicate via a control state circle, that the body-internal $mode_{M,i}$ location, which takes values in $Mode(M, i)$, may be different from the external $mode$ location, the one which triggered to enter the transition.

Fig. 5.8 Architecture diagram for ASM net rule behavior for $i = i_k$

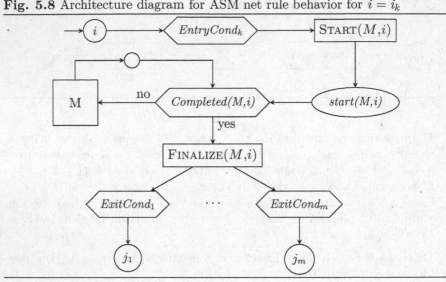

In the sequential or synchronous parallel net interpretation, the same *mode* location is used in all net transitions and in their bodies. Therefore we define:

SYNCASMNET(N) =
    forall *transition* $\in N$ NETRULE$_{sync}$(*transition*)
where
    NETRULE$_{sync}$(*transition*) =
    forall $i \in \{i_1, \ldots, i_n\}$ NETRULE(*transition*, i)

In the concurrent multi-agent interpretation, each *transition* has its own *mode* location. Therefore CONCURASMNET(N) is defined as a family of agents $a_{transition}$ equipped with program NETRULE$_{sync}$(*transition*) or agents $a_{(transition,i)}$ with program NETRULE(*transition*, i) for given i (*transition* $\in N$).

To guarantee an easy comprehension of a clear intuitive behavioral meaning of the proposed graphical notation, we do not include any of the richer and more complex actions from UML 2.0 [195] activity diagrams or from BPMN [196]. This implies however no loss of generality because such actions can be modeled separately. See [208, 209, 164, 165] where, using ASM models, a precise behavioral foundation and an execution environment is provided for the major graphical UML 2 notations.

The definition of ASM nets offers an interface to model various submachine concepts which are known from sequential or concurrent computation paradigms. We do not enter here this interesting issue.

Notational convention. Below we will use ASM transitions with only one *entry* node (furthermore with trivial *EntryCond* = *true*) and only

Fig. 5.9 Notation for One-Entry Two-Exits ASM Net Transitions

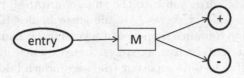

two exit nodes *plusExit* denoted $+$ and *minusExit* denoted $-$, where the exit conditions (execution success or failure, also called *PlusExitCond* resp. *MinusExitCond*) are clear from the context. In such cases we simplify Fig. 5.7 to Fig. 5.9. When linking in an ASM net a $+/-$ exit of a transition t to the unique *entry* or *start* node of another transition t', we sometimes annotate the linking arrow by $+/-$.

5.2.1 Guard-State-Milestone Approach to BPM

In [148] the so-called Guard-State-Milestone (GSM) approach to BPM is introduced as part of IBM's ArtiFact project. The 'core constructs of GSM were chosen ... to be very close to the way that the business stakeholders think—in terms of milestones and business rules' (op. cit. p. 4). According to [143] GSM forms 'the conceptual basis of the forthcoming OMG Case Management Model and Notation (CMMN) standard' [197].

Using ASM nets one can accurately model the basic GSM concepts, given their close correspondence to basic ASM notions. The two approaches both use *control states* to split a system into phases (in GSM called *stages*). A *guard*, which in GSM 'enables entry into the stage body' by launching an instance of it, is an ASM net *EntryCond*ition that enables to START(*body*). A stage body is 'intended to achieve a milestone (or one of several related milestones)' (op. cit., p. 3). They can be expressed by ASM net *ExitCond*itions, e. g. by instantiating *Completed(M)* to their disjunction.

GSM uses a 'global' state concept which is directly supported in the ASM framework:

> ... the ... information model is shared among the multiple stakeholders involved ... a design feature that fosters communication across different groups and suborganizations. This is a deliberate and significant departure from traditional SOA and object-oriented programming, where the internal data structures of a service or object are hidden.(op. cit., p. 12)

The reason is to permit to describe process behavior together with the underlying data, using the GSM *information model* where 'all business-relevant information about an entity instance' (op. cit., pp. 6–7) is held, namely data/event attributes, milestones and state information. This is captured exactly by the ASM states, which are updated explicitly by the update set each

ASM rule yields when executed. The GSM *lifecycle model*, which expresses the process behavior, corresponds to the rules of an ASM.

GSM permits nesting of stages. Atomic stage bodies (i.e. without substages) are allowed to contain a sequence of several tasks, namely assignments, an invocation of external services, a request to create a new instance or to send a response to a call or to send an event (message). Such bodies are instances of control state ASMs. The case where 'stages at the same level of nesting may execute in parallel' (op. cit., p. 7) is an instance of a SYNCASMNET(N) or of an ASYNCASMNET(N), depending on whether 'parallel' is meant as synchronous parallelism or as true concurrency. The case where 'all occurrences of substages are terminated if the parent closes' (op. cit., p. 12) can be modeled by a corresponding ASM subnet concept (though we do not do this here). The kind of 'transactional consistency discipline based on read and write locks' GSM seems to use can be accurately defined by an ASM model, see [72] for a concrete example.

So much for modeling basic GSM features by ASM nets, precisely but using only fundamental concepts all BP stakeholders can understand. Where the ASM method, besides accurately modeling, can enhance GSM is the ASM refinement concept. It can be used to make precise what in op. cit. is called to 'drill-down' into a stage. It is described there only informally as 'a central vision of Project ArtiFact', namely to develop GSM models stepwise, starting from 'intuitive, imprecise, and/or incomplete' descriptions and stepwise adding more and more details provided by the stakeholders (op. cit., p. 4). It would be interesting to develop rigorous ASM refinement support for GSM.

5.2.2 S-BPM Communication Model

In this section we illustrate how modeling for change can work in practice, using the ASM refinement method for adapting models to new requirements. We 'replay' the specification *process* for the behavior of the commercial S-BPM Workflow Engine [187] (which has an open-source version [180, 181]). After the ASM ground model for the initially given requirements had been defined to the satisfaction of the customer, further requirements were added, more than once. Each time they could be incorporated into the already existing specification using an appropriate ASM refinement. We explain in this section some of the steps of this process which concern the characteristic communication model of S-BPM.[11]

---

[11] Originally the specification has been given in terms of control state ASMs (see [109]), but using ASM nets and ambient ASMs (Sect. 4) simplifies the exposition. We also present here only the final result and do not show the various back and forth of the process, which are characteristic for each real-life requirements capture endeavor.

5.2.2.1 Subject Behavior Diagrams

A distributed subject oriented business process model (S-BPM) consists of finitely many processes P_k whose actions are performed by actors $subj_k$, called 'subjects', in ASM terminology agents. Each subject walks through an associated flowchart-like Subject Behavior Diagram SBD_k, performing in each *node* an associated action, called *service(node)*. These actions are either *internal*, concerning only locations of the agent's SBD, or Send/Receive actions involving other subjects. Therefore S-BPM processes are a class of communicating ASMs. What makes the structure of ASM nets appropriate to describe SBDs is that once an agent entered an SBD-node (read: the current process *stage*), it enters the next SBD-node (to execute the associated next action) only upon completion of the action associated with the current SBD-node. The associated actions can be anything, for example atomic steps, but also a sequence or iteration of whatever finer-grained steps executed by the subject. This leads us to the following definition.

Definition 18. A Subject Behavior Diagram *SBD* is an ASM net of a communicating ASM with exactly one *initial* node and possibly multiple *end* nodes, such that each path starting at the *initial* node leads to at least one *end* node. Each net transition has one *entry* node and possibly multiple *exit* nodes. The behavioral interpretation of the *SBD* is SYNCASMNET(*SBD*).[12]

This suffices to establish the context in which we are going to model the intended meaning of communication actions Send/Receive of S-BPM subjects. We start with listing the specific S-BPM mailbox requirements which affect the meaning of Send/Receive actions.

5.2.2.2 S-BPM Input Pools

The S-BPM mailbox of subjects is called *inputPool*.

inputPoolSizeReq. The *inputPool* has the following size restrictions, based upon an underlying classification of messages into types:

- overall capacity $maxSize \in \{0, 1, \dots\}$ (non-negative number),
- maximal number $maxFrom(sender)$ of messages allowed from a *sender* or $maxFor(type)$ of a *type*.

At configuration time the user can indicate for any *sender* and message *type* the desired *size* limit and the *sizeAction*, to be taken in case of a *size* violation.

---

[12] A single SBD is a sequential process, executed by one subject. The behavior of a distributed S-BPM process $P = (subj_k, SBD_k)_{1 \le k \le l}$ is ASYNCASMNET(P).

SizeViolationActionReq. If a message m violates a *size* restriction, one of the following *sizeActions* can be taken:

- m is dropped (not inserted into the *inputPool*),
- m is blocked (not inserted into the *inputPool*), but can be tried to be sent synchronously; *maxSize* violation (for $maxSize < \infty$) implies *action = Blocking*,
- either the *oldestMsg* or the *youngestMsg*, determined in terms of its *insertionTime* into the *inputPool*), is deleted from the *inputPool* and m is inserted.

SyncReceiveReq. $maxFrom(sender) = 0$ and/or $maxFor(type) = 0$ indicate that the owner of the *inputPool* accepts messages from the indicated *sender* and/or of the indicated *type* only via a rendezvous (synchronously). $size = 0$ implies *action = Blocking*. Positive size limits are used for asynchronous communication.

5.2.2.3 Communication of Single Messages

We start with formulating the initial requirements.

MsgPreparationReq. A communication action starts with defining the *curMsg* to be handled. For Send, this is a concrete message with its data. For Receive, it is the kind of message to look for in the *inputPool*, namely either *any* message, or a message from a particular *sender*, or a message of a particular *type*, or a message of a particular type from a particular sender.

SendActionReq. If a Send action *CanAccess* the *inputPool* of the receiver, it inserts its message m asynchronously into the *inputPool* if this implies no *SizeViolation*. If *SizeViolation*$(m) = true$, there are three possible cases: a) m is inserted if the corresponding *sizeAction*(m) is to drop the youngest or the oldest message from the *inputPool* (*CancelingSend* case), b) m is simply not inserted (*DropIncoming* case), c) m is not inserted, but an attempt is made to synchronously Send m (case *Blocking*). The Send action fails if a synchronous Send attempt is made but fails, or if the *inputPool* could not be accessed.

The *SendActionRe*quirement is captured by a SINGLESENDNET transition with unique *entry*, two exits (taken upon successful or failed completion of the action, see Fig. 5.9), body SINGLESEND defined by Fig. 5.10 and the following components.[13]

$$\text{START}(\text{SINGLESEND}, entry) = \text{PREPARE}(curMsg, entry, Send)$$

---

[13] For some intuitively clear components we skip the detailed definitions; they appear in [109].

Fig. 5.10 Body SINGLESEND of SINGLESENDNET

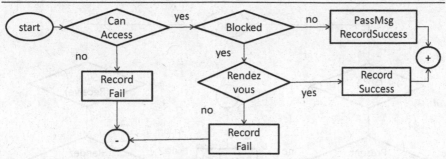

PREPARE($curMsg, entry, Send$) =
  $curMsg := composeMsg(msgData(entry))$
$CanAccess(sender, pool)$ iff
  $sender = select_{Pool}(\{subject \mid TryingToAccess(subject, pool)\})$
$Blocked$ iff $SizeViolation(curMsg) = true$ **and**
  $sizeAction(curMsg) = Blocking$
PASSMSG =
  let $pool = inputPool(receiver(curMsg))$
  if (**not** $SizeViolation(curMsg)$) **or**
    $SizeViolation(curMsg)$ **and** $sizeAction(curMsg) \neq DropIncoming$
      then INSERT($curMsg, pool$)
  if $sizeAction(curMsg) = DropYoungest$ **then**
    DELETE($youngestMsg(pool), pool$)
  if $sizeAction(curMsg) = DropOldest$ **then**
    DELETE($oldestMsg(pool), pool$)

To PREPARE the *curMsg* for a *Send* action, the needed data are specified
by an abstract function *msgData*, which accesses the database and is used to
composeMsg. It is left to the implementation to further detail these abstract
functions. For reasons of succinctness we write *curMsg* for *curMsg(entry)* and
will use the same name below also for modeling the PREPARE component for
a Receive action.

CanAccess(sender, Pool) prevents multiple senders to yield inconsistent
updates and uses for this purpose a *selection* function. Being *Blocked* means
that *curMsg* encounters a *SizeViolation* and *sizeAction(curMsg) = Blocking*.
In this case, to successfully terminate the Send action, an attempt to synchronously Send *curMsg* must be performed.

To PASSMSG means to INSERT(*curMsg, inputPool*). This includes the
deletion of the youngest or the oldest message in the pool in case of a
SizeViolation(curMsg). There is one exception to this, namely the case of
a *SizeViolation(curMsg)* where *sizeAction(curMsg) = DropIncoming*. In this
case nothing happens, but the Send action is considered to complete with

Fig. 5.11 Body SINGLERECEIVE of SINGLERECEIVENET

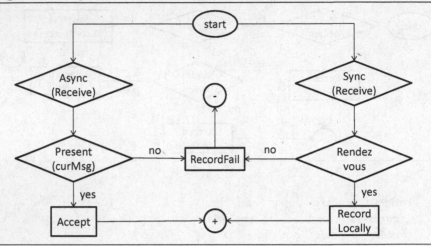

success. A FINALIZE action could be used to inform the sender about this fact.

The *Rendezvous*-with-the-receiver predicate is defined below, together with the model for an S-BPM Receive action.

ReceiveActionReq. A Receive action can be of synchronous or asynchronous kind, specified as part of the kind of expected message described in the *MsgPreparationReq*uirement. An asynchronous Receive succeeds if the *inputPool* contains a message of the kind of expected message. A synchronous Receive succeeds if there is a *sender* which tries to synchronously Send a message of the kind of expected message. Otherwise, the Receive action fails.

The *ReceiveActionReq*uirement is captured by the SINGLERECEIVENET transition with unique *entry*, two exits (taken upon successful or failed completion, see Fig. 5.9), body SINGLERECEIVE defined by Fig. 5.11 and the components defined below.

We use the name *curMsg* also for the kind *curMsg*(*entry*) of expected message the subject must PREPARE to start a Receive action. The set of *ExpectedMsgKinds* is a set of triples

$$(sender, msgType, async) \text{ or } (sender, msgType, sync)$$

where *sender* and *msgType* can also be *any*. For the expected message kind *select*ed to START(SINGLERECEIVE, *entry*), in asynchronous receive mode the machine looks for (and possibly chooses) a *Match*ing message in the *inputPool*, to locally store it, and thereby completes the action successfully (ACCEPT).

The *Rendezvous* predicate is the conjunction of the following three conditions:

- the *receiver* tries to $Sync(Receive)$,
- the *sender* which currently does *Access* the $inputPool(receiver)$ is *Blocked*,
- $Match(curMsg(sender), curMsg(receiver))$ holds.

The components are defined as follows:

$\text{START}(\text{SINGLERECEIVE}, entry) = \text{PREPARE}(curMsg, entry, Receive)$
$\text{PREPARE}(curMsg, entry, Receive) =$
  $curMsg := select_{MsgKind}(ExpectedMsgKind(entry))$
$ExpectedMsgKind(entry) \subseteq \{(s, t, r) \mid s \in Sender \cup \{any\}$ **and**
  $t \in MsgType \cup \{any\}$ **and** $r \in \{sync, async\}\}$
$Async(Receive)$ iff $third(curMsg) = async$
$Present(curMsg)$ iff
  forsome $msg \in inputPool$ $Match(msg, curMsg)$
$\text{ACCEPT} =$
  let $receivedMsg =$
    $select_{Pool}(\{msg \in inputPool \mid Match(msg, curMsg)\})$
  $\text{STORELOCALLY}(receivedMsg)$
  $\text{RECORDSUCCESS}(\text{SINGLERECEIVE}, async)$
  $\text{DELETE}(receivedMsg, inputPool)$
$Sync(Receive)$ iff $third(curMsg) = sync$
let $sender = \iota s(\{s \in Sender \mid CanAccess(s, inputPool(receiver)\}$
  $Rendezvous$ iff
    $Blocked(sender)$ **and** $Sync(Receive)(receiver)$ **and**
      $Match(curMsg(sender), curMsg(receiver))$
$\text{RECORDLOCALLY} =$
  $\text{STORELOCALLY}(curMsg(sender))$
  $\text{RECORDSUCCESS}(\text{SINGLERECEIVE}, sync)$

5.2.2.4 Communication of Multiple Messages

A first additional requirement concerned the number of messages a subject can manipulate in one Send/Receive action, namely finitely many instead of only one. Most refinement steps by which we incorporate the additional requirement into the S-BPM interpreter model are similar, if not the same, for Send and Receive, so that we use *ComAct* to denote any one of Send/Receive.

MultiComActReq. In one *ComAction*, a subject can handle a finite set *MsgToBeHandled* of messages. The *multi*tude is defined at the SBD-node where such a *MultiComAction* takes place. The entire set of *MsgToBeHandled* has to be prepared *before* the *SingleComAction* is performed for each of those messages. To complete a *MultiComAction*, the

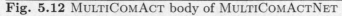

Fig. 5.12 MULTICOMACT body of MULTICOMACTNET

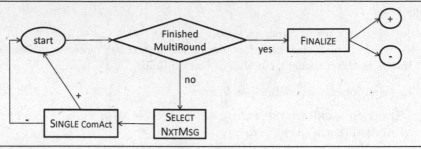

subject must Send/Receive the indicated *multi*tude of messages without
pursuing in between any other communication. If for at least one $m \in$
MsgToBeHandled the *SingleComAct* fails, then the *MultiComAct*ion
fails.

Essentially, the new requirement asks for an iteration *MultiComAct* of
*SingleComAct*ions at an SBD-node. This fits the iteration pattern of ASM
nets. To define such a MULTICOMACTNET we use *mult* as a (design-time
or run-time determined) function of the *entry* node. The PREPARE component for a single *curMsg* has to be extended to a START component
PREPAREMSG. This component defines a set *MsgToBeHandled* (together
with a copy, which is needed at the end of the *MultiRound* to check whether
the *ComAct* succeeded or not). *curMsg* will assume, one by one, each element
of this set as value to perform the *SingleComAct*. Therefore, the *MultiComAc-
tRe*quirement is captured by a MULTICOMACTNET transition with unique
entry, two exits (taken upon successful or failed completion, see Fig. 5.9),
body MULTICOMACT defined by Fig. 5.12 and the following components.

$$\text{START}(\text{MULTICOMACT}, entry) = \text{PREPAREMSG}(entry, ComAct)$$

PREPAREMSG($entry, Send$) =
    forall $1 \leq i \leq mult(entry)$
    let $m_i = composeMsg(msgData(entry, i))$
        $MsgToBeHandled := \{m_1, \dots, m_{mult(entry)}\}$
        $RoundMsg := \{m_1, \dots, m_{mult(entry)}\}$
PREPAREMSG($entry, Receive$) =
    forall $1 \leq i \leq mult(entry)$
    let $m_i = select_{MsgKind}(ExpectedMsgKind(entry), i)$
        $MsgToBeHandled := \{m_1, \dots, m_{mult(entry)}\}$
FinishedMultiRound **iff** $MsgToBeHandled = \emptyset$
SELECTNXTMSG =
    choose $m \in MsgToBeHandled$
        $curMsg := m$
        DELETE($m, MsgToBeHandled$)

FINALIZE =
   if $Success(MultiRound, ComAct, RoundMsg)$ then
      COMPLETENORMALLY($ComAct$)
      $PlusExitCond := true$
   if $Fail(MultiRound, ComAct, RoundMsg)$ then
      HANDLEMULTIROUNDFAIL($ComAct$)
      $MinusExitCond := true$
  $Success(MultiRound, ComAct, X)$ iff
    forall $m \in X$ $m \in SuccessRecord$(SINGLECOMACT)

5.2.2.5 Communication Alternatives

A later additional requirement asked for the possibility for subjects to choose
for a $ComAct$ among finitely many sets of $MsgToBeHandled$.

> $AltComActReq$. To perform an $ComAct \in \{Send, Receive\}$, a subject can
> choose the set of $MsgToBeHandled$ among finitely many $Alternatives$.
> $Alternative$ is determined by a function $alternative(entry, ComAct)$.[a] If
> the $ComAct$ succeeds for at least one $alternative$, the $AltComAct$ suc-
> ceeds and can be $Completed$ normally. If it fails, the subject chooses the
> next $alternative$ until:
>
> - either one of them succeeds or
> - all $Alternatives$ have been tried out and failed. In this case the
> $AltComAct$ fails.
>
> ---
>
> [a] In the currently implemented S-BPM diagram notation the $Alternatives$ ap-
> pear as pairs of a receiver and a message type, each labeling in the form
> $(to\ receiver, msgType)$ an arc leaving the SBD-node in question.

To incorporate this further requirement into the MULTICOMACTNET
model, we put an iterator shell around it. It tries out each element of
$Alternative$ as current $alternative$, to be executed by the MULTICOMACTNET.
For passing the chosen $alternative$ to the START component PREPAREMSG
of the MULTICOMACTNET, we take advantage of the ambient ASM notion.
We declare the two functions $composeMsg$ and $select_{MsgKind}$ to be ambient
dependent. Thereby the set of $MsgToBeHandled$, defined by PREPAREMSG,
and its copy $RoundMsg$ become parameterized by alt.

Thus, to incorporate the $AltComActRequirement$, the MULTICOMACTNET
can be adapted by extending it to a ALTNET($ComAct$) component. This
component iterates MULTICOMACTNET for the $alternatives$ until for one of
them, the MULTICOMACTion succeeds. The net has unique $entry$, two exits
(taken upon successful or failed completion, see Fig. 5.9), body ALT($ComAct$)
defined by Fig. 5.13 and the following components. It is structurally similar
to Fig. 5.12, though not identical due to the different completion predicate.

Fig. 5.13 ALT(*ComAct*) body of ALTNET(*ComAct*)

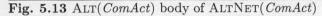

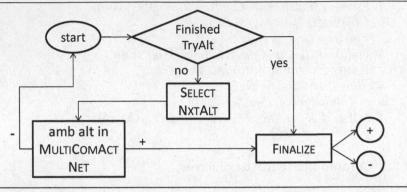

START(ALT(*ComAct*), *entry*) = INITIALIZE(*Alternative, ComAct*)
INITIALIZE(*Alternative, ComAct*) =
   Alternative := *alternative*(*entry, ComAct*)
FinishedTryAlt iff *Alternative* = ∅
SELECTNXTALT =
  choose *a* ∈ *Alternative*
   alt := *a*
   DELETE(*a, Alternative*)
FINALIZE =
  if *Success*(ALT, *ComAct*) **then**
   COMPLETENORMALLY(ALT(*ComAct*))
   PlusExitCond := *true*
  if *Fail*(ALT, *ComAct*) **then**
   HANDLEFAIL(ALT(*ComAct*))
   MinusExitCond := *true*
Success(ALT, *ComAct*) iff **forsome** *a* ∈ *Alternative*
  Success(*MultiRound, ComAct, RoundMsg*(*a*))

Exercise 53. Refine ALT(*ComAct*) to include a timeout and the possibility for the user to interrupt the action. For a solution see [53].

5.2.2.6 Alternative Actions

Another additional later requirement asked to support specifying a subject that works on alternative tasks in an order independent manner. Technically, this means to permit interleaving among a set of tasks in segments of an SBD-computation.

AltActSubdiagramReq. In an *altSplit* node, the SBD splits into finitely many SBDs $D_i \in AltBehDgm(altSplit)$ with an arrow from *altSplit* to the unique $altEntry(D_i)$ (for each $1 \leq i \leq n$) and an arrow from its unique $altExit(D_i)$ to an *altJoin* node in the SBD. See Fig. 5.14.

AltActionReq. To perform the *AltAction* associated with an *altSplit* node means to complete some of the subdiagram computations, step by step in an interleaved (order-independent) way.

CompulsoryDgmReq. Some subdiagram entries resp. exits are declared to be *Compulsory* and determine the completion predicate of the *AltAction* as follows:

- A *Compulsory* $altEntry(D_i)$ node must be entered during the run, so that the D_i-subcomputation must have been started before the *AltAction* can be *Completed*.
- A *Compulsory* $altExit(D_j)$ node must be reached in the run, for the *AltAction* to be *Completed*, if during the run the D_j-subcomputation has been entered at $altEntry(D_j)$ (whether the $altEntry(D_j)$ state is *Compulsory* or not).

At least one subdiagram has *Compulsory altEntry* and *altExit*.

CompletionReq. The *AltAction* associated with node *altSplit* is *Completed* if all subdiagrams D_i with *Compulsory* $altEntry(D_i)$ have been entered and all computations of subdiagrams D_j with *Compulsory* $altExit(D_j)$ have been *Completed*.

We capture these requirements by an AltActionNet which comes with entry node called *altSplit* and corresponding exit node called *altJoin*.[14] For the computations of the subdiagrams $D_i \in AltBehDgm(altSplit)$, the AltAction body reuses the ASM net model SyncAsmNet of SBDs, exploiting the fact that the *mode* location is implicitly parameterized by the SBD where it guides the control. Therefore, when the subject performs a step in a subdiagram D_i, the step control is in terms of $mode_{D_i}$.

As a consequence, Start(AltAction, *altSplit*) initializes for each *Compulsory* D_i the $mode_{D_i} := initial(D_i)$ to the unique *initial* node of D_i. The body AltAction remains in its $mode = start(\text{AltAction}, altSplit)$ and does nothing more than choosing either an active subdiagram to perform the next step there, or to start the computation of another not-yet-active diagram—until completion when the subject proceeds to the next SBD node by $mode := altJoin(altSplit)$.

Start(AltAction, *altSplit*) =
    forall $D \in AltBehDgm(altSplit)$
        if $Compulsory(D)$ **then** $mode_D := initial(D)$

---

[14] This structured entry/exit pair, together with the completion concept, avoid the semantical difficulties and the complexity of the.OR-Join notion in BPMN [101].

Fig. 5.14 Structure of Alternative Action nodes [109, 7.7]
© 2012 Springer-Verlag Berlin Heidelberg, reprinted with permission

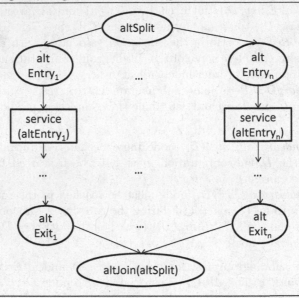

ALTACTION =
    choose $D \in AltBehDgm$
        if $Active(D)$ **then** SYNCASMNET(D)
            else $mode_D := initial(D)$ -- Start a subdiagram computation
    $Active(D)$ iff $mode_D \neq$ **undef**   -- D has been started
    $Completed(\text{ALTACTION}, altSplit)$ iff **forall** $D \in AltBehDgm(altSplit)$
        if $Compulsory(altEntry(D))$ **then** $Active(D)$
        and if $Compulsory(altExit(D))$ **then** $mode_D = altExit(D)^{15}$
    FINALIZE(ALTACTION) =
        forall $D \in AltBehDgm(altSplit)$ $mode_D :=$ **undef**
        $mode := altJoin(altSplit)$

Exercise 54. Adapt ALTACTION to the case where the subdiagrams are executed concurrently by independent agents. For a similar scheme see [52, 51].

5.3 Further BPM Applications of ASMs

There are various other applications of ASMs in the BP area which we can only mention in this book. A major one appeared in two books related to

---

[15] By the definition in Fig. 5.13 this implies that $Completed(D)$ is true.

the BPMN standard [196]. The first book [166] completes the critical work started in [78] (see also [42]) and offers an ASM-based definition of a 'purified' behavioral semantics of BPMN process diagrams. This eliminates numerous well-known deficiencies and shortcomings of the BPMN standard. The second book [167] extends this 'purified BPMN variant' by advanced interaction and communication concepts. To offer tool developers an unambiguous intuitive understanding of the intended meaning of the introduced modeling constructs, ASMs are used to define their behavior.

For a typical textbook BP example, namely the *ProcureToPay* case study in [100], an ASM ground model and a refinement to a CoreASM executable version have been presented in [246] and [245], respectively. The models illustrate in particular how by ASM refinements one can easily adapt a model to requirements changes.

Another interesting BPM use of ASM ground models shows how to cope with the request to provide a fully documented, precise, unambiguous requirements description without using technical terms (except terms the domain expert is familiar with). An invoice BP has been suggested in [115] as example for this endeavor and has been used in [56] to show how, once an ASM ground model has been developed starting from the originally given (incomplete and ambiguous) informal requirements, one can easily restate the model in accurate natural language terms. Such a reformulation maintains the correctness, completeness and consistency of the ground model ASM.

Conclusion. All these examples and the ASMs presented in this chapter illustrate how the ASM method supports the relevant features needed to appropriately model BPs and to correctly refine those models to executable code. To be mentioned in particular are the following features:

- component-based and stepwise definition,
- smooth integration of data and resource concerns into visualizable control-flow diagrams,
- treatment of timing and more generally nested interrupt/canceling issues (using the concept of cancel regions explained in Sect. 2.4.7),
- static or runtime assignment of groups of tasks to actors, where needed constrained by actor capability criteria, by allocation strategies, by the four-eyes and similar principles, etc.

Chapter 6
Modeling Distributed Systems

In this chapter we use the ASM method to model some characteristic features one finds in present-day distributed systems.[1] In Sect. 6.1 we show how to model establishing wireless communication routes between mobile independent agents of ad hoc networks. Since the structure of these networks is subject to dynamic change and is managed by the networks in a self-organizing way, without external administration, to model them involves concurrent communicating ASMs with a dynamic set of agents. In Sect. 6.2 we illustrate modeling basic elements of relaxed shared memory management for distributed systems. This involves concurrent communicating ambient ASMs, again with a dynamic set of agents. Both examples illustrate the role of ground models to provide a high-level yet complete explanation of complex system behavior, avoiding to bury behaviorally relevant design decisions into code. In Sect. 6.3 we survey some more applications of ASMs to specify complex multi-agent systems.

6.1 Routing in Mobile ad hoc Networks

In this section we develop a ground model for the basic features of the Ad hoc On-Demand Distance Vector (AODV) routing protocol proposed in [201].[2] We use the protocol as case study to illustrate how, by stepwise developing the components of an ASM model, one can explain complex intended

---

[1] For industrial-strength applications of the ASM method to programming language and virtual machine design see [232, 54, 118] and the recent survey [43].

[2] Due to the didactic purpose of this book, which is not a book on routing protocols for ad-hoc networks, we abstract from various features considered in [201]. This includes bidirectional communication, timing issues, thereby also route request repetitions in case a route request is not obtained in due time, garbage collection, and various performance-focussed features mentioned below. To obtain a full specification of the protocol one can add such features by appropriate ASM refinements.

© Springer-Verlag GmbH Germany, part of Springer Nature 2018
E. Börger, A. Raschke, *Modeling Companion for Software Practitioners*,
https://doi.org/10.1007/978-3-662-56641-1_6

system behavior from scratch, gently but accurately, supporting a correct *understanding* of the requirements by the programmers and of the high-level system behavior by the users of the system.

During the work on this case study it happened that the first author became his own guinea-pig: having no expertise with systems of communicating mobile agents, he started from scratch, namely from the requirements as formulated in the RFC document [201], trying to build an AODV ground model to make sure to fully understand the protocol. Not surprisingly, various places in this document popped up where the description is ambiguous or incomplete or where it revealed some inconsistency in the requirements. Also counter examples showed up to the argument put forward in [202, Appendix A] for the widely believed loop freedom claim for AODV. At this stage, to be able to correctly complete the ground model, we needed authoritative answers from experts of the field to clarify the critical issues. Left without answers from the protocol authors, we discovered a technical report [108] which eventually clarified all our questions. Therefore, the ground model ASM we define in this section is guided by the requirements in the RFC document [201], but informed by their professional analysis in [108].[3]

6.1.1 AODV *Machine and Data Structure*

The dynamic network of mobile agents is modeled as an undirected graph. We identify the nodes with a dynamic set of *Agent*s, also called hosts. The dynamic set of direct *Link*s (edges) defines for each agent a a dynamic set *neighb*or of other agents, with which a can communicate directly by sending messages.

If a *WantsToCommunicateWith* another agent b, it needs a communication path $a_0, a_1, \ldots, a_n$, also called a route, formed by *Active* direct links (so that in particular $a_{i+1} \in neighb(a_i)$) leading from the source node $a = a_0$ (called *originator*) to the *destination* node $b = a_n$. Node a can START COMMUNICATION WITH(b) right away if it *KnowsActiveRouteTo*(b) (see below the definition of this predicate). If it does not know an *Active* route to b, to learn about a route to b, the node will GENERATE ROUTE REQUEST

---

[3] In [108] a process algebra for AODV is defined and used for a detailed mathematical analysis. For the ambiguities and inconsistencies in the RFC document [201] various solutions (and their major implementations!) are rigorously formulated and evaluated, together with their behavioral consequences, in particular concerning loop freedom and route correctness. Also some accurately described improvements concerning certain performance-relevant shortcomings of AODV for route discovery and packet delivery are suggested. Although the compact functional process algebra notation makes it hard to grasp and check the model, especially for readers without experience with formal methods, this work is a brilliant illustration of the pragmatic, economical and not only scientific value of a precise high-level definition and analysis of accurate system models, prior to their implementation.

and BROADCAST it to all neighbors. Then a remains *WaitingForRouteTo*(b) until it receives information about a route to b, namely by receiving from some neighbor a route reply *rrep* which answers the *rrequest* by indicating how to reach b. A node may be simultaneously *WaitingForRouteTo*(b_i) for multiple agents b_i.

Thus, two roles of the ROUTER program each node is equipped with are to PROCESSROUTEREQuests and to PROCESSROUTEREPlies. Furthermore, if a node a detects a *LinkBreak* of the edge by which it was connected to a neighbor b, it should PROCESSROUTEERRor, namely GENERATEROUTEERRor and PROPAGATEROUTEERRor. At each moment the ROUTER performs at most one of these tasks, due to the single-agent nature of each ROUTER instance. This determines the overall component structure of the communicating ASM AODV $= (a, \text{AODVSPEC})_{a \in Agent}$ of agents, each one executing its own instance of the following program AODVSPEC:

AODVSPEC = **one of**   -- main program
   PREPARECOMM
   ROUTER

The submachines of the main program are defined as follows:

   PREPARECOMM =
    if *WantsToCommunicateWith*(*destination*) **then**
     if *KnowsActiveRouteTo*(*destination*)
     then
       STARTCOMMUNICATIONWITH(*destination*)
       WantsToCommunicateWith(*destination*) := *false*
       WaitingForRouteTo(*destination*) := *false*
     else
       if not *WaitingForRouteTo*(*destination*) **then**
        GENERATEROUTEREQ(*destination*)
        WaitingForRouteTo(*destination*) := *true*
   ROUTER = **one of**
    PROCESSROUTEREQ
    PROCESSROUTEREP
    PROCESSROUTEERR
   PROCESSROUTEERR = **one of**
    GENERATEROUTEERR
    PROPAGATEROUTEERR

We assume (as in [201]) that nodes can trust each other and that communication is reliable, in the sense that sent messages are not corrupted though they may not arrive at their destination, due to broken links or timeouts. We specify below only GENERATEROUTEREQUEST and the ROUTER, neither the communication trigger STARTCOMMUNICATIONWITH nor the component for the communication itself.

Since we treat AODV as a communicating ASM, all predicates and functions are private (here *WantsToCommunicateWith*, *KnowsActiveRouteTo*, *WaitingForRouteTo*, *neighb*, etc.), except the common background elements. In other words, they are implicitly parameterized by the executing agent **self**. We assume that the predicate *WantsToCommunicateWith* can be set to *true* only by the application program of each agent and to *false* only by PREPARECOMM. Note that if an agent a *WantsToCommunicateWith*(b) and does not know an *Active* route to b, it will GENERATEROUTEREQ(b) only once and enter *WaitingForRouteTo*(b) mode. However, it remains waiting to communicate with b until through a route reply received from some neighbor it *KnowsActiveRouteTo*(b). Only then a can apply its rule PREPARECOMM once more, this time to STARTCOMMUNICATIONWITH(b).

Exercise 55. The above defined rule PREPARECOMM abstracts from the feature considered in [201, Sect. 6.3] which permits a route request to be repeated (at most *RreqRetries* many times), namely if no information about the requested route is received within *NetTraversalTime*. Show how the rule can be refined to include such request repetitions.

6.1.1.1 Structure of Route Tables and Route Messages

The protocol handles generation and processing of messages of three types: *RouteRequest* messages to request a route to a destination in case no *Active* route to reach the destination is known, *RouteReply* messages to provide an answer to the *origin*ator of a route request in case a valid route to the destination has been found, and *RouteError* messages to inform about broken links in a known route. *Route control message* refers to any route request, reply or error message, as distinguished from messages which send data packets.

Route Tables. Each agent c keeps its 'knowledge' of possible communication paths in an initially empty route table RT. A route table *entry* $\in RT(c)$, which for brevity (hopefully not misleadingly) is often also called a route, provides information about a path from c to a destination, i.e. to some other network agent $d = dest(entry)$. The information comes in the form of the direction to take to reach d, indicated by a neighbor of c, called *nextHop*(*entry*), through which d can be reached (unless some link break occurred). Also the path length is recorded, called *hopCount*(*entry*), updated with each hop and intended to indicate the distance between c and d (hence the name distance vector protocol). It is a characteristic protocol feature that every route *entry* for a destination records only a *nextHop*(*entry*) to reach that destination. As a consequence, 'knowing' a route provides no direct knowledge of an entire path from c to d.

To guarantee loop freedom for the communication paths provided by the algorithm, each node maintains a local route request counter, called current sequence number and denoted *curSeqNum*(a). It is initialized with 0 and INCREMENTed (increased by 1) each time a sends out a new route request. The only other increase of $curSeqNum(a)$, in fact an INCREMENT to $curSeqNum(a) + 1$ as further explained below, may occur when a acts as destination node of a route request and generates a route reply to a new route request the *origin*ator of *req* generated after having learned that on its previously known *Active* path to a a *LinkBreak* occurred. The known information about $curSeqNum(b)$ is attached to each route request or reply message *msg* with $dest(msg) = b$. It is called $destSeqNum(msg)$ and records the highest value of $curSeqNum(b)$ the *msg* sender knows at the moment of sending, namely through route information for destination b in its route table or through the just received route request or reply with destination b. For this purpose, each $entry \in RT(a)$ for a route to b records the highest (also called latest or freshest) value of $curSeqNum(b)$ received by a as $destSeqNum(msg)$ in any route request, reply or error message *msg* concerning the destination b. The location with this information is called again destination sequence number, namely of that *entry*, and denoted $destSeqNum(entry)$.[4]

To prove that the sequence number mechanism prevents loops in communication paths established by the ROUTER, the following two properties of *destSeqNum*bers are crucial. Although a proof of the properties can be given only once the protocol rules are completely defined (see Exerc. 58), we state them already here to convey to the reader an intuitive idea about the role of destination sequence numbers.

Destination Sequence Number Lemma. In every run of AODV the following two properties hold:

Boundedness. For every route control message *msg* and every route table *entry* for a destination d, its corresponding *destSeqNum*ber never exceeds the *curSeqNum*ber of its destination—except an increase by 1 when it belongs to a not any more *Active* path to d where a *LinkBreak* occurred, formally:

$$destSeqNum(msg) \leq curSeqNum(dest(msg)) + 1$$
$$destSeqNum(entry) \leq curSeqNum(dest(entry)) + 1$$

Monotonicity. Whenever a value of a *destSeqNum*ber is refreshed or passed to a new route control message or route table entry, it is at most increased (never decreased). In other words, its given value is smaller than or equal to the refreshed or passed value.

By its definition, $destSeqNum(r)$ may be *unknown* to a when a sends a route request r with destination b. Therefore, in [201] a 'Valid Destination Sequence Number' flag is used. The reason is that a $destSeqNum(entry)$ may be defined (read: different from the value *unknown*) but not "valid", a case

---

[4] The two functions *destSeqNum* differ by the type of their arguments.

which is indicated by $known(entry) = false$, using a Boolean valued function $known$. One can then define the predicate $ValidDestSeqNum$ as follows:[5]

$ValidDestSeqNum(entry)$ **iff** $known(entry) = true$

Routes become unusable for sending data packets when a $link \in Link$ used by the route breaks, for example due to a neighbor's moving out of the range of direct reachability via this $link$. This route property is indicated using an $Active(entry)$ flag. When a link connecting a to a neighbor b breaks, each destination d of a route $entry \in RT(a)$ which uses b as $nextHop(entry)$ becomes unreachable. Therefore, the route is invalidated (for its use to send data packets in a *communication path*) by setting $Active(entry) := false$ and increasing its $destSeqNum(entry)$ by 1. $RouteError$ messages propagate the knowledge an agent a has acquired about unreachable destinations d, namely to each neighbor which has a route entry to d that uses a as $nextHop$ (see Sect. 6.1.4). These neighbors are called *precursors* and are also recorded in $RT(a)$-entries.

We therefore have the following elements of route table entries in $RT(a)$:[6]

- $dest(entry) \in Agent$
- $destSeqNum(entry) \in NAT \cup \{unknown\}$
- $known(entry) \in \{true, false\}$ indicating whether $destSeqNum(entry)$ is (in)valid
- $hopCount(entry) \in NAT$, intended as 'number of hops needed to reach destination' [201, p. 4][7]
- $nextHop(entry) \in Agent$ (a $neighbor$ of a if the link is not broken)
- $Active(entry) \in true, false$
- $precursor(entry) \subseteq Agent$ ($\subseteq neighb(a)$ if the links are not broken)

The predicate $KnowsActiveRouteTo(destination)$ in PREPARECOMM qualifies the information an agent keeps in its route table RT and is defined as follows:

$KnowsActiveRouteTo(destination)$ **iff forsome** $entry \in RT$
$dest(entry) = destination$ **and** $Active(entry)$

Each route table RT contains for each destination d at most one $entry$, namely such that $dest(entry) = d$. If it exists, we call it $entryFor(d, RT)$.

---

[5] For comparing $destSeqNumbers$ of route entries in route tables with those of route request, reply or error messages, we stipulate that $unknown < n$ for each $n \in NAT$ and $unknown + 1 = unknown$. Instead of $unknown$ one could use the ASM term **undef**.

[6] Reference [201] considers, besides $lifetime(entry)$, further route table locations keeping information on repairing invalid routes and on the network interface we abstract from here. We also abstract from the concern about $maxint$, using just NATural numbers.

[7] This declared intended meaning of $hopCount(entry)$ can be violated by the protocol. See the examples in Fig. 6.1, 6.2.

$entryFor(d, RT) =$
$$\begin{cases} entry & \textbf{if forsome } entry \in RT \; dest(entry) = d \\ \textbf{undef else} \end{cases}$$

Route Requests. Each route request $rreq \in RouteRequest$ contains information about the request $destination$ and its $origin$ator, together with the last known values of their request counters recorded as $destSeqNum(rreq)$ (whose value may be $unknown$) and $originSeqNum(rreq)$. The latter is initialized upon $rreq$ generation by the following update:

$originSeqNum(rreq) := curSeqNum(origin(rreq)) + 1.$

Each $rreq$ also keeps an information, called $hopCount$, about the distance minus 1 between an agent which receives $rreq$ and the request $origin$ator. As a consequence, $rreq$ is created with the initialization $hopCount(rreq) := 0$. Each $rreq$ is globally identified by the request $origin$ator and the current value $localId(rreq)$ of a $localReqCount$er which for this purpose is incremented by 1 when $rreq$ is generated. This yields the following derived function:

$globalId(rreq) = (localId(rreq), origin(rreq)).$

We therefore have the following elements of route requests:[8]

- $dest(rreq) \in Agent$ denoting the $dest$ination of the requested route
- $destSeqNum(rreq) \in NAT \cup \{unknown\}$
- $origin(rreq) \in Agent$ denoting the request originator
- $originSeqNum(rreq) \in NAT$
- $hopCount(rreq) \in NAT$ intended to denote the length minus 1 of the path the $rreq$uest traveled from $origin(rreq)$ to the $rreq$-receiving agent
- $localId(rreq) \in NAT$ recording the value of $localReqCount + 1$ when $rreq$ is created

Route Replies. Each route reply $rrep \in RouteReply$ contains information about the route request $origin$ator and the $dest$ination with associated well defined $destSeqNum(rrep)$. This information remains the same for each upon forwarding refreshed version $rrep'$ of $rrep$. In addition, each $rrep$ly comes with a $hopCount(rrep)$ that is updated upon forwarding a reply.[9]

- $dest(rrep) \in Agent$ denoting the $dest$ination of the detected route
- $destSeqNum(rrep) \in NAT$ with value determined upon creating $rrep$
- $origin(rrep) \in Agent$, the request originator to whom the reply is addressed
- $hopCount(rrep) \in NAT$ intended to denote the length of the current route leading from the $rrep$-sender to $dest(rrep)$

---

[8] Reference [201] considers further flags on various information (for example concerning bi-directional communication, etc.) we abstract from here.

[9] As stated above, we abstract from *lifetime* concerns, here the time 'for which nodes receiving the RREP consider the route to be valid' [201, p. 9]. We also abstract from further flags on various additional information, introduced in [201] to guarantee network traffic and performance properties.

Route Error Messages. A message *rerr* ∈ *RouteError* sent by an agent *a* indicates a set of destinations, together with their increased *destSeqNum* value, which became unreachable via *a*, i.e. cannot be reached at present using *a* as *nextHop* of a route entry. Details are explained in Sect. 6.1.4.

6.1.2 Generating and Processing Route Requests

When an agent *a* must GENERATEROUTEREQ(*destination*) it creates a new *r* ∈ *RouteRequest* message to be BROADCASTed to its *neighb*ors. It INCREMENTs both its *localReqCount* (used for *localId(r)*) and its *curSeqNum* (which is transmitted as *originSeqNum(r)*). To enable *a* to recognize (and not to answer itself to) *r*, should the message arrive via some neighbor, the request is BUFFERed, say by INSERTing it into a set of *ReceivedReq*uests. For the *lastKnownDestSeqNum* the document [201, p. 14] states that 'If no sequence number is known, the unknown sequence number flag MUST be set'. This can happen either because in *RT(a)* there is an *entry* for the *destination* with not *ValidDestSeqNum(entry)* or because there is no *entry* for the *destination*. In the second case we set *destSeqNum(r)* to *unknown* and *ValidDestSeqNum(r)* becomes *false*.

> GENERATEROUTEREQ(*destination*) =
>   **let** *r* = **new** (*RouteRequest*) **in**
>   *dest(r)* := *destination*
>   *destSeqNum(r)* := *lastKnownDestSeqNum(destination, RT)*
>   *origin(r)* := **self**
>   *originSeqNum(r)* := *curSeqNum* + 1
>   INCREMENT(*curSeqNum*)
>   *hopCount(r)* := 0
>   *localId(r)* := *localReqCount* + 1
>   INCREMENT(*localReqCount*)
>   **if** *entryFor(destination, RT)* ≠ **undef**
>   **then** *known(r)* := *known(entryFor(destination, RT))*
>   **else** *known(r)* := *false*
>   BROADCAST(*r*)
>   BUFFER(*r*)
>   **where**
>   BROADCAST(*r*) = **forall** *n* ∈ *neighb* **do** SEND(*r*, **to** *n*)
>   BUFFER(*r*) = INSERT(*globalId(r)*, *ReceivedReq*)
>   *lastKnownDestSeqNum(d, RT)* =
> $\begin{cases} destSeqNum(entry) & \textbf{if forsome } entry \in RT \ \ dest(entry) = d \\ unknown & \textbf{else} \end{cases}$
>   INCREMENT(*l*) = (*l* := *l* + 1)

To guarantee that PROCESSROUTEREQuest is performed at most once for a given route request *rreq*, upon receiving a *rreq* which at some time has been *AlreadyReceivedBefore*, the receiving agent *c* 'silently discards' [201, p. 16] (i. e., only CONSUMEs) *rreq*. Otherwise, *c* will BUILDREVERSEROUTE and either GENERATEROUTEREPLY(*rreq*)—in case it *FoundValidPathFor*(*rreq*)— or FORWARDREFRESHEDREQ(*rreq*).[10]

> PROCESSROUTEREQ(*rreq*) =
>> **if** *Received*(*rreq*) **and** *rreq* ∈ *RouteRequest* **then**
>>> **if not** *AlreadyReceivedBefore*(*rreq*) **then** -- no *rreq* processed twice
>>>> INSERT(*globalId*(*rreq*), *ReceivedReq*)
>>> **if** *HasNewReverseRouteInfo*(*rreq*) **then**
>>>> BUILDREVERSEROUTE(*rreq*)
>>>>> -- with freshest *destSeqNum* for *RT*-entry to *origin*ator)
>> **seq**
>>> **if** *FoundValidPathFor*(*rreq*)
>>> **then** GENERATEROUTEREPLY(*rreq*)
>>> **else** FORWARDREFRESHEDREQ(*rreq*)
>>>> -- with freshest *destSeqNum* in forwarded req for *dest*(*rreq*)
>> CONSUME(*rreq*)

BUILDREVERSEROUTE is defined below and serves to build a 'reverse path' from *c* back to the *origin*(*rreq*). The intention is to use this path to send a *rreply* back to the *origin*ator of *rreq*. For this purpose, *c* defines or updates a 'reverse route entry' *revEntry* with *dest*ination *origin*(*rreq*), if the *rrequest* *HasNewReverseRouteInfo*rmation. This is the reason why GENERATEROUTEREPLY can be executed only once the *nextHop* to the request *origin*ator is established, so that GENERATEROUTEREPLY sequentially follows BUILDREVERSEROUTE. Building the reverse route is done in such a way that the new *destSeqNum*(*revEntry*) holds the greatest (also called freshest) *curSeqNum*ber value *c* knows for the *rreq-origin*ator.

The receiving agent will FORWARDREFRESHEDREQ(*rreq*)—BROADCAST a *refreshed* version of the received *rrequest*—to its *neighb*ors if it had NOT *FoundValidPathFor*(*rreq*). When refreshing *rreq* to the request *r′* that has to be forwarded, the *destSeqNum*(*r′*) may be increased, passing from *destSeqNum*(*rreq*) to the *lastKnownDestSeqNum* for *dest*(*rreq*). If however the receiving agent *FoundValidPathFor*(*rreq*), it can GENERATEROUTEREPLY, a message *rreply* explained in Sect. 6.1.3 which travels back to the originator of the *rrequest* to inform it about the found path.

Reverse Route Remark. The *rreply* to the *rrequest* seems to be intended to travel along the reverse path, built by processing the *rrequest*.[11] However, the protocol as defined in [201] does not guarantee this. It can

---

[10] We leave it as Exerc. 56 to handle an entry for a route of length one from the receiver of the message to its sender. The same applies to route reply and to error messages.

[11] 'The reverse path route entries are maintained for at least enough time for the RREQ to traverse the network and produce a reply to the sender' [202, Sect. 2.1.1]. This view

happen that a reverse route, built by one *rreq*, even before being built completely, is already redirected (changed) by another route *request*, from the same originator but with different destination. See the example in Fig. 6.1. This follows from the fact that BUILDREVERSEROUTE(*rreq*) is called only if the *rrequest HasNewReverseRouteInfo*rmation.

The predicates and submachines of PROCESSROUTEREQ are defined as follows.

> *AlreadyReceivedBefore*(*req*) **iff** *globalId*(*req*) $\in$ *ReceivedReq*
> *FoundValidPathFor*(*req*) **iff**
>   *dest*(*req*) = **self or** *KnowsFreshEnoughRouteFor*(*req*, *RT*)
> *KnowsFreshEnoughRouteFor*(*req*, *RT*) **iff forsome** *entry* $\in$ *RT*
>   *dest*(*entry*) = *dest*(*req*) **and** *ValidDestSeqNum*(*entry*)
>   **and** *destSeqNum*(*entry*) $\geq$ *destSeqNum*(*req*)
>   **and** *Active*(*entry*)
> FORWARDREFRESHEDREQ(*r*) =
>   **let** *r'* = **new** (*RouteRequest*)
>   COPY(*dest, origin, originSeqNum, localId, known,* **from** *r* **to** *r'*)
>   *hopCount*(*r'*) := *hopCount*(*r*) + 1
>   *destSeqNum*(*r'*) := *max*{*destSeqNum*(*r*),   -- best known
>   *lastKnownDestSeqNum*(*dest*(*r*), *RT*)}   -- *destSeqNum*
>   BROADCAST(*r'*)
> COPY(*f₁, ..., fₙ,* **from** *arg* **to** *arg'*) =
>   **forall** $1 \leq i \leq n$ **do** $f_i(arg') := f_i(arg)$

A *rrequest* message, received by a node, *HasNewReverseRouteInfo*(*rreq*) if there is no entry for *origin*(*rreq*) in the node's route table or if there is some *entryFor*(*origin*(*rreq*), *RT*) for which the *rrequest HasNewOriginInfo*.

> *HasNewReverseRouteInfo*(*req*) **iff** *req* $\in$ *RouteRequest* **and**
>   *ThereIsNoRouteInfoFor*(*origin*(*req*), *RT*) **or**
>   (*ThereIsRouteInfoFor*(*origin*(*req*), *RT*) **and**
>   *HasNewOriginInfo*(*req*, *RT*))
> **where**
>   *ThereIsRouteInfoFor*(*d*, *RT*) **iff**
>   **forsome** *entry* $\in$ *RT dest*(*entry*) = *d*
>   *ThereIsNoRouteInfoFor*(*node*, *RT*) **iff**
>   **not** *ThereIsRouteInfoFor*(*node*, *RT*)

---

is held also by the definition in [201, p. 6] of a reverse route: 'A route set up to forward a reply (RREP) packet back to the originator from the destination or from an intermediate node having a route to the destination.' See also the explanation of the role of reverse routes where their construction is described in [201, p. 16]: 'This reverse route will be needed if the node receives a RREP back to the node that originated the RREQ'.

$HasNewOriginInfo(req, RT)$ **iff**   -- info on $curSeqNum(origin(req))$
   let $entry = entryFor(origin(req), RT)$
     $originSeqNum(req) > destSeqNum(entry)$
   or $originSeqNum(req) = destSeqNum(entry)$ **and**
     $(hopCount(req) < hopCount(entry)$ **or not** $Active(entry))$

If for a received *rrequest* $ThereIsNoRouteInfoFor(origin(rreq), RT)$, then
BUILDREVERSEROUTE(*rreq*) creates an RT-entry for the *originator* of *rreq*.
The $destSeqNum(e)$ of the new entry e records the information *rreq* carries
on the $curSeqNum(origin(rreq))$, the freshest information available on the
request count of $origin(rreq)$ (see EXTENDREVERSEROUTE).

If $ThereIsRouteInfoFor(origin(rreq), RT)$, a *revEntry* for the $origin(rreq)$
already exists and is refreshed if (and only if) the *rreq* $HasNewOriginInfo$.
This condition means that the information carried by the *rrequest* on the
*originatorSeqNum*ber is 'greater than' the information hold in *revEntry*, formally expressed by $originSeqNum(rreq) > destSeqNum(revEntry)$, or that the
two values are the same but the *rreq* knows a shorter path to the *origin*ator
or the *revEntry* is not *Active*. The update $Active(entry) := true$ guarantees
that the 'current node can use the reverse route to forward data packets in
the same way as for any other route in the routing table' [201, p. 17] (see
UPDATEREVERSEROUTE).

   BUILDREVERSEROUTE(*rreq*) =
    if $ThereIsRouteInfoFor(origin(rreq), RT)$
           -- *rreq* knows fresher $curSeqNum(origin(rreq))$ than RT
    then
      UPDATEREVERSEROUTE($entryFor(origin(rreq), RT), rreq$)
    else
      EXTENDREVERSEROUTE($RT, rreq$)
   where
    EXTENDREVERSEROUTE(RT, req) =
     let $e = $ **new** (RT)
      $dest(e) := origin(req)$
      $precursor(e) := \emptyset$
      UPDATEREVERSEROUTE(e, req)
    UPDATEREVERSEROUTE(e, req) =
     $destSeqNum(e) := originSeqNum(req)$
     $nextHop(e) := sender(req)$
     $hopCount(e) := hopCount(req) + 1$
     $Active(e) := true$
     $known(e) := true$

Fig. 6.1 shows a **redirecting reverse route** example: a_1 first generates
a route request $rreq[1]$ with $originSeqNum(rreq) = 1$ to a destination a_{n+1},
then another route request $req[2]$ with $originSeqNum(req) = 2$, to another
destination b, whose reverse path crosses at some node a_i the reverse path

segment already established by *rreq*. The arrows ← indicate a reverse route step. Initially every *curSeqNum* = 0.

The example shows that the *hopCount* of an existing and of a redirected *revEntry* can be in any relation: =, <, or >, contrary to the argument put forward in [202, Appendix A] to support the loop freedom claim.

Fig. 6.1 Redirecting Reverse Route example

(a) Reverse routes for segments of *rreq*-path from a_1 to a_{n+1} are created.

(b) a_i receives a new *req* from a_1 to another destination and redirects the *rreq* reverse route at a_i.

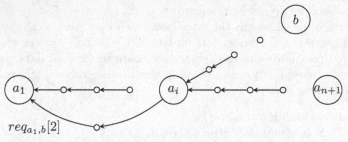

6.1.3 Generating and Processing Route Replies

An agent c is triggered to GENERATEROUTEREPLY to a *Received*(*rreq*) only when it *FoundValidPathFor*(*rreq*). This can only happen either because c is the *dest*(*rreq*) or it is an 'intermediate' node, a node which *KnowsFreshEnoughRouteFor* the *rreq* in its *RT* [201, p. 18]. The cases exclude each other because a *dest*(*rreq*) node has no *entryFor* itself in its routing table. In both cases, a new route reply *rrep* is created for *dest*(*rreq*) and *origin*(*rreq*), with a well-defined *destSeqNum*, and sent to the *nextHop* towards the message *originator*. This *nextHop* could be the *sender*(*rreq*), but not necessarily; this explains that GENERATEROUTEREPLY has to be performed after BUILDREVERSEROUTE.

The values set for *hopCount* and *destSeqNum* of *rrep* depend on whether c is the *dest*(*rreq*) or an intermediate node.

Reply generation by intermediate nodes. If c is an intermediate node, the values for *hopCount*(*rrep*) and *destSeqNum*(*rrep*) are retrieved from the

$entryFor(dest(rreq), RT(c))$. The freshness of $destSeqNum(rrep)$ is guaranteed using the fact that $c\ KnowsFreshEnoughRouteFor(rreq, RT)$.

PROCESSROUTEERR makes crucial use of this definition and the fact that this entry is also required to be *Active*. As a consequence, no node with a not *Active* $entryFor(dest(rreq), RT)$, or with a not *ValidDestSeqNum* or a too old *destSeqNum* in the $entryFor(dest(rreq), RT)$, can act as 'intermediate node' to generate a reply to a route request. In fact, if a node c with an *Active*(*entry*) for a previously established communication path between an originator a and a destination d detects a *LinkBreak* to a route neighbor $nextHop(entry)$, the node is excluded from acting as intermediate node by GENERATEROUTEERR. This machine makes *entry* inactive and increases the $destSeqNum(entry)$.[12]

Reply generation by destination nodes. If c is the $dest(rreq)$ node, a reply r is generated where $destSeqNum(r)$ is the maximum of c's *curSeqNum* and the *destSeqNum* of the *rreq*, value to which also *curSeqNum* is updated.

> GENERATEROUTEREPLY($rreq$) =
>   **let** r = **new** (*RouteReply*)
> $dest(r) := dest(rreq)$
> $origin(r) := origin(rreq)$
>   **if** $dest(rreq)$ = **self** **then**
> $hopCount(r) := 0$
> $destSeqNum(r) := max\{curSeqNum, destSeqNum(rreq)\}$
> $curSeqNum := max\{curSeqNum, destSeqNum(rreq)\}$
>   **else**
>   **let** $fwdEntry = entryFor(dest(rreq), RT)$
> $hopCount(r) := hopCount(fwdEntry)$
> $destSeqNum(r) := destSeqNum(fwdEntry)$
>   PRECURSORINSERTION($sender(rreq), fwdEntry$)[13]
>   SEND(r, **to** $nextHop(entryFor(origin(rreq), RT))$)
>   **where**
>   PRECURSORINSERTION($node, entry$) =
>   INSERT($node, precursor(entry)$)

To PROCESSROUTEREply, a node a will BUILDFORWARDROUTE if the *rreply HasNewForwardRouteInfo*. In this way, the node possibly updates its route table information about a path to the destination of the received reply message *rrep*, namely on the basis of the information provided on such a path by the message and the route table. If a *MustForward*(*rrep*) to the *origin*ator, it will FORWARDREFRESHEDREP(*rrep*) via an *Active* entry for the $origin(rrep)$. Note that if the *rrep* has no new forward route information, then the *rreply* message is "silently" discarded and not forwarded.

---

[12] Remember the stipulation that $unknown + 1 = unknown$.

[13] For Exerc. 57 one needs also a PRECURSORINSERTION of $nextHop(fwdEntry)$ into $precursor(entryFor(origin(rreq), RT))$.

PROCESSROUTEREP($rrep$) =
   if $Received(rrep)$ **and** $rrep \in RouteReply$ **then**
     if $HasNewForwardRouteInfo(rrep)$ **then**
      BUILDFORWARDROUTE($rrep$)
       if $MustForward(rrep)$ **then** FORWARDREFRESHEDREP($rrep$)
     CONSUME($rrep$)
where
   $MustForward(rep)$ **iff**
     $origin(rep) \neq$ **self** **and** $Active(entryFor(origin(rep), RT))$
   $HasNewForwardRouteInfo(rep)$ **iff** $rep \in RouteReply$ **and**
     $ThereIsNoRouteInfoFor(dest(rep), RT)$ **or**
      ($ThereIsRouteInfoFor(dest(rep), RT)$ **and**
       $HasNewDestInfo(rep, RT)$)

To BUILDFORWARDROUTE($rrep$) it must be checked whether at the receiving node $ThereIsRouteInfoFor$ the $dest(rrep)$ in a $fwdEntry \in RT$ or whether a new RT-entry has to be created.

In the first case, let $fwdEntry \in RT$ be the $entryFor(dest(rrep), RT)$. The node will UPDATEFORWARDROUTE for $fwdEntry, rrep$) since $HasNewDestInfo$ holds for ($rrep, RT$). This means that $rrep$ provides a 'fresher' destination sequence number than $fwdEntry$, or the same $destSeqNum$ber with either a shorter path to the $dest(rrep)$ or with a not $Active$ $fwdEntry$. Thus, flushing fresh information from $rrep$ to $fwdEntry$ concerns $destSeqNum$ber, $nextHop$, $hopCount$ and makes the $fwdEntry$ $Active$ with $ValidDestSeqNum$ber. Furthermore, the $nextHop$ of a reverse route in RT to $origin(rrep)$ (if there is such a route) is INSERTed into $precursor(fwdEntry)$.

In case of a new entry e that has to be created, additionally the $dest(e)$ must be defined.

BUILDFORWARDROUTE($rrep$) =
   if $ThereIsRouteInfoFor(dest(rrep), RT)$
     then UPDATEFORWARDROUTE($entryFor(dest(rrep), RT), rrep$)
     else EXTENDFORWARDROUTE($RT, rrep$)
where
   EXTENDFORWARDROUTE(RT, rep) =
     let $e =$ **new** (RT)   -- create new entry to extend forward route
      $dest(e) := dest(rep)$ -- with same $destination$ as rep
      UPDATEFORWARDROUTE(e, rep)
   UPDATEFORWARDROUTE(e, rep) =
     $destSeqNum(e) := destSeqNum(rep)$
     $nextHop(e) := sender(rep)$
     $hopCount(e) := hopCount(rep) + 1$
     $Active(e) := true$
     $known(e) := true$
     SETPRECURSOR(rep, e)

$HasNewDestInfo(rep, RT)$ **iff**   -- *entry* has either
  let $entry = entryFor(dest(rrep), RT)$
    $destSeqNum(rep) > destSeqNum(entry)$ -- older $destSeqNum$[14]
    or $(destSeqNum(rep) = destSeqNum(entry)$
      and $hopCount(rep) + 1 < hopCount(entry))$ -- or longer path
    or $(destSeqNum(rep) = destSeqNum(entry)$
      and $Active(entry) = false)$ -- or inactive route
SETPRECURSOR$(rep, e) =$
  if $MustForward(rep)$ **then**
   INSERT$(nextHop(entryFor(origin(rep), RT)), precursor(e))$

If there is no *fwdEntry* for $dest(rrep)$ in the route table RT or, for some $fwdEntry \in RT$, the predicate $HasNewDestInfo$ holds for *rrep* and *fwdEntry*, then *rrep*-data are copied not only into $entryFor(dest(rrep), RT)$ but also into the to-be-forwarded new $rrep' \in RouteReply$ with *hopCount* increased by 1. Note that if a *rreply* is received by a node which is not the $origin(rrep)$, but which has no *Active* $entryFor(origin(rep), RT)$, then the message is not forwarded (and curiously enough no error message is required to be generated).

FORWARDREFRESHEDREP$(rep) =$
  let $rep' = $ **new** $(RouteReply)$
  COPY$(dest, destSeqNum, origin,$ **from** rep **to** $rep')$
  $hopCount(rep') := hopCount(rep) + 1$
  SEND$(rep',$ **to** $nextHop(entryFor(origin(rep), RT)))$

Fig. 6.2 shows a **redirecting forward route** example. The notation is the same as explained for Fig. 6.1, arrows $\rightarrow$ indicate a forward route step. In the example, after a_1 and b have generated a route request to a_{n+1} with *originSeqNum*ber 1 and the destination node has generated a *rrep* for a_1 with $destSeqNum(rrep) = 0$, a_{n+1} generates a *rrquest* to another node z INCREMENTing its $curSeqNum(a_{n+1})$ to 1. Then node a_i receives the *reply* to *req* with $destSeqNum(rep) = 1$ before the *rreply* to *rreq*, thus redirecting the forward route built by *rrep* for communication between a_1 and a_{n+1}.

The example shows that the *hopCount* of an existing and of a redirected *fwdEntry* can be in any relation: $=, <,$ or $>$, contrary to the argument put forward in [202, Appendix A] to support the loop freedom claim.

Exercise 56. To avoid broadcasting requests for routes to neighbors the following optimization is considered in [201]. Whenever a node receives a control *message*, it will HANDLEROUTETOSENDERINFO$(message)$. This means to enter the information that the sender can be reached by a route of length 1 (possibly with *unknown* sequence number). Define this component.

---

[14] By *unknown* $< n$ for each $n = 0, 1, \ldots$ this condition includes the case $destSeqNum(entry) = unknown$, introduced by Exerc. 56.

Fig. 6.2 Redirecting Forward Route example

(a) Destination a_{n+1} answers *rreq* before *req* by *rrep*

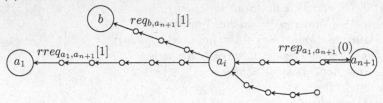

(b) a_{n+1} broadcasts a new *rrq* for destination z

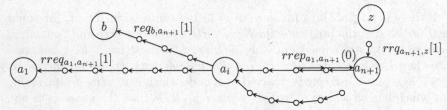

(c) a_i receives *rep* before *rrep* and increases $destSeqNum(entryFor(a_{n+1}, RT(a_i)))$

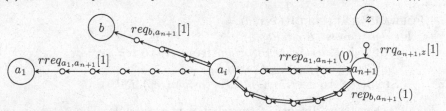

(d) FORWARDREFRESHEDREP(*rrep*) at a_i without changing $entryFor(a_{n+1}, RT(a_i))$ permits to establish the dotted communication path ($\cdots$) from a_1 to a_{n+1}

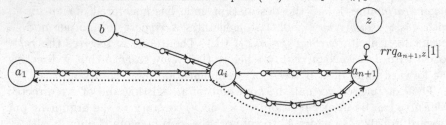

Exercise 57. In [201, Sect. 6.6.3] a feature establishing bidirectional communication is considered. It enables a destination node D to build a reverse route to the originator node O also in case an intermediate node answered the request for a route to D. By this "Gratuitous Reply", D gets a reply to build the reverse route to O without having sent a request for it. Show that, to specify this optimization, it suffices to refine GENERATEROUTEREPLY by inserting a submachine GENERATEGRATUITOUSREP(*rreq*).

6.1.4 Generating and Processing Route Error Messages

PROCESSROUTEERR performs two actions: to GENERATEROUTEERRor messages *rerr* when it detects a *LinkBreak* for a route entry for a destination, and to PROPAGATEROUTEERRor information along the *precursor* chain of route table entries. In case an *rerr* reaches an *origin*ator node that is *WaitingForRouteTo(d)* for one of the nodes which *rerr* informs to have become unreachable, the router does also REGENERATEROUTEREQ(d).

> PROCESSROUTEERR = **one of**
> GENERATEROUTEERR
> PROPAGATEROUTEERR

GENERATEROUTEERR considers every *entry* $\in$ *RT* whose direct link to *nextHop(entry)* is detected as broken. It sets *Active(entry)* := *false*, INCREMENTs *destSeqNum(entry)* and SENDs to each *node* $\in$ *precursor(entry)* the information on the unreachable destinations d which have some precursor, together with their INCREMENTed *destSeqNum(d)*; remember the stipulation that *unknown* + 1 = *unknown*. *LinkBreak* is a monitored predicate by which the ROUTER is informed about any loss of direct links to *neighb*ors, due to dynamic network changes. Since the set *UnreachEntry* is defined to contain only *Active* entries, a node never fires GENERATEROUTEERR more than once per detected *LinkBreak*, before the corresponding route *entry* becomes *Active* again.[15]

> GENERATEROUTEERR =
>   **let** *UnreachEntry* =
>   {*entry* $\in$ *RT* | *LinkBreak(nextHop(entry))* **and** *Active(entry)*}
>   **if** *UnreachEntry* $\neq \emptyset$ **then**   -- some broken link detected
>   **forall** *entry* $\in$ *UnreachEntry*
>   *Active(entry)* := *false*
>   INCREMENT(*destSeqNum(entry)*)
>   **let** *rerr* = {(*dest(e)*, *destSeqNum(e)* + 1) |
>   *e* $\in$ *UnreachEntry* **and** *precursor(e)* $\neq \emptyset$}
>   **forall** *a* $\in$ *precursor(entry)* SEND(*rerr*, **to** *a*)

PROPAGATEROUTEERR, upon receiving an *rerr* $\in$ *RouteError*, inactivates every route table *entry* which uses the *sender(rerr)* as *nextHop*, for each destination d with $(d, s) \in$ *rerr* and fresher sequence number s than *destSeqNum(entry)*, that is satisfying $s >$ *destSeqNum(entry)*. It also updates the *destSeqNum(entry)* to s and SENDs a refreshed message *rerr'* to all *precursor(entry)* nodes. *rerr'* rrestricts *rerr* to the elements of *UnreachDest* which have some precursor.

---

[15] We would have expected that in addition *precursor(entry)* is emptied, but the requirements do not mention any deletion of precursors.

If an *origin*ator node which is *WaitingForRouteTo*(d) receives an *rerr* containing some $(d, s) \in rerr$, it performs a REGENERATEROUTEREQ(d) step, which enables PREPARECOMM to fire once moreGENERATEROUTEREQ(d).

PROPAGATEROUTEERR =
  if *Received*(*rerr*) **and** *rerr* $\in$ *RouteError* **then**
    let *UnreachDest* $= \{(d, s) \in rerr \mid$ **forsome** *entry* $\in RT$
                $d = dest(entry)$ **and** *nextHop*(*entry*) = *sender*(*rerr*)
                    and *Active*(*entry*) **and** *destSeqNum*(*entry*) $< s\}$
    forall $(d, s) \in$ *UnreachDest*
      let *entry* = *entryFor*(d, RT)
        Active(*entry*) := *false*
        destSeqNum(*entry*) := s
        forall $a \in$ *precursor*(*entry*) SEND(*rerr'*, **to** a)
      if *WaitingForRouteTo*(d) **then** REGENERATEROUTEREQ(d)
    CONSUME(*rerr*)
  where
    err' $= \{(d', s') \in$ *UnreachDest* $\mid$ *precursor*(*entryFor*(d', RT)) $\neq \emptyset\}$
    REGENERATEROUTEREQ(d) = *WaitingForRouteTo*(d) := *false*

Exercise 58. Prove the Destination Sequence Number Lemma stated in Sect. 6.1.1.1 by checking each rule where a *destSeqNum*ber is updated. Formally this is an induction on runs of AODV.

Exercise 59. (Project) Refine the ASM model AODVSPEC to integrate the protocol features formulated in [201] which we have not dealt with here. Formulate and prove the corresponding correctness properties of interest.

6.2 Concurrency with Relaxed Shared Memory Model

Relaxed shared memory models can be found in various recent distributed systems. As concrete example we use the noSQL database system Cassandra [111] to illustrate modeling typical features of database management for concurrent processes, in particular data replication, distribution of replicas and background propagation of updates. In the context of ASMs it comes natural to consider bulk read- and write-requests, see the beginning of Sect. 6.2.1.2. We specify the functional data management behavior by a ground model (Sect. 6.2.1), which expresses the user request/response pattern view, and use two ASM refinements to describe in Sect. 6.2.2 some major replication policies and in Sect. 6.2.3 the internal interaction between distributed database components, called data centers. Since these components and their internal interaction remain hidden to the user, they are not included in the user view ground model. The section is based upon [221].

6.2.1 Memory Replication Ground Model

The definition of basic (Sect. 2.5) and concurrent (Definition 2) ASM runs assumes that in each step every ASM agent atomically reads and/or writes well-defined unique values in respective locations l. Due to the atomicity of read/write actions a simultaneous write of l by one agent and read of l by one or more agents are conflict-free, since the read action returns the value of l in the current state and the write action determines the value of l in the next state. Conflicts due to simultaneous writes are excluded in the ASM framework by the consistency constraint on update sets; obviously other techniques could be used, like explicit sequentialization, synchronization, insertion of mutual exclusion algorithms, etc.

But what to do in the case of the replication of every location l a machine sees and shares with other machines, namely by a family of locations $l', l'', \ldots$ in the underlying database none of the involved machines sees, but which are all considered as legitimate copies of l? Consider as extreme example the following concurrent machine IRIW (Independent Read Independent Write, see [70]) of four user agents $a_1, \ldots, a_4$ which interact with a database for reading and writing two 0-ary locations x, y by the following respective programs:

$$x := 1 \mid y := 1 \mid read(x) \text{ step } read(y) \mid read(y) \text{ step } read(x).$$

Assume that both locations x, y are replicated twice in the database by x', x'' resp. y', y''. Assume also that a) a write action to x or y triggers in the database an immediate update of one of the replicas and is followed later by an internal propagation action of the database, which performs an update also of the other replica, and that b) a read action of x, y returns the value of one of the replicas. Then it is possible that in a concurrent run which is started with value 0 for all replicas and where each agent makes once each of its possible moves, a_3 reads $x = 1, y = 0$ and a_4 reads $x = 0, y = 1$. The behavior depends on database internals, here which replica is directly affected by a write/read request of a user and what is the propagation time. Such behavior is usually considered as an undesirable database inconsistency; for example sequentially consistent runs in the sense of Lamport [170] exclude it. If in particular applications certain levels of database inconsistency may be tolerated, we would however require that the users are provided with a precise high-level computation model which allows them to understand such behavior and to evaluate whether it is acceptable for their application. We provide here an ASM describing some characteristic features of the replication-based shared memory model of the noSQL memory management system Cassandra [111] and use the model to exhibit their impact on data consistency.

6.2.1.1 Cassandra Signature

Cassandra can be seen as managing the storage of relations P_i $(i = 1, \ldots, k)$ by replicating each of them in a cluster $\mathcal{D}_i$ of data centers (read: physical machines) $d \in \mathcal{D}_i$; the clusters partition an overall data center set $\mathcal{D} = \bigcup_{i=1}^{k} \mathcal{D}_i$. Users appear as elements $(a, pgm(a))$ of a concurrent ASM USERS $= (a, pgm(a))_{a \in \mathcal{A}}$. Each of them communicates with Cassandra via a dedicated data center $home(a) \in \mathcal{D}$. We model each data center as database agent d whose program $pgm(d)$ is defined in Sect. 6.2.1.2. Essentially, a data center $home(a)$ receives read/write requests from a and responds to them, namely by returning to a values it reads resp. acknowledgments of updates it performs in the database. The characteristic replica-based database feature is that these database-internal read/write actions involve not only replicas of data kept by $home(a)$, but also replicas in other data centers (in the cluster related to the request)—feature whose details remain hidden to the user (except for a concept of read/write policies we analyze in Sect. 6.2.2).

In Cassandra relations come with primary keys through which (and only through which) data can be accessed. Thus, each P_i denotes (read: is interpreted as) a finite set of $(a_i + c_i)$-tuples, a subset of some set $K^{a_i} \times B^{c_i}$ with fixed a_i, c_i and a static set K^{a_i} of key values; a_i is called the key arity and c_i the co-arity of P_i. The interpretations of P_i are constrained as follows: the key arity a_i gives rise to a function $p_i : K^{a_i} \to B^{c_i}$ (so that K^{a_i} is called its $keyDomain(p_i)$) which is classified as agent-dependent function. Thus each pair $(p_i, \mathbf{k})$ with $\mathbf{k} \in K^{a_i}$ is considered as a location that is 'shared' in the following sense by user agents a: in every state S of a, the value of the location $(p_i, \mathbf{k})$ is determined by $eval_a^S(p_i(\mathbf{k}))$ (see Def. 8), a tuple $\mathbf{v} \in B^{c_i}$ communicated to a by its $home(a)$ data center as the current database value of some replica(s) of the location. This value in a given state may be different for different agents, triggering a consistency issue we will consider later. From the modeling point of view the agent-dependency of the function p_i means that the user machines are treated as ambient ASMs, in the sense defined in Chap. 4.

In Cassandra what is replicated are p_i-values which are associated in the database with so-called horizontal relation fragments. The fragmentation is described using static hash functions on the primary key values:

$$h_i : K^{a_i} \to [m, M] \subseteq \mathbb{Z}.$$

These functions assign a hash-key to each key value at which in the memory some value may be defined. The interval $[m, M]$ of hash-key values is partitioned into interval ranges $[m, M] = \bigcup_{j=1}^{q_i} range_j$, i.e. with $range_{j_1} < range_{j_2}$ for all $j_1 < j_2$ so that each range is again an interval. It is these range intervals that are used for the horizontal fragmentation of the function p_i into q_i fragments:

$$Frag_{j,i} = \{\mathbf{k} \in K^{a_i} \mid h_i(\mathbf{k}) \in range_j\}.$$

Therefore, the values associated in the database with elements of $Frag_{j,i}$ determine the set of all key/value pairs $(\mathbf{k}, \mathbf{v})$, where the memory for the key stores a defined[16] value $\mathbf{v}$ which may 'serve as possible value of $p_i(\mathbf{k})$'. For a tuple $\mathbf{v}$ to 'serve as possible value of $p_i(\mathbf{k})$' means that a database agent upon a read request for the location $(p_i, \mathbf{k})$ may send $\mathbf{v}$ as current value to the requesting user. We call each such set of key/value pairs with keys in $Frag_{j,i}$ a *replica* of $Frag_{j,i}$. Cassandra keeps in each data center $d \in \mathcal{D}_i$ r_i replicas of $Frag_{j,i}$. The *replication factor* r_i is defined for the cluster $\mathcal{D}_i$ to which d belongs.

To describe the effect of read/write operations on the elements of a replica let each data center $d \in \mathcal{D}_i$ consist of n_i nodes, for brevity say numbers $j' \in \{1, \ldots, n_i\}$.[17] For each node j', let $p_{i,j,d,j'}$ be (a symbol for) a dynamic function we call a *replica function*. A replica function records the value $p_{i,j,d,j'}(\mathbf{k}) = \mathbf{v}$ of replica elements $(\mathbf{k}, \mathbf{v})$ in memory. To ease the formulation and investigation of policies that guarantee certain to-be-specified levels of consistency (as known from replication in relational databases), we consider values in replicas to come with timestamps (see below for details).[18] Thus, $p_{i,j,d,j'}$ has the same arity a_i as p_i but co-arity $c_i + 1$, so that its values consist of c_i-tuples $\mathbf{v}$—called relation values—and a timestamp. It is assumed that for each relation and fragment, in each data center d, all replica functions $p_{i,j,d,j'}$ are always defined for the same keys $\mathbf{k} \in Frag_{j,i}$ though their values— either the relation value or the timestamp or both—may differ from replica to replica. Thus a fragment is always replicated as a whole.

We write $HoldsReplica(j', d, j, i)$ to denote that the node j' in the data center $d \in \mathcal{D}_i$ stores in the database a replica of $Frag_{j,i}$. The definition implies that if $HoldsReplica(j', d, j, i)$ holds and $p_{i,j,d,j'}(\mathbf{k})$ is defined, then $h_i(\mathbf{k}) \in range_j$. The assumption mentioned above for replica functions means that for each key value $\mathbf{k} \in K^{a_i}$ the following holds:

if $HoldsReplica(j', d, j, i)$ then forall $j^* \in \{1, \ldots, n_i\}$
  $p_{i,j,d,j'}(\mathbf{k})$ is defined if and only if $p_{i,j,d,j^*}(\mathbf{k})$ is defined.

When users interact with Cassandra to read or update some current p_i-values in the database, Cassandra follows a *read/writePolicy*, described in Sect. 6.2.2, to choose a set of replicas of fragments it uses to react to the user request. These replicas are formulated as a set of pairs (d', j'), which determine the replica functions $p_{i,j,d',j'}$ Cassandra will read or update. We write $ReplicaNodes_{i,j}$ for the set of all such pairs for given $Frag_{j,i}$:

---

[16] As usual in databases, a relation for a given argument may not be defined; this is often also expressed by saying that the relation for this argument has no value. In an ASM we would usually represent this by assigning the value **undef**, but see the footnote on 'undefined data' in Sect. 6.2.1.2.

[17] Obviously, nodes of different data centers are different, so we should write something like $node_{d,1}, \ldots, node_{d,n_i}$. But since we always speak about nodes in a data center which is known from the context, we simplify the notation using j' instead of $node_{d,j'}$.

[18] Cassandra assumes correct timestamps to be provided by the programs that access the database.

$ReplicaNodes_{i,j} = \{(d', j') \mid d' \in \mathcal{D}_i \text{ and } 1 \le j' \le n_i\}.$

For a proper handling of timestamps we adopt Lamport's concept of logical timestamps [169]. Thus, each data center d has a logical $clock_d$, which indicates the current time at data center d and is assumed to advance (without this being further specified). Timestamps are evaluated resp. updated by a data center when it evaluates a read request resp. receives a write request. In addition, the following requirements are assumed to be satisfied:

1. Timestamps are totally ordered.
2. Timestamps set by different data centers are different from each other.[19]
3. Timestamps respect the inherent order of message passing, i. e. when data with a timestamp t is created at data center d and sent to data center d', then at the time the message is received, the clock at d' must show a time larger than t.
4. When a timestamp is set (except when adjusted), it is increased.

When condition 3 is not met, a data center may adjust its clock for logical time synchronization [169] using the following machine:

  $\textsc{AdjustClock}(d, t) = (clock_d := t')$
    where $t' =$ the smallest possible timestamp at d with $t \le t'$

6.2.1.2 Cassandra Rules

Since in one step an ASM may read and/or write values for a set of locations, it is easy to model bulk read/write access as they appear in SQL-like query languages. For the sake of generality, given that bulk read/write access is supported also by Cassandra, we consider a) queries $write(p_i, p)$, where p may have multiple key/value-pairs, and b) queries of form $read(p_i, \varphi)$ to request the current value of locations $(p_i, \mathbf{k})$ for the set of keys $\mathbf{k} \in K^{a_i}$ which satisfy condition $\varphi(\mathbf{k})$.[20] Due to the fragmentation this set splits into subsets of $Frag_{j,i}$:

$$keyDomain(p_i) \uparrow \varphi = \{\mathbf{k} \in K^{a_i} \mid \varphi(\mathbf{k})\} = \bigcup_{j=1}^{q_i} Frag_{j,i} \uparrow \varphi$$

The ground model abstracts from the details of how the database selects replicas when reacting to read/write requests from users. It is only stipulated that the selection *Complies* with a configurable *readPolicy* or a configurable *writePolicy*. A detailed definition of some major policies Cassandra supports is given as refinement in Sect. 6.2.2. For reasons of simplicity, we assume in

---

[19] One might assume that a timestamp created by data center d has the form $n + o_d$ with a positive integer n generated by d and a real number offset $o_d \in (0, 1)$, such that offsets of different data centers are different.

[20] The special case of a single (not bulk) $read(p_i, k)$ appears as the special case of a singleton set.

the abstract model that nodes in a data center are always reachable ('alive'), so that the values they record can be retrieved. Non-reachability issues can be treated in a much simpler way when more details about the internal interaction between data centers are available, see Sect. 6.2.3.

When $home(a)$ receives a $read(p_i, \varphi)$ request from user agent a, the data center follows its $readPolicy$ to select for each $Frag_{j,i}$ a set $C_{i,j}$ of data centers $d' \in \mathcal{D}_i$ and nodes j' with replicas of $Frag_{j,i}$. This involves reading, for certain key values $\mathbf{k}$, the current database value of terms $p_{i,j,d',j'}(\mathbf{k})$. These readings yield possibly multiple time-stamped values $(\mathbf{v}, t)$. Out of those a defined value $\mathbf{v} \neq null$ with the latest (most recent) timestamp is selected and sent to a, where it is interpreted as the up-to-date value of $p_i(\mathbf{k})$.[21] Since we require that timestamps set by different data centers differ, it follows that for given $\mathbf{k}$, the value $\mathbf{v}$ with the latest timestamp is unique.

This explains ANSWERREADREQ_i, which is part of the $pgm(d)$ the data center agent $d \in \mathcal{D}_i$ executes upon receipt of a $read(p_i, \varphi)$ request.

$\text{ANSWERREADREQ}_i =$
  if $Received(read(p_i, \varphi), \textbf{from } a)$ **then**
   forall $j \in \{1, \dots, q_i\}$ -- for each fragment choose complying replicas
    choose $C_{i,j} \subseteq ReplicaNodes_{i,j}$ **with** $Complies(C_{i,j}, readPolicy)$
    let $t_{max}(\mathbf{k}) =$ -- compute most recent timestamp
     $\max\{t \mid p_{i,j,d',j'}(\mathbf{k}) = (\mathbf{v}', t) \textbf{ forsome } \mathbf{v}', (d', j') \in C_{i,j}\}$
        -- collect most recent defined values in j-th fragment
    let $\rho_{i,j} = \{(\mathbf{k}, \mathbf{v}) \mid \mathbf{k} \in Frag_{j,i} \uparrow \varphi \textbf{ and } \mathbf{v} \neq null \textbf{ and}$
       $p_{i,j,d',j'}(\mathbf{k}) = (\mathbf{v}, t_{max}(\mathbf{k})) \textbf{ forsome } (d', j') \in C_{i,j}\}$
    let $\rho = \bigcup_{j=1}^{q_i} \rho_{i,j}$ -- collect values from all fragments
    $\text{SEND}(ValFor(read(p_i, \varphi), \rho), \textbf{to } a)$
          -- send current (p_i, φ)- values
   $\text{CONSUME}(read(p_i, \varphi), \textbf{from } a)$

For a $write(p_i, p)$ request sent by agent a to data center d there is an analogous rule d executes to process the request. In all replicas of $Frag_{j,i}$ selected by a $writePolicy$ and for each key $\mathbf{k}$ at which p provides a relation value $\mathbf{v}$, older database values at $\mathbf{k}$ are updated to the fresh p-value $\mathbf{v}$[22] with the current data center time $clock_d$ as timestamp. The clocks of the corresponding data centers d' that are 'behind' this current data center time are adjusted by $clock_d$, more precisely: if the current time $t_{current}$ of the managing data center

---

[21] We treat the case of 'undefined data', i.e. of keys $\mathbf{k}$ for which the memory has no record of a value $\mathbf{v}$, by special data $(null, -\infty)$, carrying a special value $null$ and the smallest possible timestamp $-\infty$. They are considered as value of $p_{i,j,d,j'}(\mathbf{k}) = (null, -\infty)$. To delete a record, we use $p_{i,j,d,j'}(\mathbf{k}) = (null, t)$ with deletion timestamp $t > -\infty$. Deletion timestamps t become obsolete once via propagation the value $(null, t)$ has been assigned to all replicas, whereafter the physical removal of such data from the database can be performed. We abstract here from the physical removal. Should the data center find no value $\mathbf{v} \neq null$, then it returns the empty set as answer.

[22] This value may be $null$ to capture deletion.

d is later than the clock at data center d', $clock_{d'}$ is adjusted by d'. The new value $(\mathbf{v}, t_{current})$ is also propagated asynchronously to the non-selected copies (see the definition below). This explains PERFORMWRITEREQ$_i$ in $pgm(d)$, which is executed by d upon receipt of an update request $write(p_i, p)$:

> PERFORMWRITEREQ$_i =$
>   **if** $Received(write(p_i, p), \mathbf{from}\ a)$ **then**
>   **let** $t_{current} = clock_{\mathbf{self}}$ -- retrieve current data center time
>   **forall** $j \in \{1, \ldots, q_i\}$ -- for each fragment choose complying replicas
>   **choose** $C_{i,j} \subseteq ReplicaNodes_{i,j}$ **with** $Complies(C_{i,j}, writePolicy)$
>   **forall** $(d', j') \in C_{i,j}$ -- for each chosen d' and replica
>   **forall** $(\mathbf{k}, \mathbf{v}) \in p$ **with** $h_i(\mathbf{k}) \in range_j$ -- for each p-value
>   **forall** $\mathbf{v}', t$ **with** $p_{i,j,d',j'}(\mathbf{k}) = (\mathbf{v}', t)$ **and** $t < t_{current}$
> $p_{i,j,d',j'}(\mathbf{k}) := (\mathbf{v}, t_{current})$ -- update older db value
>   PROPAGATE$(i, j, \mathbf{k}, \mathbf{v}, t_{current}, C_{i,j})$
>   -- propagate p-value to non-chosen replicas
>   **if** $clock_{d'} < t_{current}$ **then** ADJUSTCLOCK$(d', t_{current})$
>   SEND$(AckFor(write(p_i, p)), \mathbf{to}\ a)$
>   CONSUME$(write(p_i, p), \mathbf{from}\ a)$

For the background propagation of updates to all non-selected replicas in any data center, each data center agent has a PROPAGATE rule. To let the propagation work asynchronously, a new agent is created. It executes a program which performs the updates and the clock adjustment for all data centers d' and nodes j' which were not considered in the policy-conform selected set $C_{i,j}$. We maintain the abstract functional ground model view by letting the background propagation program perform all the updates in one step and then kill the executing agent (by deleting it from the set of still executing agents). The asynchrony is nevertheless achieved by the fact that the newly created agent b can perform its step in a run any moment after—and only after—the step of the data center d which created b.

> PROPAGATE$(i, j, \mathbf{k}, \mathbf{v}, t, C) =$
>   **let** $b = \mathbf{new}\ (Agent)$
> $pgm(b) :=$
>   **forall** $(d', j') \in ReplicaNodes_{i,j} \setminus C$
>   **forall** $\mathbf{v}', t'$ **with** $p_{i,j,d',j'}(\mathbf{k}) = (\mathbf{v}', t')$ **and** $t' < t$
> $p_{i,j,d',j'}(\mathbf{k}) := (\mathbf{v}, t)$
>   **if** $clock_{d'} < t_{current}$ **then** ADJUSTCLOCK(d', t)
>   DELETE$(b, Agent)$[23]

---

[23] Since in the ground model the propagation is formulated as happening in parallel for all involved replicas, the propagation agent performs only this one step and thus can also kill itself right away.

Thus, in the user view of the request/response pattern interaction with Cassandra, the home data center agent $d \in \mathcal{D}_i$ executes the following program $pgm(d) = \text{DATACENTERUSERVIEW}_i$. The rules ADJUSTCLOCK and PROPAGATE defined above appear as declared rule (callable subprogram):

$\text{DATACENTERUSERVIEW}_i =$
$\quad \text{ANSWERREADREQ}_i$
$\quad \text{PERFORMWRITEREQ}_i$

Let CLUSTERUSERVIEW_i be the concurrent ASM of all data center agents $d \in \mathcal{D}_i$ with $pgm(d) = \text{DATACENTERUSERVIEW}_i$.

Obviously, in a concurrent run of USERS and CLUSTERUSERVIEW_i, simultaneous write requests by different users may yield conflicts and/or inconsistencies. This depends on timing issues (for the communication, the writes and their propagation) and in part on the replication policies we define in the next section, where we return to the consistency question.[24]

6.2.2 Replication Policy Refinement

We list here the major replication policies offered by Cassandra. In the model they appear as values of *readPolicy* and *writePolicy*, which constrain the read/write actions. We define for them the predicate *Complies* which is used in $\text{DATACENTERUSERVIEW}_i$. These definitions provide the technical details to rigorously analyze which replication policies guarantee which kind of data consistency.

A replication policy determines how many replicas are to be taken into account to perform a database read or a write requested by a user. In other words, it is about the cardinality of the selected subsets $C_{i,j} \subseteq ReplicaNodes_{i,j}$ and the data centers d at which replicas are chosen in $C_{i,j}$. The cardinality condition is indicated by *all* ('all replicas are accessed') or by a number *one, two, three*. Replicas can also be requested to be taken only locally. In this case the policy is indicated by a pair $(num, At(d))$, indicating the number of replica nodes and the data center where they have to be taken ($d = \mathbf{self}$). The policy can also be a *quorum* relation between $C_{i,j}$ and $ReplicaNodes_{i,j}$. This leads to the following definition of *Complies*:

$Complies(C, policy)$ **iff forsome** (i, j)
$\quad C \subseteq ReplicaNodes_{i,j}$ **and**
$$\begin{cases} C = ReplicaNodes_{i,j} & \text{if } policy = all \\ |C| = num & \text{if } policy = num \\ |C| = num \text{ and } C = C \uparrow d & \text{if } policy = (num, At(d)) \\ q \cdot |ReplicaNodes_{i,j}| < |C| & \text{if } policy = quorum(q) \end{cases}$$

---

[24] With a monolithic view on the database, i.e. assuming that there is a unique database agent db with $home(a) = db$ for all agents a, the consistency issue changes, see the analysis in [221].

where

$num \in \{one, two, three\}$ **and** $0 < q < 1$

$C \uparrow d = \{(d', j') \in C \mid d' = d\}$ -- replicas taken only in d

Value $q = \frac{1}{2}$ expresses that the majority of replicas is considered. In a similar way one can define local quorum versions:

$Complies(C, (quorum(q), At(d)))$ **iff**
    $Complies(C, quorum(q))$ **and** $C \models C \uparrow d$
$Complies(C, (quorum(q), At(all)))$ **iff forall** $d \in \mathcal{D}_i$
    $q \cdot |ReplicaNodes_{i,j} \uparrow d| < |C \uparrow d|$

Cassandra uses the specification of read- and write-policies to determine the degree of consistency which can be guaranteed in concurrent runs of users and cluster data center agents (so-called *tunable consistency* concept). These runs appear in the ground model as concurrent ASM runs of USERS and CLUSTERUSERVIEW$_i$. For instance, if the policy is *all* for both reads and writes, then—exploiting the atomicity of ground model actions—the following can be proved: for any set of read requests, the database returns the unique freshest value (the one with latest timestamp in the state of the database access through which the requests are elaborated); furthermore if one (and simultaneously no other) data center in a cluster receives a write request, this request triggers an update of all replicas in the database to the new value. With the *one* policy in a given database state, different replica functions may have different values so that inconsistency phenomena can occur, like the one explained for the IRIW program at the beginning of Sect. 6.2.1. For a rigorous definition and detailed analysis of a certain form of consistency one can prove in the Cassandra ground model, to be achievable with some read/write policies, we refer the reader to [221].

6.2.3 Data Center Communication Refinement

In this section we enrich the interaction model between users and Cassandra by adding the internal communication between data centers. The idea is to split for each user request each atomic ground model step ANSWERREADREQ$_i$ or PERFORMWRITEREQ$_i$ of Cassandra by a) delegating to each involved data center the work to be done at its local nodes, b) collecting the local responses, and c) sending out the final response to the requestor once the collected local responses are *Sufficient* for the underlying read/write policy. To model this we need three new rules:

- A rule to MANAGEINTERNALREQuests which arrive by internal communication from some data center $d \in \mathcal{D}_i$. By this rule, each data center elaborates and internally communicates request responses on the basis of the data stored at its own local nodes (Sect. 6.2.3.2).

- A rule to DELEGATEEXTERNALREQuest users send to their *home* data center $d \in \mathcal{D}_i$. By this rule, each data center agent d forwards the user request by internal communication to all data centers in $\mathcal{D}_i$ so that each of them will MANAGEINTERNALREQ (Sect. 6.2.3.1).
- A rule MANAGERESPONSECOLLECTION a) to collect from all data centers their local, internally communicated response to the user *request*, b) to check whether the accumulated responses are *Sufficient* for the underlying read/write policy, and c) in case they are sufficient for the *request*, to send the final answer to the requesting user agent a. To this purpose, part of DELEGATEEXTERNALREQ is the creation of a collector agent c_{req} (one for each *request*) whose role is to execute the MANAGERESPONSECOLLECTION rule (Sect. 6.2.3.3). In this way the *home*(a) data center acts as mediator (via DELEGATEEXTERNALREQ) and by MANAGEINTERNALREQ contributes to MANAGERESPONSECOLLECTION.

In this database view, the CLUSTERMANAGEMENT$_i$ appears as a concurrent ASM of data center agents $d \in \mathcal{D}_i$, each equipped with the following program CLUSTERDATACENTER$_i$, together with the response collector agents the data center agents create when they receive a request. The collector agent program MANAGERESPONSECOLLECTION appears as declared rule.

> CLUSTERDATACENTER$_i$ =
>   DELEGATEEXTERNALREQ$_i$
>   MANAGEINTERNALREQ$_i$

Decentralizing the atomic ANSWERREADREQ$_i$ and PERFORMWRITEREQ$_i$ steps provides the possibility to perform reads/writes on replicas in many different orders, affecting not only the consistency issue, but also the correctness of the refinement of CLUSTERUSERVIEW$_i$ to CLUSTERMANAGEMENT$_i$. We come back to this question at the end of Sect. 6.2.3.3.

In the next three subsections we notationally suppress the arbitrarily fixed cluster index i.

6.2.3.1 Delegation of External Requests

As the name of the rule indicates, when a *request* from some user a is *Received*, the receiving data center agent d performs two actions:

- Create a response collector agent c and INITIALIZE it appropriately. This includes equipping it with the MANAGERESPONSECOLLECTION program.
- FORWARD the *reqest*, together with the information on response collector and current data center time, to all data centers for local *reqest* handling.

When d receives an internal *request* it will HANDLELOCALLY the *request* on the basis of the replica data kept in its own nodes.

$\textsc{DelegateExternalReq} =$
  if $Received(req, \textbf{from } a)$ **then**
    let $t_{current} = clock_{\textbf{self}}$ -- retrieve current data center time
    let $c = \textbf{new } (Agent)$ -- create response collector
      $\textsc{Initialize}(c, (req, a, \textbf{self}))$ -- and initialize it
      $\textsc{Forward}(req, c, t_{current})$ -- delegate response
    $\textsc{Consume}(req, \textbf{from } a)$
  where
    $\textsc{Forward}(r, c, t) =$ -- delegate response throughout the cluster
      forall $d \in \mathcal{D}_i$ **do** $\textsc{Send}((r, c, t), \textbf{to } d)$
    $req \in \{read(p_i, \varphi), write(p_i, p)\}$ **forsome** φ, p (with fixed p_i)

The response collector c needs an initially empty set $ReadVal$, where to collect the local values for a read *request* sent by the data centers to c when they $\textsc{HandleLocally}$ the *request*. The policy compliance check is performed by counting the number of inspected replicas of the j-th fragment at data center d and the number of inspected replicas of the j-th fragment. The counting is performed using counter locations $count_c(j, d)$ and $count_c(j)$, which obviously are both initialized by 0. To send the final response to the user who originated the *request* to Cassandra, the response collector has to know the *request*, its *requestor* and the mediating data center agent $home(requestor)$. This explains the following definition:

$\textsc{Initialize}(c, (r, usr, d)) =$
  $pgm(c) := \textsc{ManageResponseCollection}$
  $ReadVal_c := \emptyset$ -- initialize set where to collect responses
  forall $d \in \mathcal{D}_i$ **forall** $1 \leq j \leq q_i$
    $count_c(j, d) := 0$ -- inspected $Frag_{j,i}$-replicas at d
    $count_c(j) := 0$ -- inspected $Frag_{j,i}$-replicas
  $request_c := r$ -- record user request
  $requestor_c := usr$ -- record user
  $mediator_c := d$ -- record $home(usr)$

6.2.3.2 Management of Internal Requests

Internal requests received by a data center contain the original *request* together with information a) on the response collector c to whom to send the response, and b) on the timestamp t with which the *request* is elaborated.

$\textsc{ManageInternalReq}_i = \textbf{if } Received(req, c, t) \textbf{ then}$
  par $(\textsc{HandleLocally}_i(req, c, t), \textsc{Consume}(req, c, t))$

$\textsc{HandleLocally}(req, c, t)$ preserves most of the corresponding ground model action except for checking the read/write policy, a check which is performed in the refined model by the response collector. Therefore, there is a read and a write request version. For both we use a monitored predicate

Alive to describe that a node in a data center is accessible, meaning for example that it replies fast enough to the request. In fact, only *Alive* nodes contribute to the number of inspected replicas.

For a $read(p_i, \varphi)$ request the receiving data center selects from all of its *Alive* replica nodes the value with locally maximal timestamp. It sends these values with their computed local timestamp to the response collector as local answer to the read request, including into the answer also the number of inspected replicas.

$\text{HANDLELOCALLY}(read(p_i, \varphi), c, t) =$
    let $d = \mathbf{self} \in \mathcal{D}_i$ -- at the local data center d
    forall $j \in \{1, \dots, q_i\}$ -- for each fragment
    let $G_{i,j,d} = \{j' \mid HoldsReplica(j', d, j, i) \textbf{ and } Alive(j', d)\}$
                             -- inspect replicas at all *Alive* d-nodes
    let $t_{max}(\mathbf{k}) =$ -- to compute their most recent timestamp
       $\max\{t \mid p_{i,j,d,j'}(\mathbf{k}) = (\mathbf{v'}, t) \textbf{ forsome } \mathbf{v'}, j' \in G_{i,j,d}\}$
    let $\rho_{i,j,d} = \{(\mathbf{k}, \mathbf{v}, t_{max}(\mathbf{k})) \mid \mathbf{k} \in Frag_{j,i} \uparrow \varphi \textbf{ and } \mathbf{v} \neq null \textbf{ and }$
               $p_{i,j,d,j'}(\mathbf{k}) = (\mathbf{v}, t_{max}(\mathbf{k})) \textbf{ forsome } j' \in G_{i,j,d}\}$
           -- collect at d most recent defined values in j-th fragment
    let $\rho_d = \bigcup_{j=1}^{q_i} \rho_{i,j,d}$ -- collect those values from all fragments
    let $\mathbf{x}_d = (|G_{i,1,d}|, \dots, |G_{i,q_i,d}|)$ -- count inspected replicas
    $\text{SEND}(LocalValFor(read(p_i, \varphi), \rho_d, \mathbf{x}_d), \textbf{to } c)$
                       -- send local values to response collector

For (p_i, p)-requests there is an analogous rule:

$\text{HANDLELOCALLY}(write(p_i, p), c, t) =$
    let $d = \mathbf{self} \in \mathcal{D}_i$ -- at the local data center d
    forall $j \in \{1, \dots, q_i\}$ -- for each fragment
    let $G_{i,j,d} = \{j' \mid HoldsReplica(j', d, j, i) \textbf{ and } Alive(j', d)\}$
                         -- inspect replicas at all *Alive* d-nodes
    forall $j' \in G_{i,j,d}$ -- for each of those replicas
      forall $(\mathbf{k}, \mathbf{v}) \in p$ **with** $\mathbf{k} \in Frag_{j,i}$ -- for each update value in p
      if $p_{i,j,d,j'}(\mathbf{k}) = (\mathbf{v'}, t')$ **with** $t' < t$ **forsome** $\mathbf{v'}, t'$
        then $p_{i,j,d,j'}(\mathbf{k}) := (\mathbf{v}, t)$ -- update older values to p-value
    if $clock_d < t$ **then** $\text{ADJUSTCLOCK}(d, t)$
    let $\mathbf{x} = (|G_{i,1,d}|, \dots, |G_{i,q_i,d}|)$ -- count inspected replicas
    $\text{SEND}(LocalAckFor(write(p_i, p), \mathbf{x}), \textbf{to } c)$
                       -- send local ack to response collector

Note that also a replica where a value with timestamp t or larger is stored—i.e. where $p_{i,j,d,j'}(\mathbf{k}) = (\mathbf{v'}, t')$ with $t \leq t'$ **forsome** $\mathbf{v'}, t'$—counts as inspected replica, i.e. it is counted for $|G_{i,j,d}|$.

6.2.3.3 Collection and Policy Check of Responses

Since the *policy* compliance cannot be checked locally but only at the cluster level, in the refined model it is the response collector's duty to test whether the local responses, already collected for its *request*, are *Sufficient(policy)*. Therefore, the collector program MANAGERESPONSECOLLECTION splits for each request type (read or write) into two rules, one to collect local responses and one to send the final response if the local responses collected so far turn out to be *Sufficient(policy)* (in which case the collector has done its job and kills itself).

> MANAGERESPONSECOLLECTION =
> COLLECTLOCALREADRESPONSES
> SENDREADRESPONSE
> COLLECTLOCALWRITERESPONSES
> SENDWRITERESPONSE

For collecting the write responses it suffices to REFRESHREPLICACOUNT (defined below), since only an acknowledgment and no values are sent to the requestor.

> COLLECTLOCALWRITERESPONSES =
> **if** $Received(LocalAckFor(write(p_i, p), \mathbf{x}), \textbf{from } d)$ **then**
> REFRESHREPLICACOUNT$(\mathbf{x}, d)$
> CONSUME$(LocalAckFor(write(p_i, p), \mathbf{x}), \textbf{from } d)$

To COLLECTLOCALREADRESPONSES means a) to INSERT into the collector's set *ReadVal$_c$* the received locally collected values with newer timestamp, and b) to DELETE the ones with older timestamp (if any).

> COLLECTLOCALREADRESPONSES =
> **if** $Received(LocalValFor(read(p_i, \varphi), \rho, \mathbf{x}), \textbf{from } d)$ **then**
> **forall k if thereissome** $(\mathbf{k}, \mathbf{v}, t) \in \rho$ **then**   -- for each key k
> **let** $(\mathbf{k}, \mathbf{v}, t) \in \rho$ -- with received local value **v**
> **if thereisno** $(\mathbf{k}, \mathbf{v}', t') \in ReadVal$ -- if key k new for collection
> **then** INSERT$((\mathbf{k}, \mathbf{v}, t), ReadVal)$ -- collect received key value
> **else let** $(\mathbf{k}, \mathbf{v}', t') \in ReadVal$ -- for k-value **v**' in collection
> **if** $t' < t$ **then**   -- with older timestamp
> DELETE$((\mathbf{k}, \mathbf{v}', t'), ReadVal)$ -- replace old value
> INSERT$((\mathbf{k}, \mathbf{v}, t), ReadVal)$ -- by new value
> REFRESHREPLICACOUNT$(\mathbf{x}, d)$
> CONSUME$(LocalValFor(read(p_i, \varphi), \rho, \mathbf{x}), \textbf{from } d)$
> **where**
> REFRESHREPLICACOUNT$(\mathbf{x}, d) =$
> **let** $(x_1, \ldots, x_{q_i}) = \mathbf{x}$
> **forall** $j \in \{1, \ldots, q_i\}$
> $count(j, d) := count(j, d) + x_j$
> $count(j) := count(j) + x_j$

The collector can SENDREADRESPONSE to a $read(p_i, \varphi)$ request when the corresponding replica *counter* function ($count^{(1)}$ or $count^{(2)}$ depending on the type of *readPolicy*, see below) shows that the values collected so far for the current *readPolicy* are *Sufficient*.

> SENDREADRESPONSE =
> **if** *Sufficient*(*readPolicy*)(*count*) **and** *IsReadReq*(*request*(**self**)) **then**
>> **let** $\rho = \{(\mathbf{k}, \mathbf{v}) \mid (\mathbf{k}, \mathbf{v}, t) \in ReadVal$ **forsome** $t\}$
>> SEND(*ValFor*(*request*(**self**), ρ),   -- send the collected values
>>> **from** *mediator*(**self**), **to** *requestor*(**self**))
>>
>> DELETE(**self**, *Agent*)   -- collector kills itself

The SENDWRITERESPONSE is simpler, since only an acknowledgment has to be sent, informing that with respect to the current *writePolicy* enough replicas have been updated by the requested write.

> SENDWRITERESPONSE =
> **if** *Sufficient*(*writePolicy*)(*count*) **and** *IsWriteReq*(*request*(**self**)) **then**
>> SEND(*AckFor*(*request*(**self**)),
>>> **from** *mediator*(**self**), **to** *requestor*(**self**))
>>
>> DELETE(**self**, *Agent*)

Policy compliance is refined to counting the number of inspected replicas. For *number* and *quorum*(q) policy the unary $count^{(1)}$ function does the work.

> $Sufficient(num)$ **iff forall** $1 \le j \le q_i$ $count(j) \ge num$[25]
> $Sufficient(all)$ **iff forall** $1 \le j \le q_i$ $count(j) = |Replicas_{i,j}|$
> $Sufficient(quorum(q))$ **iff**
>> **forall** $1 \le j \le q_i$ $q \cdot |Replicas_{i,j}| < count(j)$
>
> **where**
> $num \in \{one, two, three\}$ **and** $0 < q < 1$
> $Replicas_{i,j} = \{(d, j') \mid HoldsReplica(j', d, j, i)$ **and** $Alive(j', d)\}$[26]

For locally restricted policies the binary $count^{(2)}$ function must be used:

> $Sufficient(num, At(d))$ **iff forall** $1 \le j \le q_i$ $count(j, d) \ge num$
> $Sufficient(quorum(q), At(d))$ **iff**
>> **forall** $1 \le j \le q_i$ $q \cdot |Replicas_{i,j,d}| < count(j, d)$

---

[25] Note that the = used to define *Complies*(C, *num*) must be replaced here by $\ge$ because, due to the concurrency, when the delegate tests the predicate *Sufficient*, it may have received already more than *num* answers.

[26] Without the restriction to *Alive* nodes the delegate could send its answer only if all nodes that are needed to form the answer have been *Alive* at some moment since the to be answered request did arrive at the *home*(a) of the requesting agent a. This would contradict however the spirit of using replicas, namely to be on the safe side if some replica holding node happens to be unreachable. The Cassandra documentation does not contain enough information to reliably model the feature that messages, which are sent to nodes that are not *Alive*, are written in a log file and have to be answered when the node becomes again *Alive*.

$Sufficient(quorum(q), At(all))$ **iff forall** $d \in \mathcal{D}_i$
    forall $1 \le j \le q_i$ $q \cdot |Replicas_{i,j,d}| < count(j, d)$
where
    $Replicas_{i,j,d} = \{j' \mid HoldsReplica(j', d, j, i) \text{ and } Alive(j', d)\}$

From the above explanations it should be clear that each request/response interaction of users with their home data center in a concurrent run of USERS and CLUSTERUSERVIEW$_i$ can be simulated by a corresponding interaction in a concurrent run of USERS and CLUSTERMANAGEMENT$_i$ (see Exerc. 60). This property is called refinement completeness. For the abstract Cassandra model and its refinement by internal communication the inverse refinement correctness can be established only under additional assumptions on the serializability of read/write requests and answers, using some form of transaction, as comes out of the detailed model analysis provided in [221]. We stick here to provide a simple example on what can happen in an unrestricted concurrent run of users with the CLUSTERMANAGEMENT$_i$.

Run example for CLUSTERMANAGEMENT$_i$. Consider any location x with at least two replicas x_1 and x_2, both initialized by 0, disregarding timestamps since they play no role for the example. Assume write policy *all* and read policy *one* for one agent a_1 issuing a write request $x := 1$ and then another agent a_2 issuing two successive read requests for x. In this case the following answer scenario, which one wouldn't expect from the DATACENTERUSERVIEW$_i$ ground model, is possible with an implementation by CLUSTERMANAGEMENT$_i$:

1. The write request by a_1 leads to an immediate update of replica x_1, namely to 1 before a_2 issues its first read request, and to the later propagation of 1 to x_2, namely after the second read request has been answered.
2. The first read request by a_2 is answered by the value of replica x_1 which due to the update is 1, the second read request by the value of replica x_2 which is still 0 (due to the later propagation of 1 to it.)

Exercise 60. Each concurrent run of USERS and CLUSTERUSERVIEW$_i$— where users post requests to their home data centers which respond executing each its instance of the abstract program DATACENTERUSERVIEW$_i$—can be simulated by a concurrent run of USERS and the internally communicating concurrent ASM CLUSTERMANAGEMENT$_i$, i.e. such that for each abstract user/database interaction there is an equivalent concrete user/database interaction with same read/write effect). See [221, Sect. 4.2].

6.3 Some Comparative Case Studies

Over the years, in numerous case studies the ASM method has been tested and compared to other specification and software development approaches, with varying focus. We survey some of them here.

One of the first examples was the Production Cell case study. Numerous solutions, which use various well-known software specification and analysis methods, are published in [183] and can be directly compared to the work published for an ASM-based solution. In [64] an ASM ground model has been defined. It has been used for an inspection process as part of a Dagstuhl seminar [61]. It has been refined to C^{++} code [185], which has been extensively and successfully tested to control without failure a Production Cell simulator that had been made available in Karlsruhe for testing purposes. The properties requested as part of the requirements have been verified using PVS [124]. Joachim Schmid [223] used the example for code generation by an ASM2C^{++} compiler.

Similar work has been done later for other case studies which too were explicitly proposed to make comparative material for different specification and software development methods available. In the 90'ies the Steam Boiler [4] and the Light Control [59] case studies have been proposed to the participants of two dedicated Dagstuhl seminars [3, 60]. Recently the landing gear case study [33] has been proposed to the participants of the ABZ Conference in 2014 [11]. The reader can again compare directly the ASM solutions [25, 67, 15] with those using other (mostly formal) methods and published in the same Proceedings.

The Invoice case study [115] was focussed on how to generate, using different formal methods, a rigorous natural language specification from a precise model of an originally given informal requirements description. The ASM solution [56] exploits paraphrasing ASM rules in natural language terms (as we suggest to always do when formulating and explaining ASM rules).

Various case studies have been devoted to hardware design and verification, namely for the Transputer [51], for a special-purpose parallel architecture [50] and for pipelining schemes in DLX [63, 128, 234] and in the RISC microprocessor ARM2 [147]. The ARM2 model has been used in [238] to automatically transform register transfer descriptions of microprocessors into executable ASMs. In [237] bit-true and cycle-accurate simulators and debuggers have been derived from behavioral and structural ASM models for application-specific instruction set processors.

Part II
Implementation

Chapter 7
Syntax and Semantics of ASMs

In this chapter we provide a mathematical (not a formalized) definition of the syntax and the semantics of ASMs. We provide here only the technical definitions by which the ASM method becomes a precise mathematical design and analysis instrument; the motivation for the definitions and how they can be used for building accurate models of complex systems has been explained in the preceding chapters.

This chapter is of purely technical character and has been inserted for readers with interest in implementation issues. It defines the (rather small) conceptual basis that is needed to implement tools which offer to machine execute and debug ASM models. Therefore, we assume that the reader is familiar with the syntax and semantics of programming languages.

We proceed stepwise and first define basic single-agent ASMs and their runs (Sect. 7.2), extracting the definition from [76, Sect. 2.4]. We then apply bootstrapping to extend this definition to ambient ASMs (Sect. 7.2.1). For the extension by step controlled ASMs—**stepwise**$(P_1, \ldots, P_n)$ and P **seq** Q and their iteration constructs **while**$_{stepwise/atomic}$—we have already defined their semantics by basic ASM rules in Sect. 4.5.1, 4.5.2. Concurrent multi-agent ASMs have already been defined by Def. 2 (syntax) and Def. 6 (semantics) and the operational characterization of concurrent ASM runs by the CONCURRENCYPATTERN(*Process*) ASM in Sect. 2.4.3 (p. 73).

We complement these definitions in Chap. 9 by a meta model for the syntax and the semantics of control state diagrams (CSDs), which we use to visualize the behavior of control state ASMs.

7.1 Mathematical Structures (ASM States)

We start with a brief review of what is needed from logic to explain the basic concepts of ASM *state* and state *updates* by execution of ASM rules.

© Springer-Verlag GmbH Germany, part of Springer Nature 2018
E. Börger, A. Raschke, *Modeling Companion for Software Practitioners*,
https://doi.org/10.1007/978-3-662-56641-1_7

The *signature* or *vocabulary* of an ASM is a finite set of function names f^n, each coming with a fixed *arity* $n = 0, 1, 2, \ldots$ indicating the number of arguments of the function. We consider f^n and f^m with $n \neq m$ as different function names and notationally often omit the arity, where it is clear from the context. Function names can be *static* or *dynamic* and come with a further pragmatic classification explained below. 0-ary static functions are also called *constants*, 0-ary dynamic function names are variables of programming, not to be confused with logical variables. To simplify definitions, we identify sets and relations (also called predicates) with their Boolean-valued characteristic function. We assume each ASM signature to contain the three static constants *true*, *false* and **undef**.

Starting with constants and variables, *terms* (often also called *expressions*) are built in the usual manner inductively, applying n-ary function symbols (with $n > 0$) to terms t_i to form a new term $f(t_1, \ldots, t_n)$ (sometimes also written $ft_1 \ldots t_n$). *Formulae* (often also called Boolean-valued *expressions*) are built inductively in the usual manner from *atomic* formulae—equations $t_1 = t_2$ and predicates $P(t_1 \ldots t_n)$ (sometimes also written $Pt_1 \ldots t_n$) with terms t_i—applying propositional connectives (**not, and, or, if then, iff**) and quantifiers (**forall, forsome**).

Definition 19. An ASM *state* $\mathcal{A}$ for a given signature Σ is defined by a non-empty set A and an *interpretation* of each function symbol $f^n \in \Sigma$ by a function $f^{\mathcal{A}} : A^n \to A$ (thus $c^{\mathcal{A}} \in A$ for each 0-ary function symbol c).[1] The interpretations of *true*, *false* and **undef** are requested to be pairwise different elements and different from all other elements in A. For notational convenience they are written again *true*, *false* and **undef**. For the same reason we write f instead of $f^{\mathcal{A}}$—when it is clear from the context that not the function symbol f, but its interpretation $f^{\mathcal{A}}$ is meant.

A is called the *superuniverse* or *base* set of the state. Each set (with characteristic function symbol in Σ) is interpreted in a state as subset of the superuniverse, each predicate P^n as the set of all $(a_1, \ldots, a_n) \in A^n$ where $P(a_1, \ldots, a_n) = true$ (we also say where $P(a_1, \ldots, a_n)$ is true). In particular, ASMs use a so-called *Reserve* set, from where **new** elements are imported when 'fresh' elements are needed. **new** (X) is used as term building operator, denoting a fresh element to be fetched from *Reserve* and put into the set X, see for details below. Logical terms and formulae are interpreted in the usual manner in states. We denote by $eval(exp, \mathcal{A}, \zeta)$ the value the interpretation of exp yields in state $\mathcal{A}$, with interpretation ζ of the logical variables which occur freely in exp.

---

[1] In mathematics and logic ASM states are known as algebras or structures, where however all functions are static. In the theory of computing they are known as abstract data types, usually considered as defined axiomatically.

This concept of abstract ASM state realizes a strong information hiding principle. The internal representation of the elements of a state, in other words the structure of a superuniverse, is disregarded.[2]

As indicated by the name, **undef** represents an opaque, but well-defined distinguished element of the superuniverse. It serves to formally treat each interpreted function $f^{\mathcal{A}}$ (for logical reasons) as a *total* (i. e. everywhere defined) function, but to view it as a *partial* function , namely with *domain* consisting of all arguments $(a_1, \ldots, a_n) \in A^n$ where $f^{\mathcal{A}}(a_1, \ldots, a_n) \neq$ **undef**.

An ASM state $\mathcal{A}$ can be viewed not only as abstract data type, but also as abstract memory which maps locations to values. A *location* l (of $\mathcal{A}$) is defined as pair $(f, (a_1, \ldots, a_n))$ of a function symbol f^n and an argument $(a_1, \ldots, a_n) \in A^n$, where a_i are elements of the superuniverse A of $\mathcal{A}$, called *elements* of l . The value $f^{\mathcal{A}}(a_1, \ldots, a_n)$ is called the *content* of l. An *update* for $\mathcal{A}$ is a pair (loc, val) of a location (of $\mathcal{A}$) and an element $val \in A$, used to indicate how in the given state the indicated *loc*ation is subject to be updated to the indicated *val*ue. A set of updates is called an *update set*; it is called *consistent* if it contains no clashing updates (i. e. no two updates (l, v_1) and (l, v_2) with $v_1 \neq v_2$).

When a consistent update set U is applied to—we also say 'fired' in—a state $\mathcal{A}$, it yields a new state, denoted $\mathcal{A} + U$ and called the *sequel* of $\mathcal{A}$, where for each *loc*ation which has an update $(loc, val) \in U$ its content in $\mathcal{A}$ is replaced by the possibly new *val*ue. No other location is updated.[3]

7.2 Sequential and Concurrent ASMs

We provide here the definitions for single-agent ASMs, in terms of which concurrent runs of multi-agent ASMs have been defined already precisely by Def. 2, 6.

Definition 20. Syntactically, the rules of single-agent (also called basic or sequential) ASMs with signature Σ are defined inductively as follows. We also indicate their intended effect on producing the sequel of a given state; it is defined more precisely below in terms of update sets.

Update rule. $f(t_1, \ldots, t_n) := t$ is an ASM rule for each n-ary dynamic function symbol $f \in \Sigma$, meaning to update the value of the interpretation of f at the argument value $(t_1, \ldots, t_n)$ to the value of t.

---

[2] If two states are isomorphic to each other (i. e. if their superuniverses can be mapped to each other by a bijection and the function interpretations agree on corresponding elements), they are treated as one state. The reader can find a detailed definition of this principle in [76, pp. 66–67].

[3] This stipulation guarantees that ASMs do not suffer from the so-called frame problem of axiomatic specifications by logical formulae.

Conditional rule.   If P, Q are ASM rules, then also **if** *Condition* **then** P **else** Q is an ASM rule for each Boolean-valued expression *Condition*, meaning to execute P if the *Condition* evaluates to *true*, and to execute Q otherwise.

Let rule.   If P is ASM rule, then also **let** $x = t$ **in** P is an ASM rule for each term t, meaning to assign the value of t to x and then execute P with this value for x (call by value).

Block (also called Parallel or Par) rule.   If P, Q are ASM rules, then also P **par** Q is an ASM rule, meaning to execute P and Q in parallel (simultaneously, in the same state).

Forall rule.   If P is an ASM rule, then also **forall** x **with** *Property* **do** P is an ASM rule for each Boolean-valued expression *Property*, meaning that all $P(x)$ where x satisfies *Property*(x) are executed in parallel (simultaneously).

Choose rule.   If P is an ASM rule, then also **choose** x **with** *Property* **do** P is an ASM rule for each Boolean-valued expression *Property*, meaning that an element x that satisfies the *Property*(x) is chosen to execute $P(x)$.

Call (also called Macro) rule.   If P is an ASM rule, then also $Q(t_1, \ldots, t_n)$ is an ASM rule for terms t_i, if there is a *rule declaration* $Q(x_1, \ldots, x_n) = P$ where the free variables of P are a subset of $\{x_1, \ldots, x_n\}$. The intended meaning is to call Q with parameters $(t_1, \ldots, t_n)$ (call by name).

Sometimes also the **skip** rule is included, with the usual meaning to do nothing. It is used rarely, mainly as placeholder for some intended future refinement.

Where useful, also rules for so-called Update Instructions may be added. Their meaning is to produce a specific update or set of updates, defined instruction-wise.[4] This powerful modular specification mechanism is supported by the plug-in concept of CoreASM (see Sect. 8).

To define a single-agent ASM, we usually declare a *main rule* (without parameters, also called the *program* of the ASM) defined for a signature Σ coming with a classification of its functions, a set of rule declarations and a set of *initial* states (for Σ). Often we simply call an ASM program P, or a pair (a, P) of an agent a which executes P, an ASM, when the rest is clear from the context. By the so-called *function classification* of an ASM the roles of its functions and locations are declared, as pictorially represented by Fig. 7.1. A *static* function is a function which does not depend on any ASM state, whereas the value of a *dynamic* function for given arguments may change from state to state, as usual for variables of programming. Static functions can be defined separately from machine programs where they are used. For a given ASM program P, dynamic functions can be declared as *monitored*, which means that they provide input defined by the environment of P and are only read (never updated) by P. Similarly, *out* or output functions are

---

[4] For some examples see Sect. 3.2.2 and the communication actions in Def. 4.

Fig. 7.1 Classification of functions and locations [76, Fig. 2.4]
© 2003 Springer-Verlag Berlin Heidelberg, reprinted with permission

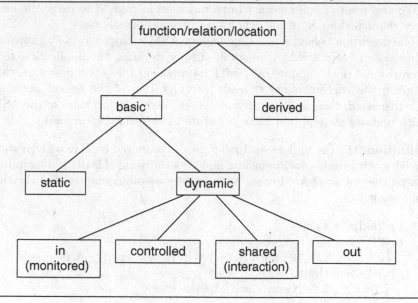

dynamic functions which serve as output in the sense that P can write but never read them. *Controlled* functions are functions only P can read and write, *shared* functions are functions both P and the environment can read and write, so that typically a protocol is needed to avoid write clashes.

For pragmatic reasons, one may also declare a function as a *derived* function that is defined by a fixed scheme (equations, axiomatic descriptions, program module, etc.), in terms of other static or dynamic functions, and can be read but not written neither by P nor its environment. Similarly, we speak about *environment independent functions* as functions f for which $f(x, e) = f(x, e')$ for all environments e, e' and all arguments x. We also use the equality in the form $f(e, x) = f(e', x)$. Sometimes we also declare an analogous classification for (sets of) locations.

For the sake of brevity and to exploit common notations, we write ASM rules also with minor syntactical variations if their meaning is clear from the context. For example, we write

> **choose** x **with** *cond* **do** P
> **ifnone do** Q

instead of

> **if forsome** x *cond* = *true*
> **then choose** x **with** *cond* **do** P
> **else** Q

In particular, we use the vertical notation instead of **par** (P, Q) and indentation instead of **in** in Let rules.

We also use the well-known **where** notation in rules R to mark the auxiliary character, for R, of the definition in the **where** clause.

The execution behavior of a single-agent ASM with program P, known as *semantics* of basic ASMs, consists in simply iterating the application to a given state $\mathcal{A}$ of the update set $Upd(P, \mathcal{A}, varEnv)$ rule P computes in state $\mathcal{A}$, given the *varEnv*ironment (read: interpretation of the logical variables with free occurrences in P). Such a step is defined below as *move* of the ASM which updates state $\mathcal{A}$ into its sequel state $\mathcal{A} + Upd(P, \mathcal{A}, varEnv)$.

Definition 21. The update set $Upd(P, \mathcal{A}, \zeta)$ computed by P in a given state $\mathcal{A}$ with given variable environment ζ and superuniverse A is defined by induction on the syntax of ASM rules. Notationally we often suppress the variable assignment.

$$Upd(\textbf{skip}, \mathcal{A}, \zeta) = \emptyset$$
$$Upd(f(t_1, \ldots, t_n) := t, \mathcal{A}, \zeta) =$$
$$\{((f, (v_1, \ldots, v_n)), eval(t, \mathcal{A}, \zeta))\} \textbf{ where } v_i = eval(t_i, \mathcal{A}, \zeta)$$
$$Upd(\textbf{if } Cond \textbf{ then } P \textbf{ else } Q, \mathcal{A}, \zeta) =$$
$$\begin{cases} Upd(P, \mathcal{A}, \zeta) \textbf{ if } eval(Cond, \mathcal{A}, \zeta) = true \\ Upd(Q, \mathcal{A}, \zeta) \textbf{ else} \end{cases}$$
$$Upd(\textbf{let } x = t \textbf{ in } P, \mathcal{A}, \zeta) = \qquad\qquad\qquad \text{-- call by value}$$
$$Upd(P, \mathcal{A}, \zeta[x \mapsto a]) \textbf{ where } a = eval(t, \mathcal{A}, \zeta)^5$$
$$Upd(P \textbf{ par } Q, \mathcal{A}, \zeta) = Upd(P, \mathcal{A}, \zeta) \cup Upd(Q, \mathcal{A}, \zeta)$$
$$Upd(\textbf{forall } x \textbf{ with } Prop \textbf{ do } P, \mathcal{A}, \zeta) = \bigcup_{a \in I} Upd(P, \mathcal{A}, \zeta[x \mapsto a])$$
$$\textbf{where } I = \{a \in A \mid eval(Prop(a), \mathcal{A}, \zeta[x \mapsto a]) = true\}$$
$$Upd(\textbf{choose } x \textbf{ with } Prop \textbf{ do } P, \mathcal{A}, \zeta) = Upd(P, \mathcal{A}, \zeta[x \mapsto a])$$
$$\textbf{if } eval(Prop(a), \mathcal{A}, \zeta[x \mapsto a]) = true \textbf{ forsome } a \in A$$
$$Upd(\textbf{choose } x \textbf{ with } Prop \textbf{ do } P, \mathcal{A}, \zeta) = \emptyset$$
$$\textbf{if } eval(Prop(a), \mathcal{A}, \zeta[x \mapsto a]) = false \textbf{ forall } a \in A$$
$$Upd(Q(t_1, \ldots, t_n), \mathcal{A}, \zeta) = Upd(P(x_1/t_1, \ldots, x_n/t_n), \mathcal{A}, \zeta)$$
$$\textbf{where } Q(x_1, \ldots, x_n) = P \text{ is a rule declaration}^6 \qquad \text{-- call by name}$$

Remark on choose. For reasons of simplicity we introduce here the functional notation $Upd(P, \mathcal{A}, \zeta)$, although it implies a systematic notational abuse: the **choose** operator may yield a multitude of update sets, namely one set $U_a = Upd(P, \mathcal{A}, \zeta[x \mapsto a])$ for each a satisfying $eval(Prop(a), \mathcal{A}, \zeta[x \mapsto a]) = true$. Therefore, a correct description is formulated in terms of a relation $yields(P, \mathcal{A}, \zeta, U_a)$ (see [76, Table 2.2] and Sect. 4.5.1). For an ASM whose rule declarations do not contain **choose**, the functional notation is formally correct, because each such rule produces at most one well-defined update

---

[5] $f[a \mapsto b]$ indicates the function obtained from f by changing $f(a)$ to b.

[6] $exp(x/t)$ denotes the result of substituting each free occurrence of x in exp by an occurrence of t.

set. It may be that no update set is defined, for example if via the call rule one introduces non terminating recursive machine calls, or if in a turbo ASM P **seq** Q the first component P yields an inconsistent update set. After all, the **choose** operator only serves to let non-determinism in an ASM rule stand out explicitly; conceptually it could be dispensed with replacing **choose** x **with** *Prop* **do** P by $P(select(Prop))$, where *select* is a choice function which selects an element satisfying the given *Property*.[7]

Remark on new. We use the **new** operator in rules of form

let $x =$ **new** (X) **in** P

which stand for deleting an element x from the *Reserve* set, making x into an element of X (by the update $X(x) := true$) and executing P with this x. It is required that parallel (simultaneous) invocations of **new** yield pairwise different new elements (and also that for the semantics of ASMs it does not matter which *Reserve* element is fetched); how this requirement can be formally satisfied is explained in detail in [76, Sect. 2.4.4].

Definition 22. We say that an ASM (with main rule) P can make a *move* or *step* from state $\mathcal{A}$ to the sequel state $\mathcal{B} = \mathcal{A} + Upd(P, \mathcal{A})$, written $\mathcal{A} \Rightarrow_P \mathcal{B}$, if the update set $Upd(P, \mathcal{A})$ is consistent. The updates in $Upd(P, \mathcal{A})$ are called *internal* to distinguish them from updates of monitored or shared locations; the sequel is called the next internal state.

A *run* or *execution* of P is a finite or infinite sequence $S_0, S_1, \ldots$ of states (of the signature of P) such that

- S_0 is an initial state of P,
- for each n either $S_n \Rightarrow_P S_n'$ and the environment produces a consistent set U of updates of monitored or shared locations such that $S_{n+1} = S_n' + U$, or P cannot make a move in state S_n (i. e. produces an inconsistent update set) in which case S_n is called the last state in the run.

7.2.1 Ambient ASMs

The syntactical Def. 20 of ASM rules is extended by an Ambient rule whereby with P also **amb** *exp* **in** P is an ASM rule, where *exp* is any expression. The function classification is extended by adding an *environment* parameter to functions f with the possibility to declare f as environment dependent or independent. Formally, f is called *EnvDependent* if $f(e, x) \neq f(e', x)$ for some environments $e \neq e'$ and some argument x, *EnvIndependent* else.

The semantics of ambient ASMs refines the semantics of basic ASMs as follows:

---

[7] The two ways to describe non-determinism differ from the logical point of view; using a *selection* function forces the designer to define the function as part of the initialization. See [76, Sect. 8.1] for details.

- by adding in Def. 21 a clause for $Upd(\textbf{amb}\ exp\ \textbf{in}\ P, \mathcal{A}, \zeta, env)$,
- by extending the *eval*uation function $eval = eval_\zeta^{\mathfrak{A}}$ inductively by an environment parameter env to a function $eval_{\zeta,env}^{\mathfrak{A}}$ (which we write again $eval$ where the parameters are clear from the context):

$$eval(f(t_1, \ldots, t_n), env) =$$
$$\begin{cases} f^{\mathfrak{A}}(env, eval(t_1, env), \ldots, eval(t_n, env)) & \textbf{if}\ EnvDependent(f) \\ f^{\mathfrak{A}}(eval(t_1, env), \ldots, eval(t_n, env)) & \textbf{else} \end{cases}$$

Here $f^{\mathfrak{A}}$ denotes the interpretation of the possibly implicitly parameterized function symbol f in state $\mathfrak{A}$.

To avoid a signature blow up that could result from dynamic environment nesting, we treat env as a stack where new environment expressions are *push*ed. This explains the inductive definition of the update set produced by an ambient ASM rule where environment *expressions are passed by value*:

$$Upd(\textbf{amb}\ exp\ \textbf{in}\ P, \mathcal{A}, \zeta, env) =$$
$$Upd(P, \mathcal{A}, \zeta, \text{PUSH}(eval(exp, \mathcal{A}, \zeta, env), env))$$

Exercise 61. Rewrite the clauses of Def. 21 with extended $eval_{\zeta,env}^{\mathfrak{A}}$ function to convince yourself that these refined clauses, together with the Ambient ASM rule, completely define the behavioral semantics of ambient ASMs.

The semantics of the special *flat-ambient* ASMs, where only the last declared (most recent) environment is kept, can be defined by a syntactical transformation to ambient-free ASMs. See Def. 9 for the technical details.

For the two versions of step controlled ASMs **stepwise**$(P_1, \ldots, P_n)$ and P **seq** Q and their **while**$_{stepwise \lceil atomic}$ constructs we have defined their semantics by appropriate basic ASM rules in Sect. 4.5.1, 4.5.2.

Chapter 8
Debugging System Design (CoreASM)

This chapter is about debugging system design, not only code, using ASMs. We explain how to refine ASMs to models which are automatically executable by the CoreASM interpreter (Sect. 8.2).

In Sect. 8.1 we specify the behavior of CoreASM by a basic ASM. In Sect. 8.3 we exploit the plug-in architecture of the tool to specify the behavior of a CoreASM debugger by a basic ASM. These specifications serve as basis for the tool manuals and have been written for readers with interest in the implementation; by their very nature they are of technical character.

The operational semantics of ASMs conceptually supports the execution of specifications. The possibility to simulate runs of ASM machines stepwise, in mind or on paper, is one of the main advantages of the approach to intellectually manage complexity that is typical in modern system design. The pseudo-code notation, together with the simple realization of parallelism by collecting simultaneous updates into an update set, allow also non-experts to comprehend and analyze a given specification. However, this mental approach is time consuming for larger specifications, furthermore an automatic (computer supported) execution mechanism facilitates error detection considerably. It also improves the communication between domain experts and specifiers, as an executable model can be used to "play around" and test different scenarios.

In this way, ambiguities, misunderstandings, omissions and similar errors can be detected and corrected more easily; a concrete real-life example has been described in Sect. 3.2. An executable specification also plays an important role in the gradual refinement from a ground model to code (see Fig. 1.1). Last but not least, sometimes executable ASM models can be integrated directly into an existing software system, in which case further refinements offer a concrete reuse of models.

Following [76, Sect. 8.3] we distinguish three ways to make ASM models executable:

- **Interpretation.** To interpret ASM rules it suffices to define a parser and an interpreter component. The parser creates an abstract syntax tree (AST) for the given ASM. To execute a step of the ASM, the interpreter component visits each node of the AST recursively. At each node, a set of updates is calculated which corresponds to the construct by which the parser has labeled the node and which may also depend on the results of the subtree(s) (if any). All these updates are added to the update set of the simulated machine step. Once the tree is evaluated, the update set (if consistent) is applied and the next step is executed.
- **Compilation.** One can compile ASMs into machine code or into an intermediate representation, for example into a program of some programming language. Particular attention has to be paid to the handling of non-deterministic constructs, e. g. **choose**, and of updates of variables. In typical imperative programming languages variable assignments result in immediate updates of their values. This is in contrast to executing accumulated update sets at the end of a simulated machine step. The compiler must generate code that simulates the 'simultaneous' execution of accumulated assignments.
- **Coding.** For a concrete ASM model one can directly write code in some programming language. This may (though not necessarily always will) result in time consuming work and may make it hard to prove that the behavior of the hand-crafted code corresponds to the behavior of the ASM model.

In each of these categories, several tools for the execution of ASMs have been developed; see Sect. 8.4 and [76, Sects. 8.3, 9.4.3] for a short overview. In this chapter, we focus on CoreASM[1], a tool mainly developed by Roozbeh Farahbod as part of his PhD thesis [104]. Its execution engine follows the interpreter approach. It consists of a small kernel that is extended by plug-ins. This architecture allows one to extend the tool with new features, in particular extending the supported input language with new constructs. It is noteworthy that the behavior of this tool is specified by a basic ASM. As a consequence one can check the execution behavior of the engine to be correct with respect to the specified one and the latter to be correct with respect to the semantics of ASMs.

In Sect. 8.1 we present such a basic ASM model for CoreASM, though due to space limits we concentrate our attention on the more interesting features and refer the reader for more details to [105]. An elaborated documentation of the language supported by CoreASM and its plug-ins can be found also in [106]. The main work involved in transforming an abstract ASM into a CoreASM executable version is refining and completing the model, an issue we address in Sect. 8.2. In Sect. 8.3 once more the flexibility of the CoreASM approach is illustrated, this time by an ASM specification of a CoreASM de-

---

[1] http://github.com/CoreASM

Fig. 8.1 General architecture of CoreASM [105]
© 2009 Roozbeh Farahbod, reprinted with permission

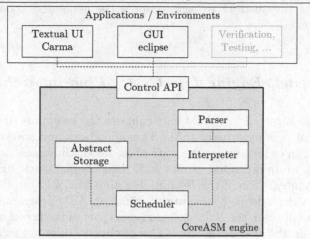

bugger which exploits the plug-in architecture. Some related tools are briefly discussed in Sect. 8.4.

8.1 The Formal Model of CoreASM

The basic idea behind the ASM interpreter CoreASM is the definition of a minimal kernel with a maximum of extendability. This way, it is possible to add new language constructs and functions easily and independently of other features. Due to space reasons, we hide at several places some technical details. Thereby we simplify the original specification [107] and focus on its overall idea and main aspects. For the complete model and more detailed information we refer to [104].

Fig. 8.1 shows the main components of CoreASM. The CoreASM engine is separated from higher level applications by the so called *Control API*[2], which is used by a textual (called Carma) and a graphical (eclipse) user interface. Any tool for e. g. verification or test case generation should use this interface, too. Inside the engine, the *Parser* is responsible for transforming a textual representation of a specification into an AST which is evaluated for each machine step by the *Interpreter*. The *Abstract Storage* keeps track of the abstract state of the ASM, providing interfaces for the *Interpreter* to get the value of any given function in the current state. The *Scheduler* manages the

---

[2] Application Programmer Interface: a collection of method signatures defining the accessible interface of a component from outside.

execution of a step when receiving a *step*-command from the Control API. It chooses the to-be executed agents, invokes the interpreter for each of them and instructs the abstract storage to apply the generated updates (if they are consistent).

8.1.1 Kernel, Engine Life Cycle, Plug-in Architecture

Kernel. The kernel of CoreASM only contains the essentials that are necessary to execute the most basic ASMs. Thus, *functions* and *universes* are part of the kernel in order to store the state of an ASM. Universes, another name for domains, are represented as sets with their characteristic function. This requires the integration of the *Boolean* domain (*true, false*) in the kernel together with the predefined value **undef**. Since an ASM program consists of a finite number of rules, the *Rules* domain is also part of the kernel and serves to record rules in the abstract storage. Three concrete rules are included in the kernel, too: *assignment*, **skip** and **import**. Without an assignment rule, there would be no possibility to produce updates and thereby change the current state. The **import** rule, which introduces new elements to the state, needs a special treatment in the implementation; this is for theoretical reasons concerning the *Reserve* set we do not explain here, see [76, Sect. 2.4.4]. Finally, the kernel provides a simple *default scheduling policy*, the "pseudo-random selection of an arbitrary set of agents [...] which is sufficient for multi-agent ASMs where no assumptions are made on the scheduling policy" [105, p. 43].

Only the domains are part of the kernel, but no operation on these domains. For example, the boolean algebra is outsourced to a plug-in, the same holds for the expression syntax for defining finite sets and operations on them, etc.

Engine life cycle The dynamic part of the kernel (called *engine life cycle*) is described by the ground model shown in Fig. 8.2. In the *engineMode Idle*, one of four rules can be executed, depending on the *newCommand* in the command queue. Commands can be sent to the engine via the Control API

Fig. 8.2 CoreASM engine life cycle ground model

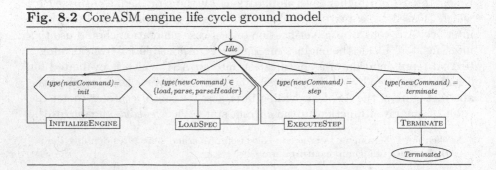

or they can be created by the engine itself. There are some dependencies among commands in these four command groups and there is also a natural order to issue the commands, which is not reflected in Fig. 8.2. Of course, the implementation of CoreASM provides appropriate error handling for senseless command sequences. Since we want to explain here the intended normal behavior, we skip the error handling in the CSDs; only for a few macros we insert a generic ERROR rule, for which we assume that it stops the current computation and returns an error message.

The mentioned dependencies are the following two: an *init* command has to be executed before any other command; a *step* command can only be executed, if a *load* command has been successfully executed before. Thus, the natural order of commands is as follows.

First, the initialization of the engine has to be performed via an *init* command. INITIALIZEENGINE sets several locations to default values and loads the catalog of available plug-ins. The catalog consists of all plug-ins that are available for the engine at the current installation of CoreASM and has to be distinguished from the set of loaded plug-ins for a concrete specification (see below). All these tasks are handled by the Control API component. For further details of this engine phase we refer to [105, Sect. 3.2.1].

Second, a specification can be loaded by the commands *load, parse*, or *parseHeader*. Sometimes, it might be useful for an external application (e. g. a modern text editor with syntax highlighting and auto completion) that a specification is only parsed and not completely initialized. This can be achieved by the *parse* command. Analogously, *parseHeader* only parses the header of a specification and stops the initialization after loading the required plug-ins. LOADSPEC is described in detail in Sect. 8.1.3.

After a complete initialization, a *step* can be executed by a *step* command. This *step* corresponds to an ASM machine step and includes the selection of agents (in case of multi-agent ASMs) and the application of updates. The refinement of EXECUTESTEP is elaborated in Sects. 8.1.4–8.1.5.

Finally, an engine can be terminated at any time by the *terminate* command. In contrast to the other rules, TERMINATE switches the *engineMode* to *Terminated*, not back to *Idle*.

Plug-in architecture. The minimal kernel of CoreASM can be extended by plug-ins in three dimensions (compare [105, Sect. 3.3]):

1. plug-ins providing new *data structures* have to extend a) the parser, in order to facilitate the use of literals, operators, static functions etc., b) the abstract storage, to provide the possibility to store elements of these data structures, and c) the interpreter, defining the semantics of the added operations. Examples for these kinds of plug-ins are the Number- or the Set-plug-in.
2. New *control structures* can extend the CoreASM language by providing new syntactic constructs. These extensions can either be syntactical sugar (i. e. short cut constructs that can also be expressed by existing language constructs) or new rule types producing updates. An example for such a

kind of extension is the **stepwise**-construct explained in Sect. 4.5.1. In order to obtain such a behavior, a plug-in must extend the parser and the interpreter.

3. The *execution model* of CoreASM itself can also be extended by so called *ExtensionPointPlugin*s. This permits e. g. to alter the scheduling policy to select agents, the instrumentation of the engine for analytical purposes like debugging (see Sect. 8.3), or the integration of meta constructs operating on update sets (for example support for invariants). This kind of extension is realized by introducing extension points into the control state diagram of the engine life cycle. At these extension points new rules and intermediate modes can be introduced right before the original machine would have switched to the next engine mode.

Formally, plug-ins are elements of the domain *Plugin*. Every plug-in has a *pluginName* and a *pluginLoadPriority*. The load priority is a number between 0 (lowest priority) and 100 (highest priority). When several plug-ins are loaded, the engine takes care of this priority. If two plug-ins have the same priority, they are loaded in an arbitrary order. The *pluginDependencySet* contains the names of all those plug-ins the current plug-in depends on. Finally, a plug-in can have a PLUGININITRULE which is called when the plug-in is loaded by the engine. In CoreASM it is also possible to package plug-ins in so called *packageplugin*s. For example, the "Standard Plug-in" contains some plug-ins for common language constructs like **if-then-else**, **let**, **forall**, Numbers, Sets, etc. The set of *enclosedPlugins(p)* for a given plugin p contains all enclosed plug-ins, if p *isPackagePlugin*.

The following sections describe the interactions between the components (Control API, parser, interpreter, scheduler, abstract storage) in more detail by refining the submachines of the engine ground model.

8.1.2 Storing Abstract Data

One of the main ideas of ASMs is to permit arbitrary data structures in the state. In order to maintain this flexibility, CoreASM introduces an abstract storage, that is able to store every possible element of a state in a flexible yet easy to handle way. This section briefly recaps the formalization of the abstract storage from [105, Sect. 4.1], as far as it is necessary to understand the following sections.

In order to distinguish the values of an ASM model from the values as represented in the abstract storage, a dedicated notation is introduced. For example, $undef_e$ denotes the value of **undef** in the abstract storage. We call these values of the abstract storage *elements* of the domain *Element*. The index e is a reminder to which domain this value belongs to, since we will introduce more domains later.

Every element is a member of some *background*. A background is a representation of the "type" of an element, such as Number, String, Set, Map, etc. The function $bkg\colon Element \to Name$ defines for every element its corresponding background. If no particular background is given, the default value of this function is Element.

The equality of two elements depends on the equality notion of their background and is defined as follows:

$$equal(e_1, e_2) \text{ iff } equal(bkg(e_1), e_1, e_2) \text{ or } equal(bkg(e_2), e_1, e_2)$$

This notion of equality can be extended by plug-ins that introduce new backgrounds. For the default background the following equation holds where $=$ denotes the equality relation for model elements:

$$\forall e_1, e_2 \in Element \quad equal(\text{Element}, e_1, e_2) \text{ iff } e_1 = e_2$$

State. The state of a simulated ASM is an element of the domain *State*. In every $s \in State$ the function $content\colon State \times Location \to Element$ returns for a given location the corresponding element. During simulation, the current state is saved in the nullary function $state\colon State$.

Locations are elements of the domain *Location*. A location is a pair of a $name_{loc}\colon Location \to Name$ and a sequence of $args_{loc}\colon Location \to List(Element)$ (often written as $(f, [a_1, \ldots, a_n])$).

Booleans. The domain *BooleanElement* only has two elements true_{be} and false_{be} representing the *Boolean* values *true* and *false*. The following two functions map boolean elements to the corresponding boolean values and vice versa:

$$booleanElement\colon Boolean \to BooleanElement$$
$$booleanValue\colon BooleanElement \to Boolean$$

The equality of two booleans is defined using their corresponding values. Furthermore for all $b \in BooleanElement$ holds $bkg(b) = \text{Boolean}$.

Functions. Function elements represent functions and are members of the domain *FunctionElement*. For every CoreASM state, a mapping of function names to function elements exists. The derived function *functions* returns the set of *FunctionElements* for a given state.

$$stateFunction\colon State \times Name \to FunctionElement$$
$$functions\colon State \to \wp(FunctionElement)$$
$$\textbf{where } functions(s) = \{f | f \in FunctionElement \textbf{ and }$$
$$\textbf{forsome } n \in Name\ stateFunction(s, n) = f\}$$

As usual, a function represents a mapping from a list of arguments to a value (or, generalized, an element):

$$value_{fe}\colon FunctionElement \times List(Element) \to Element$$

The function $class_{fe}$ returns the corresponding class of a function (see Fig. 7.1) in which *shared* is the default value if no other class is defined. $isModifiable(f)$ tells whether the function f is modifiable or not.

$$class_{fe} \colon FunctionElement \to \{monitored, controlled, out, static, derived\}$$
$$isModifiable(f) \text{ iff } class_{fe}(f) \in \{controlled, out\}$$

The assignment of a function to a specific value is done by the rule SET-VALUE. For convenience, the interface of the abstract storage provides two signatures for this rule: one with an explicit list of arguments, the other one directly with a location as parameter.

$$\text{SETVALUE}_{fe}(f, args, v) =$$
$$\quad \textbf{if } isModifiable(f) \textbf{ then } value_{fe}(f, args) := v$$

$$\text{SETVALUE}_{fe}(l, v) =$$
$$\quad \textbf{let } f = stateFunction(state, name_{loc}(l))$$
$$\quad\quad \textbf{if } f \neq \textbf{undef then } \text{SETVALUE}_{fe}(f, args_{loc}(l), v)$$

Since partial functions are avoided (see footnote on p. 49), retrieving the value of a function for an argument returns **undef** for undefined locations.

$$getValue \colon Location \to Element$$
$$getValue(l) = \begin{cases} value_{fe}(f, args_{loc}(l)), & \text{if } value_{fe}(f, args_{loc}(l)) \neq \textbf{undef} \\ \textbf{undef}_e, & \text{otherwise.} \end{cases}$$
$$\textbf{where}$$
$$\quad f = stateFunction(state, name_{loc}(l))$$

The equality of two functions is based on the extensionality, but since in its full generality this is not easily computable, CoreASM assumes two functions to be unequal, unless defined otherwise.

Universes. Universes are sets of elements. In the abstract storage *UniverseElement*s are treated similarly to functions. Actually, universes are modeled by their characteristic function so that every universe element is also a function element: *UniverseElement $\subseteq$ FunctionElement*. Additionally, for convenience, a membership function is defined:

$$member_{ue} \colon UniverseElement \times Element \to Boolean.$$

As a consequence, we need a specialized definition for *value* and SETVALUE:

$$value_{ue}(u, e) = booleanElement(member_{ue}(u, e))$$
$$\text{SETVALUE}_{ue}(u, e], b) = \text{SETVALUE}_{fe}(member_{ue}, [u, e], booleanValue(b))$$

Analogously to function elements, the function *stateUniverse* maps names of universes in a state to their universe elements and the function *universes* returns the set of universe elements in a state. The equality between two universe elements is defined as the equality of their characteristic functions with background Universe.

$$stateUniverse \colon State \times Name \to UniverseElement$$
$$universes \colon State \to \{UniverseElement\} \textbf{ where}$$
$$\quad universes(s) = \{u | u \in UniverseElement \textbf{ and}$$
$$\quad\quad\quad\quad \textbf{forsome } n \in Name \; stateUniverse(s, n) = u\}$$

Fig. 8.3 Overview of CoreASM elements of the abstract storage [105]
© 2009 Roozbeh Farahbod, reprinted with permission

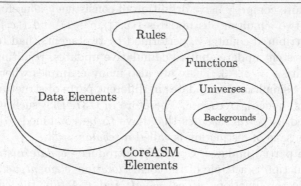

Backgrounds. Backgrounds are universes with a static membership function. This means that a background from the very beginning contains all elements it represents, e. g. the background of strings represents all possible strings. The representation of backgrounds in the abstract storage are elements of the domain *BackgroundElement*. For every background element *b* a function *newValue*(*b*) must be defined that returns a default element of *b*, e. g. an empty string.

Rules. Rules of a CoreASM specification are modeled by elements of the domain *RuleElement*. The mapping functions *stateRule*: *State* × *Name* → *RuleElement* and *rules*: *State* → {*RuleElement*} are defined for this domain and its identifier is Rule. For rule elements some more functions exist, representing the *name*, the *body* and a list of *param*eters of the rule.

$name_{rule}$: *RuleElement* → *Name*
body: *RuleElement* → *Node*
param: *RuleElement* → *List*(*Name*)

It is assumed that all names of rules, universes and functions are unique in any CoreASM state. The body of a rule points to the root node of the corresponding parse tree. The parsing process and the resulting parse tree of *Node*s are explained in the following section.

Fig. 8.3 illustrates the types of elements in the abstract storage, provided by the kernel, and their relation to each other. As one can see, backgrounds form a subset of universes which in turn form a subset of the set of functions (due to the definition of sets as given by their characteristic function). A plug-in can add new types to this bunch, like sets, maps, strings, and numbers.

Updates and update instructions. Updates are handled by the abstract storage component, too, albeit, they are not *Elements*. An update is a pair (l, v) representing a location l and its new value v. After every step, the accumulated set of updates is applied to the current state if the update set is consistent, i. e. if it contains no two updates (l, v) and (l, v') with $v \neq v'$.

Often a more comprehensive definition of consistency is useful. For example, in [52], two simultaneous updates $((c, [\,]), c + 1)$ and $((c, [\,]), c + 2)$ of the same distributed counter c, performed by two agents, had to be treated not as inconsistent updates but as cumulative updates, resulting in the one counter update $c := c + 3$. There are also many examples where one would like to specify simultaneous updates in different parts of structured elements like sets, lists, queues, trees, etc. Therefore in [137, 138] such updates have been analyzed as *partial updates* that have to be combined to one update, which for the sake of distinction is called a *regular update*.

To handle partial updates, CoreASM introduces *update instructions*. An update instruction is a triple of the form $(location, element, action)$. By appropriate selector functions $uiLoc$, $uiVal$, and $uiAction$ the corresponding components of an update instruction are accessed.[3] An $action \in Action$ defines the kind of modification that has to be performed on the $location$ to obtain a regular update.

In the CoreASM kernel only the $updateAction \in Action$ is defined. This $updateAction$ does nothing so that an update instruction $(l, v, updateAction)$ is equivalent to the regular update (l, v). Formally this comes up to extend Definition 21 from update sets $Upd(P, \mathcal{A}, \zeta)$ to multisets $UpdInstr(P, \mathcal{A}, \zeta)$ of update instructions, replacing each update $(l, v) \in Upd(P, \mathcal{A}, \zeta)$ by the equivalent $(l, v, updateAction)$ and interpreting the set operations as multiset operations.

Each plug-in P computes its specific multiset $UpdInstr(P, \mathcal{A}, \zeta)$. Instead of sets, multisets (or bags) are needed which we denote by $\{\!|$ and $|\!\}$. Multisets are needed because multiple occurrences of a partial update in a program may generate multiple occurrences of one update (read: multiple update instructions for the same location and the same update action) which together determine a regular update. For example two occurrences of a partial update $((c, [\,]), c + 1)$ for the above distributed counter generate two occurrences of the update instruction $((c, [\,]), c + 1, cumulativeCounter)$ which are then aggregated to one regular update with cumulative effect $c := c + 2$.

Another example is the *CollectionPlugin*. We call a *collection* an abstract concept of data structures that can group zero or more elements. Examples for collections are sets, maps, bags, lists, queues, stacks, etc. The generic CollectionPlugin defines two rules **add .. to ..** and **remove .. from ..** as common interface for all kinds of collections to add resp. remove elements to resp. from them. Where applicable, special update instruction actions are introduced for a concrete collection kind. These actions are *aggregated* and

---

[3] In CoreASM, additionally, *uiAgents* is defined. This function returns the set of agents that produced that update instruction. This information is necessary for the scheduler to detect if inconsistent regular updates result from updates produced by two agents or by only one. This influences whether another combination of agents can be chosen for execution or if the step has failed (see the next section).

composed during the *aggregation phase* into one regular update of the location in question.

Aggregation of update instructions. When the *aggregation phase* starts, CoreASM has computed the multiset *updateInstructions* of all generated update instructions. Starting with this multiset the *aggregator* plug-ins, those which handle an action that occurs in some of the *updateInstructions*, compute an *updateSet* that consists only of regular updates. Each plug-in *p* handles the corresponding elements of *updateInstructions* to compute its specific set *resultantUpdates(p)*. The plug-in program (or its specification) defines how multiple update instructions it must handle, which affect a same location, are combined into one regular update for that location. If this so-called aggregation succeeds, the predicate *CanBeAggregated* is set to true, otherwise (e. g. if the aggregation yields inconsistent updates) it is set to false. For an example see below the plug-in specification for the abstract machines ACTIVATE/DEACTIVATE used in Sect. 3.2.2.

This explains the following AGGREGATEUPDATES rule, which is executed just before the next state can be computed by applying the generated set of updates (see Fig. 8.6). Note that concerning the generated updates the kernel acts like a plug-in, transforming each $(l, v, updateAction)$ into the regular update (l, v).

> AGGREGATEUPDATES =
>   **if** *AggregationSuccessful* **then**
>   **let** $ap = \{a \,|\, a \in Plugin \textbf{ and } aggregator(a)\}$
>   *updateSet* :=
> $\bigcup_{p \in ap} resultantUpdates(p) \cup resultantUpdates(\mathsf{kernel})$
> **where**
>   *AggregationSuccessful* **iff**
>   **forall** $ui \in updateInstructions\ CanBeAggregated(ui) = true$
> $CanBeAggregated(ui)$ **iff** $aggStatus(ui) = successful$
> $aggregator(a)$ **iff forsome** $ui \in updateInstructions$
> $actionHandledBy(a) = uiAction(ui)$

As an example we specify an Activation plug-in that computes the set of *resultantUpdates* for the abstract machines ACTIVATE and DEACTIVATE from Sect. 3.2.2. These rules determine partial updates of the *trigger* location and yield update instructions with action *activationAction*. Formally we extend Definition 21 as follows:

> $UpdInstr(\text{ACTIVATE}(f(t_1, \ldots, t_n)), \mathcal{A}, \zeta) =$
> $\{((f, (v_1, \ldots, v_n)), true, activationAction)\}$
> $UpdInstr(\text{DEACTIVATE}(f(t_1, \ldots, t_n)), \mathcal{A}, \zeta) =$
> $\{((f, (v_1, \ldots, v_n)), false, activationAction)\}$
>   **where** $v_i = eval(t_i, \mathcal{A}, \zeta)$

The following AGGREGATE$_{\text{Activation}}$ rule specifies how to compute the *resultantUpdates*(Activation) for generated update instructions with *activationAction*. If, for any *loc*ation, there exists at least one such update instruction for that *loc*ation and its value is *true*, then $(loc, true)$ is added to the *resultantUpdates*. If all such update instructions for that *loc*ation have value *false*, the $(loc, false)$ is added to the *resultantUpdates*. All such update instructions for this *loc*ation are aggregated *successfully*.

$$\text{AGGREGATE}_{\text{Activation}}(updateInstructions) =$$
$$\textbf{forall } ui \in updateInstructions \textbf{ with } uiAction(ui) = activationAction$$
$$\textbf{let } ui = (loc, val, activationAction)$$
$$\textbf{let } s = \{u' \mid u' = (loc, val', activationAction)$$
$$\textbf{and } u' \in updateInstructions \textbf{ forsome } val'\}$$
$$\textbf{if thereissome } ui' \in s \textbf{ with } uiVal(ui') = true$$
$$\textbf{then } \text{INSERT}((loc, true), resultantUpdates(\text{Activation}))$$
$$\textbf{else } \text{INSERT}((loc, false), resultantUpdates(\text{Activation}))$$
$$\textbf{forall } ui' \in s \ aggStatus(ui') := successful$$

Remark on sequential composition. In the context of Turbo-ASMs, it could be necessary to not only aggregate update instructions but to also *compose* them. In the following example executing one step of the ASM results in adding 19 and 46 to the set *s*.

```
    par
        add 25 to s
        add 19 to s
seq
    par
        remove 25 from s
        add 46 to s
```

The two multisets of update instructions resulting from the two parts of the **seq** rule have to be composed into one multiset with respect to the order of the update instructions (introduced by the order of the two multisets). A background plug-in also has to provide a composition mechanism (if applicable). The composition is usually only applied in combination with the **seq**-rule.

For further details regarding the aggregation and composition of partial updates to regular updates see [186].

8.1.3 Parsing Specifications

After the initialization of the engine, typically a specification is *load*ed. Figure 8.4 shows the refinement of the LOADSPEC rule. The gray rounded rectangles distinguish which parts are handled by which component. When a speci-

Fig. 8.4 Refinement of LOADSPEC [105]
© 2009 Roozbeh Farahbod, reprinted with permission

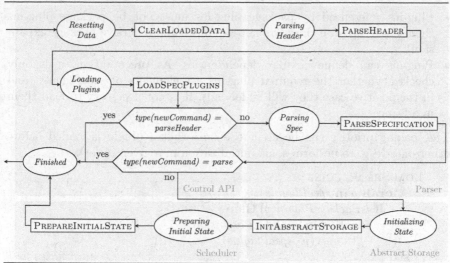

fication is loaded, all data of any previously *specHasBeenLoaded* is discarded. This means that the *loadedPlugins* and the *grammarRules* of the compound parser are reset. Furthermore, the *specification* is set to the *specToLoad* given by the user.

CLEARLOADEDDATA[4] =
    if *specHasBeenLoaded* then
        loadedPlugins := {}
        grammarRules := {}
        specification := *getSpecification*(*specToLoad*)

Next, PARSEHEADER determines the set of plug-ins required by the *specification*. It delegates the work to another rule we do not refine further here. This rule essentially specifies a simple line parser: it looks at the beginning of each line for the keyword **use** followed by a plug-in name and collects these names in a set.[5] In this way the rule computes a function *requiredPlugins*.

PARSEHEADER =
    specPlugins := *requiredPlugins*(*specification*)

In the next step, the package plug-ins are expanded and then all plug-ins are loaded, following their priority. In this step, it is also checked if the plug-in

---

[4] We slightly simplified this definition from the original specification in [105, Sect. 3.2.2] to abstract from some technical details.

[5] Although the **use**-directives can be everywhere in the file, it is recommended to put all of them at the beginning of a CoreASM specification file.

dependencies of each plug-in are satisfied. The given specification reflects the current implementation of CoreASM. This has the following consequences:

- Plug-ins referenced by package plug-ins must not be package plug-ins themselves, because those are not expanded (no recursive package expansion).
- Plug-ins can define circular dependencies. As precondition, it is only checked whether the required plug-ins are elements of *specPlugins* (and in the positive case they will be loaded). It is not necessary to load them in advance.

The loading priority can be used to ensure that a plugin is loaded before other ones (e. g. to perform some initialization in a given order).

> LOADSPECPLUGINS =
>> **forall** p **in** *specPlugins*   -- 1. expanding package plug-ins
>>> **if** *isPackagePlugin(p)* **then**
>>>> **forall** p' **in** *enclosedPlugins(p)*
>>>>> INSERT(p', *specPlugins*)
>> **seq**   -- 2. loading plug-ins with the maximum load priority first
>>> **while** $|specPlugins \setminus loadedPlugins| > 0$
>>>> **let** $toLoad = specPlugins \setminus loadedPlugins$
>>>>> **choose** p **in** *toLoad* **with** *maxPriority(p, toLoad)*
>>>>>> **if** $requiredPlugins(p) \subseteq specPlugins$ **then**
>>>>>>> LOADPLUGIN(p)
>>>>>> **else**
>>>>>>> ERROR('Cannot load p due to missing dependencies.')

The submachine LOADPLUGIN is defined as follows:

> LOADPLUGIN(p) =
>> PLUGININITRULE(p)
> **seq**
>> INSERT(p, *loadedPlugins*)
>> **if** *isParserPlugin(p)* **then**
>>> INSERT(*pluginGrammar(p)*, *grammarRules*)
>> **if** *isOperatorProvider(p)* **then**
>>> INSERT(*pluginOperators(p)*, *operatorRules*)

This rule expresses that when a plug-in p is loaded, PLUGININITRULE is executed and then p is added to the set of *loadedPlugins*. In most cases, a plug-in provides an extension to the language, and thus to the parser as well, or it provides new operators.

Traditional parsers transform a formal grammar (usually in EBNF [135, Sect. 1.8]) into a pushdown automaton. This permits to recognize a fixed language. The problem in the context of CoreASM is, that the grammar is not fixed but depends on the loaded plug-ins. Thus, the ad-hoc combined grammar must be compiled into an executable parser during runtime. Even if the automatically combined grammar is conflict free [135, Sect. 3.5.3], this task involves different tools and is complicated.

Instead, CoreASM utilizes monadic parser combinators [149] building a recursive-descent parser ad-hoc and takes advantage of the JParsec[6] library, which implements in Java many convenient functions for applying monadic parser combinators, like easier handling of operator associativity and precedence. Every CoreASM plug-in p that *isParserPlugin* provides a *pluginGrammar* (a set of partial parser functions) that is added to the set of *grammarRules*. If the plug-in *isOperatorProvider*, the *pluginOperators* are added similarly to the set of *operatorRules*. In the rule PARSESPECIFICATION, these sets of parser functions are combined into one parser and applied to the *specification*. This step is left abstract in [105].

Excursus on monadic parsers. In general, parsers are functions that get an input stream of characters and return a transformation (an element of T) of parts of the input together with the remainder of the input: $\pi\colon \Sigma^* \to (T, \Sigma^*)$. A full parser returns ε as the rest of the input.

The idea here is to combine several of those parser functions by using combinators like *sequence* or *choice*. A sequence of two (partial) parsers is realized by nesting of functions. The sequence of two parsers AB is translated by first applying parser A and passing its result to parser B. Thus, the combined parsing function for a given *input* is $B(A(inp))$.

The choice $(A|B)$ can be realized in different ways: One possibility is to first try parser A and if it fails, the complete *input* is handed over to parser function B. Another possibility is to apply both parsers to the same *input* and return a list of both results. In both ways, conflicts are handled directly. In the first case, A is prioritized over B, in the latter case, that parser is chosen which does not lead to an error in the further processing. In libraries as used by CoreASM these principal ideas are enhanced by choosing the most greedy parser, i.e. the parser that accepts the longest input.

Similarly, the *- and the $^+$-operators ("arbitrary many" and "at least one") of the EBNF syntax can be simulated by recursive functions. After the combination of all partial parsers, the resulting parser function is applied to the *input*. If the remaining input is empty, the full text has been parsed and the wanted result (the element of T in the parser function definition above) is returned. If the remaining input is not empty, the original input stream does not match the grammar and an error message is returned.

This flexible combination of different parsers is the main advantage of monadic parser combinators compared to traditional parser techniques. Disadvantages regarding the performance and the handling of left-recursive grammars do not play such an important role in this context, because specifications usually are rather small compared to programs where monadic parsers

---

[6] https://github.com/jparsec/jparsec

have been applied successfully. The potential non-termination in case of a left-recursive grammar is mitigated by additional functionality provided by the used library like the support of operator tables.
End of excursus.

Result of the parsing process. The result of the parsing process is an abstract syntax tree (AST) of *Node*s. For tree navigation, the following functions are defined on nodes:

- *first*: *Node* → *Node* returns the first abstract child node of a node.
- *next*: *Node* → *Node* returns the next abstract sibling in a list of children of a node.
- *parent*: *Node* → *Node* returns the parent of a node.

Note the emphasis on the *abstract* child or sibling node. Any token node in the sequence of children or siblings, created by the parser but with no special interest for CoreASM, is skipped. The following functions provide information about how a node was created during the parse process:

- *plugin*: *Node* → *Plugin* holds the plug-in that provided the grammar rule which is parsed at this node. This plug-in is responsible for the evaluation of this node during the interpretation.
- *grammarRule*: *Node* → *GrammarRule* returns the grammar rule that produced the given node.
- *token*: *Node* → *Token* returns the token that represents the given node (e. g. a keyword or a literal value).
- *class*: *Node* → *Class* returns the class of the corresponding grammar rule. These classes are introduced to distinguish between kinds of nodes on a higher level. Examples for classes are: Id(entifier), Rule, Expression, Declaration, UnaryOperator, BinaryOperator, and TernaryOperator (see Sect. 8.1.5 for usage of these classes).

Each node represents one kind of expression or rule that determines the specific meaning of each child node. Figure 8.5 shows an example parse tree, namely for the CoreASM rule **if** x **then** y := 5 **else skip**. The fill color of the nodes indicates by which plug-in (including the kernel) this node was created. For a uniform interface, the kernel is handled like a plug-in (i. e. the KernelPlugin). For instance, *plugin(next(first(root))) =* KernelPlugin and the *class* of that node equals Rule. One can see that the partial parsers, provided by the plug-ins, delegate the parsing of variable parts, like expressions or rules, back to the kernel resp. the main parser. The name above some of the nodes indicates the kind of the node.

PARSESPECIFICATION saves the *rootNode(specification)* returned by the parser. The next step in Fig. 8.4 is INITABSTRACTSTORAGE. It creates a new *State* in the abstract storage, initializes it and, in case of a vocabulary extension, loads the new vocabulary into the abstract storage.

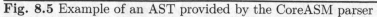

Fig. 8.5 Example of an AST provided by the CoreASM parser

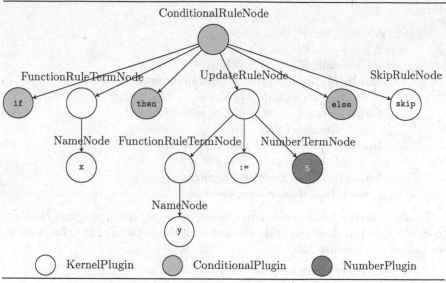

INITABSTRACTSTORAGE =
    let *newState* = **new** (*State*)
    state := *newState*
    INITIALIZESTATE(*newState*)
    LOADVOCABULARYPLUGINS(*newState*)

INITIALIZESTATE loads a set of *Agents* and a set of *programs*.[7] It resets the currently *executingAgent* and the *stepCount*er to their default values.

INITIALIZESTATE(*state*) =
    let *u* = **new** (*UniverseElement*)
    stateUniverse(*state*, Agents) := *u*
    let *f* = **new** (*FunctionElement*)
    stateFunction(*state*, program) := *f*
    -- *executingAgent* holds the value of '*self*' in the simulated machine
    executingAgent := **undef**
    stepCount := 0

LOADVOCABULARYPLUGINS loads for each plug-in which *isVocabularyExtender* the extensions of the abstract storage provided by the plug-in. The functions *pluginBackgrounds*, *pluginUniverses*, *pluginFunctions*, and *pluginRules* return the corresponding (*Name*, *Element*) pairs of the given plug-in. In this way, plug-ins can add new background or universe elements and predefined function or rule elements (for example library functions and rules)

---

[7] To conform to the CoreASM syntax we deviate here from the practice to write sets with initial capital letter.

to the abstract storage (more precisely: to the given *state* in the abstract storage).

> LOADVOCABULARYPLUGINS(*state*) =
>   **forall** $p \in$ *loadedPlugins*
>   **if** *isVocabularyExtender*(p) **then**
>   **forall** (*bkgName, bkg*) $\in$ *pluginBackgrounds*(p)
>   *stateUniverse*(*state, bkgName*) := *bkg*
>   **forall** (*uName, universe*) $\in$ *pluginUniverses*(p)
>   *stateUniverse*(*state, uName*) := *universe*
>   **forall** (*fName, f*) $\in$ *pluginFunctions*(p)
>   *stateFunction*(*state, fName*) := *f*
>   **forall** (*rName, rBody*) $\in$ *pluginRules*(p)
>   *stateRule*(*state, rName*) := *rBody*

Finally, the scheduler creates a new agent and assigns the program *initRule* to it. *initRule* is a dedicated rule marked with the keyword **init**. Its value is set during the parsing process.

> PREPAREINITIALSTATE =
>   **let** $a = new(Element)$
>   *initAgent* := a
>   SETVALUE$_{ue}$((Agents, [a]), true)
>   SETVALUE$_{fe}$((program, [a]), *initRule*)

8.1.4 Scheduling and Executing Agents

Once a specification is loaded, a *command* with *type*(*command*) = *step* triggers the execution of one step of the specification. Figure 8.6, which is explained in this subsection, is a refinement of the rule EXECUTESTEP in Fig. 8.2 and shows the sequence of tasks to be performed. After finishing the execution of one step of the specification, which for brevity we call a *simulation step*, the CoreASM engine returns to the *Idle* mode.

We consider now one simulation step as defined by Fig. 8.6. First, the rule STARTSTEP resets the multiset of *updateInstructions* and the *selectedAgentsSet* of those agents which in the simulation step are selected out of the *agentSet* to perform one step of their program. The *agentSet* is the set of all available agents. In step 0 it consists only of the *initAgent*, in later steps it consists of those agents that have a defined *program*.

> STARTSTEP =
>   *updateInstructions* := {||}
>   *selectedAgentsSet* := {}
>   **if** *stepCount* < 1   -- initially *stepCount* = 0
>   **then** *agentSet* := {*initAgent*}
>   **else** *agentSet* :=
>   {$a \mid a \in$ *getValue*(Agents, []) **and** *getValue*(program, [a]) $\neq$ undef}

If there is no agent with an associated program to select ($agentSet = \emptyset$), CoreASM considers the simulation step as successfully completed. If the termination condition (see Sect. 8.2) of the CoreASM run is not chosen appropriately, this results in an infinite loop of CoreASM.

CREATESCHEDULE, based on a *currentSchedulingPolicy* and the set of available agents, defines a *schedule* which serves to determine the value of *selectedAgentsSet* (by the rule SELECTAGENTS described below). Scheduling policies can be provided by plug-ins, offering to select among various algorithms to CREATESCHEDULE. For this purpose the *currentSchedulingPolicy* can be determined as part of a CoreASM program, namely as parameter of a keyword **schedulingPolicy** provided by the "SchedulingPoliciesPlugin". In CREATESCHEDULE the function *getNewSchedule* yields a schedule determined by the *currentSchedulingPolicy*. If no *currentSchedulingPolicy* is set in the specification and/or no schedule plug-in is loaded, CoreASM creates as default schedule the set of non-empty subsets of all available agents.

> CREATESCHEDULE =
>   **if** *currentSchedulingPolicy* = **undef**
>   **then** *schedule* := $\wp(agentSet) \setminus \{\emptyset\}$[8]
>   **else** *schedule* := *getNewSchedule(currentSchedulingPolicy)*

Remark on scheduling policies. In the BIOMICS project[9] a derivation of CoreASM has been developed, called CoreASIM. As described in [207], one of the extensions is to allow "dynamic" schedules. This permits to calculate the schedule for the next simulation step as part of the current simulation step (remember: simulation steps are steps of the executed specification). This mechanism permits to define scheduling algorithms that may depend on the current state of an ASM.

SELECTAGENTS assigns to *selectedAgentsSet* the *nextAgentsSubset* that is available in the current *schedule* (if any). The definition of the selection function *nextAgentsSubset* depends on how *schedule* is implemented. For example, if *schedule* is implemented as a list, *nextAgentsSubset* returns the *head* of the list. If *schedule* values are sets, as is the case with the default schedule, *nextAgentsSubset* simply selects a subset of *agentSet*. SELECTAGENTS directly reflects the set P_n of agents which in a given state S_n of a concurrent ASM run perform the computation of the next state S_{n+1} (see Definition 6).

> SELECTAGENTS =
>   *selectedAgentsSet* := *nextAgentsSubset(schedule)*
>   *schedule* := DELETE(*nextAgentsSubset(schedule)*, *schedule*)

---

[8] In the case of the default scheduling policy, we exclude $\emptyset$ from the *schedule* to avoid that it could become a possible value of *selectedAgentsSet*. Other scheduling policies might permit an empty agent set to appear.

[9] Biological and Mathematical Basis of Interaction Computing (http://www.biomicsproject.eu).

Fig. 8.6 Refined control state diagram of EXECUTESTEP

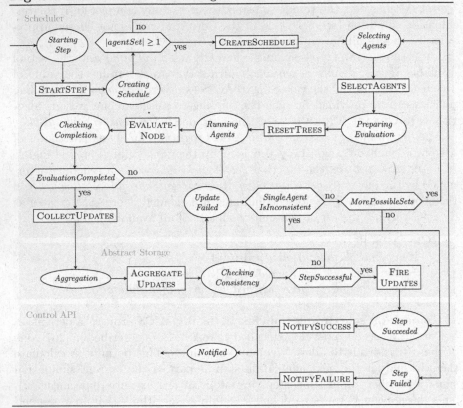

In order to calculate the resulting updates of the execution of an agent's program, its AST is used as evaluation tree. The function *pos* indicates for each agent the current position during the depth-first evaluation. In RESET-TREES, for each agent *a* of the *selectedAgentsSet*, *pos(a)* is initialized by the AST *root* node of the allocated program *p*. CLEARTREE removes any information that remained in the AST from a previous evaluation.

> RESETTREES =
>   **forall** $a \in selectedAgentsSet$
>   **let** $p = getValue(\mathsf{program}, [a])$
> $pos(a) := root(p)$
>   CLEARTREE(p)

Next, for each agent of the *selectedAgentsSet* the next node is evaluated by EVALUATENODE until the evaluation is completed. Completion of the evaluation means that the *root* nodes of all agents' programs have been *Evaluated*.

EVALUATENODE determines which plug-in is responsible for the current node and delegates the interpretation to the corresponding *pluginRule* or handles the node by the KERNELINTERPRETER. After the evaluation of a node, the interpretation is returned to its *parent* node (if it exists).

> EVALUATENODE =
>   **forall** $a \in selectedAgentsSet$
>   **let** $p = getValue(\textsf{program}, [a])$
>   **if not** $Evaluated(pos(a))$ **then**
>   **if** $plugin(pos(a)) \neq$ **undef then**
>   **let** $R = pluginRule(plugin(pos(a)))$
> $R(a)$
>   **else**
>   KERNELINTERPRETER(a)
>   **else**
>   **if** $parent(pos(a)) \neq$ **undef then**
> $pos(a) := parent(pos(a))$

> *EvaluationCompleted* **iff**
>   **forall** $a \in selectedAgentsSet$
> $Evaluated(root(getValue(\textsf{program}, [a]))) = true$

Finally, the calculated update instructions of each agent are added to the global multiset *updateInstructions* by the rule COLLECTUPDATES. More details about the interpretation of the AST (especially about the used data structures) are provided in the next Sect. 8.1.5.

> COLLECTUPDATES =
>   **forall** $a \in selectedAgentsSet$
>   **let** $p = getValue(\textsf{program}, [a])$
>   INSERT$(updates(root(p)), updateInstructions)$

The next step in executing a simulation step is the aggregation of updates as described in Sect. 8.1.2 where the predicate *AggregationSuccessful* is defined. A step is considered as successful, if all *updateInstructions* have been handled successfully and the resulting *updateSet* is consistent.

> *StepSuccessful* **iff**
>   *AggregationSuccessful* **and** *Consistent(updateSet)*

If *StepSuccessful* holds, FIREUPDATES applies all updates to the current state creating a new state and then can NOTIFYSUCCESS, concluding the successful step by incrementing the *stepCount*.

> FIREUPDATES =
>   **forall** $(l, v) \in updateSet$
>   SETVALUE$_{fe}(l, v)$
> NOTIFYSUCCESS =
> $stepCount := stepCount + 1$

Otherwise, the mode *UpdateFailed* is entered. In this mode, a deeper insight into the reason for the failed update is gained in order to decide, whether it is worth trying another subset of agents or not. A *SingleAgentIsInconsistent* if the contradicting updates are produced by one agent. In that case, there is a problem in the program of that agent, which is reported to the user by NOTIFYFAILURE. In this way the inconsistency does not remain hidden to the user and the selection of a different set of agents, which could be tried out for the currently simulated step, is interrupted. Otherwise, if the inconsistent update is produced by the combination of selected agents, another set of agents is tried out, if there are options left in the *schedule*. *MorePossibleSets* checks whether applying *nextAgentsSubset* to the *schedule* yields a new subset of agents or not. [10]

> *SingleAgentIsInconsistent* **iff**
>   **forsome** $ui, ui' \in updateSet$
> $uiLoc(ui) = uiLoc(ui')$ **and** $uiVal(ui) \neq uiVal(ui')$
>   **and** $uiAgent(ui) = uiAgent(ui')$
> *MorePossibleSets* **iff** $nextAgentsSubset(schedule) \neq$ **undef**

Remark. In the CoreASM implementation the parallel execution of all agents of the *selectedAgentsSet* is spread over several tasks. These tasks could be executed concurrently if the concurrent execution is supported by the underlying platform (e. g. in a multi-core environment).

8.1.5 Interpreting a Flexible Language

The task of the CoreASM interpreter is to compute, using the AST representation of the given ASM and the current state information, the set of updates produced by the ASM step in the current state. The computation consists of a tree traversal during which at evaluated nodes n a triple denoted by $[\![n]\!]$ is computed. $[\![n]\!]$ consists of a) the affected location, b) a multiset of update instructions accumulated at n and in its subtree, and c) a value associated with the node. Each of these elements can be **undef**, depending on the kind of node whose interpretation created the triple. The following selector functions are used to access the different components of the interpretation result $[\![n]\!]$ for a given node n:

---

[10] This behavior has been specified in [104, p.59] and corresponds to the current implementation of CoreASM. It privileges the analysis of single-agent behavior over multi-agent behavior. To implement the recently proposed [70] notion of concurrent ASM runs, which we use in this book (see Definition 6) and which was not known at the time of Farahbod's thesis work, it would be desirable to let CoreASM enter mode *StepFailed* and NOTIFYFAILURE ONLY if there are no *MorePossibleSets*. In addition, it would be desirable to let CoreASM report to the user an information on every unsuccessful combination of agents.

- $loc(n)$ returns the first component $loc(n) = firstComponent(\llbracket n \rrbracket)$, a location or l-value (left value).
- $updates(n)$ returns the multiset of update instructions. This multiset also contains all accumulated update instructions of the subtree of n.
- $value(n)$ returns the value (also called the r-value or right value) associated with the given node.
- $Evaluated(n)$, defined by $Evaluated(n)$ **iff** $\llbracket n \rrbracket \neq$ **undef**, indicates whether the node n has been evaluated.

A *pattern* returns the symbolic name for the grammar pattern represented by a node (e. g. IfThen represents the pattern **if ... then ...**). Patterns are needed to distinguish between different kinds of nodes provided by plug-ins or by the kernel. The notation $(\!| \, pattern \, |\!) \Rightarrow actions$ is a short form for the ASM rule "**if** $conditions(pattern)$ **then** $actions$", where $conditions(pattern)$ depends on the pattern. If the $conditions$ hold for the current AST-node, the $actions$ are performed on this node.

The following example illustrates the notation where pos stands for the node currently evaluated by the *agent*, $pos(agent)$. For the sake of brevity we omit the *agent* parameter when *agent* is clear from the context or not relevant.

$$(\!| \, true \, |\!) \; \Rightarrow \; \llbracket pos \rrbracket := (\mathbf{undef}, \mathbf{undef}, \mathsf{true}_e)$$

expresses that as result of the interpretation of a node at an AST-position pos which represents the literal $true$, if the $conditions(true)$ hold, then to the node the triple is assigned with no (**undef**) location (resp. l-value), no update instructions[11] and element true as value (r-value).

The expression "$conditions(true)$", which describes the rule guard, is defined by $class(pos) \neq$ Id **and** $pattern(pos) = $ true. The role of the identifier condition $class(pos) \neq$ Id is explained below.

The interpretation of *false* and **undef** is defined analogously. The interpretation of **self** returns the value of the current *agent*:

$$(\!| \, \mathbf{self} \, |\!) \; \Rightarrow \; \llbracket pos(agent) \rrbracket := (\mathbf{undef}, \mathbf{undef}, agent) \, .$$

In order to write more complex patterns concisely, the following special notations for different kinds of nodes are introduced:

- ⟦?⟧ denotes a generic node, whether evaluated or not.
- ☐ denotes a generic unevaluated node. For mnemonic reasons, small letters in the box remind the reader of the expected result. For example, the result of a node ⟦l⟧ should concern a location, more precisely it is expected to consist of a triple where the first component is defined and is a location. We abbreviate this by saying that '⟦l⟧ should result in a location'. Similarly, ⟦u⟧ should result in a multiset of update instructions, typically due to the interpretation of a rule. ⟦v⟧ should result in a value, typically due to the interpretation of an expression.

---

[11] In this context, **undef** stands for the default value ∅.

- The same letters but without boxes are used in order to identify nodes that are already evaluated. For example, v is used for an evaluated expression node whose *value* is not **undef**.
- Small Greek letters are used to indicate the children of the current *pos* in the AST which do not represent a keyword node. For example, in the pattern **if** $^\alpha e$ **then** $^\beta u$ the letter α denotes the condition node and β denotes the **then**-part of a conditional rule.

Table 8.1 from [105] summarizes the abbreviations with their equivalent ordinary notation, depending on their occurrence in a *pattern* or in the *actions*.

Table 8.1 Abbreviations in syntactic pattern-matching rules [105]

Abbreviation	Translation as *pattern* part	Translation as *actions* part
α, β etc.		$first(pos), next(first(pos))$, etc.
$^\alpha\boxed{?}$	$class(\alpha) \neq \mathsf{Id}$	
$^\alpha\square$	$class(\alpha) \neq \mathsf{Id} \wedge \neg Evaluated(\alpha)$	
$^\alpha\boxed{l}, {}^\alpha\boxed{u}, {}^\alpha\square\,^*$	$class(\alpha) \neq \mathsf{Id} \wedge \neg Evaluated(\alpha)$	
$^\alpha x$	$class(\alpha) = \mathsf{Id}$	$token(\alpha)$
$^\alpha l$	$loc(\alpha) \neq \mathbf{undef}$	$loc(\alpha)$
$^\alpha u$	$updates(\alpha) \neq \mathbf{undef}$	$updates(\alpha)$
$^\alpha v$	$value(\alpha) \neq \mathbf{undef}$	$value(\alpha)$

With these notations, complex patterns can be written in a compact form. For instance, $(\!| \text{ } \mathbf{if} \,^\alpha\boxed{v} \text{ } \mathbf{then} \,^\beta\boxed{u} \text{ } |\!) \Rightarrow pos := \alpha$ is a short form for the following rule:

> **let** $\alpha = first(pos), \beta = next(first(pos))$
>   **if** $class(pos) \neq \mathsf{Id}$ **and** $pattern(pos) = \mathsf{IfThen}$
>   **and** $class(\alpha) \neq \mathsf{Id}$ **and not** $Evaluated(\alpha)$
>   **and** $class(\beta) \neq \mathsf{Id}$ **and not** $Evaluated(\beta)$
>   **then**
> $pos := first(pos)$

This rule checks whether the node at the current *position* of the interpretation process does not represent an identifier but an IfThen-rule, and whether its two children do not represent an identifier and are not evaluated yet. If this rule guard is true, the interpretation process proceeds with the interpretation of the first child node (where in this case an expression has to be evaluated). For identifiers a special treatment is required which is explained below.

This example illustrates the first step of the interpretation of a conditional rule. The next step depends on the value of the condition:

> $(\!| \text{ } \mathbf{if} \,^\alpha v \text{ } \mathbf{then} \,^\beta\boxed{u} \text{ } |\!) \Rightarrow$
>   **if** $v = \mathbf{true}_e$ **then** $pos := \beta$ **else** $[\![pos]\!] := (\mathbf{undef}, \{ | \}, \mathbf{undef})$

If the guard is true, the subtree under the β-node is evaluated, otherwise, the conditional rule behaves like a **skip**-node. In the first case, once the the subtree has calculated its update set, this update set must be recorded to be passed to the parent node:

$$(\!|\, \mathbf{if}\,^{\alpha}v \,\mathbf{then}\,^{\beta}u\,|\!) \;\Rightarrow\; [\![pos]\!] := (\mathbf{undef}, \mathit{updates}(u), \mathbf{undef})$$

The update of the *position* to lead back to the parent node is performed by the rule EXECUTETREE whenever the node of the current *position* has finished its evaluation (indicated by $\mathit{Evaluated}(pos) = \mathit{true}$).

The handling of identifiers must distinguish three cases:

1. The identifier is part of a local environment, introduced e. g. by an **import** or a **let** rule,
2. the identifier is a global function (nullary or with arguments), or
3. the identifier is unknown, yet. In this case, a new function element is created in the abstract storage.

In each of these cases, the value of the identifier is returned as *value*. If the identifier represents a global (modifiable) function resp. a location, this is returned as *loc*ation in the triple, too. The local value of an identifier x can be looked up via the function $\mathit{env}(x)$ which is organized as stack, in order to allow overriding in different scopes. An *UndefinedToken* is neither a function nor a rule nor a universe. The following rule captures this behavior:

$$
\begin{aligned}
(\!|\,^{\alpha}x\,|\!) \to \quad &\mathbf{if}\ \mathit{env}(x) \neq \mathbf{undef}\ \mathbf{then} \quad\quad\quad\quad \text{-- } x \text{ is a local identifier}\\
&\quad [\![pos]\!] := (\mathbf{undef}, \mathbf{undef}, \mathit{env}(x))\\
&\mathbf{else}\\
&\quad \mathbf{if}\ \mathit{isFunctionName}(x)\ \mathbf{then}\\
&\quad\quad \mathbf{let}\ l = (x, [\,])\\
&\quad\quad\quad [\![pos]\!] := (l, \mathbf{undef}, \mathit{getValue}(l))\\
&\quad \mathbf{if}\ \mathit{UndefinedToken}(x)\ \mathbf{then}\\
&\quad\quad \text{HANDLEUNDEFINEDIDENTIFIER}(pos, x, [\,])\\
&\mathbf{where}\\
&\quad \mathit{UndefinedToken}(x)\ \mathbf{iff}\\
&\quad\quad \mathbf{not}\ (\mathit{isFunctionName}(x)\ \mathbf{or}\ \mathit{isRuleName}(x)\ \mathbf{or}\ \mathit{isUniverseName}(x))
\end{aligned}
$$

The rule HANDLEUNDEFINEDIDENTIFIER queries all *loadedPlugins* if one of them can handle this identifier. This way, it is possible for plug-ins to introduce new functions, rules, or literals. If none of the plug-ins can handle this identifier, KERNELHANDLEUNDEFINEDIDENTIFIER creates a new function element with the initial value **undef** at the given location.

$$
\begin{aligned}
&\text{KERNELHANDLEUNDEFIDENTIFIER}(pos, x, args) =\\
&\quad \mathbf{let}\ f = \mathbf{new}\ (\mathit{FunctionElement})\\
&\quad\quad \mathit{stateFunction}(state, x) := f\\
&\quad\quad [\![pos]\!] := ((x, args), \mathbf{undef}, \mathsf{undef}_e)
\end{aligned}
$$

For n-ary functions, the behavior is very similar to nullary functions, except that all arguments are evaluated first in an arbitrary order. This is realized by choosing any not yet *Evaluated* node of the list of arguments and setting the interpreter *pos*ition to this node until all arguments are evaluated. Obviously, this realizes a call-by-value semantics for function calls. Note, that this is not the case for rule calls, where a call-by-substitution semantics is used instead.

$$(\, {}^{\alpha}x({}^{\lambda_1}\boxed{?}_1, \ldots, {}^{\lambda_n}\boxed{?}_n) \,) \rightarrow$$
$$\quad \textbf{if } isFunctionName(x) \textbf{ then}$$
$$\quad\quad \textbf{choose } i \in [1..n] \textbf{ with not } Evaluated(\lambda_i)$$
$$\quad\quad\quad pos := \lambda_i$$
$$\quad\quad \textbf{ifnone} \qquad\qquad \text{-- left/righthandside are both evaluated}$$
$$\quad\quad\quad \textbf{let } l = (x, [value(\lambda_1), \ldots, value(\lambda_n)])$$
$$\quad\quad\quad [\![pos]\!] := (l, \textbf{undef}, getValue(l))$$
$$\quad\quad \textbf{if } UndefinedToken(x) \textbf{ then}$$
$$\quad\quad\quad \textsc{HandleUndefinedIdentifier}(pos, x, [\lambda_1, \ldots, \lambda_n])$$

As last example, we show how the assignment rule is realized. Again, left and right side of the assignment rule are evaluated in an arbitrary order. If both sides are evaluated, the *loca*tion of the left hand side is not **undef**. Since the location is modifiable, an update is produced which sets this location to the value of the right hand side node. Otherwise, appropriate error messages are generated.

$$(\, {}^{\alpha}\boxed{?} := {}^{\beta}\boxed{?} \,) \rightarrow$$
$$\quad \textbf{choose } \tau \in \{\alpha, \beta\} \textbf{ with not } Evaluated(\tau)$$
$$\quad\quad pos := \tau$$
$$\quad \textbf{ifnone}$$
$$\quad\quad \textbf{if } loc(\alpha) \neq \textbf{undef} \textbf{ then}$$
$$\quad\quad\quad \textbf{if } isModifiable(stateFunction(state, name_{loc}(loc))) \textbf{ then}$$
$$\quad\quad\quad\quad [\![pos]\!] := (\textbf{undef}, \{\!\!\{(loc(\alpha), value(\beta))\}\!\!\}, \textbf{undef})$$
$$\quad\quad\quad \textbf{else } \textsc{Error}(\text{'Cannot update a non-modifiable function'})$$
$$\quad\quad \textbf{else } \textsc{Error}(\text{'Cannot update a non-location'})$$

Every plug-in that extends the language provides a partial parser that produces the node constellation in the AST according to the appropriate patterns. The partial interpreter knows how to deal with these nodes and evaluates them by setting the current *pos*ition in the AST to the corresponding node. If all (sub-)nodes are evaluated, a triple for this node is generated which leads to the continuation of the evaluation of the parent node.

A simulation step is completed once the *root* node of the AST is *Evaluated*. The multiset *updates(root)* is the multiset *updateInstructions* of the complete simulation step. As explained above, this multiset has to be aggregated into the *updateSet* which (if consistent) will be applied by CoreASM to the current state to yield the next state.

Fig. 8.7 shows an intermediate situation of the interpretation of the AST in Fig. 8.5. Node β is *Evaluated*, the interpretation result

$$(\textbf{undef}, \{\!\!\{((y, [\,]), 5_e, updateAction)\}\!\!\}, \textbf{undef})$$

can be assigned to the node *pos*, and the interpreter control can be returned to the parent node.

Fig. 8.7 Intermediate interpreter situation

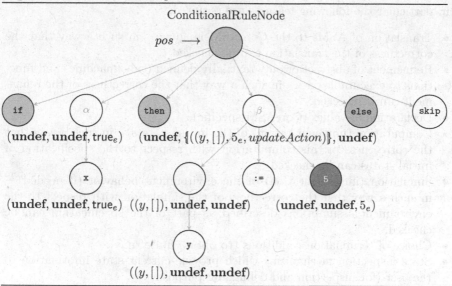

ConditionalRuleNode

$pos \longrightarrow$

if α then β else skip

(**undef, undef**, true_e) (**undef**, $\{((y, [\,]), 5_e, \mathit{updateAction})\}$, **undef**)

x := 5

(**undef, undef**, true_e) (($y, [\,]$), **undef, undef**) (**undef, undef**, 5_e)

y

(($y, [\,]$), **undef, undef**)

8.2 Translating Abstract to CoreASM Executable Models

In this section we describe the necessary steps to transform an abstract model into a CoreASM-executable one and their rationale.

Machine processing of a model permits to exploit two facts: a) machines are much better than humans at identifying syntactical errors, like name or type inconsistencies, typos, etc., b) conceptual problems or errors can be discovered by experiments with the model, namely via execution of test cases and analysis of their results. On the other side, the main problem with machine processing of a specification is that an abstract model, to become executable, has to be translated into a machine-readable form. This implies that the free choice of abstraction level is lost. It is, for example, not enough to state in natural language that "a list of elements shall be sorted", but one has to specify the exact algorithm how this is achieved.

The specifications presented in this book use algorithmic and mathematical concepts and notation as well as precise natural language elements. The "literate" [163] style (mixing formal parts with explaining text) eases the understanding of the specifications for humans and is crucial to intellectually manage (the complexity of) a system, but to obtain an executable model the abstract model must be translated into a concrete execution language. To maintain a system understanding also for the executable code and to be useful in practice, such a translation besides its semantical correctness must also satisfy some basic pragmatic properties. For translating ASMs to CoreASM in particular the following features are required:

- Translation of ASMs to the CoreASM language—in such a way that the correctness of the translation can be checked.
- Refinement of abstract or only textually defined (sub-)machines and functions to executable ones—in such a way that the correctness of the refinement can be checked.
- Declaration of values (CoreASM specific).
- Computation (implementation) of the initial state(s)—in such a way that the correctness of this computation with respect to the specification of initial states can be checked.
- Simulation (implementation) of the environment behavior (if needed)—in such a way that the correctness of the simulation with respect to the environment assumptions described as part of the specification can be checked.
- Choice of termination conditions (to obtain finite runs).
- State inspection mechanisms which provide current state information to the user (for inspection and debugging purposes).

First, we illustrate how the **translation of ASMs into the CoreASM language** works. As mentioned in Sect. 8.1.3, a parser must be able to process the specification. Usually parsers work on plain text and thus, all mathematical symbols must be replaced by appropriate keywords. To distinguish between mathematical ASM syntax and CoreASM syntax, CoreASM code is typeset in `typewriter` font. The syntax offered by CoreASM is rather intuitive and has been chosen to be as close as possible to the mathematical notation. In the following, we only illustrate some characteristic features of the syntax. For a detailed definition of the supported language, we refer to the user manual of CoreASM [106].

As first example, we translate the definition of SPONTANEOUSLYDO (see the Termination Detection algorithm in Sect. 3.2):

$$\text{SPONTANEOUSLYDO}(\mathcal{M}) =$$
$$\textbf{choose } R \in \mathcal{M} \cup \{\textbf{skip}\} \textbf{ do } R$$

The symbols $\in$ and $\cup$ are replaced by the keywords **in** resp. **union**. A rule declaration is introduced by the keyword **rule**.

```
rule SpontaneouslyDo(M) =
  choose R in M union {@Skip} do
    R

rule Skip =
  skip
```

Note that the body of any rule consists of exactly one rule. In case several rules shall be executed, one has to surround them with, for example, a

par-construct (for parallel execution) or a **seq**-construct (for sequential execution). Currently, CoreASM does not support indentation sensitive syntax, but supports braces ({ }) and brackets ([]) as less verbose alternatives for **par** resp. **seq**.

Nevertheless, we can omit the **par/endpar** in the example above, because SpontaneouslyDo consists of only one **choose**-rule which again contains only one rule R. The keyword **skip** can not be used as reference to the **skip** rule. Instead, we have to encapsulate it in a separate rule Skip that can be referenced with its identifier in the set.

To illustrate a **refinement of abstract (sub-) machines** we use the traffic light SWITCH rule from Sect. 2.1.1. SWITCH(l) = ($l := l'$) sets the parameter l to the opposite value l'. What 'opposite' means has to be made explicit to the machine:

```
rule Switch(l) =
  par
    if l = on then l := off
    if l = off then l := on
  endpar
```

This example also illustrates the need to **declare values**. CoreASM assumes every unknown identifier to be a location. Thus, if on and off are not explicitly defined to be values, CoreASM would treat them as (initially **undef**ined) locations. That would imply that none of the two rules is executed if l has a value different from **undef**. Values can be defined either by plug-ins, which introduce a new *background* (for example the *NumberPlugin* provides numbers to CoreASM), or by using the *SignaturePlugin* which provides the possibility to define universes and enumerations.

Universes are sets that can be declared with initial values. Membership is realized by their characteristic functions. In the following example, on and off are defined as values of the universe Light.

```
universe Light = {on, off}
```

One can add new elements to a universe. In the Light example the rule AddDefect imports a new element and adds it to the universe Light. In order to provide the possibility to explicitly access this new element, the generated value must be stored in a location, say defect. The rule guard prevents a second execution of the rule; would it be omitted, each call to AddDefect would add a new element and redirects the location defect to this new value. Then the universe Light would grow with each execution step.

```
rule AddDefect =
  if Light(defect) != true then
    import newElem do par
      Light(newElem) := true
      defect := newElem
    endpar
```

Enumerations are a fixed set of values that can not be changed. The syntax is similar to that for universes:

```
enum Light = {on, off}
```

The characteristic function of an enumeration is treated as a static (not modifiable) function. Nevertheless, it is possible to check the membership via **if** Light(on) = **true then** .... Every value identifier must be unique over the entire specification, such that there is no ambiguity concerning the membership.

Without **computation of the initial state** all locations have value **undef**. The initial state in CoreASM can be established in two ways. An initial value can be provided directly with the declaration of a location, as in the universe Light example above. It can also be provided dynamically by executing the *initial rule*. The initial rule is an ordinary rule elected by the keyword **init**, followed by its name.

In the Termination Detection example of Sect. 3.2, the initial state is described declaratively as follows:

> **forall** $m \in Machine$
> $\quad mode(m) \in \{active, passive\}$ *-- InitializationReq*
> $\quad color(m) \in \{black, white\}$ -- any initial machine coloring
> $\quad hasToken(master) = true$ -- the master *hasToken*
> $\quad$ **if** $m \neq master$ **then** $hasToken(m) = false$ -- ... and nobody else
> $\quad Triggered(m) = false$ -- meaning: NoMsgsAround
> $\quad tokenColor = black$ -- triggers *master* to start a probe
> **where**
> $\quad Machine = \{m_0, \ldots, m_{N-1}\}$
> $\quad master = m_0$
> $\quad number(m_i) = i \bmod N$

This leads to the following **init** rule in CoreASM. It establishes the initial state of the location and creates agents by setting the predefined characteristic functions of Agents to true. Each agent gets also a program assigned. Note the definition of a constant as a derived function.

```
enum COLORS = {BLACK, WHITE}
enum MODES = {ACTIVE, PASSIVE}

init InitialState

derived N = 8
derived machines =
    {a | a in Agents with number(a) != undef}

rule InitialState =
  par
    forall i in [0..(N−1)] do
```

```
        import m do
          par
            Agents(m) := true
            program(m) := @TerminationDetection
            number(m) := i
            choose s in MODES do
              mode(m) := s
            if i = 0 then
              par
                hasToken(m) := true
                color(m) := WHITE
                master := m
              endpar
            else
              par
                hasToken(m) := false
                choose c in COLORS do
                  color(m) := c
              endpar
            Triggered(m) := false
          endpar
        tokenColor := BLACK
        program(self) := undef
      endpar
```

The last line `program(self) := undef` disables the initial agent that executes the initial rule. This ensures that the rule is executed only once. After the initialization phase, the multi-agent machine is executed.

Now assume that `TerminationDetection` and all other rules are defined appropriately for execution by CoreASM. The reactive character of the ASM implies that the execution of this specification in CoreASM will run forever. In practice, this is not very useful. The CoreASM eclipse environment provides the possibility to **choose between different termination conditions**:

- A simulation step returns an empty update set.
- A simulation step returns the same update set as the previous one.
- There is no agent with a defined program.
- After a certain number of simulation steps have been executed.

In case of the Termination Detection, we want to stop execution when a termination has been detected. To achieve this, the following code is added to the specification:

```
rule CheckTermination =
  if TerminationDetected then
    StopASM
```

```
derived TerminationDetected =
  self = master and hasToken(master)
    and mode(master) = PASSIVE
    and color(master) = WHITE and tokenColor = WHITE

rule StopASM =
  forall m in Agents do
    program(m) := undef
```

CheckTermination is added to the TerminationDetection-rule and the termination condition "there is no agent with a defined program" is chosen.

Now, we can run this model and it will stop should TerminationDetected evaluate to true.

What is still missing is the ability to observe the current state, which is useful for debugging purposes or just for tracing the execution. A **state inspection mechanism** which provides current state information to the user is supported in CoreASM in three ways. First, the CoreASM eclipse environment offers the possibility to log information about the current execution state (end of a step, current step number, last update set, dump of the complete state, and the selected set of agents) after each step. Second, a special rule **print** provided by the *IO*-plug-in allows for logging arbitrary information (strings or values of the current state, not of the to-be-calculated one) to the console. Third, using a debugging component like the one we specify in the following section. Usually, a combination of all three options is used.

As an example, one could add the following line to StopASM, in parallel to the **forall** rule.

```
print ''global termination detected''
```

In some cases, a dedicated **behavior of the environment** is assumed. This is not the case for the *TerminationDetection*, since all behavior (sending messages, getting passive, etc.) of each machine is already integrated in the rules. If this is not the case, it is necessary to model an environmental behavior in ASMs to allow for a useful simulation. Sometimes this task is even more complex than modeling the algorithm itself. An example of such a complex behavior is the simulation of the network traffic and movement of communicating nodes for executing the AODV routing protocol presented in Sect. 6.1.

Final remarks. In general, the usage of an integrated development environment (IDE) is recommended, since its tools help to increase the productivity. The eclipse plug-in of CoreASM for example provides a special editor component with features like syntax highlighting, code completion, indication of warnings and errors, a debugging component, comfortable execution, and much more.

The *SignaturePlugin* provides the possibility to declare used functions with their type signature. This enables CoreASM to perform type checks during runtime. Additionally, all identifiers in the specification that are not declared are marked with a warning. This avoids otherwise hard to find typos or other simple mistakes that might lead to strange behavior.

The possibility to monitor and inspect in a detailed way the current state is very important in order to verify the correct behavior of a specification. The following example illustrates this. In a first version of the termination detection algorithm, the ACTIVATE and DEACTIVATE rules were realized just by assigning *true* resp. *false* to the trigger (without using the *ActivationPlugin*). In every run, the termination was detected correctly without reporting an inconsistent update. But one would expect an inconsistency in case one agent performs an ACTIVATE and simultaneously another agent performs DEACTIVATE. A detailed look into the log showed the reason why CoreASM did not report the encountered inconsistencies: inconsistent updates did occur, but these cases were discarded due to the default scheduling policy of CoreASM which chooses another set of agents if the current one yields an inconsistent update set. As a result, none or only very few messages were sent among the agents.

Exercise 62. Refine the 1WayTrafLightSpec model to a CoreASM executable one.

Exercise 63. Using the CoreASM model of 1WayTrafLightSpec from Exerc. 62 define a CoreASM executable version for 1WayTrafLightCtl and the environment ASM LightUnitResponse.

Exercise 64. Refine Refined1WayTrafLightCtl to a CoreASM executable model.

8.3 Exploiting the Flexibility: A Debugger for CoreASM

In this section we apply the ASM method to extend the ASM model of Core-ASM by an ASM model of a debugger, to debug (the CoreASM refinement of) ASM *models*. This illustrates also how the component-based architecture of CoreASM supports to introduce a new component by rigorously defining its behavior and its interaction with the given machine.

As is well-known, a debugger permits to stop the execution of a program (here: a CoreASM executable specification) at a specific point (*breakpoint*), to get the program executed step by step, to inspect the program state, maybe to modify it, and finally to resume the execution. One could think of it as a slow-motion program execution aiming at providing detailed insight into the program and at detecting bugs. To specify a debugger for CoreASM one has to define exactly a) what can be useful breakpoints and actions to debug an ASM and b) how the defined debugging behavior is integrated into CoreASM.

For the integration we exploit the plug-in architecture of CoreASM. Table 8.2 shows the different kinds of plug-ins supported by CoreASM, most of which have been mentioned in the previous sections of this chapter.

Table 8.2 CoreASM Plug-in Interfaces (from [105])

Plug-in Interface	Extends	Description
Parser Plug-in	Parser	provides additional grammar rules to the parser
Interpreter Plug-in	Interpreter	provides new semantics to the Interpreter
Operator Provider	Parser, Interpreter	provides grammar rules for new operators along with their precedence levels and semantics
Vocabulary Extender	Abstract Storage	extends the state with additional predefined functions, universes, and backgrounds
Aggregator	Abstract Storage	aggregates partial updates into basic updates
Scheduler Plug-in	Scheduler	provides new scheduling policies for multi-agent ASMs
Extension Point Plug-in	all components	extends the control state model of the engine

The CoreASM debugger component can be specified using plug-ins for *Extension Points*. By CoreASM *ExtensionPoints* we understand those control states $c = engineMode$ of the CoreASM engine for which new rules may be introduced by some *ExtensionPointPlugins*, rules which must be executed right after the execution of the *kernelRule(c)* defined in Sect. 8.1. This means to refine each CoreASM *kernelRule(c)* by switching, after its execution, to the machine HANDLEEPPLUGIN(c) described below. This machine extends CoreASM at c by executing every *ExtensionPointPlugin* p that is registered for execution when *engineMode = c*. Therefore, in CoreASM as defined in Sect. 8.1, each rule **if** *engineMode = c* **and** *Cond* **then** *rule* is refined to:

> **if** *engineMode = c* **and** *Cond* **then**
>   *rule* **seq** [12]
>   **if** *ExtensionPoint(c)* **and** *PluginRegisteredFor(p, c)* **forsome** *p*
>   **then**
>   *engineMode := ExecutingEpPlugin*
>   **forall** *p* **with** *PluginRegisteredFor(p, c)*
>   *lastEngineCallMode(p) := c*   -- record breakpoint

and the following rule is added to the main rule of CoreASM:

> **if** *engineMode = ExecutingEpPlugin* **then**
>   HANDLEEPPLUGIN

Obviously the possible *engineMode* value *Terminated* in Fig. 8.2 is declared not to be an *ExtensionPoint*. But for example, *kernelRule(Idle)* refers to the control state diagram rule in Fig. 8.2. Depending on the received input command, executing this rule leads to a successor *engineMode* *InitializingKernel* or *ResettingData* or *StartingStep* or *Terminating* (see Figs. 8.4, 8.6, and [105]).

---

[12] **seq** permits overwriting *engineMode*.

In HANDLEEPPLUGIN, first all *ExtensionPointPlugin*s that are registered for the given mode c are *marked* for execution and recorded in the set *CalledPlugins*. Then the set of *marked* plug-ins is executed in the inverse order of their priority. Each plug-in rule has its own *internalMode*s and when *Done* is assumed to have suggested a *nextEngineMode* to return to. Due to the sequential (stepwise) execution, the plug-in with the highest priority will therefore decide about this next say 'genuine' *engineMode*, in which the Core-ASM engine will take over again once the extension point plug-ins at c have been executed[13].

We use the **step** and not the **seq** construct of Sect. 4.5 because we want the plug-ins to be able to wait for user input.

> HANDLEEPPLUGIN =
>   **forall** $p \in ExtensionPointPlugin$
>   -- first, all plug-ins registered for this state transition are marked
> $marked(p) := PluginRegisteredFor(p, lastEngineCallMode(p))$
>   INSERT$(p, CalledPlugins)$ -- record plug-ins called for execution
>   **step**
>   **while**$_{stepwise}$ $marked(p) = true$ **forsome** $p \in ExtensionPointPlugin$
>   **let** $eps = \{p \in ExtensionPointPlugin \mid marked(p)\}$
>   **choose** $p' \in minPriority(eps)$ -- eps element of minimal priority
>   **let** $R = pluginExtensionRule(p')$
>   **if** $Done(p')$ **then**
> $marked(p') := false$ -- proceed with next *marked* plug-in
> $Done(p') := false$ -- reset *Done* for next call of plug-in
> $internalMode(p') :=$ **undef**
>   **else** R -- execute one step of R
>   **step**   -- return to CoreASM engine
>   **choose** p **in** $CalledPlugins$ **with**
>   **forall** $p' \in CalledPlugins$ $priority(p') \leq priority(p)$
> $engineMode := nextEngineMode(p)$
> $CalledPlugins := \emptyset$ -- reset *CalledPlugins* for next ExtensionPoint
>   **where**
> $priority(p) = pluginCallPriority(p, c)$

The values of the functions *PluginRegisteredFor(p,c)*, *pluginCallPriority(p)*, and *pluginExtensionRule(p)* must be provided by the extension point plug-in p.

By keeping the predicate *Done* false, a plug-in can remain in the loop as long as necessary. In this way it becomes possible to execute plug-in rules right before any genuine CoreASM mode, to skip existing genuine engine

---

[13] The attentive reader who is familiar with CoreASM might have noticed that we deviate from the CoreASM specification [104] at this point. According to the E(xtensible)FSM specification [104, p. 95], an extension point plugin can not determine the subsequent *engineMode*, although the text suggests this. With this restriction, it would not have been possible to define the debugger component as it is done here.

modes, and also to introduce new modes that are handled by the plug-in itself. It is up to the developer of a plug-in to guarantee that the resulting state transition system does not end in a dead end or interfere unexpectedly with other extension point plug-ins and (if wanted) still contains the original engine state transitions.

For breakpoints and steps we specify a generalized and more abstract version than the one in the debugger described in [87]. We plan to adapt the current implementation of the debugging component to match the definition presented here.

A breakpoint denotes a specific point in the executed specification or program. If a breakpoint is hit, the execution is paused such that the user can examine the current state, modify it, and execute the specification step by step or just resume until the next breakpoint is hit or the execution terminates. The set *Breakpoints* contains all breakpoints introduced by the user. We define the following three (common) kinds (subsets) of *Breakpoints*:

- *Watchpoint.* A watchpoint can be defined for a universe, an enumeration, a derived function, or a location. It suspends the execution whenever the interpreter evaluates a node that reads or writes the corresponding element. The function *name*(*bp*) returns the linked identifier of a watchpoint *bp*.
- *RuleBreakpoint.* A rule breakpoint is bound to a macro rule and suspends the execution whenever the corresponding rule is called.
- *NodeBreakpoint.* A node breakpoint sticks to a specific node of the AST and the execution pauses right before this node shall be evaluated.

In implementations, the typical user interface to the user is a text editor which may have several limitations concerning the selection of identifiers for watchpoints or the definition of a node breakpoint. Possible workarounds are to interpret the breakpoint at a function signature declaration as watchpoint or to choose the first node in the partial tree the current (textual) line corresponds to. Of course, one could think of a more sophisticated user interface to overcome these limitations.

Once the execution of the specification is suspended, using the *stepResume* command it is possible to just resume the execution until the next breakpoint is hit. Another possibility is to request that the execution proceeds step by step. For the 1-step simulation by CoreASM of the parallel rules of an ASM, we exploit for debugging purposes that parallel execution is semantically equivalent to execution "in any order". This is realized by the behavior of the CoreASM interpreter which evaluates the nodes of the AST one after the other. So we make this correspond to one minimal step, called *stepMicro*, of the debugger.

Between these two extreme kinds of execution control, several intermediate levels can be defined: *stepOver*, *stepInto* and *stepReturn* steps.

A *stepOver* step bypasses the step-by-step execution of a rule call. Instead, the subtree of the macro rule call is evaluated as a whole and the debugger stops right before the evaluation of the next (sub-)rule in the current parallel or sequential rule.

A *stepInto* step stops before the first rule inside the called macro rule is executed.

If the current execution is paused in the body of a macro rule, *stepReturn* allows one to jump out of the macro rule to the next rule of the caller, without stepping over (but still executing) each AST node of the current macro rule.

Whereas *stepReturn* only deals with macro rule calls, *stepSubtree* behaves similarly but for any arbitrary subtree of the current node. Once a machine step is finished or another set of agents is chosen because of an inconsistent update, the stepping mechanism is canceled and again only breakpoints are considered as stop points.

The following example illustrates the indicated behavior of the different steps. Assume a node breakpoint is set at the node that represents the macro call to rule B. Thus, the execution suspends right before the evaluation of this node. If the user performs a *stepOver*, the interpreter will stop right before the evaluation of the node representing the call to A or C, depending on which node has not been evaluated yet, thus depending on the order chosen by the interpreter. If all rules are already evaluated, the **par**-node itself is chosen.

```
rule B =
    par
      R1
      if x+2*4 < y then
        R2
      else
        R3
    endpar

rule Start =
    par
      A
      B
      C
    endpar
```

If the user in the initial situation instead performs a *stepInto*, the interpreter will stop right before the evaluation of the **par**-node of rule B. Then, several *stepMicros* will eventually reach the node representing the operator "<" inside the term "x+2*4 < y". A subsequent *stepSubtree* command will stop after the evaluation of this complete term which means right before the evaluation of R2 or R3 depending on the result of this term. In any case, a *stepReturn* will continue the execution until the evaluation of rule B is finished. It will stop before the execution of A or C or even **par** inside the rule Start, as already discussed in the case of *stepOver*.

We now show how the debugger behavior sketched above can be specified by an ASM model, to be implemented by a CoreASM debugger plug-in. We define the different kinds of breakpoints as elements of corresponding sets *WatchBreakpoint*, *RuleBreakpoint*, *NodeBreakpoint*. The set *Breakpoint* is defined as the union of these sets. For each of these breakpoint types, the following functions are defined:

- *name*(*wbp*) returns the name of the location to which the watch breakpoint *wbp* is linked.
- *ruleName*(*rbp*) returns the name of the rule to which the rule breakpoint *rbp* is attached.
- *node*(*nbp*) returns the AST node that is linked to this node breakpoint.
- *Enabled*(*bp*) indicates whether the breakpoint *bp* is enabled or temporarily disabled.

  The possibility to manually disable a breakpoint temporarily during debugging is in some cases convenient for the user. It is also possible to enable a breakpoint only if a condition is true, e. g. that **self** equals to a specific agent or that a location in the current state has a specific value. For the sake of brevity, we leave this predicate abstract.

In its PLUGININIT-rule (see the specification of LOADPLUGIN on p. 264) the Debugger plug-in is registered to be called in the two *engineMode*s *PreparingEvaluation* and *CheckingCompletion* (see Fig. 8.6). Formally, we define:

> **forall** $c \in \{PreparingEvaluation, CheckingCompletion\}$
> $PluginRegisteredFor(\mathsf{Debugger}, c) := true$

The rule DEBUGGER is assigned to *pluginExtensionRule*(Debugger) as its program. It consists of calls to four submachines, determined by the current mode. If CoreASM is in *engineMode* = *PreparingEvaluation*, the *schedule* has just determined a (possibly new) *selectedAgentsSet* for execution, so that the engine can proceed to execute a machine step for each selected agent. In this case, according to the above requirements, the debugger is called and first of all clears all possible intermediate stop positions (*nextStopPos*). Then it enters *CheckingInterruption* mode to CHECKINTERRUPT-POINTS, inspecting for each selected agent its current AST, whereafter it enters *WaitingForStepCommand* mode to execute WAITFORSTEPCOMMAND.

The submachines are described in more detail below. This includes the machine CHECKSTEPPING, performed if *engineMode* = *CheckingCompletion* has been reached.

> DEBUGGER =
>   **if** *lastEngineCallMode*(Debugger) = *PreparingEvaluation* **then**
>   **forall** $a \in selectedAgentsSet$
>   *nextStopPos*(*a*) := **undef**   -- clear stop positions
>   *paused*(*a*) := *false*   -- initially no agent is paused
>   *lastEngineCallMode*(Debugger) := **undef**   -- switch to Debugger
>   *internalMode*(Debugger) := *CheckingInterruption*

> **if** $internalMode(\mathsf{Debugger}) = CheckingInterruption$ **then**
>   CHECKINTERRUPTPOINTS   -- report interrupts to user
> $internalMode(\mathsf{Debugger}) := WaitingForStepCommand$
> **if** $internalMode(\mathsf{Debugger}) = WaitingForStepCommand$ **then**
>   WAITFORSTEPCOMMAND
> **if** $lastEngineCallMode(\mathsf{Debugger}) = CheckingCompletion$ **then**
>   CHECKSTEPPING
> $lastEngineCallMode(\mathsf{Debugger}) := $ **undef**

In CHECKINTERRUPTPOINTS, for all selected agents the current *position* in their AST is checked against breakpoints and the *nextStopPosition*. If either a breakpoint is hit or the stepping requires an interrupt, the execution is *paused* and the current stop position is recorded and indicated to the user by the abstract macro rule MARKINSPEC.

> CHECKINTERRUPTPOINTS =
>   **forall** $a \in selectedAgentsSet$
>   **let** $p = getValue(\mathsf{program}, [a])$
>   **if** $IsBreakpointEnabled(pos(a))$ **or** $pos(a) = nextStopPos(a)$ **then**
> $paused(a) := true$
> $lastStopPos(a) := pos(a)$ -- record current stop position
>   MARKINSPEC($pos(a)$)   -- report current stop position to user
> **where**
> $IsBreakpointEnabled(pos)$ **iff**
> $pattern(pos) = \mathsf{Id}$ **and**   -- watch breakpoint
> $(isFunction(first(pos))$ **or** $isUniverse(first(pos)))$ **and**
>   **thereissome** $bp \in WatchBreakpoint$ **with**
> $(name(pos) = name(bp)$ **and** $Enabled(bp))$
>   **or** $pattern(pos) = \mathsf{RuleCall}$ **and**   -- rule breakpoint
>   **thereissome** $bp \in RuleBreakpoints$ **with**
> $(name_{rule}(ruleValue(first(pos))) = ruleName(bp)$ **and**
> $Enabled(bp))$
>   **or thereissome** $bp \in NodeBreakpoints$ **with**   -- node breakpoint
> $(Matches(pos, node(bp))$ **and** $Enabled(bp))$

In the predicate *IsBreakpointEnabled* the matching of the current position to any breakpoint is handled by accessing the information stored in the AST. The function *name(pos)* returns the name (i. e. token) of the identifier of the AST node *pos*. The comparison of two nodes is outsourced to an abstract predicate *Matches* in order to correctly handle any copies of the node (due to recursion, etc.).

WAITFORSTEPCOMMAND returns control to the interpreter (by changing mode to *RunningAgents*, see Fig. 8.6) if no agent is *paused* (any more). If *paused(a)* is *true* for some agent a, WAITFORSTEPCOMMAND does not progress (read: the debugger remains active, waiting for a step command) until a *stepCommand* becomes available. A *stepCommand* is a message sent by the user via an appropriate interface. It is CONSUMEd by the debugger when it triggers the execution of the rule WAITFORSTEPCOMMAND. The *type* of a *stepCommand* corresponds to the above mentioned kinds of debugging steps *stepResume*, *stepMicro*, *stepInto*, *stepOver*, *stepReturn*, and *stepSubtree*. Additionally, a *stepCommand* is only performed for just one *paused* agent which is selected by the user. That means that a breakpoint may stop many agents, but a *stepCommand* only resumes one agent.

Now assume some agent is *paused* and there is a *StepCommandAvailable*. If it is a *stepResume* command, the *nextStopPos* is cleared such that the interpreter becomes enabled to continue the execution until the next breakpoint is hit. In any case, the *paused* agent is resumed and the *selectedAgentsSet* is filtered such that EVALUATENODE only executes programs of not paused agents (including the currently released agent a). The debugger is deactivated and returns control to the CoreASM interpreter.

> WAITFORSTEPCOMMAND =
>   **if thereissome** $a' \in selectedAgentsSet$ **with** $paused(a') = true$
>   **if** $StepCommandAvailable(stepCommand)$ **then**
>   **let** $a = agent(stepCommand)$
>   **if** $type(stepCommand) = stepResume$
>   **then**
> $nextStopPos :=$ **undef**   -- cancels stepping
>   **else**
> $lastStepCommand := stepCommand$
> $paused(a) := false$ -- resume agent
> $originalSelectedAgentsSet := selectedAgentsSet$
> $selectedAgentsSet :=$ -- filter out paused selected agents
> $\{a\} \cup \{s \in selectedAgentsSet \mid paused(s) = false\}$
> $nextEngineMode(\mathsf{Debugger}) := RunningAgents$
>   -- return to interpreter
> $Done(\mathsf{Debugger}) := true$ -- deactivate debugger
>   CONSUME($stepCommand$)
>   **else**   -- return to interpreter if no agent paused
> $nextEngineMode(\mathsf{Debugger}) := RunningAgents$
> $Done(\mathsf{Debugger}) := true$

EVALUATENODE (see Fig. 8.6 and p. 270) executes one micro step for each uninterrupted agent and turns the mode into *CheckingCompletion*. In that mode the kernel checks whether *EvaluationCompleted* became true and in that case collects the update instructions of all agents. CHECKSTEPPING publishes the result of the last node evaluation to the user and resets the *selectedAgentsSet*. If the machine step is not yet completed, CHECKSTEPPING switches back to the *internalMode CheckingInterruption* to close the debugger loop. In this case, depending on the *lastStepCommand* the *nextStopPos* is set. *nextStopPos* behaves like a dynamic node breakpoint realizing the different stepping mechanisms.

CHECKSTEPPING =
   PUBLISHUPDATES($pos(a)$)   -- inform user about node evaluation
   $selectedAgentsSet := originalSelectedAgentsSet$
   if *EvaluationCompleted* **then**
      $nextEngineMode(\text{Debugger}) := Aggregation$
      $Done(\text{Debugger}) := true$
   else
      $internalMode(\text{Debugger}) := CheckingInterruption$
      if $lastStepCommand \neq$ **undef** **then**
        let $a = agent(lastStepCommand)$
        let $step = type(lastStepCommand)$
          if $step = stepMicro$ **then**
            if not $Evaluated(pos(a))$ **then**
              $nextStopPos(a) := pos(a)$
            else -- only if $pos(a) = root(a)$ signaling end of machine step
              skip
          if $step = stepInto$ **then**
            if $pattern(lastStopPos(a)) = \mathsf{RuleCall}$ **then**
              $nextStopPos(a) := bodyOfCalledRule(lastStopPos(a))$
            else
               $nextStopPos(a) := pos(a)$ -- same behavior as *stepMicro*
          if $step = stepOver$ **then**
            STOPATNEXTSIBLINGOFPARORSEQRULE(a)
          if $step = stepReturn$ **then**
            STOPATNEXTSIBLINGAFTERCALLER(a)
          if $step = stepSubtree$ **then**
            STOPATNEXTUNEVALUATEDPARENT(a)
  where
     $bodyOfCalledRule(pos) = next(first(pos))$

In the simplest case, the *lastStepCommand* was a *stepMicro*, *nextStopPos* is the current node itself. In case of a *stepInto*, the behavior is different only if the currently evaluated node represents a rule call. Then, the *nextStopPos* is the rule of the body of the called rule (typically a **par** rule). One could think of an improved usability in this case by jumping over **par** and **seq** rules directly to their first rule (which is usually intended by the user).

stepOver, *stepReturn*, and *stepSubtree* demand a more complex calculation of the *nextStopPosition*. We only show as an example the behavior of *stepOver* in the rule *StopAtNextSiblingOfParOrSeqRule*. The behavior of the two other rules is only described textually, its formalization is left for Exerc. 65.

STOPATNEXTSIBLINGAFTERCALLER sets *nextStopPos* to the next (not yet evaluated) sibling of that rule call node up the AST which caused the call of this rule. If the root node is reached, *nextStopPos* is set to **undef**. STOPATNEXTUNEVALUATEDPARENT uses the closest predecessor node of the current node that has not yet been evaluated for the *nextStopPos*. This means that the complete subtree of the current node is evaluated at the next interruption.

In STOPATNEXTSIBLINGOFPARORSEQRULE we use **while**$_{atomic}$ to simulate recursion, given the inductive AST data structure. The AST is traversed in direction to the root node until a **par**- or **seq**-rule is found as parent node. Then the next sibling of the current node is chosen as *nextStopPos*. Some special cases have to be dealt with like reaching the root node or if no *lastStopPos*ition was set.

> STOPATNEXTSIBLINGOFPARORSEQRULE(a) =
>> **par**
>>> *curPos* := *lastStopPos*(a)
>>> *prevPos* := *curPos*
>>> *found* := *false*
>> **seq**
>>> **while**$_{atomic}$ *found* = *false* **do**
>>>> **if** *Evaluated*(*curPos*) **then**
>>>>> *curPos* := *parent*(*curPos*)
>>>>> *prevPos* := *curPos*
>>>> **if** *pattern*(*curPos*) ∈ {Par, Seq} **then**
>>>>> *nextStopPos*(a) := *next*(*prevPos*)
>>>>> *found* := *true*
>>>> **if** *curPos* = *root*(a) **then**
>>>>> *nextStopPos*(a) := **undef**
>>>>> *found* := *true*

Whereas the debugging in CoreASM could be used just by loading the debugger plug-in in a specification, in reality it is a little bit more complicated, mainly due to the required interaction. Therefore, it is necessary to provide an appropriate debugging user interface that permits to toggle breakpoints on various levels, trigger the step commands, and present the current state and update set. That means, the implementation of the debugger component needs a tighter integration into a development environment so that one can switch the debugging on and off by convenient features of this environment.

Besides the mentioned functionality, a debugger component could offer the possibility to change the current state in order to observe the system behavior in that particular state. Another idea realized in [87] is to collect the states of the different machine steps and permit to jump back and forth in the list of previous states. The implementation of the debugger component in CoreASM deviates from this formal description mainly due to implementation specific details, but it offers similar functionality.

Exercise 65. Define the rules STOPATNEXTSIBLINGAFTERCALLER and STOPATNEXTUNEVALUATEDPARENT used in CHECKSTEPPING.

8.4 Related Tools

Various tools to execute models belonging to specific classes of ASMs have been developed since the 90'ies for use in concrete industrial applications, preceding the design of CoreASM [84] and Asmeta [16]. We mention a few of them and refer for more information to [76, Sect. 9.4.3]. The historically first appeared in [157, 158, 81], an interpreter of basic ASMs, developed in Prolog (to execute in particular the models of Prolog in [36, 37]) and used in a time- and security-critical coal mining application. The *Workbench* [88] tool environment has been developed for use in the railway domain project Falko [65] at Siemens. It has also been adopted in [194] to provide an executable semantics for UML. Notably, it includes a transformation of ASMs into FSMs which can be model checked using SMV [89]. *AsmGofer* [222, 224] was developed to execute the ASM models of Java and the JVM in [232]. It has been used in an industrial ASIC design and verification project at Siemens (where also a compiler from ASM to VHDL has been developed) and in the Light Control Case Study [67]. *AsmL* [112] has been developed at Microsoft Research and has been used successfully in various projects, for example to specify, simulate, and test the interfaces of Microsoft COM components [18, 20], but it is no longer maintained.

More recently the open source tools CoreASM [84], an interpreter approach, and Asmeta [16], a meta-model approach, have been developed to support design, analysis and execution of ASMs.

CoreASM. The flexibility and expandability of the CoreASM language and of the engine itself is one of its strengths. They enable users to implement their own plug-ins and extensions. This paves the way for domain specific applications of the CoreASM engine. An example is the extension of CoreASM by a scheduling plug-in, developed under the name of Abstract State Interaction Machines in the BIOMICS project [207] and applied in the recent INTERLACE project with the Sardex company (see https://www.interlaceproject.eu/). However, this flexibility also has a price. Extending components (parser, abstract storage, interpreter) enriches their behavioral capabilities and thereby makes them more complex. Due to the indirection via plug-ins, each component depends on the plug-ins loaded for the specifications in question so that there is only a small fixed base—the kernel and standard plug-ins—a tool developer can rely upon. This may make a correct understanding of extended components more difficult. It also has an impact on further processing of ASM specifications. Imagine besides execution one wants to model check an ASM against given properties (as done in [89, 243]), or prove properties to hold for ASMs using some theorem prover (as done for example in [228], in the Verifix project [131, 99, 98] using PVS, in numerous projects using KIV [218, 139, 219, 140]), or generate code (as done in [223, 103, 231]), or provide and analyze test cases. Then one needs appropriate translations of (parts of) the specification to the language of the tool one wants to adopt. But since the CoreASM language is extensible, not fixed, each of these translations has to be defined separately for the kernel and for each used plug-in.

The package plugin *StandardPlugin*, which collects the most common language constructs, already contains 20 plugins. An interesting future extension of CoreASM could come with a richer common language, through which other tools can be addressed or created with less effort, but keeping the experimental character of CoreASM due to its further extendability where needed.

Asmeta. The name stands for a meta-model based tool environment for working with ASM models, formulated in the AsmetaL language. It provides, besides an interpreter, various tools which support the validation and verification of properties of ASMs belonging to various classes.

A model checker tool AsmetaSMV allows one to model check temporal properties of ASMs. Technically, this is realized by a translation of (high-level) ASM programs to (for efficiency reasons low-level) NuSMV[14] programs. This model checker is used by a tool, called AsmetaMA (Model Advisor), which allows one to check certain general properties of ASMs. Examples are consistency—that never any inconsistent updates are required to be performed in a state—or that no update $s := t$ is always trivial, trivial meaning $s = t$, etc. Such properties are formalized by temporal logic formulas to be model checked by NuSMV.

For validation purposes also a test generator called ATGT is available. It uses Spin[15] to generate tests from ASMs and supports structural based testing, fault based testing and combinatorial testing. A related validation tool AsmetaV allows one to validate AsmetaL specifications by UML use-case like scenarios, similar to the treatment of scenarios in *AsmL* [19] or in CoreASM by the Bârun plug-in [9].

A refinement correctness prover AsmRefProver allows one to prove the correctness of a certain form of refinement steps. It is based on an SMT solver.

The Asmeta tool set also includes a graphical front-end (implemented as eclipse plug-in) to edit and manipulate ASMs and a tree-representation of basic ASM rules. Recently also a C^{++} code generator for some class of ASMs has been announced.

All these tools operate on a meta model instance, generated by one common parser and based upon a fixed language. It would be interesting to provide precise high-level specifications of the behavior of these tools, e. g. by some ASMs which would help to check and understand the conceptual correctness of the work performed by the tools.

In the last years, an attempt has been started to define a Unified Abstract State Machine (UASM) core language on which the development of ASM

---

[14] http://nusmv.fbk.eu/

[15] http://spinroot.com

supporting tools can be based [13]. The goal is to agree upon a stable language kernel for the ASM language with a formally defined semantics, so that present (CoreASM and Asmeta) and future ASM-based tools can be made interoperable.

Chapter 9
Control State Diagrams
(Meta Model)

In this chapter we illustrate an ASM-based metamodeling approach to define the syntax and semantics of a domain specific language. We consider a graphical language, namely of *Control State Diagrams* (CSDs) we used throughout the book. In Sect. 9.1-9.3 we define their language and in Sect. 9.4 an ASM specification for a compiler of CSDs to basic ASMs.

Analogous ASM-based definitions have been provided in [103] for SDL and in [208] for UML activity diagrams. The CSD material presented here is based upon the master thesis [179]. The thesis contains also the description of a graphical editor which has been implemented prototypically with code generation for CoreASM syntax. Similarly to Chap. 8, this chapter illustrates for readers who are interested in implementation issues how to use an ASM model to rigorously specify a tool—here the CSD2ASM translator—before writing the code.

For control state ASMs, textually defined in Sect. 2.5, we have worked in this book with the flowchart-like visualization indicated in Fig. 2.29, which is borrowed from [76, Sect. 2.2.6]. Pragmatic reasons led us to permit to use not only the seven basic ASM constructs and their standard notation, as defined in Chap. 2, but also commonly used variations and extensions, as long as they come with a clear meaning and can unambiguously be reduced to the core constructs. For the same reasons we have adopted also numerous slight graphical variations of Fig. 2.29, which can easily and unambiguously be reduced to the flowchart type in Fig. 2.29. Also in the literature one can find several versions of control state diagrams, e. g. in [64, 191]. In [14] a translation of textual ASMs to a similar graphical notation is presented.

In this chapter, we experiment with a definition of *canonical* CSDs which uniformly captures all graphical elements used in this book. We provide an ASM which specifies how to compile canonical CSDs into basic ASMs in such a way that further extensions by additional graphical notations can be added easily, namely by preprocessors (which translate the new graphical elements to canonical CSDs) or by refining the translator ASM.

We adopt the metamodeling approach [133] which separates the following parts in the definition of a language [129]:

- The **static structure** (abstract syntax) with its **constraints**. They describe the elements of the language with their properties and their relations to each other.
- The **behavior** which describes the semantics of the language constructs.
- The **representation** (concrete syntax) which builds the interface to the user, typically in form of keywords or graphical symbols.

In the traditional approach to the definition of languages, their concrete and abstract syntax are defined together by a grammar. Metamodeling separates the definition of the abstract and the concrete syntax. Therefore, we first list the sets and functions, which constitute the elements of the static structure of the CSD metamodel (Sect. 9.1), together with their constraints (Sect. 9.3), which ensure the intended well-formedness of CSDs. Then we define the concrete syntax of CSDs (Sect. 9.2). By this definition, a concrete CSD becomes an instance of the meta-model, formed by concrete sets with corresponding concrete functions. Finally, we define the dynamic behavior of CSDs. This could be done by defining an interpreter, which directly associates a meaning with the abstract sets and functions. It can also be described by a translation of every meta-model instance to an ASM, whose behavior is taken as defining the semantics of the instance. We choose to define the behavior of CSDs by compiling them into textual basic ASMs (Sect. 9.4).

Replacing parts of CSDs by subdiagrams is related to ASM refinements. In this book we cannot develop this interesting theme further, but to trigger the interest of some readers we define in Sect. 9.5 one natural way to integrate subdiagrams into CSDs.

As leading example consider the following translation for a part of the SLUICEGATEOPERATOR diagram SGO in Fig. 2.10.

> SLUICEGATEOPERATOR =
>   if $mode = fullyClosed$ then
>   if $Event(Raise)$ then
>   STARTTORAISE
> $mode := rising$
>   if $mode = rising$ then
>   if $Event(top)$ then
>   STOPMOTOR
> $mode := fullyOpen$
>   if $Event(Stop)$ then
>   STOPMOTOR
> $mode := middle$
>   if $mode = fullyOpen$ then
>   if $Event(Lower)$ then
>   . . .

The translation results in one large textual ASM SGO^*. Each circle (or ellipse) in the diagram, with control state label l, is translated as a distinct value l of a 0-ary location *mode*, which indicates the current control state (or phase) of SGO^*. For each edge outgoing a control state *node* with label *lab*, SGO^* has a conditional rule of the form **if** $mode = lab$ **then** M, where M depends on the diagram part between *node* and the next reachable control state node(s) in the diagram. Since all these rules are guarded by $mode = l$, for some l, in SGO^* they appear on the same hierarchical level (i. e. indentation), so that in each step SGO^* executes them in parallel.

9.1 Static CSD Graph Structure

A CSD is a directed graph and as such consists of nodes and edges. The set of *Nodes* is constrained to be a disjoint union of three sets *Mode* (read: set of control states), *Rule* (read: set of ASM rules), and *Condition* (read: set of rule guards). Nodes in these sets are called mode nodes or rule nodes or condition nodes (or shortly modes, rules, conditions), respectively. The set of directed *Edges* consists of ordered pairs (*source*, *target*) of *Nodes*. An edge has one of the three *edgeType*s in $\{yes, no, empty\}$, which are needed to distinguish the three different kinds of outgoing edges of *Conditions*. Edge type *empty* stands for an edge which at runtime is followed unconditionally. One $node \in Mode$ is designated as a start point for a diagram, called *initialMode*.

The *Rule* set is constrained to be a disjoint union of some subsets, among which we consider here the basic ones: *UpdateRule*, *ParallelRule*, *MacroRule*, *ForallRule*, *ChooseRule*, *LetRule*. Nodes in these sets are called update rule nodes, parallel rule nodes, etc., or simply update rules, parallel rules, etc. The complete list is defined in [179]. Conditional rules do not appear in the list because they need a separate treatment. Each set contains concrete instantiations of the described concept. For example, the update rules $\boxed{x := 5}$ and $\boxed{f(x, y) := true}$ are elements of *UpdateRule* (see the concrete syntax below).

For nodes in *ForallRule*, *ChooseRule*, and *LetRule* we permit to define the included rule not only textually, but also by somehow restricted CSDs (see for example Fig. 2.25 on p. 82). We call them *EmbeddedCSD*s and require that their nodes and edges are elements of *Node* and *Edge* resp. their corresponding subsets. The parameterized functions *nodes*(*csd*), *edges*(*csd*), *modes*(*csd*), etc., retrieve the corresponding subsets for a given $csd \in EmbeddedCSD$. A function *startNode*(*csd*) returns the unique node of an embedded CSD that is designated as the starting point of its translation. Differently from *initialMode*, *StartNode*s are not necessarily mode nodes.

Further constraints on these sets define what we want to permit as valid graphs. We require that a *ValidCSD* consists only of valid nodes (with a correct number and correct types of in- and outgoing edges, corresponding to the node type) with *ValidSuccessors* and that the CSD has *NoInvalidLoops*. If the CSD contains *EmbeddedCSD*s, these have to be valid, too.

> *ValidCSD* **iff**
> *ValidModesAndRules* **and** *ValidConditions* **and** *NoInvalidLoops*
> **and** *ValidSuccessors* **and** *ValidEmbeddedCSDs*

We now define these constraints in detail.

Each mode or rule node must have at least one incoming edge, unless it is an *initialMode* or $startNode(csd) \in StartNode$ for some *csd*. The number of outgoing edges can be arbitrary (even 0), but no outgoing edge is conditioned by a *yes* or *no* type (formally: each outgoing edge has an *empty* type).

> *ValidModesAndRules* **iff forall** $n \in Mode \cup Rule$
> $(|Incoming(n)| \geq 1$ **or** $n \in StartNode)$
>   -- at least one incoming edge (except for *StartNodes*)
> **and forall** $e \in Outgoing(n)$ $edgeType(e) = empty$
>   -- outgoing edges (if any) are followed unconditionally
> **where**
> $Incoming(n) = \{(s, n) \mid (s, n) \in Edge\}$
> $Outgoing(n) = \{(n, t) \mid (n, t) \in Edge\}$
> $StartNode =$
> $\{startNode(csd) \mid csd \in EmbeddedCSD\} \cup \{initialMode\}$

The constraint on incoming edges is similar for condition nodes, but these nodes must have at least one outgoing edge. The outgoing edges may be conditioned by edge type *yes* or *no*.

> *ValidConditions* **iff forall** $n \in Condition$
> $(|Incoming(n)| \geq 1$ **or** $n \in StartNode)$
>   -- at least one incoming edge (except for *StartNodes*)
> **and** $|Outgoing(n)| \geq 1$ -- at least one outgoing edge

Loops between mode nodes are permitted, but we do not permit loops among rule or condition nodes between two mode nodes. Such loops would result in a non-terminating translation. The *NoInvalidLoops* constraint can be checked by the ASM CHECKFORSECONDARYLOOP(m) in Sect. 4.5.2, page 172, which computes the value of the function *loopfree*(m) we use to express the constraint:

> *NoInvalidLoops* **iff forall** $m \in Mode$ $loopfree(m) = true.$

To prevent some obvious inconsistencies we impose some simple constraints on the successors of nodes, although the consistency problem in its full generality is obviously undecidable (see the remark at the end of Sect. 9.4 and Exerc. 67). For example, if an edge connects two mode nodes n, n', there should be no other edge leading from n to another mode node n'', because in that case the translation in Sect. 9.4 would yield two inconsistent updates to the *mode* location. Slightly more generally, we stipulate that nodes with more than one outgoing edge are not allowed to have mode nodes as successors, except condition nodes. For condition nodes we permit only one outgoing edge typed *yes*, and only one outgoing edge typed *no*, as edge which leads to a mode successor. For outgoing edges of condition nodes type *empty* is treated as *yes*.

> *ValidSuccessors* **iff forall** $n \in Node$
>   **if** $n \in Mode \cup Rule$ **then**
>   **if** $|Outgoing(n)| > 1$ **then**
>   **thereisno** $(n, t) \in Edge$ **with** $t \in Mode$
>   **else**   -- n is condition node
>   **if** $|OutgoingYes(n)| > 1$ **then**
>   **thereisno** $(n, t) \in OutgoingYes$ **with** $t \in Mode$
>   **and if** $|OutgoingNo(n)| > 1$ **then**
>   **thereisno** $(n, t) \in OutgoingNo$ **with** $t \in Mode$
>   **where**
> $OutgoingYes(n) =$
> $\{e \mid e \in Outgoing(n)$ **and** $edgeType(e) \in \{yes, empty\}\}$
> $OutgoingNo(n) = \{e \mid e \in Outgoing(n)$ **and** $edgeType(e) = no\}$

As stated already above, *EmbeddedCSD*s must have a designated *startNode*. To ensure a closed scope, no edges are permitted from or to the surrounding CSD and also no mode nodes with outgoing edges.

> *ValidEmbeddedCSDs* **iff forall** $csd \in EmbeddedCSD$
>   -- each embedded CSD has...
> $startNode(csd) \neq$ **undef**   -- a well-defined startpoint,
>   **and** $ClosedSubgraph((nodes(csd), edges(csd)), (Node, Edge))$
>   **and forall** $node \in modes(csd)$ $|Outgoing(node)| = 0$
>   -- no mode node with outgoing edges
> **where**
> $EmbeddedCSD^1 =$
> $\{forallBody(node) \mid node \in ForallRule$
>   **and** $forallBody(node) \in CSD\}$
> $\cup \{chooseBody(node) \mid node \in ChooseRule$
>   **and** $chooseBody(node) \in CSD\}$
> $\cup \{letBody(node) \mid node \in LetRule$ **and** $letBody(node) \in CSD\}$
> $ClosedSubgraph((Node', Edge'), (Node, Edge))$ **iff**
> $Node' \subseteq Node$ **and** $Edge' \subseteq Edge$
>   **and thereisno** $(s, t) \in Edge'$ **with** -- no edge leading out of and...
> $s \in Node'$ **and** $t \in Node \setminus Node'$
>   **and thereisno** $(s, t) \in Edge'$ **with** -- no edge leading into subgraph
> $s \in Node \setminus Node'$ **and** $t \in Node'$

---

[1] The functions *forallBody*, *chooseBody*, and *letBody* are defined in Table 9.1 in the next section.

The above constraints concern the syntactic structure of CSDs. Some more constraints are defined below to guarantee a correct translation of CSDs to textual ASMs.

9.2 Concrete Syntax of CSDs

Table 9.1 lists the graphical elements we use to define the concrete syntax. Most of them have already been introduced by diagrams in the preceding chapters of the book.

We use various functions to access the content of graphical elements. For example, *modeLabel*: *Mode* → *String* denotes a function which provides for each mode node its label, represented as a *String*. In this context, a *String*

Table 9.1 Symbols of CSD elements

Symbol	Description
mode	A mode is represented as a circle or an ellipse. The textual label can be retrieved by *modeLabel*: *Mode* → *String*.
cond	A condition is represented as a hexagon with a conditional term. The textual ASM representation of the conditional term is given by the function *guardExp*: *Condition* → *String*.
RULE	A macro call rule just contains the name RULE. The function *calledRule*: *MacroCallRule* → *String* returns this name as text.
$f := t$	An update rule just contains the update rule itself. The function *assignment*: *UpdateRule* → *String* returns a textual representation of the given update rule.
$rule_1$ ⋮ $rule_n$	A parallel rule is represented as a rectangle with n rows divided by solid lines. Each row contains an arbitrary rule and all rules are executed in parallel. To get the set of these rules, the function *parRules*: *ParallelRule* → *Set*(*String*) can be used.
forall x **with** *cond* / *body*	A forall rule is split into two parts: In the first line, the keyword **forall** marks this as a **forall**-rule. In the second part, the body of the forall rule is given. The content of the upper row can be retrieved by the function *forallExp*: *ForallRule* → *String* and the second one by *forallBody*: *ForallRule* → *String* ∪ *EmbeddedCSD*.
choose x **with** *cond* / *body*	A choose rule is defined analogously to the forall rule. The two access functions are *chooseExp*: *ChooseRule* → *String* and *chooseBody*: *ChooseRule* → *String* ∪ *EmbeddedCSD*.
let $x = t$ / *body*	A let rule is also defined analogously to the forall and the choose rule. The content of the upper row can be retrieved by the function *letExp*: *LetRule* → *String* and the second one by *letBody*: *LetRule* → *String* ∪ *EmbeddedCSD*.

is a list of characters including also special characters like line breaks and white spaces. This allows us to use all possibilities the ASM syntax offers (e. g. indentation and arbitrary ASM expressions in nodes).

For outgoing edges of condition nodes (and only for those) it must be indicated which edge should be taken if the evaluation of the condition returns the value *true* (take the edges labeled *yes*) or *false* (take the edges labeled *no*), respectively. Where the context is clear, we sometimes omit the labels and in this case interpret the edges as for the *yes* case.

As body of *ForallRules*, *ChooseRules*, and *LetRules* we permit textual ASMs and CSDs. Therefore, the rule body retrieving functions return an element of *String* or of *EmbeddedCSD*.

The values of all these access functions are constrained by appropriate correctness conditions, mostly reflecting ASM syntax properties, so that they can be used in the translation process without any further check. For example, the content of a condition node, say *exp*, will be passed to the translated text (the textual ASM code) without any test whether *exp* is a legal conditional expression.

Edges are represented as solid arrows ($\longrightarrow$). For documentation and visualization purposes, we allow symbols with colored background and similar means to indicate some grouping of nodes (see for example Fig. 8.4). Additionally, for example, several edges with the same target are permitted to be joined together to form one single edge. Initial modes or start nodes of embedded CSD are marked with a small arrow pointing to them.

9.3 Additional Constraints on CSDs Labels

Here we add to the above structural (graph) constraints some constraints which deal with the labels of nodes. These constraints must be satisfied to guarantee that the result of the translation of a CSD into textual ASMs is a legal ASM. CSDs which satisfy all these contraints are called *canonical* CSDs.

NoEmptyNodes requires that the content (label, body) of each node is not empty:

> *NoEmptyNodes* **iff forall** *node* $\in$ *Node*   -- some label is defined
>   **if** *node* $\in$ *Mode* **then** *modeLabel(node)* $\neq$ **undef**
>   **if** *node* $\in$ *Condition* **then** *guardExp(node)* $\neq$ **undef**
>   **if** *node* $\in$ *MacroRule* **then** *calledRule(node)* $\neq$ **undef**
>   **if** *node* $\in$ *UpdateRule* **then** *assignment(node)* $\neq$ **undef**
>   **if** *node* $\in$ *ParallelRule* **then** *parRules(node)* $\neq$ **undef**
>   **if** *node* $\in$ *ForallRule* **then**
>   *forallExp(node)* $\neq$ **undef and** *forallBody* $\neq$ **undef**
>   **if** *node* $\in$ *ChooseRule* **then**
>   *chooseExp(node)* $\neq$ **undef and** *chooseBody* $\neq$ **undef**
>   **if** *node* $\in$ *LetRule* **then**
>   *letExp(node)* $\neq$ **undef and** *letBody* $\neq$ **undef**

As already stated at the end of the previous section, we require that in canonical CSDs each non-empty label comes in correct ASM syntax. The translation process, described in the next section, would also work if any of these label constraints is not satisfied, but then the result of the translation would not be a valid ASM. This is because during the translation we just "copy" the labels into the resulting text.

Remark. In an *UpdateRule* node, the mode variable could be assigned to a new mode. Although we do not explicitly forbid this, it is strongly discouraged to do so, because this results in a *mode* change that is not reflected in the graphical representation and could be compared to a hidden "goto" in programming languages. Nevertheless, it is possible to access the mode variable read-only, for example to distinguish several cases. For an example of this use see the definition of HANDLEFAILURE in Sect. 2.4.7.

9.4 Behavior of CSDs (Translation to ASMs)

For a given CSD, we translate each of its combinations of nodes and edges by appropriate rules into a textual ASM. We have chosen this definition over an interpreter approach because it allows the reader to inspect the correctness of the translation piecemeal (formally by an induction on run steps of the translator ASM TRANSLATECSD defined below), considering the rules one by one. To describe the different combinations succinctly, in an easily legible way, we use a graphical shorthand notation, formulated by patterns. Similar to the pattern notation in Sect. 8.1.5, a pattern describes, for a given *node*, a possible constellation of the graph elements between the *node* and its successor nodes.

To be precise, $(\!| pattern(node) |\!) \Rightarrow actions$ is a short form for the ASM rule **if** $cond(pattern(node))$ **then** $actions$, where $cond$ depends on the pattern and represents the aforementioned combination of nodes and edges. For example, for a specific *node*, the pattern $(\!| \boxed{m_1} \rightarrow \boxed{m_2} |\!)$ results in the condition

if $node = \boxed{m_1}$ **and** $\boxed{m_1} \in Mode$ **and** $\boxed{m_2} \in Mode$
and $(\boxed{m_1}, \boxed{m_2}) \in Edge$ **then**
        . . .

Typically, the *actions* are also parameterized, e. g. by the *node*. Where necessary to guarantee disjoint pattern conditions, also checks for non-outgoing edges are added to the condition.

We use a function $status: Node \rightarrow \{\textbf{undef}, active, closed\}$ to indicate whether the given node can be handled by the translation (*active*), whether it has already been handled (*closed*), or whether it has not been activated yet (**undef**). We assume that initially, $status(n) = \textbf{undef}$ for all nodes n.

The final result of the translation will be a textual ASM representation of the CSD. During the translation process, often partial translations are included into some already existing text. The function $positions\colon Node \rightarrow \wp(Position)$ holds a set of positions in the text where the translation of some part of the given node has to be included. We leave the definition of $Position$ abstract. Possible definitions may be an offset in a text file or a node in an abstract syntax tree.

We define the translation by an ASM program TRANSLATECSD. For the initial state of the machine we only assume $notInitialized = true$.

The first step serves to INITIALIZETRANSLATOR. This rule uses a (here not furthermore specified) macro CREATETEXTUALASM($text$), which creates a new textual representation with its argument $text$. The created textual representation begins with the name of the CSD which is to be translated; this name is provided to the translator by an input function $titleCSD$. The rest of the $text$ argument is an equality sign, followed by the position β where the textual ASM code has to be inserted that will result from the translation.

INITIALIZETRANSLATOR =
  let $\beta = $ **new** ($Position$)
    CREATETEXTUALASM(

$$\boxed{titleCSD} = \atop \boxed{\beta}$$)

$nextModePos := \beta$
$status(initialMode) := active$

In the following, we have to deal with quoting and unquoting of values that represent the text and of functions which for given arguments yield text that should be inserted. Notationally, we put a frame around textual ASM code. This is to distinguish what we call the 'translated code' from the ASM code of the translator TRANSLATECSD. In the call below of the macro CREATETEXTUALASM, the monitored function $titleCSD$ is placed outside the box to indicate that what is inserted into the text is the value of the 0-ary function and not its name $titleCSD$. In the following, for the sake of succinctness and where applicable, we write just the value of such auxiliary function terms inside the box to indicate that what is inserted into the textual representation is (not the term, but) the value of the function at the moment of its insertion.

β defines a new element of the set of $Positions$ which is inserted into the textual representation created by CREATETEXTUALASM. Later, all occurrences of such $positions$ will be replaced by some $text$, namely when ADDTEXTUALASM($pos, text$), defined below, is called with the $text$ to be inserted. The function $nextModePos$ indicates the next position where the translation for a next mode node has to be added. Last but not least, the $initialMode$ has to be set to $active$, so that TRANSLATE can start there with $nextModePos = \beta$.

After the initialization step, TRANSLATECSD chooses in each step an *active* *node* and calls TRANSLATE with this *node* and one of its *positions*, where the part corresponding to *pos* of the translation of this *node* has to be inserted. The translation is complete, if no *active* node is found any more.

TRANSLATECSD =
  if *notInitialized* = *true* **then**
    INITIALIZETRANSLATOR
    notInitialized := *false*
  if *notInitialized* = *false* **then**   -- translate node by node
    choose *node* ∈ *Node* **with** *status*(*node*) = *active*
      if *node* ∈ *Mode* **then**
        TRANSLATE(*node*, *nextModePos*)
        status(*node*) := *closed*   -- a *mode* node is immediately closed
      else
        choose *pos* ∈ *positions*(*node*)   -- translate pos by pos
          TRANSLATE(*node*, *pos*)
          DELETE(*pos*, *positions*(*node*))
          if *positions*(*node*) \ {*pos*} = ∅ **then**
            status(*node*) := *closed* -- if no *positions* left, *node* is *closed*

The mode node cases can be treated independently of each other, because all conditional rules which translate mode nodes in the diagram appear in the translation code at the same hierarchical level (see the example $SGO*$ at the end of the introduction to this chapter).

We now define the submachines used for the translation. The general scheme of the TRANSLATE rule is as follows.

TRANSLATE(*node*, *pos*) =
  ⦇ *pattern*$_1$(*node*) ⦈ ⇒ *actions*$_1$(*node*, *pos*)
    ⋮
  ⦇ *pattern*$_n$(*node*) ⦈ ⇒ *actions*$_n$(*node*, *pos*)

The set of 'pattern rules' ⦇ *pattern*$_i$(*node*) ⦈ ⇒ *actions*$_i$(*node*, *pos*) depends on *node* and *pos*. In a step of TRANSLATE(*node*, *pos*), for each *pattern* that matches, the corresponding *actions* are executed.

Figure 9.1 gives an overview of the patterns that can occur in a valid CSD. To avoid pattern repetitions, when a same scheme works for any kind of rule or condition node, we write the pattern using the symbol $\boxed{rc}$ to indicate any *Rule* or *Condition* node. In the following, we provide for some characteristic pattern rules a detailed definition of their meaning.

Modes. A transition from one mode to another mode is translated as follows. Where the context is clear, we use, for example, *m* as a placeholder for the value of *modeLabel*($\widehat{m}$). Since for every mode node an individual rule is created, each mode node is translated only once. This explains why the target mode is only activated if it is not yet closed and different from the

Fig. 9.1 Possible combinations of nodes in a CSD

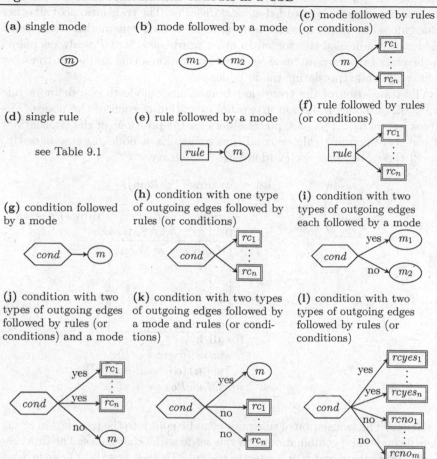

(a) single mode

(b) mode followed by a mode

(c) mode followed by rules (or conditions)

(d) single rule

see Table 9.1

(e) rule followed by a mode

(f) rule followed by rules (or conditions)

(g) condition followed by a mode

(h) condition with one type of outgoing edges followed by rules (or conditions)

(i) condition with two types of outgoing edges each followed by a mode

(j) condition with two types of outgoing edges followed by rules (or conditions) and a mode

(k) condition with two types of outgoing edges followed by a mode and rules (or conditions)

(l) condition with two types of outgoing edges followed by rules (or conditions)

source node. In fact, in case $m_1 = m_2$ holds, the transition does not change the mode value. Since TRANSLATECSD closes the source node m_1, setting simultaneously the status of the target node $m_2 = m_1$ to *active* would result in an inconsistent update.

$$
(\!| m_1 \rightarrow m_2 |\!) \Rightarrow \textbf{let } \beta = \textbf{new } (Position)
$$

ADDTEXTUALASM(pos,

> **if** $mode = m_1$ **then**
> $\quad mode := m_2$
> β

)

if $m_1 \neq m_2$ **and** $status(m_2) \neq closed$ **then**
$\quad status(m_2) := active$
$\quad nextModePos := \beta$

Observe that for mode nodes, no *positions* are maintained. The translations of these nodes are always added at *nextModePos*. The translations of all other nodes along the paths from a mode *m* to its subsequent modes are inserted inside the conditional rule for *m*. In other words, *nextModePos* always points to the end of the current "mode-related" conditional rule and is set to a new value only while translating mode nodes.

.The translation of the transition from a mode node to one or more rule or condition nodes results in a parallel execution of each. of the nodes. The Greek letters $\alpha_1, \ldots, \alpha_n$ are placeholders for the positions of the translations of the corresponding rule or condition nodes. Each node rc_i is assigned to one of these positions; their order can be arbitrary.

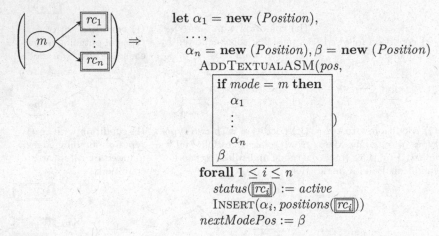

Rules. The translation of rule nodes can be split into the translation of single rule nodes and combinations of a rule node with other nodes. The first case is straight forward and is delegated to the rule TRANSLATESINGLE(*node, pos*).

$(\!|\,\fbox{$rule$}\,|\!)\ \Rightarrow\ $ TRANSLATESINGLE($\fbox{$rule$}, pos$)

In TRANSLATESINGLE for *MacroCallRules*, *UpdateRules* and *ParallelRules*, the value of the label resp. the set of labels is just copied into the textual representation.[2]

The translations of *ForallRules*, *ChooseRules* and *LetRules* follow a pattern which we explain for *LetRules*. There are two cases to consider, depending on whether the body is a textual ASM or an *EmbeddedCSD*. In the first case, the ASM text again is copied and only the keyword **in** is inserted between the *letExp* and the *letBody*.

In the second case, the *letExp* with the keyword **in** is copied as well, but in order to mark the position, where the translation of the embedded CSD

---

[2] Since the translations of a macro call rule and an update rule follow the same pattern (modulo the involved function name), one could combine these two rules into one rule with a corresponding textual ASM as label.

shall be inserted, a new position α is inserted. This position is added to the *positions* of the *startNode* of the *csd* and its *status* is set to *active* such that the *startNode* and thus, the whole *csd* is considered in the translation process.

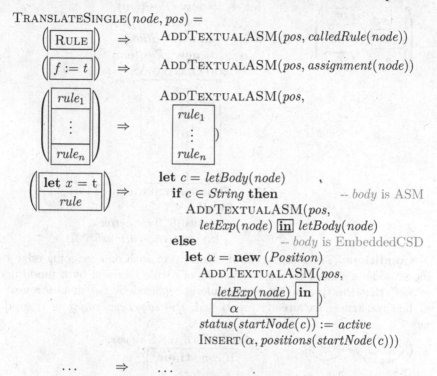

In contrast to the translation of a single rule, for the combination of a rule node with successor nodes we distinguish two cases, depending on the target node type. If a rule node is followed by a mode node with label m, the rule node is translated and the *mode* function in the translated code is set to m. The correctness of this translation is based on the constraint that in this case only one outgoing edge is allowed.

In case a rule node is followed by one or several rule or condition nodes, this combination is treated as sequential execution. This means that the single *rule* is executed and then followed by the parallel execution of all target node rules or conditions ($rc_1, \ldots, rc_n$). To achieve this, n positions are created and added to the textual ASM. Then, for each node $\boxed{rc_i}$ one of these positions is added to its set of positions. Note that the order is arbitrary due to the intended parallel execution. Finally, the *status* for every successor node is set to *active*.

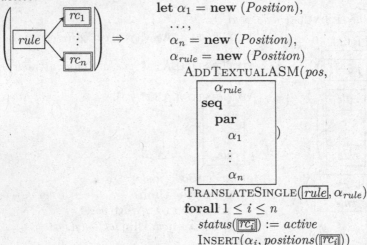

$$\text{let } \alpha_1 = \textbf{new } (Position),$$
$$\dots,$$
$$\alpha_n = \textbf{new } (Position),$$
$$\alpha_{rule} = \textbf{new } (Position)$$
$$\text{ADDTEXTUALASM}(pos,$$

$$\boxed{\begin{array}{l} \alpha_{rule} \\ \textbf{seq} \\ \quad \textbf{par} \\ \quad\quad \alpha_1 \\ \quad\quad \vdots \\ \quad\quad \alpha_n \end{array}}\;)$$

$$\text{TRANSLATESINGLE}(\boxed{rule}, \alpha_{rule})$$
$$\textbf{forall } 1 \leq i \leq n$$
$$status(\boxed{rc_i}) := active$$
$$\text{INSERT}(\alpha_i, positions(\boxed{rc_i}))$$

Conditions. The translation of a condition with one outgoing edge to a mode node is similar to the translation of a rule followed by a mode node, except, that the translation of the rule is replaced by the generation of an if-then construct. As already mentioned, the *edgeType empty* is treated as *yes*.

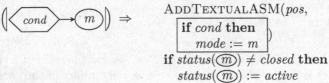

$$\text{ADDTEXTUALASM}(pos,$$
$$\boxed{\begin{array}{l} \textbf{if } cond \textbf{ then} \\ \quad mode := m \end{array}}\;)$$
$$\textbf{if } status(\boxed{m}) \neq closed \textbf{ then}$$
$$status(\boxed{m}) := active$$

In the case of two outgoing edges with mode nodes as successors, the if-then construct is replaced by an if-then-else construct.

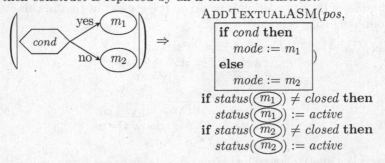

$$\text{ADDTEXTUALASM}(pos,$$
$$\boxed{\begin{array}{l} \textbf{if } cond \textbf{ then} \\ \quad mode := m_1 \\ \textbf{else} \\ \quad mode := m_2 \end{array}}\;)$$
$$\textbf{if } status(\boxed{m_1}) \neq closed \textbf{ then}$$
$$status(\boxed{m_1}) := active$$
$$\textbf{if } status(\boxed{m_2}) \neq closed \textbf{ then}$$
$$status(\boxed{m_2}) := active$$

Finally, the translation of a condition node followed by multiple nodes introduces new positions, where the translations of the successor nodes into a parallel machine are started. Depending on the *edgeType*, these positions are set in the **then**- or in the **else**-branch.

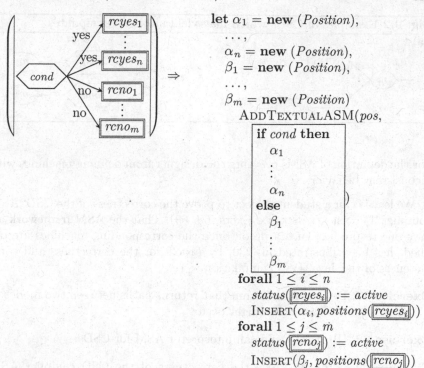

$$\text{let } \alpha_1 = \textbf{new } (Position),$$
$$\dots,$$
$$\alpha_n = \textbf{new } (Position),$$
$$\beta_1 = \textbf{new } (Position),$$
$$\dots,$$
$$\beta_m = \textbf{new } (Position)$$

ADDTEXTUALASM(*pos*,

> **if** *cond* **then**
> α_1
> $\vdots$
> α_n
> **else**
> β_1
> $\vdots$
> β_m
)

forall $1 \leq i \leq n$
$status(\boxed{rcyes_i}) := active$
INSERT$(\alpha_i, positions(\boxed{rcyes_i}))$
forall $1 \leq j \leq m$
$status(\boxed{rcno_j}) := active$
INSERT$(\beta_j, positions(\boxed{rcno_j}))$

The translation patterns of the other cases are omitted here; they are straightforward variations of the cases we have explained. We encourage the reader to define the missing translations patterns as an exercise (see Exerc. 66).

Exercise 66. Define the patterns for the remaining kinds of ASM rules, together with their translation scheme.

Remarks. The above translation scheme is designed in such a way, pattern by pattern, that it is easy to grasp for the human reader, for whom it serves as a—both precise and intuitive—definition for the meaning of the graphical constructs. Of course, this specification can and should be optimized for an executable translation, e. g. to yield fewer conditions, less rule replications, etc.

If a given CSD may lead to inconsistent updates, so will the translated textual ASM. For example, consider two paths which start at a mode and do not end up in the same successor mode, as depicted in Fig. 9.1a. The two rules RULE$_1$ and RULE$_2$ are executed in parallel and yield two updates of the *mode* location, namely by m_1 and m_2, which are inconsistent if $m_1 \neq m_2$. In Fig. 9.1b a similar inconsistency can happen, but it is less visible because it depends on whether the two conditions *cond*$_1$ and *cond*$_2$ overlap. If they are disjoint, no inconsistent update can show up. Neither the definition of CSDs

Fig. 9.2 Examples of CSDs which may yield inconsistent updates

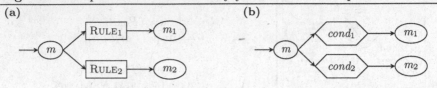

(a)

(b)

nor the definition of ASMs prevents the designer from defining machines with inconsistent behavior.

We leave it for a student project to prove the correctness of the CSD2ASM compiler TRANSLATECSD (see Exers. 68, 69). That the ASM framework allows one to produce such a proof, once the corresponding machines are defined, has been illustrated in [232] by proofs for the correctness and completeness of the Java2JVM compilation.

Exercise 67. Design an algorithm that returns paths between two modes of a CSD where inconsistencies might occur.

Exercise 68. (Project) Define an interpreter ASM for CSDs.

Exercise 69. (Project) Prove the correctness of the CSD compiler ASM TRANSLATECSD with respect to the interpreter ASM for CSDs defined in Exerc. 68.

9.5 Subdiagram Replacements to Refine CSDs

Since CSDs are a graphical representation of control state ASMs, the questions arises whether ASM refinements of control state ASMs, which add or change rules, have a visual correspondence in terms of adding or replacing CSD subdiagrams. In this book we have visualized various ASM refinements by introducing subdiagrams into previously defined control state ASM flowcharts, see for example Figs. 2.3, 2.4, 2.10, 2.12, 2.14, and Sect. 2.4, to mention a few.

In this section we propose a simple subdiagram replacement definition, which captures the subdiagrams used in this book to visualize some ASM refinements. We hope to trigger some interest in a thorough investigation of the relation between graph operations on CSDs and ASM refinements. It would be interesting to find out whether sophisticated graph rewriting techniques can be helpful in this context.

To replace a subgraph D_1 of a given graph D by some other subgraph D_2, one has to describe how the incoming and outgoing edges of D_2 replace those

Fig. 9.3 Examples of replaceable subCSDs

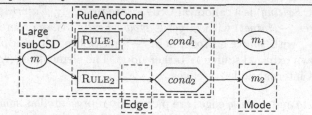

of D_1 in D. First of all we declare which CSD subdiagrams we permit to be replaced and which diagrams we permit as their substitute.

Definition 23. Let $D = (Node, Edge)$ be a canonical CSD. We call $D' = (Node', Edge')$ a *replaceable subCSD* of D if $D' \setminus (Entry(D') \cup Exit(D'))$ is a canonical CSD and a closed subgraph of D. $Entry(D')$ and $Exit(D')$ are defined as ordered sets of all edges which enter resp. leave (some internal nodes of) D':

$Entry(s) =$
$\quad \{(ext, int) \in Edge \mid ext \notin Node' \text{ and } int \in Node'\}$
$Exit(s) =$
$\quad \{(int, ext) \in Edge \mid int \in Node' \text{ and } ext \notin Node'\}$

We intend a singleton set consisting only of an edge to be included into this definition. In this case $Entry(D')$ and $Exit(D')$ are defined as the singleton set of this edge.

A replaceable subCSD is pictorially indicated by a dashed polygon around the included nodes and edges. For reference purposes, we usually also include a label which names the scope. This label can be accessed via a function $subCsdRef(D')$. Figure 9.3 shows some examples of replaceable subCSDs. For the sake of brevity, we indicate in one figure different replaceable subCSDs.[3] The dashed polygon around $\textsc{Rule}_1$ has no label, because in this case the name of the rule can be used to identify the subCSD. Since the definition of a macro call rule as replaceable subCSD is a rather common case, we permit to skip the dashed rectangle around a *rule* and to further detail (or redefine) it in a subdiagram which carries the name of the given *rule*. We used such subCSDs already in Fig. 2.12.

Sometimes we draw $\lceil\textsc{Rule}\rfloor$ to indicate that $\textsc{Rule}$ is an abstract rule and has to be refined by a subdiagram in order to become a canonical CSD (see for example Fig. 2.20).

Definition 24. Let $D = (Node, Edge)$ be a graph without distinguished *initialMode* or *startNodes*. We call it an *InOutCSD* if it comes with a pair

---

[3] The subCSDs in the figure have some overlap, although in the case of simultaneous replacements we consider only replacements without overlap.

(*Entering, Exiting*) of incoming and outgoing edges such that (*Node, Edge* ∪ *Entering*∪*Exiting*) is a canonical CSD. More precisely, *Entering* is an ordered set of edges (−, *target*) with *target* ∈ *Node, Exiting* is an ordered set of edges (*source*, −) with *source* ∈ *Node*; here "−" plays the role of a placeholder for an unknown external source or target node. The elements of *Node* resp. *Edge* are called internal nodes or edges.

Entering and *Exiting* edges are pictorially represented as small arrows with either no source resp. no target node. Figure 2.9 shows two simple *InOutCSD* examples, each with one incoming and one outgoing edge.

To replace a subCSD by an *InOutCSD*, the incoming and outgoing edges must be mapped in an order preserving way. For a replaceable subCSD D' of some D and an *InOutCSD* with sets *Entering, Exiting* we say that their incoming and outgoing edges are compatible if their cardinalities match, that is if $|Entry(D')| = |Entering|$ and $|Exit(D')| = |Exiting|$.

Definition 25. Let $D_1 = (Node_1, Edge_1)$ be a replaceable subCSD of some $D = (Node, Edge)$ with $Entry(D_1) = \{(source_{1,i}, enter_{1,i}) \mid 1 \leq i \leq n\}$ and $Exit(D_1) = \{(leave_{1,j}, target_{1,j}) \mid 1 \leq j \leq m\}$, with the indicated order. Let $InOutCSD = (Node_2, Edge_2)$ with compatible sets $Entering = \{(-, target_{2,i}) \mid 1 \leq i \leq n\}$ and $Exiting = \{(source_{2,j}, -) \mid 1 \leq j \leq m\}$.

We say that a CSD D^* is a *CSD-refinement* of D if D^* results from D by replacing a replaceable subCSD D_1 of D by an *InOutCSD* D_2 with compatible incoming and outgoing edges.

To replace D_1 by D_2 in D means the following:

- Delete all D_1-internal edges and nodes from D, that is the elements of $Node_1$ and $Edge_1$.
- Add all D_2-internal edges and nodes to D, that is the elements of $Node_2$ and $Edge_2$.
- Connect the source/target nodes of order-corresponding $Entry(D_1)$ and *Entering* edges. This means to add $(source_{1,i}, target_{2,i})$ to Edge for each $1 \leq i \leq n$ (redirecting *Entry* targets to the corresponding *Entering* targets).
- Connect the source/target nodes of order-corresponding $Exit(D_1)$ and *Exiting* edges. This means to add $(source_{2,j}, target_{1,j})$ to Edge for each $1 \leq j \leq m$ (redirecting *Exiting* targets to the corresponding *Exit* targets).

The order information for redirecting corresponding edges can be visualized in various ways. In this book we do it by indicating for each incoming resp. outgoing node also the source resp. target nodes of the enclosing diagram D. Figure 9.4 shows an example for the subdiagram RuleAndCond of the CSD in Fig. 9.3 with two incoming and two outgoing edges. Observe the indication of the mode nodes m and m_1, m_2 outside the dashed boundary of the *InOutCSD* to indicate how the incoming/outgoing edges have to be connected when performing the replacement.

Fig. 9.4 Subdiagram RuleAndCond with boundary of *InOutCSD*

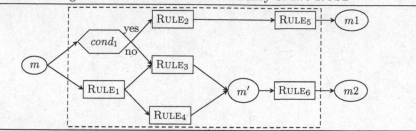

Formally, the replacement of D_1 by D_2 in D can be defined by the following ASM SUBSTITUTION(D_1, D_2, D). We disregard the special case with exactly one incoming and one outgoing subdiagram edge.

SUBSTITUTION$(D_1, D_2, D) =$
    forall $(source_1, enter_1) \in Entry(D_1)$ -- reallocate all incoming edges
        let $(-, target_2)$ be the corresponding element in *Entering*
          INSERT$((source_1, target_2), Edge)$
          DELETE$((source_1, enter_1), Edge)$
    forall $(leave_1, target_1) \in Exit(D_1)$ -- reallocate all outgoing edges
        let $(source_2, -)$ be the corresponding element in *Exiting*
          INSERT$((source_2, target_1), Edge)$
          DELETE$((leave_1, target_1), Edge)$
    forall $node \in Node_1$ -- remove D_1-nodes/edges
        DELETE$(node, Node)$
    forall $edge \in Edge_1$
        DELETE$(edge, Edge)$
    forall $node \in Node_2$ -- add D_2-nodes/edges
        INSERT$(node, Node)$
    forall $edge \in Edge_2$
        INSERT$(edge, Edge)$

Remark. Sometimes we use diagrams which provide a control-state-ASM-like overview of a system. An example is Fig. 2.16, which represents an architecture view of the system components and their (in this case sequentially ordered) interaction. Once all the components have been unfolded, the diagram becomes a CSD (see Fig. 2.28), for which the above translation to a textual ASM does work.

Epilogue

The Introduction (Sect. 1) concluded with the statement that we view the ASM modeling and analysis method not as a stand-alone method, but as to-be-integrated into industrial-strength software development frameworks which care about high-level design and analysis. A candidate par excellence are model-based engineering (MBE) frameworks which provide tools to support some, if not all, of the activities from requirements to code. Often they provide also support for pragmatic needs, like combining textual and graphical definition techniques, tracing requirements (so that one can effectively check their complete coverage), version management, etc. So what additional value can the ASM method bring to such frameworks?

Remember the ASM method offers a) a semantically well-defined, pseudo code language that is familiar to the software practitioner, and b) a mathematically precise yet simple technique

- to **B**uild systems **accurately at any desired level of abstraction**, providing well-documented, systematically inspectable and executable system *blueprints* one can use to **E**xplain, **D**ebug (validate and verify) and maintain (**E**xplore/**E**xtend and **R**euse) designs (**BEDER**),
- to **accurately link designs at different levels of abstraction**, supporting not only the stepwise implementation of application domain concepts (by ASM refinement), but also a rigorous experimental and mathematical analysis to debug the implementation steps (by validation and verification at any needed level), see Fig. 1.1,
- to **intellectually manage** the tremendous **complexity** of software intensive systems of today.

Coping with complexity is a well-known problem in software engineering. It triggered a huge number of industrial frameworks and proposals to turn programming into something that is closer to the *system designer's understanding* of the underlying problem (and how to solve it) than to *explaining to machines* how they should execute the solution. The above mentioned MBE

© Springer-Verlag GmbH Germany, part of Springer Nature 2018
E. Börger, A. Raschke, *Modeling Companion for Software Practitioners*,
https://doi.org/10.1007/978-3-662-56641-1

approach is an example of such an endeavor and comes with extensive tool support. Among ASM's benefits are:

- **Accurate high-level descriptions of the behavior of tools**, descriptions which are rarely found in current software engineering frameworks, can be provided as ASM models. This could also improve the quality of manuals. The lack of a clear behavioral model can make it hard for the users to grasp a correct understanding of what a tool does and to use it correctly. It may hinder the interoperability of tools. Not surprisingly, the best tools come with and need extensive, time consuming (and expensive!) training programs and technical support by the tool developer.[4]

- **Inspection and debugging of designs**, not only of code,[5] can be done *at whatever level of abstraction* using ASMs, thereby contributing to make complex systems understandable and circumventing the necessarily limited expressivity of tools. It increases the chances to detect *conceptual errors* which are easily missed by code debuggers.

- **Definition of variations of tool behavior patterns** by ASM refinements can help to cope with the multitude of frameworks which offer tools with similar, often slightly different, functionality but with different interfaces. Besides the dependency on the tool vendor (vendor lock-in), this multitude may create also a language and version dependency a *general* modeling framework—in particular if open-source—better avoids. Defining ASM models for tool cores and describing their variations by refinements can change this.[6] In combination with a standardization effort for functionality and interfaces of modeling-supporting tools, this can raise the abstraction level of tools and make them better interoperable.

- **Precise conceptual support for divide-and-conquer techniques** is offered by ASM refinements, allowing one to effectively and accurately combine models which have been defined step- and component-wise, possibly passing through a hierarchy of levels of abstraction.

Although the use of ASMs and their tools has proved to be useful in various industrial applications (some of which have been mentioned in this book), existing academic tools for ASMs are only a first step. Every contribution to reach the challenging goal of an open source and where useful standardized ASM-based software development tool environment is welcome.[7]

---

[4] See for example the lessons learned about the use of modeling tools in various MBE projects, reported in [159, 34] with numerous further references.

[5] 'system design errors are increasingly the cause of major accidents' [182, Sect. 2.1]

[6] An example of what we refer to is the abstract object-oriented programming language semantics model in [77]. The C# [54] and Java [232] models appear as variations of that one ASM.

[7] The joint venture the first author had proposed at the end of 1999 to Siemens and Microsoft Research, to create an ASM-based software design, analysis (debugging by validation and verification), documentation and maintenance framework, could have made building software-intensive systems more reliable and more effective than it is still today.

Appendix A
Some Complete Models in a Nutshell

We reformulate here without further explanations the complete models for a few machines described in the book, the final result of their didactically motivated piecemeal construction and explanation. They are the starting point for the refinement to CoreASM executable models. We concentrate on rewriting the rules and refer for the signature, the underlying initialization and similar assumptions to the main text where the machines are introduced. We do not repeat machines whose rules have been written out as one piece in the main text, in particular the following ones:

- 1WAYSTOPGOLIGHTSPEC (Sect. 2.1.1) with its horizontally refined model 1WAYSTOPGOORANGELIGHTSPEC (Sect. 2.1.3) and the data and vertically refined TIMED2WAYSTOPGOLIGHTSPEC (Sect. 2.1.4)
- PACKAGEROUTER ground model (end of Sect. 2.3.1)
- CONCURRENCYPATTERN (end of Sect. 2.4.3),
- ATM top level machine (Fig. 2.28),
- CONCUREXTREMAFINDING (Sect. 3.1.2),
- TERMINATIONDETECTOR for diffusing computations (Sect. 3.3.1.2),
- LOCALSYNCTRANSFORMER with SYNCSHELL(p) and SYNCHRONIZER(p) programs (Sect. 3.3.2),
- THREADPOOLEXECUTOR for J2SE 5.0 consisting of two submachines HANDLENEWTASK and HANDLEQUEUEDTASK (Sect. 4.2.2.2),
- ASMs for various bilateral, multilateral, asynchronous and synchronous communication patterns (Sect. 4.4),
- the S-BPM communication model with its characteristic integration of textual and graphical control-state diagram descriptions (Sect. 5.2.2).

We also do not repeat the ASM rules which specify CoreASM, with its debugger plug-in (Chap. 8), and the Control State Diagrams (Chap. 9).

© Springer-Verlag GmbH Germany, part of Springer Nature 2018
E. Börger, A. Raschke, *Modeling Companion for Software Practitioners*,
https://doi.org/10.1007/978-3-662-56641-1

A.1 TerminationDetection (Sect. 3.2)

TerminationDetection =   -- main program
  StartProbe   -- done by *master* if *ProbeNotSuccessful*
  TriggerActivation   -- spontaneously if *active* without token
  BecomeActive   -- if *hasMessage*
  BecomePassive   -- spontaneously if not *hasMessage*
  PassToken   -- if *passive* and not the *master*

A.1.1 Token Passing Components

StartProbe =
  if *ProbeNotSuccessful* **and** **self** = *master* **then**
    if **self** = *master* **then** *tokenColor* := *white*   -- ColorToken
    else if *color*(**self**) = *black* **then** *tokenColor* := *black*
    ForwardToken
    color(**self**) := *white*   -- GetWhite
PassToken =
  if *hasToken* **and** *mode* = *passive* **and** **self** ≠ *master* **then**
    if *color*(**self**) = *black* **then** *tokenColor* := *black*   -- ColorToken
    ForwardToken
    color(**self**) := *white*   -- GetWhite

A.1.2 Activation Related Components

BecomeActive =
  if *Triggered* **then**   -- *hasMessage*(**self**)
    mode := *active*
    Deactivate(*Triggered*)   -- delete the trigger
BecomePassive =
  if not *Triggered*   -- not *hasMessage*(**self**)
    then SpontaneouslyDo
      if *mode* = *active* **then** *mode* := *passive*
TriggerActivation =
  if *mode* = *active* **then** SpontaneouslyDo   -- TriggerAct
    if not *hasToken* **then**
      choose *m* ∈ *Machine*   -- SendMessage to *m*
        Activate(*Triggered*(*m*))
        if *number*(*m*) > *number*(**self**) **then** *color*(**self**) := *black*

A.1.3 Some Auxiliary Definitions

$Machine = \{m_0, \ldots, m_{N-1}\}$ $master = m_0$ $number(m_i) = i \bmod N$
FORWARDTOKEN =
   $hasToken(\textbf{self}) := false$ -- forward token from machine nr. $i+1$
   $hasToken(pred(\textbf{self})) := true$ -- ... to predecessor machine nr. i
$ProbeNotSuccessful$ iff $hasToken(master)$ **and**
   $(tokenColor = black$ **or** $color(master) = black)$
ACTIVATE$(trigger) =$ -- update instruction
   $trigger := true$ -- even if in parallel with DEACTIVATE$(trigger)$
DEACTIVATE$(trigger) =$ -- update instruction
  $\begin{cases} trigger := false \text{ \textbf{if} not executed in parallel with ACTIVATE}(trigger) \\ \textbf{skip} \qquad\qquad \textbf{else} \end{cases}$

A.2 VIRTUALPROVIDER (Sect. 5.1)

VIRTUALPROVIDER = **one of**   -- main program
  ({PROCESS, RECEIVEREQ, SENDREQ, RECEIVEANSW, SENDANSW})

A.2.1 Communication Components

SENDREQ = SENDANSW =   -- SENDPATTERN, see Sect. **4.4.1**
  if $readyToSend(m)$ **then**   -- trigger predicate $ToSend(m)$
    if $OkSend(m)$ **then**
     SEND(m)
     if $AckRequested(m)$ **then**
      SETWAITCOND(m)
     if $BlockingSend(m)$ **then**
      $status := awaitAck(m)$
    else
     HANDLESENDFAILURE$(m, notOkSend)$
     $readyToSend(m) := false$ -- DONE(m)

RECEIVEPATTERN$(m) =$ -- see Sect. **4.4.1**
  if $Arriving(m)$ **then**
    if $ReadyToReceive(m)$ **then**
     RECEIVE(m)
     if $ToBeAcknowledged(m)$ **then**
      SEND$(Ack(m), sender(m))$
    elseif $ToBeDiscarded(m)$ **then**
     DISCARD(m)

> **if** $ToBeAcknowledged(m)$ **then**
>> SEND($Ack(m, discarded)$, $sender(m)$)
>
> **else**
>> **if** $ToBeBuffered(m)$ **then** $--$ BUFFER(m)
>>> INSERT(m, $buffer$)
>>> SETTIMER($insertBuffer(m)$)
>>
>> **if** $ToBeAcknowledged(m)$ **then**
>>> SEND($Ack(m, buffered)$, $sender(m)$)
>
> **if** $TimeOut(insertBuffer(m))$ **then**
>> RECEIVE(m)
>> DELETE(m, $buffer$)

RECEIVEREQ = RECEIVEPATTERN
> **where** $--$ instantiation of RECEIVEPATTERN abstractions
>> **if** $ReadyToReceive(m)$ **then** $m \in InReqMssg$
>> RECEIVE(m) =
>>> CONSUME(m)
>>> **let** r = **new** ($ReqObj$) **in** $--$ CREATEREQOBJ(m)
>>> $status(r) := start$ $--$ INITIALIZE(r, m)
>>> $reqMsg(r) := m$

RECEIVEANSW = RECEIVEPATTERN
> **where** $--$ instantiation of RECEIVEPATTERN abstractions
>> **if** $ReadyToReceive(m)$ **then** $m \in InAnswMssg$
>> RECEIVE(m) =
>>> INSERT(m, $AnswerSet(subRequestor(m))$)
>>> CONSUME(m)

A.2.2 PROCESS *Component*

PROCESS =
> **choose** $r \in ReqObj$ **with** $status(r) = start$
>> **let** a = **new** ($Agent$) $--$ CREATESUBREQHANDLER(r)
>> $pgm(a) := $ HANDLESUBREQ
>> $handler(r) := a$ $--$ INITIALIZE(a, r)
>> $req(a) := r$
>> $subReq(a) := head(seqSubReq(r))$ $--$ current subrequest
>> $status(r) := handleSubReq$
>> $AnswerSet(r) := \emptyset$ $--$ INITIALIZE($AnswerSet(r)$)

The HANDLESUBREQ program with which the new subrequest handler is equipped is defined by Fig. A.1. It comes with three submachines:

Fig. A.1 HANDLESUBREQ component of VP PROCESS

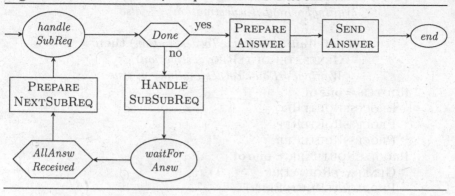

HANDLESUBSUBREQ =
 forall $r \in (parSubReq(subReq))$ -- PREPAREBROADCAST
  $readyToSend(outReq2Msg(r)) := true$
  $AnswerSet(subReq) := \emptyset$ -- INITIALIZE($AnswerSet(subReq)$)
PREPARENEXTSUBREQ =
 $subReq := next(subReq, seqSubReq(req), AnswerSet(subReq))$
 ADD($AnswerSet(subReq), AnswerSet(req(\mathbf{self})))$
PREPAREANSWER = **let** $req = req(\mathbf{self})$
 $readyToSend(outAnsw2Msg(answer(req, AnswerSet(req)))) := true$

Some auxiliary definitions:

AllAnswReceived **iff**
 forall $q \in toBeAnswered(parSubReq(subReq))$
  thereissome $m \in AnswerSet(subReq)$ **with** $IsAnswer(m, q)$
Done **iff** $subReq = done$ -- $done \notin SubReq$

A.3 AODVSPEC (Sect. 6.1)

AODVSPEC = **one of**   -- main program
 PREPARECOMM
 ROUTER
where
 PREPARECOMM =
  if $WantsToCommunicateWith(destination)$ **then**
   if $KnowsActiveRouteTo(destination)$
    then
     STARTCOMMUNICATIONWITH($destination$)

$\qquad$ $\textit{WantsToCommunicateWith}(\textit{destination}) := \textit{false}$
$\qquad$ $\textit{WaitingForRouteTo}(\textit{destination}) := \textit{false}$
$\quad$ **else**
$\qquad$ **if not** $\textit{WaitingForRouteTo}(\textit{destination})$ **then**
$\qquad\quad$ GENERATEROUTEREQ($\textit{destination}$)
$\qquad\quad$ $\textit{WaitingForRouteTo}(\textit{destination}) := \textit{true}$
ROUTER $=$ **one of**
$\quad$ PROCESSROUTEREQ
$\quad$ PROCESSROUTEREP
$\quad$ PROCESSROUTEERR
PROCESSROUTEERR $=$ **one of**
$\quad$ GENERATEROUTEERR
$\quad$ PROPAGATEROUTEERR

A.3.1 Route Request Components of AODVSPEC

GENERATEROUTEREQ($\textit{destination}$) $=$
$\quad$ **let** $r = $ **new** ($\textit{RouteRequest}$) **in**
$\quad$ $\textit{dest}(r) := \textit{destination}$
$\quad$ $\textit{destSeqNum}(r) := \textit{lastKnownDestSeqNum}(\textit{destination}, \textit{RT})$
$\quad$ $\textit{origin}(r) := $ **self**
$\quad$ $\textit{originSeqNum}(r) := \textit{curSeqNum} + 1$
$\quad$ $\textit{curSeqNum} := \textit{curSeqNum} + 1$ $\qquad$ -- INCREMENT($\textit{curSeqNum}$)
$\quad$ $\textit{hopCount}(r) := 0$
$\quad$ $\textit{localId}(r) := \textit{localReqCount} + 1$
$\quad$ $\textit{localReqCount} := \textit{localReqCount} + 1$ -- INCREMENT($\textit{localReqCount}$)
$\quad$ **forall** $n \in \textit{neighb}$ **do** SEND(r, **to** n) $\qquad$ -- BROADCAST(r)
$\quad$ INSERT($\textit{globalId}(r)$, $\textit{ReceivedReq}$) $\qquad$ -- BUFFER(r)
$\quad$ **if** $\textit{entryFor}(\textit{destination}, \textit{RT}) \neq$ **undef**
$\qquad$ **then** $\textit{known}(r) := \textit{known}(\textit{entryFor}(\textit{destination}, \textit{RT}))$
$\qquad$ **else** $\textit{known}(r) := \textit{false}$

PROCESSROUTEREQ($\textit{rreq}$) $=$
$\quad$ **if** $\textit{Received}(\textit{rreq})$ **and** $\textit{rreq} \in \textit{RouteRequest}$ **then**
$\qquad$ **if not** $\textit{AlreadyReceivedBefore}(\textit{rreq})$ **then** -- no $\textit{rreq}$ processed twice
$\qquad$ INSERT($\textit{globalId}(\textit{rreq})$, $\textit{ReceivedReq}$)
$\qquad$ **if** $\textit{HasNewReverseRouteInfo}(\textit{rreq})$ **then**
$\qquad\quad$ BUILDREVERSEROUTE($\textit{rreq}$)
$\qquad\qquad$ -- with freshest $\textit{destSeqNum}$ for $\textit{RT}$-entry to $\textit{originator}$
$\qquad$ **seq if** $\textit{FoundValidPathFor}(\textit{rreq})$
$\qquad\qquad$ **then** GENERATEROUTEREPLY($\textit{rreq}$)
$\qquad\qquad$ **else** FORWARDREFRESHEDREQ($\textit{rreq}$)
$\quad$ CONSUME($\textit{rreq}$)

BUILDREVERSEROUTE($rreq$) =
  if $ThereIsRouteInfoFor(origin(rreq), RT)$
                    -- $rreq$ knows fresher $curSeqNum(origin(rreq))$ than RT
    then UPDATEREVERSEROUTE($entryFor(origin(rreq), RT), rreq$)
    else EXTENDREVERSEROUTE($RT, rreq$)

EXTENDREVERSEROUTE(RT, req) =
  let e = **new** (RT)
    $dest(e) := origin(req)$
    $precursor(e) := \emptyset$UPDATEREVERSEROUTE($e, req$)
UPDATEREVERSEROUTE(e, req) =
  $destSeqNum(e) := originSeqNum(req)$
  $nextHop(e) := sender(req)$
  $hopCount(e) := hopCount(req) + 1$
  $Active(e) := true$
  $known(e) := true$

FORWARDREFRESHEDREQ(r) =
  let r' = **new** $(RouteRequest)$
    COPY($dest, origin, originSeqNum, localId, known,$ **from** r **to** r')
    $hopCount(r') := hopCount(r) + 1$
    $destSeqNum(r') := max\{destSeqNum(r),$ -- best known
      $lastKnownDestSeqNum(dest(r), RT)\}$ -- $destSeqNum$
    forall $n \in neighb$ SEND($r',$ **to** n)   -- BROADCAST(r')

Some auxiliary definitions:

$lastKnownDestSeqNum(d, RT)$ =
  $\begin{cases} destSeqNum(entry) & \text{if \textbf{forsome} } entry \in RT \; dest(entry) = d \\ unknown & \textbf{else} \end{cases}$

$AlreadyReceivedBefore(rreq)$ **iff** $globalId(rreq) \in ReceivedReq$

$HasNewReverseRouteInfo(req)$ **iff** $req \in RouteRequest$ **and**
  $ThereIsNoRouteInfoFor(origin(req), RT)$ **or**
  ($ThereIsRouteInfoFor(origin(req), RT)$ **and**
    $HasNewOriginInfo(req, RT)$)

$HasNewOriginInfo(req, RT)$ **iff**   -- info on $curSeqNum(origin(req))$
  let $entry = entryFor(origin(req), RT)$
    $originSeqNum(req) > destSeqNum(entry)$
    or $originSeqNum(req) = destSeqNum(entry)$ **and**
      ($hopCount(req) < hopCount(entry)$ **or not** $Active(entry)$)

$ThereIsRouteInfoFor(d, RT)$ **iff**
  forsome $entry \in RT \; dest(entry) = d$

ThereIsNoRouteInfoFor(*node, RT*) **iff**
   not *ThereIsRouteInfoFor*(*node, RT*)

FoundValidPathFor(*rreq*) **iff**
   dest(*rreq*) = **self or** *KnowsFreshEnoughRouteFor*(*rreq, RT*)

KnowsFreshEnoughRouteFor(*rreq, RT*) **iff forsome** *entry* ∈ *RT*
   dest(*entry*) = *dest*(*rreq*) **and** *ValidDestSeqNum*(*entry*)
      and *destSeqNum*(*entry*) ≥ *destSeqNum*(*rreq*)
         and *Active*(*entry*)

A.3.2 Route Reply Components of AODVSPEC

GENERATEROUTEREPLY(*rreq*) =
   let *r* = **new** (*RouteReply*)
      dest(*r*) := *dest*(*rreq*)
      origin(*r*) := *origin*(*rreq*)
      if *dest*(*rreq*) = **self then**
         hopCount(*r*) := 0
         destSeqNum(*r*) := *max*{*curSeqNum, destSeqNum*(*rreq*)}
         curSeqNum := *max*{*curSeqNum, destSeqNum*(*rreq*)}
      else
         let *fwdEntry* = *entryFor*(*dest*(*rreq*), *RT*)
            hopCount(*r*) := *hopCount*(*fwdEntry*)
            destSeqNum(*r*) := *destSeqNum*(*fwdEntry*)
            PRECURSORINSERTION(*sender*(*rreq*), *fwdEntry*)
      SEND(*r*, **to** *nextHop*(*entryFor*(*origin*(*rreq*), *RT*)))
   where
      PRECURSORINSERTION(*node, entry*) =
         INSERT(*node, precursor*(*entry*))

PROCESSROUTEREP(*rrep*) =
   if *Received*(*rrep*) **and** *rrep* ∈ *RouteReply* **then**
      if *HasNewForwardRouteInfo*(*rrep*) **then**
         BUILDFORWARDROUTE(*rrep*)
         if *MustForward*(*rrep*) **then** FORWARDREFRESHEDREP(*rrep*)
      CONSUME(*rrep*)

BUILDFORWARDROUTE(*rrep*) =
   if *ThereIsRouteInfoFor*(*dest*(*rrep*), *RT*)
      then UPDATEFORWARDROUTE(*entryFor*(*dest*(*rrep*), *RT*), *rrep*)
      else EXTENDFORWARDROUTE(*RT*, *rrep*)

$\textsc{ExtendForwardRoute}(RT, rep) =$
  let $e = \textbf{new}\ (RT)$ -- create new entry to extend forward route
    $dest(e) := dest(rep)$ -- with same *destination* as *rep*
    $\textsc{UpdateForwardRoute}(e, rep)$
$\textsc{UpdateForwardRoute}(e, rep) =$
  $destSeqNum(e) := destSeqNum(rep)$
  $nextHop(e) := sender(rep)$
  $hopCount(e) := hopCount(rep) + 1$
  $Active(e) := true$
  $known(e) := true$
  $\textsc{SetPrecursor}(rep, e)$

$\textsc{SetPrecursor}(rep, e) =$
  if $MustForward(rep)$ **then**
    $\textsc{Insert}(nextHop(entryFor(origin(rep), RT)), precursor(e))$

$\textsc{ForwardRefreshedRep}(rep) =$
  let $rep' = \textbf{new}\ (RouteReply)$
  $\textsc{Copy}(dest, destSeqNum, origin, \textbf{from}\ rep\ \textbf{to}\ rep')$
  $hopCount(rep') := hopCount(rep) + 1$
  $\textsc{Send}(rep', \textbf{to}\ nextHop(entryFor(origin(rep), RT)))$

Some auxiliary definitions:

$HasNewForwardRouteInfo(rep)$ **iff** $rep \in RouteReply$ **and**
  $ThereIsNoRouteInfoFor(dest(rep), RT)$ **or**
  $(ThereIsRouteInfoFor(dest(rep), RT)$ **and**
    $HasNewDestInfo(rep, RT))$
$HasNewDestInfo(rep, RT)$ **iff**   -- *entry* has either
  let $entry = entryFor(dest(rrep), RT)$
  $destSeqNum(rep) > destSeqNum(entry)$ -- older *destSeqNum*
  or $(destSeqNum(rep) = destSeqNum(entry)$
    and $hopCount(rep) + 1 < hopCount(entry))$ -- or longer path
  or $(destSeqNum(rep) = destSeqNum(entry)$
    and $Active(entry) = false)$ -- or inactive route
  $MustForward(rep)$ **iff**
    $origin(rep) \neq \textbf{self}$ **and** $Active(entryFor(origin(rep), RT))$

A.3.3 Route Error Components of AodvSpec

$\textsc{GenerateRouteErr} =$
  let $UnreachEntry =$
  $\{entry \in RT \mid LinkBreak(nextHop(entry))$ **and** $Active(entry)\}$
  if $UnreachEntry \neq \emptyset$ **then**   -- some broken link detected

forall $entry \in UnreachEntry$
  $Active(entry) := false$
  $destSeqNum(entry) := destSeqNum(entry) + 1$
                    -- INCREMENT($destSeqNum(entry)$)
  let $rerr = \{(dest(e), destSeqNum(e) + 1) \mid$
            $e \in UnreachEntry$ **and** $precursor(e) \neq \emptyset\}$
    forall $a \in precursor(entry)$ **do** SEND($rerr$, **to** a)

PROPAGATEROUTEERR =
  if $Received(rerr)$ **and** $rerr \in RouteError$ **then**
    let $UnreachDest = \{(d, s) \in rerr \mid$ **forsome** $entry \in RT$
            $d = dest(entry)$ **and** $nextHop(entry) = sender(rerr)$
            and $Active(entry)$ **and** $destSeqNum(entry) < s\}$
    forall $(d, s) \in UnreachDest$
      let $entry = entryFor(d, RT)$
        $Active(entry) := false$
        $destSeqNum(entry) := s$
        forall $a \in precursor(entry)$ SEND($rerr'$, **to** a)
      if $WaitingForRouteTo(d)$ **then** REGENERATEROUTEREQ(d)
    CONSUME($rerr$)
  where
    $err' = \{(d', s') \in UnreachDest \mid precursor(entryFor(d', RT)) \neq \emptyset\}$
    REGENERATEROUTEREQ(d) = $WaitingForRouteTo(d) := false$

A.4 Relaxed Shared Memory Model (Sect. 6.2)

For the given data center system $\mathcal{D} = \bigcup_{i=1}^{k} \mathcal{D}_i$, partitioned into clusters $\mathcal{D}_i$ of data centers users interact with, two concurrent ASMs have been defined, a CLUSTERUSERVIEW$_i$ which expresses how the user is invited to perceive its interaction with the database and a CLUSTERMANAGEMENT$_i$ which describes how Cassandra manages internally the users' read and write requests.

CLUSTERUSERVIEW$_i = (d, \text{DATACENTERUSERVIEW}_i)_{d \in \mathcal{D}_i}$
CLUSTERMANAGEMENT$_i = (d, \text{CLUSTERDATACENTER}_i)_{d \in \mathcal{D}_i}$

A.4.1 DATACENTERUSERVIEW$_i$

DATACENTERUSERVIEW$_i =$ -- main program of any $d \in \mathcal{D}_i$
  ANSWERREADREQ$_i$
  PERFORMWRITEREQ$_i$

ANSWERREADREQ$_i =$
  if $Received(read(p_i, \varphi), \textbf{from } a)$ **then**
    forall $j \in \{1, \dots, q_i\}$ -- for each fragment choose complying replicas

$\quad$**choose** $C_{i,j} \subseteq ReplicaNodes_{i,j}$ **with** $Complies(C_{i,j}, readPolicy)$
$\quad\quad$**let** $t_{max}(\mathbf{k}) =$ $\quad\quad\quad\quad\quad\quad$ -- compute most recent timestamp
$\quad\quad$ $\max\{t \mid p_{i,j,d',j'}(\mathbf{k}) = (\mathbf{v}', t)$ **forsome** $\mathbf{v}', (d', j') \in C_{i,j}\}$
$\quad\quad\quad\quad\quad\quad$ -- collect most recent defined values in j-th fragment
$\quad\quad$**let** $\rho_{i,j} = \{(\mathbf{k}, \mathbf{v}) \mid \mathbf{k} \in Frag_{j,i} \uparrow \varphi$ **and** $\mathbf{v} \neq null$ **and**
$\quad\quad\quad\quad p_{i,j,d',j'}(\mathbf{k}) = (\mathbf{v}, t_{max}(\mathbf{k}))$ **forsome** $(d', j') \in C_{i,j}\}$
$\quad\quad$**let** $\rho = \bigcup_{j=1}^{q_i} \rho_{i,j}$ $\quad\quad\quad$ -- collect values from all fragments
$\quad\quad$ SEND($ValFor(read(p_i, \varphi), \rho)$, **to** a)
$\quad\quad\quad\quad\quad\quad\quad\quad\quad$ -- send current (p_i, φ)- values
$\quad$ CONSUME($read(p_i, \varphi)$, **from** a)

PERFORMWRITEREQ$_i =$
$\quad$**if** $Received(write(p_i, p)$, **from** $a)$ **then**
$\quad\quad$**let** $t_{current} = clock_{\mathbf{self}}$ $\quad\quad\quad$ -- retrieve current data center time
$\quad\quad$**forall** $j \in \{1, \dots, q_i\}$ -- for each fragment choose complying replicas
$\quad\quad$**choose** $C_{i,j} \subseteq ReplicaNodes_{i,j}$ **with** $Complies(C_{i,j}, writePolicy)$
$\quad\quad\quad$**forall** $(d', j') \in C_{i,j}$ $\quad\quad$ -- for each chosen d' and replica
$\quad\quad\quad\quad$**forall** $(\mathbf{k}, \mathbf{v}) \in p$ **with** $h_i(\mathbf{k}) \in range_j$ $\quad$ -- for each p-value
$\quad\quad\quad\quad\quad$**forall** $\mathbf{v}', t$ **with** $p_{i,j,d',j'}(\mathbf{k}) = (\mathbf{v}', t)$ **and** $t < t_{current}$
$\quad\quad\quad\quad\quad$ $p_{i,j,d',j'}(\mathbf{k}) := (\mathbf{v}, t_{current})$ $\quad\quad$ -- update older db value
$\quad\quad\quad\quad\quad$ PROPAGATE($i, j, \mathbf{k}, \mathbf{v}, t_{current}, C_{i,j}$)
$\quad\quad\quad\quad\quad\quad$ -- propagate p-value to non-chosen replicas
$\quad\quad$**if** $clock_{d'} < t_{current}$ **then** ADJUSTCLOCK($d', t_{current}$)
$\quad\quad$ SEND($AckFor(write(p_i, p))$, **to** a)
$\quad\quad$ CONSUME($write(p_i, p)$, **from** a)

PROPAGATE($i, j, \mathbf{k}, \mathbf{v}, t, C$) =
$\quad$**let** $b =$ **new** $(Agent)$
$\quad\quad$ $pgm(b) :=$
$\quad\quad\quad$**forall** $(d', j') \in ReplicaNodes_{i,j} \setminus C$
$\quad\quad\quad\quad$**forall** $\mathbf{v}', t'$ **with** $p_{i,j,d',j'}(\mathbf{k}) = (\mathbf{v}', t')$ **and** $t' < t$
$\quad\quad\quad\quad$ $p_{i,j,d',j'}(\mathbf{k}) := (\mathbf{v}, t)$
$\quad\quad\quad\quad$**if** $clock_{d'} < t_{current}$ **then** ADJUSTCLOCK(d', t)
$\quad\quad$ DELETE($b, Agent$)[1]

A.4.2 CLUSTERDATACENTER$_i$

CLUSTERDATACENTER$_i =$ $\quad\quad\quad\quad\quad$ -- main program of any $d \in \mathcal{D}_i$
$\quad$ DELEGATEEXTERNALREQ$_i$
$\quad$ MANAGEINTERNALREQ$_i$

---

[1] Since in the ground model the propagation is formulated as happening in parallel for all involved replicas, the propagation agent performs only this one step and thus can also kill itself right away.

A.4.2.1 Request Delegation Rules

$\text{DELEGATEEXTERNALREQ}_i =$
  if $Received(req, \textbf{from } a)$ **then**   -- any read/write $request$
    let $t_{current} = clock_{\textbf{self}}$ -- retrieve current data center time
    let $c = \textbf{new } (Agent)$ -- create response collector
      $\text{INITIALIZE}_i(c, (req, a, \textbf{self}))$ -- and initialize it
      $\text{FORWARD}_i(req, c, t_{current})$ -- delegate response
    $\text{CONSUME}(req, \textbf{from } a)$
  where
    $req \in \{read(p_i, \varphi), write(p_i, p)\}$ **forsome** φ, p

Two component rules for request delegation:

$\text{FORWARD}_i(r, c, t) =$ -- delegate response throughout the cluster
  forall $d \in \mathcal{D}_i$
    $\text{SEND}((r, c, t), \textbf{to } d)$

$\text{INITIALIZE}_i(c, (r, usr, d)) =$
  $pgm(c) := \text{MANAGERESPONSECOLLECTION}_i$ -- see below
  $ReadVal_c := \emptyset$ -- initialize set where to collect responses
  forall $d \in \mathcal{D}_i$
    forall $1 \leq j \leq q_i$
      $count_c(j, d) := 0$ -- inspected $Frag_{j,i}$-replicas at d
      $count_c(j) := 0$ -- inspected $Frag_{j,i}$-replicas
  $request_c := r$ -- record user request
  $requestor_c := usr$ -- record user
  $mediator_c := d$ -- record $home(usr)$

A.4.2.2 Internal Request Management Rules

$\text{MANAGEINTERNALREQ}_i =$
  if $Received(req, c, t)$ **then**
    $\text{HANDLELOCALLY}_i(req, c, t)$ -- comes with read/write versions
    $\text{CONSUME}(req, c, t)$

$\text{HANDLELOCALLY}_i(read(p_i, \varphi), c, t) =$
  let $d = \textbf{self} \in \mathcal{D}_i$ -- at the local data center d
  forall $j \in \{1, \ldots, q_i\}$ -- for each fragment
  let $G_{i,j,d} =$ -- inspect replicas at all *Alive* d-nodes
    $\{j' \mid HoldsReplica(j', d, j, i) \textbf{ and } Alive(j', d)\}$
  let $t_{max}(\mathbf{k}) =$ -- to compute their most recent timestamp
    $\max\{t \mid p_{i,j,d,j'}(\mathbf{k}) = (\mathbf{v}', t) \textbf{ forsome } \mathbf{v}', j' \in G_{i,j,d}\}$
  let $\rho_{i,j,d} =$
    $\{(\mathbf{k}, \mathbf{v}, t_{max}(\mathbf{k})) \mid \mathbf{k} \in Frag_{j,i} \uparrow \varphi \textbf{ and } \mathbf{v} \neq null \textbf{ and }$
    $p_{i,j,d,j'}(\mathbf{k}) = (\mathbf{v}, t_{max}(\mathbf{k})) \textbf{ forsome } j' \in G_{i,j,d}\}$
       -- collect at d most recent defined values in j-th fragment
  let $\rho_d =$ -- collect those values from all fragments
    $\bigcup_{j=1}^{q_i} \rho_{i,j,d}$
  let $\mathbf{x}_d =$ -- count inspected replicas
    $(|G_{i,1,d}|, \ldots, |G_{i,q_i,d}|)$
    $\text{SEND}(LocalValFor(read(p_i, \varphi), \rho_d, \mathbf{x}_d), \textbf{to } c)$
       -- send local values to response collector

$\text{HANDLELOCALLY}_i(write(p_i, p), c, t) =$
  let $d = \textbf{self} \in \mathcal{D}_i$ -- at the local data center d
  forall $j \in \{1, \ldots, q_i\}$ -- for each fragment
  let $G_{i,j,d} = \{j' \mid HoldsReplica(j', d, j, i) \textbf{ and } Alive(j', d)\}$
       -- inspect replicas at all *Alive* d-nodes
  forall $j' \in G_{i,j,d}$ -- for each of those replicas
  forall $(\mathbf{k}, \mathbf{v}) \in p$ **with** $\mathbf{k} \in Frag_{j,i}$ -- for each update value in p
    if $p_{i,j,d,j'}(\mathbf{k}) = (\mathbf{v}', t')$ **with** $t' < t$ **forsome** $\mathbf{v}', t'$
      then $p_{i,j,d,j'}(\mathbf{k}) := (\mathbf{v}, t)$ -- update older values to p-value
  if $clock_d < t$ **then** $\text{ADJUSTCLOCK}(d, t)$
  let $\mathbf{x} = (|G_{i,1,d}|, \ldots, |G_{i,q_i,d}|)$ -- count inspected replicas
    $\text{SEND}(LocalAckFor(write(p_i, p), \mathbf{x}), \textbf{to } c)$
       -- send local ack to response collector

A.4.2.3 Response Collection Rules

$\text{MANAGERESPONSECOLLECTION}_i =$
  $\text{COLLECTLOCALREADRESPONSES}_i$
  SENDREADRESPONSE
  $\text{COLLECTLOCALWRITERESPONSES}_i$
  SENDWRITERESPONSE

$\text{COLLECTLOCALREADRESPONSES}_i =$
  if $Received(LocalValFor(read(p_i, \varphi), \rho, \mathbf{x}), \textbf{from } d)$ **then**
    forall k **if thereissome** $(\mathbf{k}, \mathbf{v}, t) \in \rho$ **then**   -- for each key k
      let $(\mathbf{k}, \mathbf{v}, t) \in \rho$ -- with received local value $\mathbf{v}$
        if thereisno $(\mathbf{k}, \mathbf{v}', t') \in ReadVal$ -- if key k new for collection

  then INSERT$((\mathbf{k}, \mathbf{v}, t), ReadVal)$ -- collect received key value

  else let $(\mathbf{k}, \mathbf{v}', t') \in ReadVal$ -- for k-value $\mathbf{v}'$ in collection

   if $t' < t$ **then**   -- with older timestamp

    DELETE$((\mathbf{k}, \mathbf{v}', t'), ReadVal)$ -- replace old value

    INSERT$((\mathbf{k}, \mathbf{v}, t), ReadVal)$ -- by new value

 REFRESHREPLICACOUNT$_i(\mathbf{x}, d)$

 CONSUME$(LocalValFor(read(p_i, \varphi), \rho, \mathbf{x}),$ **from** $d)$

COLLECTLOCALWRITERESPONSES =

 if $Received(LocalAckFor(write(p_i, p)), \mathbf{x}),$ **from** $d)$ **then**

 REFRESHREPLICACOUNT$_i(\mathbf{x}, d)$

 CONSUME$(LocalAckFor(write(p_i, p), \mathbf{x}),$ **from** $d)$

SENDREADRESPONSE =

 if $Sufficient(readPolicy)(count)$ **and** $IsReadReq(request(\mathbf{self}))$ **then**

 let $\rho = \{(\mathbf{k}, \mathbf{v}) \mid (\mathbf{k}, \mathbf{v}, t) \in ReadVal$ **forsome** $t\}$

 SEND$(ValFor(request(\mathbf{self}), \rho),$ -- send the collected values

  from $mediator(\mathbf{self}),$ **to** $requestor(\mathbf{self}))$

 DELETE$(\mathbf{self}, Agent)$ -- collector kills itself

SENDWRITERESPONSE =

 if $Sufficient(writePolicy)(count)$ **and** $IsWriteReq(request(\mathbf{self}))$ **then**

 SEND$(AckFor(request(\mathbf{self})),$

  from $mediator(\mathbf{self}),$ **to** $requestor(\mathbf{self}))$

 DELETE$(\mathbf{self}, Agent)$

Auxiliary rule for replica count update:

REFRESHREPLICACOUNT$_i(\mathbf{x}, d) =$

 let $(x_1, \ldots, x_{q_i}) = \mathbf{x}$

  forall $j \in \{1, \ldots, q_i\}$

   $count(j, d) := count(j, d) + x_j$

   $count(j) := count(j) + x_j$

References

1. Abrial, J.R.: The B-Book. Cambridge University Press, Cambridge (1996) 10, 25, 164
2. Abrial, J.R.: Modeling in Event-B: System and Software Engineering. Cambridge University Press, Cambridge (2010) 10, 14, 36, 164
3. Abrial, J.R., Börger, E., Langmaack, H. (eds.): Methods for Semantics and Specification, *Dagstuhl Seminar Report*, vol. 117. Schloss Dagstuhl - Leibniz-Zentrum für Informatik (1995) 239
4. Abrial, J.R., Börger, E., Langmaack, H. (eds.): Formal Methods for Industrial Applications. Specifying and Programming the Steam Boiler Control, *LNCS*, vol. 1165. Springer (1996) 239
5. Abrial, J.R., Glässer, U. (eds.): Rigorous Methods for Software Construction and Analysis (Börger Festschrift), *LNCS*, vol. 5115. Springer (2009) VI
6. Altenhofen, M., Börger, E.: Concurrent Abstract State Machines and ^+CAL Programs. In: A. Corradini, U. Montanari (eds.) Proc. of 19th International Workshop on Recent Trends in Algebraic Development Techniques (WADT 2008), *LNCS*, vol. 5486, pp. 1–17. Springer (2009) 174, 178, 179, 180
7. Altenhofen, M., Börger, E., Lemcke, J.: A High-Level Specification for Mediators (Virtual Providers). In: C. Bussler, A. Haller (eds.) Business Process Management Workshops: BPM 2005 International Workshops BPI, BPD, ENEI, BPRM, WSCOBPM, BPS, *LNCS*, vol. 3812, pp. 116–129. Springer (2006) 183, 187, 188
8. Altenhofen, M., Börger, E., Lemcke, J.: System and a method for mediating within a network. US Patent US7984188 B2 (2011). https://www.google.de/patents/US7984188. See also DE602005008557D1, EP1715653A1, EP1715653B1, US20060259605 182
9. Altenhofen, M., Farahbod, R.: Bârun: A Scripting Language for CoreASM. In: M. Frappier, U. Glässer, S. Khurshid, R. Laleau, S. Reeves (eds.) Proc. of 2nd International ABZ Conference ASM, Alloy, B and Z (ABZ 2010), *Theoretical Computer Science and General Issues*, vol. 5977, pp. 47–60. Springer (2010) 294
10. Altenhofen, M., Friesen, A., Lemcke, J., Börger, E.: A High-Level Specification for Virtual Providers. Int. J. Business Process Integration and Management **1**(4), 267–278 (2006) 182
11. Ameur, Y.A., Schewe, K.D. (eds.): Proc. of 4th International ABZ Conference ASM, Alloy, B, TLA, VDM, and Z (ABZ 2014), *LNCS*, vol. 8477. Springer (2014) VI, 239
12. Angluin, D., Aspnes, J., Diamadi, Z., Fischer, M.J., Peralta, R.: Computation in networks of passively mobile finite-state sensors. Distributed Computing **18**(4), 235–253 (2006) 72

13. Arcaini, P., Bonfanti, S., Dausend, M., Gargantini, A., Mashkoor, A., Raschke, A., Riccobene, E., Scandurra, P., Stegmaier, M.: Unified Syntax for Abstract State Machines. In: M. Butler, K.D. Schewe, A. Mashkoor, M. Biro (eds.) Proc. of 5th International ABZ Conference ASM, Alloy, B, TLA, VDM, Z (ABZ 2016), *LNCS*, vol. 9675, pp. 231–236. Springer (2016) 295

14. Arcaini, P., Bonfanti, S., Gargantini, A., Riccobene, E.: Visual Notation and Patterns for Abstract State Machines. In: P. Milazzo, D. Varró, M. Wimmer (eds.) Proc. of Conference on Software Technologies: Applications and Foundations (STAF 2016), Collocated Workshops: DataMod, GCM, HOFM, MELO, SEMS, VeryComp, *LNCS*, vol. 9946, pp. 163–178. Springer (2016) 297

15. Arcaini, P., Gargantini, A., Riccobene, E.: Modeling and Analyzing Using ASMs: The Landing Gear System Case Study. In: F. Boniol, V. Wiels, Y.A. Ameur, K.D. Schewe (eds.) ABZ 2014: The Landing Gear Case Study, *Communications in Computer and Information Science*, vol. 433. Springer (Cham) (2014) 239

16. The Asmeta website. `http://asmeta.sourceforge.net` (since 2006). Consulted 01/08/2018 10, 113, 293

17. Back, R., Kurki-Suoni, R.: Decentralization of Process Nets with Centralized Control. Tech. Rep. Ser. A No. 58, Department of Computer Science at Abo Akademi, Abo (1988) 9

18. Barnett, M., Campbell, C., Schulte, W., Veanes, M.: Specification, Simulation and Testing of COM Components using Abstract State Machines. In: R. Moreno-Díaz, A. Quesada-Arencibia (eds.) Formal Methods and Tools for Computer Science (Local Proc. of Eurocast 2001), pp. 266–270 (2001) 293

19. Barnett, M., Grieskamp, W., Schulte, W., Tillmann, N., Veanes, M.: Validating use-cases with the AsmL test tool. In: Proc. of 3rd International Conference on Quality Software (QSIC'03), pp. 238–246. IEEE Computer Society (2003) 294

20. Barnett, M., Schulte, W.: Runtime Verification of .NET Contracts. J. Systems and Software **65**(3), 199–208 (2003) 293

21. Barros, A., Börger, E.: A Compositional Framework for Service Interaction Patterns and Communication Flows. In: K.K. Lau, R. Banach (eds.) Proc. of 7th International Conference on Formal Engineering Methods (ICFEM 2005), *LNCS*, vol. 3785, pp. 5–35. Springer (2005) 150, 151, 157, 159

22. Batory, D., Börger, E.: Feature Modularized Theorems in Software Product Lines. In: A. Prinz (ed.) Proc. of 14th International Worskhop on Abstract State Machines (ASM'2007) (2007) 63

23. Batory, D., Börger, E.: Modularizing Theorems for Software Product Lines: The Jbook Case Study. J. Universal Computer Science **14**(12), 2059–2082 (2008) 10, 141

24. Beauquier, D., Börger, E., Slissenko, A. (eds.): Proc. of the 12th International on Workshop on Abstract State Machines (ASM 2005) (2005) VI

25. Beierle, C., Börger, E., Durdanović, I., Glässer, U., Riccobene, E.: Refining Abstract Machine Specifications of the Steam Boiler Control to Well Documented Executable Code. In: J.R. Abrial, E. Börger, H. Langmaack (eds.) Formal Methods for Industrial Applications. Specifying and Programming the Steam-Boiler Control, no. 1165 in LNCS, pp. 62–78. Springer (1996) 239

26. Beierle, C., Finthammer, M., Potyka, N., Varghese, J., Kern-Isberner, G.: A framework for versatile knowledge and belief management operations in a probabilistic conditional logic. IFCoLog Journal of Logics and their Applications **4**(7) (2017) 9

27. Beierle, C., Kern-Isberner, G.: Modeling conditional knowledge discovery and belief revision by Abstract State Machines. In: E. Börger, A. Gargantini, E. Riccobene (eds.) Proc. of 10th International Workshop on Abstract State Machines: Advances in Theory and Practice (ASM 2003), *LNCS*, vol. 2589, pp. 186–203. Springer (2003) 9

28. Beierle, C., Kern-Isberner, G.: An ASM refinement and implementation of the Condor system using ordinal conditional functions. In: A. Prinz (ed.) Proc. of 14th International Worskhop on Abstract State Machines (ASM'2007) (2007) 9

29. Beierle, C., Kern-Isberner, G.: A high-level implementation of a system for automated reasoning with default rules (system description). In: A. Armando, P. Baumgartner, G. Dowek (eds.) Proc. of 4th International Joint Conference on Automated Reasoning (IJCAR-2008), *LNCS*, vol. 5195, pp. 147–153. Springer (2008) 9

30. Beierle, C., Kern-Isberner, G.: A verified AsmL implementation of belief revision. In: E. Börger, M. Butler, J.P. Bowen, P. Boca (eds.) Proc. of 1st International ABZ Conference ASM, B and Z (ABZ 2008), *LNCS*, vol. 5238, pp. 98–111. Springer (2008) 9

31. Beierle, C., Kern-Isberner, G.: A conceptual agent model based on a uniform approach to various belief operations. In: B. Mertsching, M. Hund, Z. Aziz (eds.) Proc. of 32nd Annual German Conference on AI: Advances in Artificial Intelligence, *Lecture Notes in Artificial Intelligence*, vol. 5803, pp. 273–280. Springer (2009) 9

32. Böhm, C., Jacopini, G.: Flow diagrams, Turing Machines, and Languages with only two Formation Rules. Commun. ACM **9**(5), 366–371 (1966) 172

33. Boniol, F., Wiels, V., Y.Ait-Ameur, Schewe, K.D. (eds.): Proc. of ABZ 2014: The Landing Gear Case Study, Case Study Track, held at the 4th International ABZ Conference ASM, Alloy, B, TLA, VDM, and Z, *Communications in Computer and Information Science*, vol. 433. Springer (2014) 239

34. Bordeleau, F., Liebel, G., Raschke, A., Stieglbauer, G., Tichy, M.: Challenges and Research Directions for Successfully Applying MBE Tools in Practice. In: Proc. of MODELS 2017 Satellite Events: MDETOOLS 2017 (2017) 318

35. Borek, M., Katkalov, K., Moebius, N., Reif, W., Schellhorn, G., Stenzel, K.: Integrating a Model-Driven Approach and Formal Verification for the Development of Secure Service Applications. In: B. Thalheim, K.D. Schewe, A. Prinz, B. Buchberger (eds.) Correct Software in Web Applications and Web Services, Texts and Monographs in Symbolic Computation, pp. 44–81. Springer (2015) 87

36. Börger, E.: A Logical Operational Semantics for Full Prolog. Part I: Selection Core and Control. In: E. Börger, H. Kleine Büning, M.M. Richter, W. Schönfeld (eds.) Proc. of 3rd Workshop on Computer Science Logic (CSL'89), *LNCS*, vol. 440, pp. 36–64. Springer (1990) 293

37. Börger, E.: A Logical Operational Semantics of Full Prolog. Part II: Built-in Predicates for Database Manipulation. In: B. Rovan (ed.) Mathematical Foundations of Computer Science, *LNCS*, vol. 452, pp. 1–14. Springer (1990) 293

38. Börger, E.: The Origins and the Development of the ASM Method for High-Level System Design and Analysis. J. Universal Computer Science **8**(1), 2–74 (2002) 14

39. Börger, E.: The ASM Refinement Method. Formal Aspects of Computing **15**, 237–257 (2003) 11

40. Börger, E.: Modeling Workflow Patterns from First Principles. In: C. Parent, K.D. Schewe, V. Storey, B. Thalheim (eds.) Proc. of 26th International Conference on Conceptual Modeling (ER 2007), *LNCS*, vol. 4801, pp. 1–20. Springer (2007) 189

41. Börger, E.: The Abstract State Machines method for high-level system design and analysis. In: P. Boca, J. Bowen, J. Siddiqi (eds.) Formal Methods: State of the Art and New Directions, pp. 79–116. Springer (2010) 17, 20, 33, 42, 43, 45, 52, 53

42. Börger, E.: Approaches to Modeling Business Processes. A Critical Analysis of BPMN, Workflow Patterns and YAWL. J. Software and Systems Modeling **11**(3), 305–318 (2012) 189, 205

43. Börger, E.: The Abstract State Machines Method for Modular Design and Analysis of Programming Languages. J. Logic and Computation **27**(2), 417–439 (2014) VI, 14, 207

44. Börger, E.: Modeling distributed algorithms by Abstract State Machines compared to Petri Nets. In: M. Butler, K.D. Schewe, A. Mashkoor, M. Biro (eds.) Proc. of

5th International ABZ Conference ASM, Alloy, B, TLA, VDM, Z (ABZ 2016), *LNCS*, vol. 9675, pp. 3–34. Springer (2016) 125

45. Börger, E., Bolognesi, T.: Remarks on Turbo ASMs for Computing Functional Equations and Recursion Schemes. In: E. Börger, A. Gargantini, E. Riccobene (eds.) Proc. of 10th International Workshop on Abstract State Machines: Advances in Theory and Practice (ASM 2003), *LNCS*, vol. 2589, pp. 218–228. Springer (2003) 171

46. Börger, E., Butler, M., Bowen, J.P., Boca, P. (eds.): Proc. of 1st International ABZ Conference ASM, B and Z (ABZ 2008), *LNCS*, vol. 5238. Springer (2008) VI

47. Börger, E., Cisternino, A., Gervasi, V.: Ambient Abstract State Machines with Applications. J. Computer and System Sciences **78**(3), 939–959 (2012) 135, 137, 140

48. Börger, E., Cisternino, A., Gervasi, V.: Modeling Web Applications Infrastructure with ASMs. Science of Computer Programming **94**(2), 69–92 (2014) 181, 182

49. Börger, E., Craig, I.: Modeling an Operating System Kernel. In: V. Diekert, K. Weicker, N. Weicker (eds.) Informatik als Dialog zwischen Theorie und Anwendung, pp. 199–216. Vieweg+Teubner (2009) 162, 168

50. Börger, E., Del Castillo, G.: A formal method for provably correct composition of a real-life processor out of basic components (The APE100 Reverse Engineering Study). In: B. Werner (ed.) Proc. of 1st IEEE International Conference on Engineering of Complex Computer Systems (ICECCS'95), pp. 145–148. IEEE (1995) 239

51. Börger, E., Durdanović, I.: Correctness of compiling Occam to Transputer code. Computer Journal **39**(1), 52–92 (1996) 10, 204, 239

52. Börger, E., Durdanović, I., Rosenzweig, D.: Occam: Specification and Compiler Correctness. Part I: Simple Mathematical Interpreters. In: U. Montanari, E.R. Olderog (eds.) Proc. of IFIP Working Conference on Programming Concepts, Methods and Calculi (PROCOMET'94), pp. 489–508. North-Holland (1994) 204, 260

53. Börger, E., Fleischmann, A.: Abstract State Machine Nets. Closing the Gap between Business Process Models and their Implementation. In: J. Ehlers, B. Thalheim (eds.) Proc. of 7th International Conference on Subject-Oriented Business Process Management (S-BPM One 2015), S-BPM ONE '15, pp. 1:1–1:10. ACM (2015) 190, 202

54. Börger, E., Fruja, G., Gervasi, V., Stärk, R.: A high-level modular definition of the semantics of C#. Theoretical Computer Science **336**(2–3), 235–284 (2005) 4, 63, 135, 207, 318

55. Börger, E., Gargantini, A., Riccobene, E. (eds.): Proc. of 10th International Workshop on Abstract State Machines: Advances in Theory and Practice (ASM 2003), *LNCS*, vol. 2589. Springer (2003) VI

56. Börger, E., Gargantini, A., Riccobene, E.: Abstract State Machines. A Method for System Specification and Analysis. In: M. Frappier, H. Habrias (eds.) Software Specification Methods: An Overview Using a Case Study, pp. 103–119. HERMES Sc. Publ. (2006) 205, 239

57. Börger, E., Glässer, U., Müller, W.: The Semantics of Behavioral VHDL'93 Descriptions. In: J. Mermet (ed.) Proc. of European Design Automation Conference (EURO-DAC'94) with EURO-VHDL'94, pp. 500–505. IEEE Computer Society Press (1994) 4

58. Börger, E., Glässer, U., Müller, W.: Formal Definition of an Abstract VHDL'93 Simulator by EA-Machines. In: C. Delgado Kloos, P.T. Breuer (eds.) Formal Semantics for VHDL, pp. 107–139. Springer (1995) 4

59. Börger, E., Gotzhein, R.: The Light Control Case Study. J. Universal Computer Science **6**(7), 580–585 (2000) 239

60. Börger, E., Hörger, B., Parnas, D.L., Rombach, D. (eds.): Requirements Capture, Documentation, and Validation, *Dagstuhl Seminar Report*, vol. 241. Schloss Dagstuhl - Leibniz-Zentrum für Informatik (1999) 239

61. Börger, E., Joannou, P., Parnas, D.L. (eds.): Practical Methods for Code Documentation and Inspection, *Dagstuhl Seminar Report*, vol. 178. Schloss Dagstuhl - Leibniz-Zentrum für Informatik (1997) 239

62. Börger, E., Leuschel, M.: A compact encoding of sequential ASMs in Event-B. In: M. Butler, K.D. Schewe, A. Mashkoor, M. Biro (eds.) Proc. of 5th International ABZ Conference ASM, Alloy, B, TLA, VDM, Z (ABZ 2016), *LNCS*, vol. 9675, pp. 119–134. Springer (2016) 10

63. Börger, E., Mazzanti, S.: A Practical Method for Rigorously Controllable Hardware Design. In: J.P. Bowen, M.B. Hinchey, D. Till (eds.) ZUM'97: The Z Formal Specification Notation, *LNCS*, vol. 1212, pp. 151–187. Springer (1997) 239

64. Börger, E., Mearelli, L.: Integrating ASMs into the Software Development Life Cycle. J. Universal Computer Science **3**(5), 603–665 (1997) 239, 297

65. Börger, E., Päppinghaus, P., Schmid, J.: Report on a Practical Application of ASMs in Software Design. In: Y. Gurevich, P. Kutter, M. Odersky, L. Thiele (eds.) Proc. of International Workshop on Abstract State Machines: Theory and Applications (ASM 2000), *LNCS*, vol. 1912, pp. 361–366. Springer (2000) 164, 293

66. Börger, E., Prinz, A.: Special ASM Issue with Selected Papers from ASM 2007. J. Universal Computer Science **14**(12) (2008) VI

67. Börger, E., Riccobene, E., Schmid, J.: Capturing Requirements by Abstract State Machines: The Light Control Case Study. J. Universal Computer Science **6**(7), 597–620 (2000) 239, 293

68. Börger, E., Rosenzweig, D.: A Mathematical Definition of Full Prolog. Science of Computer Programming **24**, 249–286 (1995) 4, 31

69. Börger, E., Rosenzweig, D.: The WAM – Definition and Compiler Correctness. In: C. Beierle, L. Plümer (eds.) Logic Programming: Formal Methods and Practical Applications, *Studies in Computer Science and Artificial Intelligence*, vol. 11, chap. 2, pp. 20–90. North-Holland (1995) 4, 10, 31

70. Börger, E., Schewe, K.D.: Concurrent Abstract State Machines. Acta Informatica **53**(5), 469–492 (2016) 73, 132, 225, 272

71. Börger, E., Schewe, K.D.: Communication in Abstract State Machines. J. Universal Computer Science **23**(2), 129–145 (2017) 115, 126

72. Börger, E., Schewe, K.D., Wang, Q.: Serialisable Multi-Level Transaction Control:A Specification and Verification. Science of Computer Programming **131**, 42–85 (2016) 82, 194

73. Börger, E., Schmid, J.: Composition and Submachine Concepts for Sequential ASMs. In: P. Clote, H. Schwichtenberg (eds.) Proc. of 14th International Workshop on Computer Science Logic (CSL 2000), *LNCS*, vol. 1862, pp. 41–60. Springer (2000) 171

74. Börger, E., Slissenko, A. (eds.): Special ASM Issue of Fundamenta Informaticae with Selected Papers from ASM 2005. IOS Press (Amsterdam) (2007) VI

75. Börger, E., Sörensen, O.: BPMN Core Modeling Concepts: Inheritance-Based Execution Semantics. In: D. Embley, B. Thalheim (eds.) Handbook of Conceptual Modelling. Theory, Practice, and Research Challenges, pp. 287–332. Springer (2011) 141

76. Börger, E., Stärk, R.F.: Abstract State Machines. A Method for High-Level System Design and Analysis. Springer (2003) VI, VIII, XI, 13, 25, 33, 75, 90, 91, 120, 148, 154, 166, 172, 243, 245, 247, 248, 249, 251, 252, 254, 293, 297

77. Börger, E., Stärk, R.F.: Exploiting Abstraction for Specification Reuse. The Java/C# Case Study. In: F.S. de Boer, M.M. Bonsangue, S. Graf, W.P. de Roever (eds.) Formal Methods for Components and Objects: Second International Symposium (FMCO 2003), *LNCS*, vol. 3188, pp. 42–76. Springer (2004) 318

78. Börger, E., Thalheim, B.: A Method for Verifiable and Validatable Business Process Modeling. In: E. Börger, A. Cisternino (eds.) Advances in Software Engineering, *LNCS*, vol. 5316, pp. 59–115. Springer (2008) 205

79. Börger, E., Zenzaro, S.: Business Process Modeling for Reuse and Change via Component-Based Decomposition and ASM Refinement. In: J. Ehlers, B. Thalheim (eds.) Proc. of 7th International Conference on Subject-Oriented Business Process Management (S-BPM One 2015), S-BPM One. ACM (2015) 65, 66, 68, 70, 71, 75, 83, 84, 86

80. Bosa, K.: Formal modeling of mobile computing systems based on ambient Abstract State Machines. In: K.D. Schewe, B. Thalheim (eds.) Proc. of 5th International Workshop Semantics in Data and Knowledge Bases (SDKB 2011), *LNCS*, vol. 7693, pp. 18–49. Springer (2013) 135

81. Burgard, W., Cremers, A.B., Fox, D., Heidelbach, M., Kappel, A.M., Lüttringhaus-Kappel, S.: Knowledge-enhanced CO-monitoring in Coal Mines. In: Proc. of International Conference on Industrial and Engineering Applications of Artificial Intelligence and Expert Systems (IEA-AIE), pp. 511–521 (1996) 293

82. Butler, M., Schewe, K.D., Mashkoor, A., Biro, M. (eds.): Proc. of 5th International ABZ Conference ASM, Alloy, B, TLA, VDM, and Z (ABZ 2016), *LNCS*, vol. 9675. Springer (2016) VI

83. Cardelli, L., Gordon, A.: Mobile Ambients. Theoretical Computer Science **240**(1), 177–213 (2000) 135

84. The CoreASM Project. `http://www.coreasm.org` and `https://github.com/coreasm/` (since 2005). Consulted 01/08/2018 10, 96, 103, 113, 293

85. Craig, I., Börger, E.: Synchronous Message Passing and Semaphores: An Equivalence Proof. In: M. Frappier, U. Glässer, S. Khurshid, R. Laleau, S. Reeves (eds.) Proc. of 2nd International ABZ Conference ASM, Alloy, B and Z (ABZ 2010), *LNCS*, vol. 5977, pp. 20–33. Springer (2010) 150, 159, 164

86. da Cruz, F.: Kermit: A File Transfer Protocol. Digital Press (1986). See also the Kermit Web site `http://www.columbia.edu/kermit` 4

87. Dausend, M., Stegmaier, M., Raschke, A.: Debugging Abstract State Machine Specifications: An Extension of CoreASM. In: F. Mazzatini, G. Trentanni (eds.) Proc. of Posters & Tool demos Session, held at 9th International Conference on Integrated Formal Methods and 3rd International ABZ Conference ASM, Alloy, B, VDM, Z (iFM 2012 & ABZ 2012), pp. 21–25 (2012) 286, 292

88. Del Castillo, G.: The ASM Workbench. A Tool Environment for Computer-Aided Analysis and Validation of Abstract State Machine Models. Ph.D. thesis, Universität Paderborn (2001) 293

89. Del Castillo, G., Winter, K.: Model Checking Support for the ASM High-Level Language. In: S. Graf, M. Schwartzbach (eds.) Proc. of the 6th International Conference on Tools and Algorithms for the Construction and Analysis of Systems (TACAS 2000), *LNCS*, vol. 1785, pp. 331–346. Springer (2000) 293

90. Denvir, T., Oliveira, J., Plat, N.: The Cash-Point (ATM) 'Problem'. Formal Aspects of Computing **12**(4), 211–215 (2000) 64

91. Derrick, J., Fitzgerald, J.S., Gnesi, S., Khurshid, S., Leuschel, M., Reeves, S., Riccobene, E. (eds.): Proc. of 3rd International ABZ Conference ASM, Alloy, B, VDM and Z (ABZ 2012), *LNCS*, vol. 7316. Springer, Pisa (Italy) (2012) VI

92. Dijkstra, E.W.: A note on two problems in connexion with graphs. Numerische Mathematik **1**(1), 269–271 (1959) 75

93. Dijkstra, E.W.: Guarded commands, non-determinacy and formal derivation of programs. Commun. ACM **18**(8), 453–457 (1975). Also available as EWD 472 9

94. Dijkstra, E.W.: Shmuel Safra's version of termination detection. In: M. Broy, R. Steinbrüggen (eds.) Proc. of NATO Advanced Study Institute on Calculational System Design, pp. 297–301 (1999) 106, 109, 111, 114

95. Dijkstra, E.W., J.Feijen, W.H., van Gasteren, A.J.M.: Derivation of a termination detection algorithm for distributed computations. Information Processing Letters **16**(5), 217–219 (1983). Known also as EWD 840 103, 106, 108, 109, 111, 112, 113, 115

96. Dijkstra, E.W., Scholten, C.S.: Termination detection for diffusing computations. Information Processing Letters **11**(1), 1–4 (1980). Known also as EWD 687a 121, 122, 124

97. Dmitirev, S.: Language Oriented Programming: The Next Programming Paradigm. http://www.jetbrains.com (2004) 12

98. Dold, A.: A Formal Representation of Abstract State Machines Using PVS. Verifix Technical Report Ulm/6.2, Universität Ulm (1998) 10, 293

99. Dold, A., Gaul, T., Zimmermann, W.: Mechanized Verification of Compiler Back-Ends. In: T. Margaria, B. Steffen (eds.) Proc. of the International Workshop on Software Tools for Technology Transfer (STTT'98) (1998) 293

100. Dumas, M., Rosa, M.L., Mendling, J., Reijers, H.: Fundamentals of Business Process Management, chap. Introduction to Business Process Management, pp. 1–31. Springer (2013) 205

101. E. Börger O. Sörensen, B.T.: On defining the behavior of OR-joins in business process models. J. Universal Computer Science **15**(1), 3–32 (2009) 203

102. Eschbach, R.: A Termination Detection Algorithm: Specification and Verification. In: J. Wing, J.C.P. Woodcock, J. Davies (eds.) Proc. of International Conference on Formal Methods in the Development of Computing Systems (FM'99), Vol. II, *LNCS*, vol. 1709, pp. 1720–1737. Springer (1999) 106, 109, 111, 113, 114

103. Eschbach, R., Glässer, U., Gotzhein, R., v. Löwis, M., Prinz, A.: Formal Definition of SDL-2000 – Compiling and Running SDL Specifications as ASM Models. J. Universal Computer Science **7**(11), 1025–1050 (2001) 4, 293, 297

104. Farahbod, R.: CoreASM: an extensible modeling framework & tool environment for high-level design and analysis of distributed systems. Ph.D. thesis, Simon Fraser University (2009) 252, 253, 272, 285

105. Farahbod, R.: Design and Specification of the CoreASM Execution Engine and Plugins. https://github.com/CoreASM/coreasm.core/wiki/Documentation (2010) 252, 253, 254, 255, 256, 259, 263, 265, 274, 284

106. Farahbod, R., Dausend, M.: CoreASM Language User Manual. https://github.com/CoreASM/coreasm.core/wiki/Documentation (2016) 252, 278

107. Farahbod, R., Gervasi, V., Glässer, U.: CoreASM: An Extensible ASM Execution Engine. Fundamenta Informaticae XXI **77**(1-2), 71–103 (2007) 253

108. Fehnker, A., van Glabbeek, R., Hoefner, P., McIver, A., Portmann, M., Tan, W.L.: A process algebra for wireless mesh networks used for modelling, verifying and analysing AODV. Tech. Rep. 5513, NICTA, Brisbane (Australia) (2013) 208

109. Fleischmann, A., Schmidt, W., Stary, C., Obermeier, S., Börger, E.: Subject-Oriented Business Process Management. Springer (2012). http://www.springer.com/978-3-642-32391-1 (Open Access Book) 90, 117, 157, 182, 194, 196, 204

110. Fleischmann, A., Stary, C.: Whom to talk to? A stakeholder perspective on business process development. Universal Access in the Information Society **11**(2), 125–150 (2012) 90, 181

111. Foundation, A.S.: Apache Cassandra 2.0 – Documentation. http://cassandra.apache.org/ (2016). Consulted 01/08/2018 224, 225

112. Foundations of Software Engineering Group, Microsoft Research: AsmL. Web pages at https://www.microsoft.com/en-us/research/project/asml-abstract-state-machine-language/, consulted 01/08/2018 (2001) 293

113. Franklin, R.: On an Improved Algorithm for Decentralized Extrema Finding in Circular Configurations of Processors. Commun. ACM **25**(5), 336–337 (1982) 96, 100

114. Frappier, M., Glässer, U., Khurshid, S., Laleau, R., Reeves, S. (eds.): Proc. of 2nd International ABZ Conference ASM, Alloy, B, and Z (ABZ 2010), *LNCS*, vol. 5977. Springer (2010) VI

115. Frappier, M., Habrias, H. (eds.): Software Specification Methods: An Overview Using a Case Study. ISTE (2006) 205, 239

116. Friesen, A., Börger, E.: A High-Level Specification for Semantic Web Service Discovery Services. In: O. Pastor, O.Corcho, P. Sampaio, G.J. Houben, D. Schwabe, A. Wombacher (eds.) Workshop Proc. of the 6th International Conference on Web Engeneering (ICWE'06). Joint Workshop on Web Services Modeling and Implementation using Sound Web Engineering Practices and Methods, Architectures and Technologies for e-Service Engineering (SMIWEP-MATeS'06). ACM (2006) 182

117. Fruja, N.G.: The correctness of the definite assignment analysis in C#. Journal of Object Technology **3**(9), 29–52 (2004) 135

118. Fruja, N.G.: Type Safety of C# and .NET CLR. Ph.D. thesis, ETH Zürich (2006) 4, 207

119. Fruja, N.G.: Towards proving type safety of .NET CIL. Science of Computer Programming **72**(3), 176–219 (2008) 135

120. Fruja, N.G., Börger, E.: Modeling the .NET CLR Exception Handling Mechanism for a Mathematical Analysis. J. of Object Technology **5**(3), 5–34 (2006) 135

121. Fruja, N.G., Stärk, R.F.: The hidden computation steps of Turbo Abstract State Machines. In: E. Börger, A. Gargantini, E. Riccobene (eds.) Proc. of 10th International Workshop on Abstract State Machines: Advances in Theory and Practice (ASM 2003), *LNCS*, vol. 2589, pp. 244–262. Springer (2003) 172

122. Gamma, E., Helm, R., Johnson, R., Vlissides, J.: Design Patterns. Addison-Wesley (1994) 137, 145, 146, 147, 148, 149

123. Gardner, M.: Mathematical games. Scientific American **223**, 120–123 (1970) 63

124. Gargantini, A., Riccobene, E.: Encoding Abstract State Machines in PVS. In: Y. Gurevich, P. Kutter, M. Odersky, L. Thiele (eds.) Proc. of International Workshop on Abstract State Machines: Theory and Applications (ASM 2000), *LNCS*, vol. 1912, pp. 303–322. Springer (2000) 10, 239

125. Gervasi, V.: An ASM Model of Concurrency in a Web Browser. In: J.D. et al. (ed.) Proc. of 3rd International ABZ Conference ASM, Alloy, B, VDM, and Z (ABZ 2012), *LNCS*, vol. 7316, pp. 79–93. Springer (2012) 181

126. Gervasi, V., Riccobene, E.: From English to ASM: On the process of deriving a formal specification from a natural language one. Dagstuhl Report **3**(9), 85–90 (2013) 103, 111, 112, 113

127. Ghezzi, G., Jazayeri, M., Mandrioli, D.: Fundamentals of Software Engineering. Prentice-Hall (1991) 33

128. Giese, M., Kempe, D., Schönegge, A.: KIV zur Verifikation von ASM-Spezifikationen am Beispiel der DLX-Pipelining Architektur. Tech. Rep. 16/97, Universität Karlsruhe, Fakultät für Informatik (1997) 10, 239

129. Gjøsæter, T., Prinz, A., Scheidgen, M.: Meta-model or Grammar? Methods and Tools for the Formal Definition of Languages. In: Nordic Workshop on Model Driven Engineering (NW-MoDE 2008), pp. 67–82. University of Iceland Press (2008) 298

130. Glässer, U., Gurevich, Y., Veanes, M.: Abstract communication model for distributed systems. IEEE Transactions on Software Engineering **30**(7), 458–472 (2004) 158

131. Goerigk, W., Dold, A., Gaul, T., Goos, G., Heberle, A., von Henke, F.W., Hoffmann, U., Langmaack, H., Pfeifer, H., Ruess, H., Zimmermann, W.: Compiler Correctness and Implementation Verification: The Verifix Approach. In: P. Fritzson (ed.) Proceedings of the Poster Session of International Conference on Compiler Construction (CC '96), pp. 65 – 73. IDA Technical Report LiTH-IDA-R-96-12, Linköping (1996) 293

132. Goncalves, R.C., Batory, D., Sobral, J.L., Riché, T.L.: From Software Extensions to Product Lines of Dataflow Programs. Software & Systems Modeling **16**(4), 929–947 (2017) 13

133. González-Pérez, C.A.: Metamodelling for Software Engineering. J. Wiley (2008) 298

134. Granger, C.: Coding is not the new literacy. http://www.chris-granger.com/2015/01/26/coding-is-not-the-new-literacy/ (2015). Consulted 01/08/2018 VII, 7

135. Grune, D., Reeuwijk, K.v., Bal, H., Jacobs, C., Langendoen, K.: Modern Compiler Design, 2nd edn. Springer (2012) 264, 265

136. Gurevich, Y.: Evolving algebras 1993: Lipari Guide. In: E. Börger (ed.) Specification and Validation Methods, pp. 9–36. Oxford University Press (1995) 132

137. Gurevich, Y., Tillmann, N.: Partial Updates: Exploration. J. Universal Computer Science 7(11), 918–952 (2001) 260

138. Gurevich, Y., Tillmann, N.: Partial Updates. Theoretical Computer Science 336(2-3), 311–342 (2005) 260

139. Haneberg, D., Grandy, H., Reif, W., Schellhorn, G.: Verifying Smart Card Applications: An ASM Approach. In: Proc. of International Conference on Integrated Formal Methods (iFM 2007), LNCS, vol. 4591. Springer (2007) 91, 293

140. Haneberg, D., Junker, M., Schellhorn, G., Reif, W., Ernst, G.: Simulating a Flash File System with CoreASM and Eclipse. In: H.U. Hei, P. Pepper, H. Schlingloff, J. Schneider (eds.) INFORMATIK 2011. Informatik schafft Communities, LNI, vol. 192. Bonner Köllen Verlag (2011) 91, 293

141. Haneberg, D., Moebius, N., Reif, W., Schellhorn, G., Stenzel, K.: Mondex: Engineering a Provable Secure Electronic Purse. International Journal of Software and Informatics 5(1), 159–184 (2011) 10, 91

142. Haneberg, D., Schellhorn, G., Grandy, H., Reif, W.: Verification of Mondex electronic purses with KIV: from transactions to a security protocol. Formal Aspects of Computing 20(1), 41–59 (2008) 10, 91

143. Heath, F., Boaz, D., Gupta, M., Vaculín, R., Sun, Y., Hull, R., Limonad, L.: Barcelona: A design and runtime environment for declarative artifact-centric BPM. In: S. Basu, C. Pautasso, L. Zhang, X. Fu (eds.) Proc. of 11th International Conference on Service-Oriented Computing (ICSOC 2013), LNCS, vol. 8274, pp. 705–709 (2013) 193

144. Hohpe, G., Woolf, B.: Enterprise Integration Patterns: Designing, Building, and Deploying Messaging Solutions. Addison-Wesley (2003) 182

145. Hommel, G.: Vergleich verschiedener Spezifikationsverfahren am Beispiel einer Paketverteilanlage. Tech. Rep. KfK-PDV 186, Kernforschungszentrum Karlsruhe (1980) 52, 55, 56, 59, 61, 62

146. Huggins, J.: Kermit: Specification and Verification. In: E. Börger (ed.) Specification and Validation Methods, pp. 247–293. Oxford University Press (1995) 4

147. Huggins, J., Van Campenhout, D.: Specification and Verification of Pipelining in the ARM2 RISC Microprocessor. ACM Trans. Des. Autom. of Electron. Syst. 3(4), 563–580 (1998) 239

148. Hull, R., Damaggio, E., Fournier, F., Gupta, M., Heath, F., Hobson, S., Linehan, M., Maradugu, S., Nigam, A., Sukaviriya, P., Vaculin, R.: Introducing the Guard-Stage-Milestone Approach for Specifying Business Entity Lifecycles. In: M. Bravetti, T. Bultan (eds.) Proc. of 7th International Workshop on Web Services and Formal Methods (WS-FM 2010), LNCS, vol. 6551, pp. 1–24. Springer (2011) 90, 181, 193

149. Hutton, G., Meijer, E.: Monadic Parsing in Haskell. Journal of Functional Programming 8(4), 437–444 (1998) 265

150. IEEE: IEEE Standard VHDL Language Reference Manual (1993). IEEE Std 1076-1993 4

151. ISO: Prolog-Part 1: General Core. ISO Standard Information Technology–Programming Languages ISO/IEC 13211-1, ISO/ICE (1995) 4

152. ISO/IEC: Vienna Development Method — Specification Language — Part 1: Base language (1996). Information Technology ISO/IEC 13817-1 Standard 164

153. ISO/IEC: Z Formal Specification Notation âĂŤ Syntax, Type System and Seman-
     tics. http://www.iso.org/iso/catalogue_detail?csnumber=21573 (2002). Infor-
     mation Technology ISO/IEC 13568 Standard 164

154. ITU-T: SDL Formal Semantics Definition. ITU-T Recommendation Z.100 Annex
     F, International Telecommunication Union (2000). http://www.sdl-forum.org 4

155. Jackson, M.: Problem Frames: Analyzing and Structuring Software Development
     Problems. Addison-Wesley (2001) 14, 17, 42, 47, 48

156. Jones, C., Hayes, I.J., Jackson, M.A.: Specifying systems that connect to the phys-
     ical world. Tech. Rep. CS-TR-964, University of Newcastle upon Tyne (2006) 46

157. Kappel, A.M.: Implementation of Dynamic Algebras with an Application to Prolog.
     Diploma thesis, Universität Dortmund (1990) 293

158. Kappel, A.M.: Executable Specifications Based on Dynamic Algebras. In:
     A. Voronkov (ed.) Proc. of 4th International Conference on Logic Programming and
     Automated Reasoning (LPAR'93), *LNAI*, vol. 698, pp. 229–240. Springer (1993)
     293

159. Karg, S., Raschke, A., Tichy, M., Liebel, G.: Model-driven Software Engineering
     in the openETCS Project: Project Experiences and Lessons Learned. In: Proc.
     of the 19th ACM/IEEE International Conference on Model Driven Engineering
     Languages and Systems (MODELS'16), MODELS '16, pp. 238–248. ACM, New
     York, NY, USA (2016) 318

160. Kern-Isberner, G.: Conditionals in Nonmonotonic Reasoning and Belief Revision,
     LNAI, vol. 2087. Springer (2001) 9

161. The KIV System. http://www.isse.uni-augsburg.de/en/software/kiv/ (since
     2013). Consulted 01/08/2018 32, 91

162. Knuth, D.: Structured Programming with goto Statements. ACM Computing Sur-
     veys **6**(4), 261–301 (1974) 35, 67

163. Knuth, D.E.: Literate Programming. Comput. J. **27**(2), 97–111 (1984) 277

164. Kohlmeyer, J.: Eine formale Semantik für die Verknüpfung von Verhaltensbeschrei-
     bungen in der UML 2. Ph.D. thesis, Universität Ulm (2009) 192

165. Kohlmeyer, J., Guttmann, W.: Unifying the Semantics of UML 2 State, Activity
     and Interaction Diagrams. In: A. Pnueli, I. Virbitskaite, A. Voronkov (eds.) Proc.
     of the 7th International Andrei Ershov Memorial Conference on Perspectives of
     Systems Informatics (PSI 2009), *LNCS*, vol. 5947, pp. 206–217. Springer (2010)
     192

166. Kossak, F., Illibauer, C., Geist, V., Kubovy, J., Natschläger, C., Ziebermayr, T.,
     Kopetzky, T., Freudenthaler, B., Schewe, K.D.: A Rigorous Semantics fo BPMN
     2.0 Process Diagrams. Springer (2014) 4, 205

167. Kossak, F., Illibauer, C., Geist, V., Natschläger, C., Ziebermayr, T., Freudenthaler,
     B., Kopetzky, T., Schewe, K.D.: Hagenberg Business Process Modelling Method.
     Springer (2016) 205

168. Lamport, L.: A New Solution of Dijkstra's Concurrent Programming Problem.
     Commun. ACM **17**(8), 453–455 (1974) 133

169. Lamport, L.: Time, Clocks, and the Ordering of Events in a Distributed System.
     Commun. ACM **21**(7), 558–565 (1978) 117, 127, 156, 228

170. Lamport, L.: How to Make a Multiprocessor Computer That Correctly Executes
     Multiprocess Programs. IEEE Trans. Computers **28**(9), 690–691 (1979) 225

171. Lamport, L.: On Interprocess Communication. Part I: Basic Formalism. Part II:
     Algorithms. Distributed Computing **1**(2), 77–101 (1986) 133

172. Lamport, L.: A Fast Mutual Exclusion Algorithm. ACM Transactions of Computer
     Systems **5**(1), 1–11 (1987) 180

173. Lamport, L.: Specifying Systems: The TLA+ Language and Tools for Hardware
     and Software Engineers. Addison-Wesley (2003) 164

174. Lamport, L.: A +CAL User's Manual.P-Syntax Version. http://lamport.
     azurewebsites.net/tla/p-manual.pdf (2017) 176, 177, 178

175. Lamport, L.: The +CAL algorithm Language. http://lamport.azurewebsites.
net/pubs/pluscal.pdf (2017) 172, 174, 176

176. Lampson, B.W.: Principles of Computer Systems. MIT Lecture Notes 6.826,
http://bwlampson.site/48-POCScourse/48-POCS2006.pdf (2006). Consulted
01/07/2018 165

177. Langmaack, H.: An ALGOL-view on TURBO ASM. In: W. Zimmermann, B. Thalheim (eds.) Proc. of 11th International Workshop on Abstract State Machines: Advances in Theory and Practice (ASM 2004), *LNCS*, vol. 3052, pp. 20–37. Springer
(2004) 172

178. Leibniz, G.W.: Dialogus de connexione inter res et verba. G. W. Leibniz:
Philosophische Schriften (1677). Edited by Leibniz-Forschungsstelle der Universität Münster, Vol. 4 A, n. 8. Akademie Verlag 1999 7

179. Leitz, M.: Definition of the formal semantics of Control State Diagrams and implementation of a graphical editor. Master's thesis, Ulm University, Ulm (2018) 297,
299

180. Lerchner, H.: Open S-BPM Workflow Engine. http://www.i2pm.net/interest-
groups/open-s-bpm, consulted 01/08/2018 (2013) 182, 194

181. Lerchner, H., Stary, C.: An Open S-BPM Runtime Environment Based on Abstract State Machines (CBI 2014). In: Proc. of 16th IEEE Conference on Business
Informatics 2014, vol. 1, pp. 54–61 (2014). See http://www.i2pm.net/interest-
groups/open-s-bpm/sub-projects/open-s-bpm-workflow-engine 182, 194

182. Leveson, N.G.: Engineering a Safer World: Systems Thinking Applied to Safety.
Engineering Systems. MIT Press (2012) 5, 7, 318

183. Lewerentz, C., Lindner, T.: Formal Development of Reactive Systems. Case Study
"Production Cell", *LNCS*, vol. 891. Springer (1995) 239

184. Lynch, N.: Distributed Algorithms. Morgan Kaufmann (1996) 117, 119, 125, 126

185. Mearelli, L.: Refining an ASM Specification of the Production Cell to C++ Code.
J. Universal Computer Science **3**(5), 666–688 (1997) 164, 239

186. Memon, M.: Specification Language Design Concepts: Aggregation and Extensi-
bility in CoreASM. Master thesis, Simon Fraser University (2006) 262

187. Metasonic: Metasonic Tool Suite (2017). https://www.metasonic.de/en/s-bpm,
consulted 01/08/2018 182, 194

188. Monteverdi, C.: Quinto libro di madrigali a 5 voci: prefazione. Claudio Monteverdi
(1605) V

189. Monteverdi, G.C. (ed.): Scherzi Musicali di Claudio Monteverdi, chap. Dichiara-
tione della lettera stampata nel quinto libro dei suoi madrigali (1607) V

190. Moore, E.F.: The Shortest Path Through a Maze. In: Proc. Int. Sympos. on Theory
of Switching, *The Annals of the Computation Laboratory of Harvard University*,
vol. 30. II. Harvard University Press (1959) 75

191. Mukala, P., Cerone, A., Turini, F.: An abstract state machine (ASM) representation of learning process in FLOSS communities. In: C. Canal, A. Idani (eds.)
Software Engineering and Formal Methods. Proc. of Colocated Workshops HOFM,
SAFOME, OpenCert, MoKMaSD, WS-FMDS (SEFM 2014), *LNCS*, vol. 8938, pp.
227–242. Springer (2014) 297

192. Naur, P.: Programming as theory building. Microprocessing and Microprogram-
ming **15**(5), 253–261 (1985) 5

193. Oaks, S., Wong, H.: Java Threads, third edn. O'Reilly (2004). See also
https://docs.oracle.com/javase/7/docs/api/java/util/concurrent/
ThreadPoolExecutor.html 140, 141

194. Ober, I.: More Meaningful UML Models. In: Proc. of 37th International Conference
on Technology of Object-Oriented Languages and Systems (TOOLS-Pacific 2000),
pp. 146–157. IEEE Computer Society Press (2000) 293

195. Object Management Group (OMG): UML 2.0 Superstructure Specification. http:
//www.omg.org/cgi-bin/doc?formal/05-07-04 (2004) 192

196. Object Management Group (OMG): Business Process Model and Notation (BPMN). Version 2.0. http://www.omg.org/spec/BPMN/2.0 (2011). Formal/2011-01-03 4, 141, 185, 189, 192, 205

197. Object Management Group (OMG): Case Management Model and Notation (CMMN). Version 1.0 Beta 1. http://www.omg.org/spec/CMMN/1.0/Beta1 (2013) 193

198. Orwell, G.: Politics and the English Language. Horizon **13**(76), 252–265 (1946) X

199. Ousterhout, J.: Tcl and the Tk Toolkit. Addison-Wesley (1994). See also the TCL developer site http://www.tcl.tk 139

200. Parnas, D., Lawford, M.: The Role of Inspection in Software Quality Assurance. IEEE Transactions on Software engineering **29**(8), 674–676 (2003) 12

201. Perkins, C., Belding-Royer, E., Das, S.: Ad hoc On-Demand Distance Vector (AODV) Routing. RFC 3561, Copyright (C) The Internet Society, Network Working Group (2003). URL http://tools.ietf.org/html/rfc3561 207, 208, 209, 210, 211, 212, 213, 214, 215, 216, 217, 218, 221, 222, 224

202. Perkins, C., Royer, E.: Ad-hoc On-Demand Distance Vector Routing. In: Proc. of the 2nd IEEE Workshop on Mobile Computer Systems and Applications (WMCSA'99), pp. 90–100 (1999) 208, 215, 218, 221

203. Petre, L., Sekerinski, E.: From Action Systems to Distributed Systems: The Refinement Approach. Chapman and Hall/CRC (2016) 9

204. Popper, K.: Logik der Forschung. Springer (1935) 8

205. Riccobene, E., Reeves, S.: Selected and extended papers from ABZ 2012. Special Issue of *Science of Computer Programming* **94**(2) (2014) VI

206. Riccobene, E., Scandurra, P.: A formal framework for service modeling and prototyping. Formal Aspects of Computing **26**(6), 1077–1113 (2014) 156

207. Rothstein, E., Schreckling, D.: Execution Framework for Interaction Computing (2016). Deliverable D5.2. Available from http://www.biomicsproject.eu/file-repository/category/BIOMICS-d52-FinalVersion.pdf, consulted 01/08/2018 269, 293

208. Sarstedt, S.: Semantic Foundation and Tool Support for Model-Driven Development with UML 2 Activity Diagrams. Ph.D. thesis, Universität Ulm (2006) 192, 297

209. Sarstedt, S., Guttmann, W.: An ASM Semantics of Token Flow in UML 2 Activity Diagrams. In: I. Virbitskaite, A. Voronkov (eds.) Proc. of the 6th International Andrei Ershov Memorial Conference on Perspectives of System Informatics (PSI 2006), *LNCS*, vol. 4378, pp. 349–362. Springer (2007) 192

210. Sasaki, H.: A Formal Semantics for Verilog-VHDL Simulation Interoperability by Abstract State Machines. In: Proc. of IEEE Conference on Design, Automation and Test in Europe (DATE'99), pp. 353–357 (1999) 4

211. Sasaki, H., Mizushima, K., Sasaki, T.: Semantic Validation of VHDL-AMS by an Abstract State Machine. In: Proc. of the IEEE/VIUF International Workshop on Behavioral Modeling and Simulation (BMAS'97), pp. 61–68 (1997) 4

212. Schellhorn, G.: Verifikation abstrakter Zustandsmaschinen. Ph.D. thesis, Universität Ulm (1999) 32, 91

213. Schellhorn, G.: Verification of ASM Refinements Using Generalized Forward Simulation. J. Universal Computer Science **7**(11), 952–979 (2001) 32, 91

214. Schellhorn, G.: ASM Refinement and Generalizations of Forward Simulation in Data Refinement: A Comparison. Theoretical Computer Science **336**(2-3), 403–435 (2005) 32, 91

215. Schellhorn, G.: ASM Refinement Preserving Invariants. J. UCS **14**(12), 1929–1948 (2008) 32, 91

216. Schellhorn, G.: Completeness of ASM Refinement. Electr. Notes Theor. Comput. Sci. **214**, 25–49 (2008) 32, 91

217. Schellhorn, G.: Completeness of fair ASM refinement. Sci. Comput. Program. **76**(9), 756–773 (2011) 32, 91

218. Schellhorn, G., Ahrendt, W.: The WAM Case Study: Verifying Compiler Correctness for Prolog with KIV. In: W. Bibel, P.H. Schmitt (eds.) Automated Deduction – A Basis for Applications, vol. 10, pp. 165–194. Springer (1998) 10, 91, 293

219. Schellhorn, G., Grandy, H., Haneberg, D., Moebius, N., Reif, W.: A Systematic Verification Approach for Mondex Electronic Purses Using ASMs. In: J.R. Abrial, U. Glässer (eds.) Rigorous Methods for Software Construction and Analysis: Essays Dedicated to Egon Börger on the Occasion of His 60th Birthday, *LNCS*, vol. 5115, pp. 93–110. Springer (2009) 10, 293

220. Schewe, K.D., Ferrarotti, F., Tec, L., Wang, Q., An, W.: Evolving Concurrent Systems: Behavioural Theory and Logic. In: Proc. of the Australasian Computer Science Week Multiconference (ACSW 2017), pp. 77:1–77–10. ACM (2017) 165

221. Schewe, K.D., Prinz, A., Börger, E.: Concurrent computing with Shared Memory Models. submitted for publication (2017) 224, 231, 232, 238

222. Schmid, J.: Executing ASM Specifications with AsmGofer. Web pages at `https://tydo.eu/AsmGofer` (1999). 293

223. Schmid, J.: Compiling Abstract State Machines to C++. J. Universal Computer Science **7**(11), 1069–1087 (2001) 239, 293

224. Schmid, J.: Refinement and Implementation Techniques for Abstract State Machines. Ph.D. thesis, University of Ulm (2002) 293

225. Schönegge, A.: Extending Dynamic Logic for Reasoning about Evolving Algebras. Technical Report 49/95, Universität Karlsruhe, Fakultät für Informatik (1995) 10

226. Soldani, J.: Modeling Franklin's Improved Algorithm For Decentralized Extrema Finding In Circular Configurations Of Processors (2014). The CoreASM code for the algorithm can be accessed via `https://github.com/szenzaro/WebASM/blob/master/src/main/ide/ExtremaFinding.casm` 96, 100, 102

227. Somers, J.: The Coming Software Apocalypse. The Atlantic (2017). URL `https://www.theatlantic.com/technology/archive/2017/09/saving-the-world-from-code/540393/`. Consulted 01/09/2018 7

228. Stärk, R.F.: Formal specification and verification of the C# thread model. Theoretical Computer Science **343**(3), 482–508 (2005) 10, 141, 293

229. Stärk, R.F., Börger, E.: An ASM Specification of C# Threads and the .NET Memory Model. In: W. Zimmermann, B. Thalheim (eds.) Proc. of 11th International Workshop on Abstract State Machines: Advances in Theory and Practice (ASM 2004), *LNCS*, vol. 3052, pp. 38–60. Springer (2004) 141

230. Stärk, R.F., Nanchen, S.: A Logic for Abstract State Machines. J. Universal Computer Science **7**(11), 980–1005 (2001) 10, 172

231. Stärk, R.F., Schmid, J.: Completeness of a Bytecode Verifier and a Certifying Java-to-JVM compiler. J. of Automated Reasoning **30**(3), 323–361 (203) 10, 293

232. Stärk, R.F., Schmid, J., Börger, E.: Java and the Java Virtual Machine: Definition, Verification, Validation. Springer (2001) VIII, 4, 10, 30, 63, 135, 140, 207, 293, 312, 318

233. Stegmaier, M.: Analyse und Implementierung der erweiterten Semantik eines universellen Kontrollkonstrukts für Abstract State Machines. Master's thesis, Ulm University (2015) 165

234. Stegmüller, M.M.: Formale Verifikation des DLX RISC-Prozessors: Eine Fallstudie basierend auf abstrakten Zustandsmaschinen. Master thesis, University of Ulm (1998) 10, 239

235. Stroetmann, K.: The Constrained Shortest Path Problem: A Case Study In Using ASMs. J. Universal Computer Science **3**(4), 304–319 (1997) 75, 164

236. Tanenbaum, A.S.: Modern Operating Systems: Design and Implementation. Prentice-Hall (1987) 159

237. Teich, J.: Project Buildabong at University of Paderborn. `https://www.cs12.tf.fau.de/forschung/projekte/buildabong/` (2001) 239

238. Teich, J., Kutter, P., Weper, R.: Description and Simulation of Microprocessor Instruction Sets Using ASMs. In: Y. Gurevich, P. Kutter, M. Odersky, L. Thiele (eds.) Proc. of International Workshop on Abstract State Machines: Theory and Applications (ASM 2000), *LNCS*, vol. 1912, pp. 266–286. Springer (2000) 239

239. Thalheim, B., Zimmermann, W. (eds.): Proc. of 11th International Workshop on Abstract State Machines: Advances in Theory and Practice (ASM 2004), *LNCS*, vol. 3052. Springer (2004) VI

240. Wainwright, R.T.: Life is Universal. In: Proc. of Winter Simulation Conference (WSC/SIGSIM), vol. 2, pp. 449–459 (1974) 63

241. Wegner, P.: Why Interaction is More Powerful Than Algorithms. Commun. ACM **40**(5), 80–91 (1997) 27

242. Weske, M.: Business Process Management: Concepts, Languages, Architectures. Springer (2007) 141

243. Winter, K.: Model Checking Abstract State Machines. Ph.D. thesis, Technical University of Berlin (2001) 293

244. Zenzaro, S.: A CoreASM refinement implementing the ATM ground model. Available at `http://modelingbook.informatik.uni-ulm.de` (2014) 65, 79, 83

245. Zenzaro, S.: A CoreASM refinement of the P2P ground model. In: S-BPM ONE 2015 Special Session on Comparative Case Studies (2015). Available at `http://modelingbook.informatik.uni-ulm.de` 205

246. Zenzaro, S.: An ASM model for the Procure To Pay Case Study. In: J. Ehlers, B. Thalheim (eds.) Proc. of 7th International Conference on Subject-Oriented Business Process Management (S-BPM One 2015), S-BPM ONE. ACM (2015) 205

247. Zenzaro, S.: On modularity in Abstract State Machines. Ph.D. thesis, Università di Pisa, Pisa (2016) 135, 137, 165

248. Zenzaro, S., Gervasi, V., Soldani, J.: Web ASM: An Abstract State Machine Execution Environment for the Web. In: Y.A. Ameur, K.D. Schewe (eds.) Proc. of 4th International ABZ Conference ASM, Alloy, B, TLA, VDM, and Z (ABZ 2014), *LNCS*, vol. 8477, pp. 216–221. Springer (2014) 96

249. Zimmerman, W., Gaul, T.: On the Construction of Correct Compiler Back-Ends: An ASM Approach. J. Universal Computer Science **3**(5), 504–567 (1997) 10

Index

A

Abstract Syntax Tree
  AST 252
action system 9
alternating bit protocol 154
AODV 207
ASM 3
  ambient 57, 117, 136
  asynchronous 95
  await 174
  basic 16, 88, 245
  call 70
  communicating 116
  concurrent 95
  control state 16, 89
  CSD refinement 314
  declaration 70
  execution 89, 249
  flat-ambient 137
  flattened 167
  hierarchical-ambient 137
  instance 95
  multi-agent 94
  named 70
  net 190
  net transition 190
  parameterization 95
  program 22, 87
  refinement 90
  rule 9, 22, 87
  rule guard 9
  run 10, 24, 89, 249
  semantics 248
  seq 171
  sequential 16, 87, 88, 245
  state 244

  step 23, 88
  synchronous 95
  transition 22
  turbo 172
assignment 22
await
  global 175
  local 176
  step-compatible 175

B

background 26
base set 244
BP 181
BPM 181

C

call
  by name 70
  by value 70
computation
  internal 132
concurrency pattern 73
constant 88
Control State Diagram 22, 89, 297
CoreASM 40, 253
  debugger 283
  plug-in 255
CSD 22, 89, 297
  canonical 303

D

diffusing system 121

© Springer-Verlag GmbH Germany, part of Springer Nature 2018
E. Börger, A. Raschke, *Modeling Companion for Software Practitioners*,
https://doi.org/10.1007/978-3-662-56641-1

Printed in the United States
By Bookmasters